T0192034

Communications in Computer and Information Science 1225

Commenced Publication in 2007
Founding and Former Series Editors:
Simone Diniz Junqueira Barbosa, Phoebe Chen, Alfredo Cuzzocrea,
Xiaoyong Du, Orhun Kara, Ting Liu, Krishna M. Sivalingam,
Dominik Ślęzak, Takashi Washio, Xiaokang Yang, and Junsong Yuan

More information about this series at http://www.springer.com/series/7899

Constantine Stephanidis ·
Margherita Antona (Eds.)

HCI International 2020 - Posters

22nd International Conference, HCII 2020
Copenhagen, Denmark, July 19–24, 2020
Proceedings, Part II

 Springer

Editors
Constantine Stephanidis
University of Crete
and Foundation for Research
and Technology – Hellas (FORTH)
Heraklion, Crete, Greece

Margherita Antona
Foundation for Research
and Technology – Hellas (FORTH)
Heraklion, Crete, Greece

ISSN 1865-0929 ISSN 1865-0937 (electronic)
Communications in Computer and Information Science
ISBN 978-3-030-50728-2 ISBN 978-3-030-50729-9 (eBook)
https://doi.org/10.1007/978-3-030-50729-9

This Springer imprint is published by the registered company Springer Nature Switzerland AG
The registered company address is: Gewerbestrasse 11, 6330 Cham, Switzerland

Foreword

The 22nd International Conference on Human-Computer Interaction, HCI International 2020 (HCII 2020), was planned to be held at the AC Bella Sky Hotel and Bella Center, Copenhagen, Denmark, during July 19–24, 2020. Due to the COVID-19 coronavirus pandemic and the resolution of the Danish government not to allow events larger than 500 people to be hosted until September 1, 2020, HCII 2020 had to be held virtually. It incorporated the 21 thematic areas and affiliated conferences listed on the following page.

A total of 6,326 individuals from academia, research institutes, industry, and governmental agencies from 97 countries submitted contributions, and 1,439 papers and 238 posters were included in the conference proceedings. These contributions address the latest research and development efforts and highlight the human aspects of design and use of computing systems. The contributions thoroughly cover the entire field of human-computer interaction, addressing major advances in knowledge and effective use of computers in a variety of application areas. The volumes constituting the full set of the conference proceedings are listed in the following pages.

The HCI International (HCII) conference also offers the option of "late-breaking work" which applies both for papers and posters and the corresponding volume(s) of the proceedings will be published just after the conference. Full papers will be included in the "HCII 2020 - Late Breaking Papers" volume of the proceedings to be published in the Springer LNCS series, while poster extended abstracts will be included as short papers in the "HCII 2020 - Late Breaking Posters" volume to be published in the Springer CCIS series.

I would like to thank the program board chairs and the members of the program boards of all thematic areas and affiliated conferences for their contribution to the highest scientific quality and the overall success of the HCI International 2020 conference.

This conference would not have been possible without the continuous and unwavering support and advice of the founder, Conference General Chair Emeritus and Conference Scientific Advisor Prof. Gavriel Salvendy. For his outstanding efforts, I would like to express my appreciation to the communications chair and editor of HCI International News, Dr. Abbas Moallem.

July 2020   Constantine Stephanidis

HCI International 2020 Thematic Areas and Affiliated Conferences

Thematic areas:

- HCI 2020: Human-Computer Interaction
- HIMI 2020: Human Interface and the Management of Information

Affiliated conferences:

- EPCE: 17th International Conference on Engineering Psychology and Cognitive Ergonomics
- UAHCI: 14th International Conference on Universal Access in Human-Computer Interaction
- VAMR: 12th International Conference on Virtual, Augmented and Mixed Reality
- CCD: 12th International Conference on Cross-Cultural Design
- SCSM: 12th International Conference on Social Computing and Social Media
- AC: 14th International Conference on Augmented Cognition
- DHM: 11th International Conference on Digital Human Modeling and Applications in Health, Safety, Ergonomics and Risk Management
- DUXU: 9th International Conference on Design, User Experience and Usability
- DAPI: 8th International Conference on Distributed, Ambient and Pervasive Interactions
- HCIBGO: 7th International Conference on HCI in Business, Government and Organizations
- LCT: 7th International Conference on Learning and Collaboration Technologies
- ITAP: 6th International Conference on Human Aspects of IT for the Aged Population
- HCI-CPT: Second International Conference on HCI for Cybersecurity, Privacy and Trust
- HCI-Games: Second International Conference on HCI in Games
- MobiTAS: Second International Conference on HCI in Mobility, Transport and Automotive Systems
- AIS: Second International Conference on Adaptive Instructional Systems
- C&C: 8th International Conference on Culture and Computing
- MOBILE: First International Conference on Design, Operation and Evaluation of Mobile Communications
- AI-HCI: First International Conference on Artificial Intelligence in HCI

Conference Proceedings Volumes Full List

1. LNCS 12181, Human-Computer Interaction: Design and User Experience (Part I), edited by Masaaki Kurosu
2. LNCS 12182, Human-Computer Interaction: Multimodal and Natural Interaction (Part II), edited by Masaaki Kurosu
3. LNCS 12183, Human-Computer Interaction: Human Values and Quality of Life (Part III), edited by Masaaki Kurosu
4. LNCS 12184, Human Interface and the Management of Information: Designing Information (Part I), edited by Sakae Yamamoto and Hirohiko Mori
5. LNCS 12185, Human Interface and the Management of Information: Interacting with Information (Part II), edited by Sakae Yamamoto and Hirohiko Mori
6. LNAI 12186, Engineering Psychology and Cognitive Ergonomics: Mental Workload, Human Physiology, and Human Energy (Part I), edited by Don Harris and Wen-Chin Li
7. LNAI 12187, Engineering Psychology and Cognitive Ergonomics: Cognition and Design (Part II), edited by Don Harris and Wen-Chin Li
8. LNCS 12188, Universal Access in Human-Computer Interaction: Design Approaches and Supporting Technologies (Part I), edited by Margherita Antona and Constantine Stephanidis
9. LNCS 12189, Universal Access in Human-Computer Interaction: Applications and Practice (Part II), edited by Margherita Antona and Constantine Stephanidis
10. LNCS 12190, Virtual, Augmented and Mixed Reality: Design and Interaction (Part I), edited by Jessie Y. C. Chen and Gino Fragomeni
11. LNCS 12191, Virtual, Augmented and Mixed Reality: Industrial and Everyday Life Applications (Part II), edited by Jessie Y. C. Chen and Gino Fragomeni
12. LNCS 12192, Cross-Cultural Design: User Experience of Products, Services, and Intelligent Environments (Part I), edited by P. L. Patrick Rau
13. LNCS 12193, Cross-Cultural Design: Applications in Health, Learning, Communication, and Creativity (Part II), edited by P. L. Patrick Rau
14. LNCS 12194, Social Computing and Social Media: Design, Ethics, User Behavior, and Social Network Analysis (Part I), edited by Gabriele Meiselwitz
15. LNCS 12195, Social Computing and Social Media: Participation, User Experience, Consumer Experience, and Applications of Social Computing (Part II), edited by Gabriele Meiselwitz
16. LNAI 12196, Augmented Cognition: Theoretical and Technological Approaches (Part I), edited by Dylan D. Schmorrow and Cali M. Fidopiastis
17. LNAI 12197, Augmented Cognition: Human Cognition and Behaviour (Part II), edited by Dylan D. Schmorrow and Cali M. Fidopiastis

38. CCIS 1224, HCI International 2020 Posters - Part I, edited by Constantine Stephanidis and Margherita Antona
39. CCIS 1225, HCI International 2020 Posters - Part II, edited by Constantine Stephanidis and Margherita Antona
40. CCIS 1226, HCI International 2020 Posters - Part III, edited by Constantine Stephanidis and Margherita Antona

http://2020.hci.international/proceedings

HCI International 2020 (HCII 2020)

The full list with the Program Board Chairs and the members of the Program Boards of all thematic areas and affiliated conferences is available online at:

http://www.hci.international/board-members-2020.php

HCI International 2021

The 23rd International Conference on Human-Computer Interaction, HCI International 2021 (HCII 2021), will be held jointly with the affiliated conferences in Washington DC, USA, at the Washington Hilton Hotel, July 24–29, 2021. It will cover a broad spectrum of themes related to Human-Computer Interaction (HCI), including theoretical issues, methods, tools, processes, and case studies in HCI design, as well as novel interaction techniques, interfaces, and applications. The proceedings will be published by Springer. More information will be available on the conference website: http://2021.hci.international/.

General Chair
Prof. Constantine Stephanidis
University of Crete and ICS-FORTH
Heraklion, Crete, Greece
Email: general_chair@hcii2021.org

http://2021.hci.international/

Contents – Part II

Virtual, Augmented and Mixed Reality

Virtual Humans and Motion Modelling and Tracking

Learning Technology

Virtual, Augmented and Mixed Reality

Improving Cooperation Between Spatially Separated Operators Using Augmented Reality

Patrick Baber[1]([✉]), Marcel Saager[2], and Bertram Wortelen[1]

[1] OFFIS e. V., Escherweg 2, 26121 Oldenburg, Germany
{patrick.baber,wortelen}@offis.de
[2] Humatects GmbH, Marie-Curie-Str. 1, 26129 Oldenburg, Germany
saager@humatects.de
https://www.offis.de
https://www.humatects.de

Abstract. The technologies for the use of augmented reality are maturing more and more and seem to offer many possible applications. There is also a lot of research and development in the industrial and business environment to increase productivity, improve communication or minimize errors. This work focuses on the use of augmented reality in the cooperation between spatially separated operators working on a common task. AR is intended to present spatial information to the operator being instructed, thus relieving the operator of tasks involving spatial orientation. In a study that is currently being planned, we want to find out whether the use of AR can support the operator in a search-and-rescue scenario at sea and thus reduce the time needed to perform tasks. AR will be compared to the way information is presented on traditional displays.

Keywords: Distributed cooperative systems · Situation awareness · Spatial orientation and localization

1 Introduction

When it comes to working on a common overarching task, cooperation and communication between the actors plays a decisive role. In these situations the team members are sometimes physically separated from each other. An example of this is operators in a control center (control room operator) and operators at the scene of an incident (field operator).

It is likely that spatial separated actors use different tools and devices. This can cause a loss of information because the data availability and presentation differs from each other, which in turn can cause errors based on communicative misunderstandings between the parties involved [1].

This paper presents the concept of a study to evaluate whether and how the use of AR on mobile devices can support the field operator in the execution of a

© Springer Nature Switzerland AG 2020
C. Stephanidis and M. Antona (Eds.): HCII 2020, CCIS 1225, pp. 3–8, 2020.
https://doi.org/10.1007/978-3-030-50729-9_1

distributed cooperative task and improve the distributed situational awareness of the team [5].

We are working on the development of an AR application that is visualizing spatial data relevant to a task in a maritime use case. The presentation of spatial data in AR can be useful when the task is performed on site, as the perception of the field operator can be enhanced by useful information. Due to their many embedded position sensors such as GPS, magnetometers or accelerometers, mobile devices are suitable for spatial AR applications [2, 7]. The intention is that the control room operator transmits information that has a spatial reference for the field operator and supports the field operator to carry out specific tasks. Thus, the application could extend reality in the sense that it marks objects in space, displays distances between the object and the searching operator and other useful information.

Augmented Reality support is intended to relieve the field operator of certain tasks or to provide support. This support can take the form of markers, so that the field operator does not have to locate the objects he is looking for again or keep his focus on them. This allows the field operator to concentrate on other tasks to be performed. We believe that such support from AR can reduce the overall time needed to complete a higher-level task and can give the field operator more confidence in the execution of the task.

2   Related Work

In other domains, similar approaches to the one presented in this work have already been researched. These include Argus, a human-to-human cooperation application via technological support. In Argus, they use Drones as technical support for the central to gain information about the situation to send to the rescue-personnel. Therefore situational awareness (the state in which an individual knows about the environment [5]) is also a central aspect in Argus, as the principle is to be applied to the rescue of people from house fires. Hence, the setup could be adapted in case of drone example from the Argus-Paper [4].

A maritime example for the usage of AR-technology is given by Vasilijevic et al. [6]. The authors gave an overview of the potential of AR-Technologies in the maritime sector. They mentioned AR in dynamic positioning from different agents in a partly virtual environment. The approach of the following sections could solve the problem, that there is a time delay in rescue missions, the authors have not accomplished.

Besides, Geo AR is a very promising technology, which is embedded in smartphones. Michel is giving examples in his work of possible use cases and proposes a framework for designing a Geo AR application. For this paper, the usage of Geo AR in smartphone applications is a technology to discuss and embed in the AR-App prototype [2].

According to the described works before, there is no approach to help people in an accident by sea. A combination of Geo AR and a distribution in situational awareness like in Argus is possible. This paper provides a study design, based on a scenario. This scenario is focused on-site coordination with augmented reality in a maritime rescue use case.

3   AR Support for On-Site Tasks

There are many situations in which spatially separated workers work on a common higher-level task. The respective operators have both common and independent tasks. On the one hand, there is the Control Room Operator. This operator is often located in a control center from where he manages and monitors the higher-level task. Part of his area of responsibility is often also the delegation of other sub tasks. On the other hand, there is the Field Operator. His area of responsibility includes tasks that have to be processed on-site during the incident. Between the two groups of operators mentioned above, there is often a bidirectional communication and information flow. Due to the work in the field, a common aspect of the tasks of the field operator, which is fundamentally different from the tasks of the control room operator, is that the field operator has to orient himself in the environment and locate places and objects within the area. An example would be the firefighter who has to locate the fire of a burning building or the people to be rescued and then enter the building while maintaining focus and orientation. Or a technician who has to identify the correct lines, valves and switches. Identification, localization and orientation on site can cost valuable time and mean additional tasks.

In order to shorten this critical time, the use of perception-enhancing technologies could support the field operator in performing tasks related to identification, localization and orientation. The support of drones or the use of augmented reality would be conceivable here. Augmented Reality has the potential to expand the consciousness and perception of humans [3]. If the advantages of these technologies are exploited, the potential exists to make various optimizations such as reducing workload, effort, response time or time-on-task in safety critical situations by adding specific location-related information to the field operator's field of view.

Figure 1 shows a generic model that depicts parts of a control room operator's and a field operator's tasks when working on a common large-scale task. An important task group is the communication between CRO and FO. Here the FO is instructed by the CRO and learns about the situation. Through the feedback channel, he can also return information to the CRO. This increases the distributed situation awareness. Furthermore, the operators each have their own additional tasks that they have to complete in order to close the overall task. These are represented here by "...". For orientation on-site, the FO has to bring together several pieces of information. This includes the information he receives from the CRO about the situation, as well as the information he has about the environment he is in at the time of completing the task. These tasks are outlined in the model.

To illustrate the task steps in the orientation, we take the example of a Search-And-Rescue (SAR) scenario in the maritime domain. In the event of a

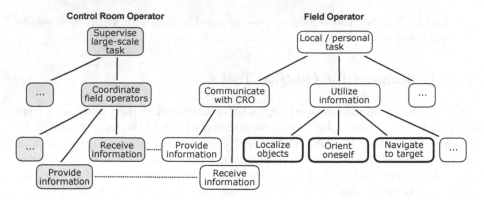

Fig. 1. Model of control room operator's and field operator's tasks

ship accident, emergency calls are received at a Maritime Rescue Coordination Centre (MRCC). Information about the incident is then forwarded to an FO and the rescue operation begins. With the information received, the FO makes his way to the scene of the incident and has to find the objects (people, ships or boats) to be searched for, orientate himself and still get there. This task can be made more difficult by other objects at sea that cover the target or by environmental influences like rain, fog or darkness. If several objects have to be picked up, there is also a constant need for reorientation in the environment.

In this example, saving time can be very important. We believe that the use of augmented reality and the associated increase in awareness and assistance can help here. Further conceivable in this and similar search-and-rescue scenarios would be the use of drones as an aid. If these drones are scanned and scanned in advance, they can identify the objects to be rescued even before the rescue ship is on site. The identified objects can then be sent to the FO in the form of geo-coordinates, which can then be displayed in augmented reality in the FO's field of vision.

In comparison to classical representations of geo-spatial data and 3d-environments, such as a map, a circuit diagram or a description, augmented reality can display objects directly in the field of view of the operator, so there is no need to translate the geo-spatial information representation into the field operator's frame of reference [3].

4   Planned Study

Based on our assumptions, we expect that the use of Augmented Reality at the incident site has a positive effect on the processing time of the tasks of a field operator, since AR supports orientation tasks and the FO can thus focus and concentrate on other tasks. Therefore, the following hypothesis results:

Hypothesis: *The processing time of on-scene tasks is shortened by the use of augmented reality compared to classical displays.*

To test this hypothesis, we are planning a study. In this study we want to go out with a German maritime search-and-rescue organization with a boat and have the test persons search for objects in the water. For this purpose, objects are to be let into the water that are equipped with a GPS transmitter and can thus communicate their position. A test run is to be carried out with the help of an application that shows the own position and the position of the objects in a classical map view. The second test run will then take place using an augmented reality application that displays the position of the objects to be searched for in space through the field of view of the FO.

The GPS transmitters thus simulate that a drone scans the environment and identifies the objects to be searched for. This information is then transmitted to the FO on his mobile device. The data that is transmitted indicates the geo-position so that it can be spatially displayed on a device equipped with sensors.

Here we measure the time it takes to identify the object and then collect it. By eliminating the tasks of identifying and focusing on the objects to be searched for, we assume that by using augmented reality the time needed to complete all tasks is altogether shorter than without perception-enhancing technologies.

5 Conclusion

The presented concept and the study should improve the cooperation between spatially separated operators. The use of mobile technologies and augmented reality offers a lot of potential for this. Further research will continue on this topic and will also focus more on the distribution of information and feedback channels in order to achieve greater distributed situation awareness.

Acknowledgements. The authors acknowledge the financial support by the Federal Ministry for Economic Affairs and Energy of Germany in the project Intellimar (project number 03SX497).

References

1. Maritime Forschungsstrategie 2025. Bundesministerium für Wirtschaft und Energie, June 2018. https://www.bmwi.de/Redaktion/DE/Publikationen/Technologie/maritime-forschungsstrategie-2025.pdf
2. Michel, T.: On mobile augmented reality applications based on geolocation. Ph.D. thesis, Université Grenoble Alpes (2017). https://tel.archives-ouvertes.fr/tel-01868246
3. Mou, W., Biocca, F., Owen, C.B., Tang, A., Xiao, F., Lim, L.: Frames of reference in mobile augmented reality displays. J. Exp. Psychol. Appl. **10**(4), 238–244 (2004). https://doi.org/10.1037/1076-898X.10.4.238
4. Sadhu, V., Salles-Loustau, G., Pompili, D., Zonouz, S., Sritapan, V.: Argus: smartphone-enabled human cooperation via multi-agent reinforcement learning for disaster situational awareness. In: 2016 IEEE International Conference on Autonomic Computing (ICAC). IEEE, July 2016. https://doi.org/10.1109/icac.2016.43

5. Salmon, P.M., Walker, G.H., Jenkins, D.D.P., Stanton, P.N.A.: Distributed Situation Awareness. Taylor & Francis Ltd., Abingdon (2009)
6. Vasilijevic, A., Borović, B., Vukić, Z.: Augmented reality in marine applications. Brodogradnja **62**, 136–142 (2011)
7. Wnorowski, J., Łebkowski, A.: Ship information systems using smartglasses technology. Sci. J. Silesian Univ. Technol. Ser. Transp. **100**, 211–222 (2018). https://doi.org/10.20858/sjsutst.2018.100.18

Immersive Virtual Reality App to Promote Healthy Eating in Children

Esteban M. Fuentes[1]([⊠]) (iD), José Varela-Aldás[1,2]([⊠]) (iD),
Guillermo Palacios-Navarro[2] (iD), and Iván García-Magariño[3] (iD)

[1] Grupo de Investigación en Sistemas Industriales, Software y Automatización
SISAu, Facultad de Ingeniería y Tecnologías de la Información y la
Comunicación, Universidad Tecnológica Indoamérica, Ambato, Ecuador
tebanfuentes@gmail.com, josevarela@uti.edu.ec
[2] Department of Electronic Engineering and Communications,
University of Zaragoza, Saragossa, Spain
guillermo.palacios@unizar.es
[3] Department of Software Engineering and Artificial Intelligence,
Complutense University of Madrid, Madrid, Spain
igarciam@ucm.es

Abstract. An immersive virtual reality application was developed as a serious game to support children on their decisions about food, the system was composed by the Gear VR (Viewer and controller), and a phone which contains the mobile application developed in Unity, providing the immersive environment, the platform was based on a path where the player has to go through it choosing between different sort of meals and also between different physical activities, the effect of balanced diet plus adequate physical activity seems reflected on the avatar previously chosen by the user, the app was tested on 12 children between 8 and 10 years old during one week, children participated on the study after receiving an informed consent, analyzing the tendencies of food choice on children before and after, a notorious positive effect could be seen on the users according to the avatar analyzed at the end of the round, besides a System usability ore was also applied to evaluate the degree of usability of the app, reaching a ore of 88.33% which rates the app as very usable, this results were even better than what was planned at the beginning of the experience.

Keywords: Virtual reality · Nutrition · Children · Serious game

1 Introduction

Food intake nowadays it's been taken in count as a very important part of public health even on developed countries due to the influence which has with the creation of tissues along the children growing up process, besides the influence over the metabolism which can have the food intake with a huge caloric content, we have to take in count that one of the major health problems that the world deals with is obesity or some problems linked to the diet habits. Lack of physical activity plus a very rich carbohydrate, sugar or fat

© Springer Nature Switzerland AG 2020
C. Stephanidis and M. Antona (Eds.): HCII 2020, CCIS 1225, pp. 9–15, 2020.
https://doi.org/10.1007/978-3-030-50729-9_2

food intake through fast food, junk food, sweets or pastries are the perfect recipe to develop health troubles and even worse if it is between young ages [1–5].

The best way to deal with health troubles such as obesity or children diabetes is education, but taking in count that technology is all the way around us, why not to take advantage of it and its positive proved effects over young population and to use is as a support tool, for example the Virtual Reality which is one of the new tendencies and has converted on a main trend specially when talking about video games or different sorts of therapy, so it is been widely applied on different topics than nutrition mainly on cerebral palsy [6, 7], but could have an amazingly positive effect over children at the moment of making food choices [8–14].

This work describes an immersive virtual reality application to encourage healthy eating in children on a friendly way, using the Gear VR as a head-mounted display (HMD) device. The results present the virtual environment developed and the children's response.

2 Materials and Methods

For the development of the present study a previous informed consent was requested to the parents of the participant children, the immersive virtual reality application was performed on 12 children between 8 and 10 years of both genders, to whom a questionnaire of food preferences was applied before and after using the virtual reality system, for a week, the motivation for the participation was mainly the use of technology and the novelty of the device for the children use.

The objective was to develop a serious game which allows the user, to make decisions about food intake and relate it to its effects over an avatar, the user in this case was focused on children and the platform let the child to choose between two food options, consequently, the avatar seems to be affected physically and emotional according to the food intake or even related to the physical activity that is another variable which affects the state of the avatar such as the old virtual pets

The Fig. 1 presents the system components, where the child interacts with the virtual reality application using the Gear VR (Viewer and controller), in addition, a phone contains the mobile application developed in Unity which is going to provide the immersive environment.

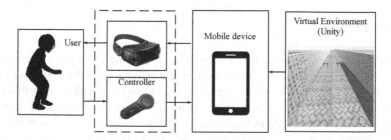

Fig. 1. Components of the Immersive virtual reality application

The game consists of a corridor platform to be followed while encountering the different feeding options, the user's interaction with the virtual environment was carried out using a handheld controller and the movements of the user are made on first person using the touchpad, when the user finds the foods, a selection laser is enabled which allows to point towards the desired food, and is finally chosen by pulling the trigger of the hand controller; as explained before the choice can be taken from two types of meals, one characterized as healthy food such as vegetables, fruits and dishes with balanced proportions of nutrients (carbohydrates, vitamins, proteins) that can be understood at simple eye, on the other side we can find junk food, such as French fries, pizza, hamburgers and hyper caloric foods.

As a plus we can find through the path some physical activities characterized by games where children can have body movement and some fun, then the realization of these activities will be reflected also on the avatars shape and mood.

The avatar is presented in the upper right of the user's view as an image of a boy or girl (according to the previous configuration), and changes its appearance with the user's decisions along the course of the tour. Principal effects when choosing junk food, can be seen as illness symptoms over the child avatar, nuanced by overweight by the shape of the avatar, sadness expressed by facial expressions and darkness on the environment, progressively; on the other side, when choosing healthy foods, the avatar has a robust strong shape, healthy and happy appearance related with the facial expression of the avatar and a shiny environment. Additionally, the avatar image uses red, orange and green background colors to highlight in health status; bad, regular and good, respectively.

A System Usability ale (SUS) was employed to each child with the help of their own parents, SUS was applied to verify or in our case, to define the usability of the Immersive Virtual reality application for the use of children [15–17].

3   Results

System tests were performed over children between 8 to 10 years, Fig. 2 presents a girl using the application (left) and the virtual reality environment (right).

Fig. 2. Immersive virtual reality test application

The proposal was evaluated by 12 children with an average age of 9 years, to whom a questionnaire of food preferences was applied before the use of the application where was clear the preference for non-healthy foods and low interest for physical activities was notorious (Table 1).

Table 1. Responses collected before de Immersive virtual reality test application

Question	Sc1	2	3	4	5	6	7	8	9	10	11	12	Count	%
When you are hungry, ¿What do you think is healthier?:														
Plate of meat, salad, rice, sauce	1												1	8
Hot dog, French fries		1	1	1	1	1	1	1	1	1	1	1	11	92
When you are thirsty ¿What would you prefer?														
Fruit juice/water	1		1	1				1					4	33
Cola, powder juice, ice tea		1			1	1	1		1	1	1	1	8	67
When you will get a snack, ¿What do you think is better for your health?														
Fruit				1					1		1		3	25
Potato chips, cookies	1	1	1		1	1	1	1		1		1	9	75
On your Spare Time ¿What would you prefer?														
Stay in Bed/watch TV	1	1				1		1			1		5	42
Go to exercise, play sports			1	1	1		1		1	1		1	7	58

To analyze the effect after using the virtual reality system for a week, the data collected is presented in the Table 2. where a highly notorious change can be seen, in a good way children accept and differentiate between what is tasty but certainly not that healthy as nutritive food specially o the snack where the 100% decided to choose a fruit.

Table 2. Responses collected after de Immersive virtual reality test application

Question	Sc1	2	3	4	5	6	7	8	9	10	11	12	Count	%
When you are hungry, ¿What do you think is healthier?														
Plate of meat, salad, rice, sauce	1	1	1	1	1	1		1		1	1	1	10	83
Hot dog, French fries							1		1				2	17
When you are thirsty ¿What would you prefer?														
Fruit juice/water	1		1	1		1		1		1	1		7	58
Cola, powder juice, ice tea		1			1		1		1			1	5	42
When you will get a snack, ¿What do you think is better for your health?														
Fruit	1	1	1	1	1	1	1	1	1	1	1	1	12	100
Potato chips, cookies													0	0
On your spare time, ¿What would you prefer?														
Stay in Bed/watch tv		1					1				1		3	25
Go to exercise, play sports	1		1	1	1	1		1	1	1		1	9	75

In addition, application data was obtained regarding the selection of food in the game. The results showed a tendency to choose healthier foods as they use the application, although at first they preferred the most harmful foods for health related to good taste and lack of interest by physical activities (Table 3).

Table 3. Differences on the children choices before and after the Immersive virtual reality test application

Question	Before (%)	After (%)	Dif. (%)
When you are hungry, ¿What do you think is healthier?			
Plate of meat, salad, rice, sauce	8	83	75
Hot dog, French fries	92	17	−75
When you are thirsty, ¿What would you prefer?			
Fruit juice/water	33	58	25
Cola, powder juice, ice tea	67	42	-25
When you will get a snack, ¿What do you think is better for your health?			
Fruit	25	100	75
Potato chips, cookies	75	0	−75
On your spare time, ¿What would you prefer?			
Stay in Bed/watch tv	42	25	−17
Go to exercise, play sports	58	75	17

The application of the SUS showed results even better than expected, being an Immersive virtual reality application characterized as very usable (88.33%) data was collected and presented on the Table 4, which includes the Scores for every user, the application of the SUS was made with the help and presence of the parent of every child and confirmed that the application was very friendly with the user and generated a good impact.

Table 4. Scores obtained by the SUS application and the estimated SUS.

Question	Sc1	2	3	4	5	6	7	8	9	10	11	12	Mean	Operation
1. I think I would like to use this system frequently	5	4	3	4	5	3	3	5	4	4	4	3	3,92	2,92
2. I find this system Unnecessarily complex	1	2	1	2	1	1	2	2	1	2	1	2	1,5	3,5
3. I think the system is easy to use	5	5	4	5	4	5	4	5	4	4	4	5	4,5	3,5
4. I think you would need technical support to make use of the system	1	1	1	1	1	1	1	1	1	1	1	1	1	4

(*continued*)

Table 4. (*continued*)

Question	Sc1	2	3	4	5	6	7	8	9	10	11	12	Mean	Operation
5. I find the various functions of the system quite well integrated	4	5	5	4	4	5	3	4	5	4	4	4	4,25	3,25
6. I have found too much inconsistency in this system	1	1	1	1	1	1	1	1	1	1	1	1	1	4
7. I think most people would learn to make use of the system quickly	5	5	5	5	5	5	5	5	5	5	5	5	5	4
8. I found the system quite uncomfortable to use	1	1	2	1	1	2	2	1	1	2	1	1	1,33	3,67
9. I have felt very safe using the system	5	4	4	5	4	6	3	4	5	4	5	5	4,5	3,5
10. I would need to learn a lot of things before I can manage the system	1	2	3	1	1	2	3	3	2	3	2	1	2	3
												Add	35,33
												Factor	2,5
												SUS	**88,33**

4   Conclusions

Due to globalization, trends on food intake are going favorably to the consumption of hyper caloric diets. The current food trend is to consume fast food foods harmful to health, so it is important to develop technological tools that promote healthy eating. The immersive virtual reality application developed helps instruct children in the consequences of poor nutrition, promoting changing food tastes in a fun way. The results obtained through the application and the questionnaire indicate a positive influence on food preference.

References

1. Velardo, S., Drummond, M.: Australian children's discourses of health, nutrition and fatness. Appetite **138**, 17–22 (2019). https://doi.org/10.1016/j.appet.2019.03.014
2. Ambroszkiewicz, J., Che, M., Szamotulska, K.: Bone status and adipokine levels in children on vegetarian and omnivorous diets. 1–8 (2018). https://doi.org/10.1016/j.clnu.2018.03.010
3. Castro, M.A.De, Verly-jr, E., Fisberg, M., Fisberg, R.M.: ienceDirect Children's nutrient intake variability is affected by age and body weight status according to results from a Brazilian multicenter study. Nutr. Res. **34**, 74–84 (2014). https://doi.org/10.1016/j.nutres.2013.09.006
4. Jílková, M., Kaupová, S., Alena, Č., Polá, L., Br, J., Velemínský, P.: Archives of oral biology early medieval diet in childhood and adulthood and its reflection in the dental health of a Central European population (Mikulčice, 9th – 10th centuries, Czech Republic) p. 107 (2019). https://doi.org/10.1016/j.archoralbio.2019.104526

5. Koutoukidis, D.A., Jebb, S.A.: Public health nutrition in the UK Key points. Medicine (Baltimore), pp. 1–5 (2018). https://doi.org/10.1016/j.mpmed.2018.12.006
6. Luiza, J., et al.: Complement. Ther. Clin. Pract. (2019). https://doi.org/10.1016/j.ctcp.2019.02.014
7. Rathinam, C., Mohan, V., Peirson, J., Skinner, J., Nethaji, K.S., Kuhn, I.: Effectiveness of virtual reality in the treatment of hand function in children with cerebral palsy: a systematic review. J. Hand Ther. **32**, 426–434.e1 (2019). https://doi.org/10.1016/j.jht.2018.01.006
8. Watt, R.G., et al.: An exploratory randomised controlled trial of a public health nutrition intervention delivered in children's centres in Islington and Cornwall. Lancet **382**, S100 (2010). https://doi.org/10.1016/S0140-6736(13)62525-8
9. Giap, H.B.: Can virtual reality, interactive game, and body motion sensors be a replacement for general anesthesia in children receiving radiation therapy? Radiat. Oncol. Biol. **102**, S149 (2018). https://doi.org/10.1016/j.ijrobp.2018.06.361
10. Tychsen, L., Foeller, P.: Effects of immersive virtual reality headset viewing on young children: visuomotor function, postural stability and motion sickness. Am. J. Ophthalmol. (2019). https://doi.org/10.1016/j.ajo.2019.07.020
11. Sigitov, A., Hinkenjann, A., Roth, T.: Towards VR-based systems for hool experiments. Procedia - Procedia Comput. i. **25**, 201–210 (2013). https://doi.org/10.1016/j.procs.2013.11.025
12. Bakr, A.F., Tarek, Z., Sayad, E., Makram, S., Thomas, S.: Virtual reality as a tool for children's participation in kindergarten design process. Alexandria Eng. J. **57**, 3851–3861 (2018). https://doi.org/10.1016/j.aej.2018.10.003
13. Willis, R.E., Gomez, P.P., Ivatury, S.J., Mitra, H.S., Sickle, K.R.Van: Virtual reality simulators: valuable surgical skills trainers or video games? J. Surg. Educ. **71**, 426–433 (2014). https://doi.org/10.1016/j.jsurg.2013.11.003
14. Bailey, J.O., Bailenson, J.N., Obradovi, J., Aguiar, N.R.: Virtual reality's effect on children's inhibitory control, social compliance, and sharing. J. Appl. Dev. Psychol. **64** (2019). https://doi.org/10.1016/j.appdev.2019.101052
15. Brooke, J.: SUS-A quick and dirty usability scale. Usability Eval. Ind. **189**, 4–7 (1996)
16. Sauro, J.: Measuring usability with the system usability scale (SUS). Meas. Usability. (2011)
17. Finstad, K.: The usability metric for user experience. Interact. Comput. (2010). https://doi.org/10.1016/j.intcom.2010.04.004

How to Improve the Immersiveness in VR by Changing the Time Expansion Coefficient

A Study on the Narrative Immersion for VR

Zichun Guo[✉], Jinghan Zhao, and Zihao Wang

Communication University of China, Beijing, China
596708006@qq.com, banruoheihei@qq.com,
wzh970517@126.com

Abstract. We introduce Time Expansion Coefficient (that is, α), which refers to the ratio of the actual time to the VR image time, in this paper. VR film designers adjust time expansion coefficient according to different narrative types in VR films to optimize users' immersive perception. We evaluated five types of narrative which include linear narrative with fixed shot, linear narrative with moving shot, circular narrative, multi-view narrative and interactive narrative. The results show that circular narrative and multi-view narrative are most affected by the time expansion coefficient. Interactive narrative and multi-view narrative are almost equally affected while linear narrative is less affected. In addition, when time expansion coefficient is greater than 1 (that is, $\alpha > 1$), immersion in all five narrative types we refer to is improved.

Keywords: Immersion · VR film · Immersive narrative strategy · VR time expansion coefficient

1 Introduction

The film "Top Player" directed by Spielberg vividly explains the picture of human survival in the VR world. The digital waves have brought the digital revolution from our real-world activities to the virtual world. The vision of VR has been to create worlds that look, sound, act, and feel real [14]. Since Facebook bought Oculus for 2 billion dollars in 2014, virtual reality (VR) has been on the centre-stage of commercial applications and research because of its promise to provide a highly immersive audio-visual experience. Much of the excitement centred on immersive VR—complex technologies that replaced real-world sensory information with synthetic stimuli such as 3D visual imagery, spatialized sound, and force or tactile feedback [10]. While researchers have long focused on the potential of VR technology for emotion feedback [11], embodied interaction [12, 13] and applications, they have only limited knowledge about what facilitates these immersive VR experiences, and specifically how time as an element contributes to the immersive experience in VR films. People's feeling about time in the virtual world is certainly different from that in the real world. The emergence of VR technology has accelerated the pace of development of this situation.

© Springer Nature Switzerland AG 2020
C. Stephanidis and M. Antona (Eds.): HCII 2020, CCIS 1225, pp. 16–29, 2020.
https://doi.org/10.1007/978-3-030-50729-9_3

For storytelling, the potential of narrative in VR films which mainly focuses on interactive narrative also provides a creative way for users. Many researchers believe that interactive traits open the closed link of narrative text and realize the interaction between user and narrative. In contrast, theoretical research combining immersion with narrative techniques is relatively rare. Ryan, Marie-Laure [2] believed that it is possible to generate plots in a virtual reality digital environment dynamically, and it is necessary to achieve a balance between immersion and interaction, i.e., Immersive-Interactive Narrative. The increase in interactive dimension will undoubtedly weaken the immersive dimension and vice versa. The exact perfect combination of immersion and interactivity will be the ultimate goal of virtual reality narrative, which Ryan, Marie-Laure likens to "Total Art."

Thus, in such background, we still lack a complete scientific understanding of how the degree of immersive experience changes by time in VR in different narratives. In this paper, we will use VR films as the studying object, and try to introduce the concept of Time Expansion Coefficient to quantify the relationship between VR time and actual time. We have deduced a VR immersive model by combining the traditional narrative theory with time expansion in VR films, and by adjusting time expansion coefficient for different narrative styles, VR film designers could strengthen the user's immersive perception.

Studies suggest that, when we are drawn into narrative time so entirely that we lose track of presentation time, we are immersed [3]. The emergence of VR technology has accelerated the pace of development of this situation. The longer the user stays in the VR image space, the more the boundary between the actual time (β) and the VR image time (θ) will be blurred, and as a result, the user will use the VR image time as a criterion to measure the narrative time. The author named the ratio of VR time to actual time as the time expansion coefficient (α), i.e., $\alpha = \beta/\theta$.

In this paper, we present a series of experiments to explore the time expansion coefficient as a direct factor influencing the degree of immersive experiences in VR films with various narrative types. The goal is to use time expansion coefficient to clarify the relationship between immersion and narrative types and also propose a more effective way for VR image designers to create rather than just rely on picture-perfect computing to improve immersion as before. The contribution of our work is as follows:

- Concept, design and implementation of the time expansion coefficient (α) for immersion in VR films;
- Discovery that interactivity and immersion in VR films are antagonistic;
- Three sorts of time expansion coefficient (α) strategies for VR films with five different narrative types.

2   Related Work

The work presented in this paper explores how time expansion coefficient improves users' immersion perception in VR films with different narrative styles. Here we summarize some most directly related works in the area of VR films, clarify the concept of immersion in VR narrative modes by distinguishing immersion degree in different kinds of media, and lay the foundation for the experiments of time expansion coefficient applied in different narrative styles.

2.1 Immersion

As Janet Murray states, "We seed the same feeling from a psychologically immersive experience that we do from a plunge in the ocean or swimming pool: the sensation of being surrounded by a completely other reality, as different as water is from air, that takes over all of our attention, our whole perceptual apparatus." [5] When the activity is challenging enough to indulge people in their perception, they will forget elapsed time and miss themselves in a virtual world, then immersion is triggered. Immersion, therefore, is something more than sensory experience for us human beings. It is a process of suspending consciousness of the real world and then entering a narrative world intentionally [6].

VR images have great potential for immersion because its time and space dimensions can go far beyond the real world. The world in VR images is not a fixed and limited space, but an infinitely interconnected macrocosm. For humans, immersion is accompanied by their way of existence because the real world itself is immersive. This immersive perception entirely depends on nature. However, the VR image space contains not only the immersive perception of the real world but also that created by the computer.

This phenomenon is explained in narratology by the concept of minimal departure. It refers that a completely fictional story-world is comprehensible to readers because it resembles or derived from the real world they live, from which they could find clues to fill in gaps [6]. So the goal of immersion in VR is to let users experience a virtual environment (VE) as if they were truly there.

The virtual reality environment gives users an immersive narrative because the users' perceptions are all immersed and surrounded by computer-controlled media. The emergence of VR technology enables users to wear an immersive helmet display with head position tracking to view the three-dimensional content constructed by virtual reality, and the user can rotate the head arbitrarily in a virtual environment and move around a small area to change the viewing position.

During the viewing process, users may be sitting in a fixed position or randomly moving through the virtual scene by preference, and change their viewing angle and position arbitrarily. Users can see their limbs in the virtual environment and use limbs to interact with the virtual world. While head-mounted displays are still popularly used, now there are also walls such as the ALIVE space at the MIT Media Lab1 and entire rooms with projected imagery responsive to users [3], where visual tracking of body parts and position is achieved through sophisticated real-time computer vision systems instead of data gloves [7].

The key to defining virtual reality in terms of human experience rather than technological hardware is the concept of presence. Presence can be thought as one's experience in a physical environment; it refers not to the existence in the physical world, but to the perception of surroundings as mediated by both automatic and controlled mental processes [8].

As a psychological element of perceptual existence, immersion in virtual reality images becomes a breakthrough point different from other media. In addition to giving users an immersive visual sense of space, immersion has also changed the concept of time. Besides the actual time, sometimes also called the presentation time, in the external narrative experience, there is another kind of time in inner narrative experience [3].

Narrative time plays a crucial and decisive role in narrative strategy. In traditional literary media, readers can be immersive in stories, which will lead to inconsistency between time in stories and reality. Later, the narrative mode of traditional images has improved immersion greatly when compared with traditional paper media. The non-identity between time in images and reality is more apparent than that between time in stories and reality. Recently, the immersion brought by virtual reality technology has become more and more perfect. So the non-identity between time in VR images and reality is much more apparent than that between time in images and reality.

2.2 The Relationship Between Narrative and Immersive

For immersive narrative, VR is a newly emerging form that combines real-world, fictional and non-fictional elements with computer-generated elements to present an immersive experience. Seeing the stereoscopic graphics popping out of the screen, picking up a virtual object with a real hand, and moving heads to change viewing angle in the virtual world all give users a unique experience [10]. Immersion is brought by the complete wrapping of the scene constructed by the virtual reality. Users' sense of vision, hearing, touch, and even taste and smell are all controlled by fictional contents, thereby achieving the purpose of being isolated from the real environment. Immersive perception in VR images presents more possibilities than traditional media, as shown in Fig. 1.

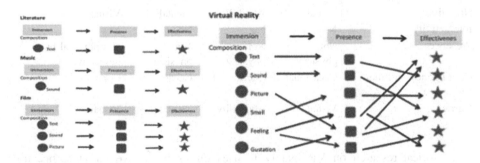

Fig. 1. Comparison of the narrative elements between VR narrative and traditional narrative

In the early days of VR, a head-mounted display provided users with a cartoon-like world to wrap around them visually. Accompanying sound provided by computer added a 3D sound-scape to the experience and data gloves connected computer with user's hand-eye coordination, allowing them to virtually grasp and manipulate objects in the virtual environment [3].

Some studies have suggested that the narrative has a considerable impact on users' immersive degree in VR images. Reliability degree is estimated with the help of internal consistency index (Cronbach's alpha) [4], and the alpha value is evaluated in a reliable criterion above 0.6. Table 1 presents the reliability coefficient estimated by each factor's low scale. Reliability index at satisfactory level ranges from 0.786 to 0.916.

Table 1. Presentation of the reliability coefficient estimated by each factor's low scale

Factors	VR with narration video	VR without narration video
Security concern perception	0.916	0.897
Ability	0.862	0.847
Benevolence	0.874	0.856
Integrity	0.807	0.786
Trust	0.889	0.891
Risk accepting	0.837	0.823

2.3 Narratives in VR Films

Studying the development of narrative theories in cinematic, theatrical and literary research, one predictably finds that different forms of narrative theories have drawn upon each other to reach specific goals [9]. It is challenging to summarize all of VR narrative theories because the narrative characteristics of VR images are much more than that in traditional novels, dramas, and movies, including features such as time, space, performance, interaction and so on. Table 2 below shows the comparison of different media on narrative, interactivity, presence, and contingency on time and space.

Table 2. Comparison of different media

	Cinema	Music	Literature	VR
Narrative	Visual	Audibility	Mental	Visual
Interactivity	No	No	No	Yes
Presence	Not physical	Not physical	Not physical	Not physical but immersive
Contingency on time and space	Occasional	Occasional	Occasional	Common
Narrative	Visual	Audibility	Mental	Visual

Historical research on VR mainly focuses on its interactive narrative because human-computer interaction can expand the possibility of narrative from multiple dimensions. In contrast, the study of immersive narrative strategies is rare. The development of narrative methods in different media often reflects the continual improvement of immersion. The development from radio to film only completes the progression from sound to image, while the development from film to virtual reality image is a leap from a single sense to multiple senses, which brings users much deeper immersion.

Linear Narrative. The earliest definition of linear narrative can be traced back to Aristotle's "Poetics". Linear narrative is a classic narrative mode, which pays attention to the integrity of the story, the unity of time and space, the causality of the plot, and the narrative and is easily understood.

Linear narrative is the most common strategy in VR images of the old days. It can be completed without interaction mechanism. For example, in a VR movie about a meteorite falling from outer space, the user will intervene the storyline in the perspective of the monster, the leading role of the movie. There is no clip from beginning to ending.

In some sense, VR movies of this narrative mode are like a 360-degree surround movie, which focuses more on narrative than interactivity. The first-person viewpoint of VR gives users an imaginary correlation with characters in the story. However, due to the absence of the third person's spectator perspective, users will quickly lose the subject, and the story will move into wrong plots.

Circular Narrative. The circular narrative generally used in traditional movies mainly refers to the film or film segment in which some plots and paragraphs have neither clear beginnings nor explicit endings, complement each other as the story extends, and express a continuous narrative structure.

When the VR film is in the structure of the circular narrative, due to its control of three-dimensional engine and program, the ring structure like the game level can be achieved in the movie. The user can choose to trigger the organ and enter an updated storyline when the film needs to be progressed.

This narrative style of ring structure is quite common in various games. In this kind of game, players need to complete tasks one by one and may return to the previous game node when failing a task. The VR film draws on the pattern of this ring structure, which breaks the boundary of the passive view of traditional film viewers and gives users rights to select and control the plot. However, if VR movie imitates the game type too much and never simplifies plots or paragraphs when designing, users may abandon the movie because of obstacles they meet or tiredness for looking for an updated story node. So this structure needs to be arranged ingeniously during the design process. For example, Fire Escape tells a story of the escape of families in the whole building when a fire broke out suddenly. In the plot arrangement, the user can view each family from a third-person omniscient perspective through the glass of the building. In the entire narrative from catching fire to the final escape, each family's story is independent. Every story, meanwhile, is connected with each other as a small part of the whole story. Therefore, in the ring structure narrative, designers need not only consider the nodes of the story turn, but more importantly, leave the viewer more space to explore. But remember it must not be too complicated.

Multi-perspective Narrative. One of the major challenges of virtual reality movies is the visual guide for audiences. It needs to help audiences focus on the main things in VR images and guide them to follow the development of the story. The balance between the sense of story and substitution requires a combination of the third perspective and the first perspective.

Johnnie Ross, the director of the Oculus studio, has come up with a variety of perspective cross-narrative solutions that can help guide users. As shown in Fig. 2, he divides the surrounding environment into multiple parts: a perspective containing the main plot, multiple perspectives containing second plots, and an interactive perspective for users to interact. As the user tries to explore the surrounding environment and move from the primary perspective across the boundary line to the second perspective, the scenes and characters within the primary perspective will enter a pause. At this time, the user can freely explore the secondary scene for environmental exploration and observation; when the viewer enters the interactive perspective, interactive contents can selectively influence contents in other perspectives; and only when the viewer go back to the primary perspective, things in the main scene will continue to move and the plot will continue to develop.

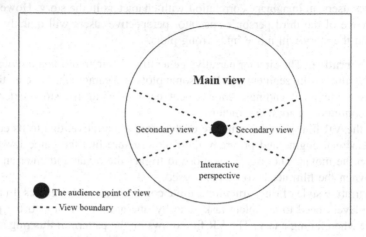

Fig. 2. Variety of perspective

3 Design

Immersion is the experience through which a fictional world acquires the presence of an autonomous language-independent reality populated with live human beings.

– Mary Laure-Ryan, Narrative as Virtual Reality

In the Parameters Design part, we will introduce the relevant parameters before the experiment, and define the three variables – VR expansion coefficient, immersion level and narrative type. In Experiment Design part, we used two methods to test how time expansion coefficient influences the immersion level in different narrative types. One is called intervention study and the other is carried out with the help of Immersion Experience Questionnaire (IEQ) [10].

3.1 Parameters Design

VR Time Expansion Coefficient. We refer to the ratio of the actual time (that is, β) to the VR image time (that is, θ) as the time expansion coefficient (that is, α, $\alpha = \beta/\theta$). When $\alpha = 1$, the VR image time is equal to the actual time; When $\alpha > 1$, the actual time is greater than the VR image time; when $\alpha < 1$, the actual time is less than the VR image time; the change of the time expansion coefficient will inevitably lead to change in the degree of immersion perception, and further influence the choice of narrative strategy.

Immersion Level. In this study, we get inspiration from the Flow theory, which was first proposed by American psychologist Csikszentmihalyi in 1975. It mainly explains how people filter out all unrelated sensations, achieve a high concentration of attention and then go into an immersive state. Therefore, in order to test whether someone is in a state of immersion, we only need to examine whether he or she is indeed in the process of watching VR movies and measure his or her ability to filter out irrelevant external information. During the experiment, we will interfere with the tester through some external ringtones during the unit test time. Specifically, we averaged five interruptions per test unit.

The fewer ringtones the tester hear, the stronger he or she feels immersive, and vice versa. The smaller the number of interferences we obtained, the stronger the immersion is (that is 0 = week, 5 = strong), and vice versa.

Narrative Strategy. Our research aims to help VR designers choose different VR time expansion coefficients to optimize users' immersion in VR movies with different narrative styles. Therefore, during the experiment, we first include three immersive narrative strategies based on related work. There are linear narrative, circular narrative and multi-view narrative. Second, in the linear narrative type, we further divide it into two types, moving shot and fixed shot, to analyze the effect of lens motion on immersion. Finally, we compare the results drawn from our experiments with previous results concerning interactive narratives to analyze the relationship between interactive narrative strategies and immersive narrative strategies.

3.2 Experiment Design 1

This experiment yielded an intervention study through external disturbances.

Time Expansion Coefficient. The experiment was conducted in a controlled laboratory environment, with the device of the HTC Vive Pro model. The test time for each tester is 120 s; that is, the real-world time (β) is 120 s. Such a short time is to avoid the discomfort caused by prolonged testing, which may lead to misjudgment of immersion. What's more, as shown in Table 3, the deviation between the value of α and one shouldn't be too large. Otherwise, testers' rational judgment will be too obvious to give an objective judgement of the immersion level, which may lead to wrong experiment results. In this experiment, we set the values of θ to 105 s, 120 s, and 135 s, i.e., time expansion coefficient (α) greater than one, equal to one and less than one respectively. The experiment was conducted in an area of 2 m multiplied by 2 m to avoid signal instability caused by excessive area. Before the test began, we asked each tester to stand at the same designated test point. The initial angle of each lens in the VR glasses was set at 55°, which was in line with the domain of human eye and users were asked to adjust it for the most comfortable angle of view (Table 4).

Table 3. Time trend chart of discomfort in VR movie watching

Age	Neck pain of time	Dizzy of time
Under the age of 20	10 min	9 min
20 to 30 years old	8 min	7 min
30 to 40 years old	7 min	5 min
40 to 50 years old	4 min	3 min
More than 60	3 min	2 min

Table 4. Experimental data settings

Parameters	$\alpha < 1$	$\alpha = 1$	$\alpha > 1$
Θ (VR time)	105 s	120 s	135 s
α (VR time expansion coefficient)	1.142	1	0.888
β (Actual time)	120 s	120 s	120 s

Stimulus and Test Films. Test films are divided into four types, namely linear narratives, circular narratives, multi-view narratives, and interactive narratives. Among them, the linear narrative is divided into two types according to the motion and non-motion of the picture lens. So there was a total of five test films in our experiment.

As shown in Table 5, five films were set to three time expansion coefficients during the test. Therefore, each tester needed watching 15 films in total. In the process of the test, we used five weak ringtones as external disturbances and stimuli randomly in 120 s.

Table 5. Experimental VR movies

Narrative strategy		The Name of Test VR
Multi-perspective narrative		*Waves of Grace*
Circular narrative		*Fire Escape*
Linear narrative	Moving shot	*Help*
	Fixed shot	*Alien Invasion*
Interactive narrative		*Raising a Rukus*

After the test, we recorded the number of rings heard by each tester. It was used to measure their immersion level.

Participants. We recruited 12 participants (7 male, 5 female) with an average age of 26.93 (SD = 4.74). All the participants have watched VR films before: Six reported watching a few times (less than 5) a year, and another six watching more than six times a year on average. All participants professed to have a keen interest in VR films (SD = 1.88). Five of the participants have even played VR games before.

Procedure. After briefly informed the procedure, participants were asked to bring a VR device at the designated location to begin testing. During the testing process, the testers were sorted in a cross-over manner to prevent the same tester from continuously testing 15 films. The total time for each participant was approximately 60 min. After 30 s from the start of the test, we started interfering the tester with an average of 5 external disturbances. When the test was over, they were asked to immediately report the number of ringtones they heard to the experimenter.

Results. We analyze the experimental results through three dimensions: the effect of time expansion coefficient on linear narrative strategy, the effect of time expansion coefficient on immersion in VR movies with five different narrative types and the relationship between interactivity and immersion.

The Results of Linear Narrative Strategy Test. The quantitative experiment data for liner narrative is shown in Table 6. For VR linear narratives, moving shot is more immersive than fixed shot. Immersion in fixed shot when the time expansion coefficient is greater than 1(that is, $\alpha > 1$) is the best.

Table 6. Linear narrative strategy test results

Linear narrative	Time expansion coefficient	Number of interference												Number of interference (AVG)
		No. 1	No. 2	No. 3	No. 4	No. 5	No.6	No. 7	No. 8	No. 9	No. 10	No. 11	No. 12	
Moving shot	$\alpha = 0.888$	5	4	2	3	4	4	3	5	4	2	4	4	3.667
	$\alpha = 1$	1	3	3	4	3	3	4	3	3	3	1	3	2.833
	$\alpha = 1.142$	2	2	2	4	3	3	2	3	4	3	2	2	2.667
Fixed shot	$\alpha = 0.888$	1	3	2	4	3	3	1	4	3	3	2	3	2.667
	$\alpha = 1$	2	2	2	4	3	4	2	4	2	3	2	4	2.833
	$\alpha = 1.142$	0	3	1	3	3	2	1	3	0	2	3	3	2

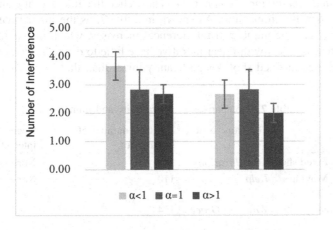

Fig. 3. Comparison of moving shot and fixed shot

As can be seen in Fig. 3, the average number of interferences of the moving shot decreases as time expansion coefficient increases. Moreover, the average number of interferences of the fixed shot is the largest when the time expansion coefficient is equal to 1 (that is, $\alpha = 1$).

Influence of Time Expansion Coefficient. To what extent the five films are affected by the time expansion coefficient varies. As shown in Fig. 4, circular narrative and multi-view narrative are the two styles affected most by time expansion coefficient. The effects of time expansion coefficients on interactive narratives and multi-view narratives are roughly the same. Linear narratives are least affected by the coefficient of time expansion. In addition, when the time expansion coefficient is greater than 1 (that is, $\alpha > 1$), the number of interferences of all the five films shows a downward trend, which means the immersion is improved.

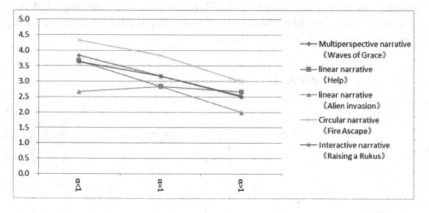

Fig. 4. Rate of influence of time expansion coefficient

Interactivity and Immersion Comparison. The richer the interactivity and lens language, the weaker the immersion. As shown in Table 7, as the interactivity in all the five films increases, the number of interferences increases, which means immersion is weakened. The two films with linear narrative have little to do with interaction, among which interference in fixed shot is significantly lower than that in moving shot.

Table 7. Comparison of interactivity and immersion

Type		The name of test VR	The total number of interference	Degree of interactivity
Linear narrative	Fixed shot	*Alien Invasion*	80	None
	Moving shot	*Help*	110	None
Multi-perspective narrative		*Waves of Grace*	114	Weak
Circular narrative		*Fire Escape*	134	Medium
Interactive narrative		*Raising a Rukus*	136	Strong

3.3 Experiment Design 2

This experiment yielded a quantitative comparison of subjective immersion ratings through a questionnaire, a qualitative method.

Experiment 2 shared the same parameters, participants and test films with Experiment1. We just replaced the number of interferences with the scores in immersion questionnaires to measure users' immersion level in this experiment.

We conducted our experiment with the help of a validated questionnaire, Immersion Experience Questionnaire (IEQ) [10]. It was created based on Brown and Cairns (2004)'s conceptualization and aimed at providing a general measure of immersive experience in VR games.

The IEQ consists of 32 questions. We ruled out 11 questions concerning player behaviour and used the other 21 questions in our research. Participants were asked to answer this questionnaire using the 5-point Likert scale (ranging from 1 (Strongly Disagree) to 5 (Strongly Agree)) to describe their feelings in films [1]. The immersion level is measured by the mean score of the 21 questions in this questionnaire.

Results. The mean score of all the 12 participants for the immersion level of the linear narrative is shown in Fig. 5. We can see scores of fixed shot are all higher than those of moving shot. When the time expansion coefficient is greater than 1(that is, $\alpha > 1$), the immersion score of both the two types is the highest. The result is the same as that in Experiment 1. Also, Fig. 6 shows that immersion scores increase as the time expansion coefficient increases, the same as what Fig. 4 shows.

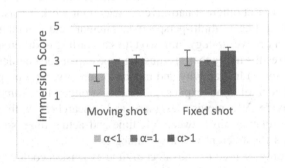

Fig. 5. Comparison of moving shot and fixed shot

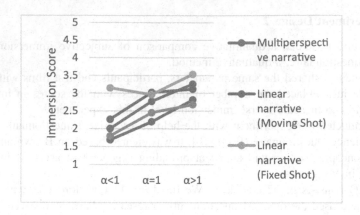

Fig. 6. Rate of influence of time expansion coefficient

The results of the two experiments verify each other and clarify how time expansion coefficient affects immersion in VR movies with different narrative types.

4 Conclusion

This paper presented a study on how time expansion coefficient influences the immersion of VR user at different narrative strategy. Our work involved four narrative strategies, including linear, multi-perspective, circular and interactive. We further divided the linear narrative strategy into two types according to different kinds of shots. The experimental results imply that 1) adjusting time expansion coefficient can improve immersion efficiency. 2) Interactivity and immersion are inversely proportional. 3) The higher the coefficient of time expansion is, the stronger the immersion is. These findings can provide VR movie designers and researchers with a reference for understanding the relationship between VR time and actual time, so as to help them adjust VR contents for different narrative strategies.

This research only focused on the effect of time expansion coefficient on immersion in a small scale ($\alpha = 0.888-1.142$), and only tested on four narrative types. In fact, it is only a small part as there are various kinds of VR movies. Future research can extend to more types of narrative techniques, even to those combined with audiovisual languages in different narrative techniques. In addition to studying the ontology of the narrative strategy, further expanding the test range of time expansion coefficient can help VR creators select an appropriate narrative strategy more accurately and more efficiently. In future studies, we will continue to explore the relationship between time expansion coefficient, user immersion and narrative strategy.

References

1. Swarajya, G., Reddy, H.: Empirical Investigation on Measurement of Game Immersion using Real World Dissociation Factor (2016)
2. Ryan, M.-L.: Narrative as Virtual Reality 2: Immersion and Interactivity in Literature and Electronic Media. Johns Hopkins University Press, Baltimore (2015)
3. Brooks, K.: There is Nothing Virtual About Immersion: Narrative Immersion for VR and Other Interfaces. Motorola Labs/Human Interface Labs
4. Liang, H., Chang, J.: Puppet Narrator: utilizing motion sensing technology in storytelling for young children. In: Ismail Khalid Kazmi - International Conference on Games & Virtual Worlds for Serious Applications (2015)
5. Murray, J.H.: Hamlet on the Holodeck - The Future of Narrative in Cyberspace. The Free Press, New York (1997)
6. Herman, D., Manfred, J., Marie-Laure, R.: Routledge Encyclopedia of Narrative Theory. Routledge, Abingdon (2007)
7. Sparacino, F.: INTER_FACE Body Boundaries, issue editor: Emanuele Quinz, Anomalie n. 2, Paris, France, Anomos (2001)
8. Steuer, J.: Defining virtual reality: dimensions determining telepresence. J. Commun. **42**(4) (Autumn), 73–93 (1992)
9. Aylett, R., Louchart, S.: Towards a narrative theory of virtual reality. Virtual Reality **7**, 2–9 (2003)
10. Bowman, D.A., McMahan, R.P.: Virginia Tech. Virtual Reality: How Much Immersion Is Enough?. Published by the IEEE Computer Society (2007)
11. Lin, J.-H.T.: Fear in virtual reality (VR): fear elements, coping reactions, immediate and next-day fright responses toward a survival horror zombie virtual reality game. Comput. Hum. Behav. **72** (2017), 350–361 (2017)
12. Begault, D.R., Trejo, L.J.: 3-D sound for virtual reality and multimedia (2000)
13. Rogers, K., Ribeiro, G., Wehbe, R.R., Weber, M., Nacke, L.E.: Vanishing importance: studying immersive effects of game audio perception on player experiences. In: Virtual Reality CHI 2018, 21–26 April 2018, Montreal, QC, Canada (2018). ©2018 Copyright is held by the owner/author(s). Publication rights licensed to ACM
14. Sutherland, I.E.: The ultimate display. Multimedia: From Wagner to virtual reality (1965)

Enabling Interaction with Arbitrary 2D Applications in Virtual Environments

Adrian H. Hoppe[1]([✉]), Florian van de Camp[2], and Rainer Stiefelhagen[1]

[1] Karlsruhe Institute of Technology (KIT), Karlsruhe, Germany
{adrian.hoppe,rainer.stiefelhagen}@kit.edu
[2] Fraunhofer IOSB, Fraunhofer Institute of Optronics, System Technologies
and Image Exploitation, Karlsruhe, Germany
florian.vandecamp@iosb.fraunhofer.de

Abstract. Virtual environments (VE) provide immersive experiences
that allow users to perceive and interact with three dimensional (3D)
content. Yet, the 3D applications are often tailored for specific tasks
and hardware setups such as a virtual or augmented reality (VR/AR)
head mounted display (HMD). This limits the range of available content, because not every standard application (e.g. web browser, calender,
office) that is available on a 2D desktop PC can be easily accessed using
VR or AR. As commonly used by other systems, we capture arbitrary 2D
windows from a desktop PC and display them as a 2D surface in the VE.
Furthermore, we provide different techniques that aim to allow easy and
fast interaction with the 2D applications in VR. For example, the work
bench tool allows to copy and paste subsections of a 2D window. The
copied sections are fully interactable and can be moved around and scaled
to provide easy access to small menus. With the macro tool, users can
create shortcuts to frequently used functions that are executed by cursor presses or hotkeys. The provided tools yield new ways of interacting
with 2D interfaces. By allowing the user to easily interact with already
available 2D applications, the productivity of VEs increases strongly.

Keywords: Virtual reality · 2D application · Screen capture ·
Interaction

1 Introduction

VR and AR allow users to experience information in immersive VEs. The technologies with their stereoscopic rendering are especially suitable for viewing
spatial data. VR and AR find use in the areas of data visualization, modeling, designing and planning, training and education, telepresence, cooperative
working, and entertainment [4, 15].

VR and AR HMDs require specially designed applications that utilize stereoscopic rendering and often use gesture- or wand-based interaction. Yet, not all
applications benefit from the advantages of a 3D representation and, on the con-
trary, are well suited for 2D visualization and interaction, e.g. a web browser

© Springer Nature Switzerland AG 2020
C. Stephanidis and M. Antona (Eds.): HCII 2020, CCIS 1225, pp. 30–36, 2020.
https://doi.org/10.1007/978-3-030-50729-9_4

or spreadsheet application. However, a user might want to explore 3D data and then quickly browse the internet for information or check her/his calendar. In order not to force the user to constantly switch between her/his 2D work space and the 3D VE by putting on and taking off the HMD, the 2D applications need to be accessible within VR/AR. Current PC-powered VR headsets allow the user to access the desktop as a 2D window and interact with it using a ray-casting interaction [7]. But, those approaches do not fully explore the possibilities of improving the visualization of and the interaction with 2D windows. The methods presented below focus on these two aspects and aim to provide an efficient and easy-to-use way to integrate existing 2D applications into VEs. They target to extend the functional range and increase the usability of VR and AR environments.

2   Related Work

In order to display a 2D application inside a VE without reimplementing the software for 3D, a screen capturing method can be used. The application is filmed, converted to a texture and then displayed on top of an object, e.g. a (curved) plane or flattened cube, inside the VE. GDI [17] is an application programming interface, which captures the desktop or even single windows, and is used for example by the Open Broadcaster Software (OBS) [13]. Other systems include the Desktop Duplication API [16] or WindowsGraphicsCapture [19]. Current VR implementations provide the user with a way to interact with their whole desktop or separate windows while using their PC-powered VR HMD. Examples are SteamVR [24], Oculus Dash [9], Windows Mixed Reality home [18], Bigscreen [6], uDesktopDuplication [10], and Virtual Desktop [26].

Angus and Sowizral [3] map a 2D application to a hand-held tablet. By using a stylus or the user's virtual finger, touch events are send to the application. WebVR [5] is a virtual web browser that extracts the image of a web browser and displays it inside the VE. Barsoum and Kuester display more than one browser window so that the user can use several virtual screens at the same time. Regenbrecht et al. [21] create an AR environment that displays virtual windows within the real world. They track different fiducial markers in the physical environment to position and align the virtual windows. Users can move the markers to setup their work space. The PC's mouse can be picked up to serve as a 3D ray-casting device. Toyama et al. [23] integrate web browser windows into a larger VE. Different browser windows can be placed side by side to allow parallel tasks, or at different places to allow content-based grouping. They found that users rely on environmental landmarks to facilitate placement and retrieval of windows. They also use a ray-casting technique to interact with the browser window.

Even-though the majority of the presented work uses a ray-casting technique to interact with a 2D virtual window, this might not be the ideal solution. The 3D interaction reduces the performance of traditional interaction techniques [8]. Ray-casting techniques can be difficult to use on smaller surfaces or larger distances because of their sensible reaction to changes in the rotation of the virtual laser pointer's origin. Techniques that try to minimize this precision problem are for example a bending ray-cast that always selects the closest interactable object [1, 22, 25]. However, when capturing an arbitrary application the positions and extends of buttons and other menu items might be unknown. Other approaches position virtual windows (e.g. as a tablet) relative to the user's body [2, 11, 14, 20, 27] or use the available keyboard and mouse [5, 12, 21] to utilize smaller distances or proprioception to increase precision.

3 Tools for Interaction with 2D Applications

Current approaches, such as ray-casting or hand-held windows, often do not change the visual appearance of the 2D window, but only apply position, rotation, or scale transformations. Our approach extends the state of the art by exploring different techniques for visualizing and interacting with 2D windows inside a VE.

As a first step, we implemented a screen capturing feature using GDI. This allows us to display any 2D window or the whole screen of the operating system inside a VR application. The window is captured as a texture and mapped to a mesh, e.g. a plane or a cube. Since GDI does not capture the cursor, a cursor image is rendered at the respective location inside the texture. We then added a ray-casting interaction that is based on the texture coordinates of the mesh. The texture coordinates are transformed into application space coordinates by a simple linear interpolation between the window's corners. Based on the interactive virtual windows we implemented the following mechanisms.

3.1 Duplicated Windows

Users might quickly switch between a distant and a close-up (hand-held or floating in-air) interaction with a movable virtual window. However, users need to move and scale the windows or use a snapping mechanism in order to combine the benefits of having an overview over a large window, and a precise interaction with a hand-held window. Since virtual windows can be duplicated at will, this method can be used for a parallel display of a close-up and distant version of the window. Users do not need to rearrange one window, but can work with different copies of it (see Fig. 1). This can easily be achieved by displaying the texture of the application on different meshes. Users can also interact with any copy of the virtual window.

In addition to that, several copies of one window can be used to implement multi-user interaction. A larger overview window can be used for group discussions and each user can work with her/his own close-up copy of the window. To prevent users from interfering with each other, a user can lock the interaction for other users if required.

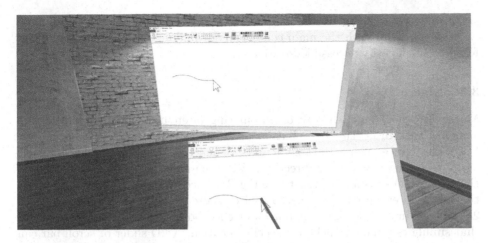

Fig. 1. The user uses a copy of the captured window directly in front of her/him instead of the window on the wall.

3.2   Work Bench Tool

Besides duplicating the whole window, users can also choose to duplicate only a specific part. This allows the user to manipulate different sections of a window, like the window's toolbar or main content, individually. The various sub-windows can be scaled up and brought into a comfortable position close to the body to interact with them (see Fig. 2). This is especially useful to increase speed and precision for frequently used features or small menus, or to extract and enlarge specific information. Also this avoids the need of constantly changing the size of a window, because some parts are large enough while other parts are too

Fig. 2. The user extracted the save, redo and undo buttons, the brush panel, and the color panel from the original window to setup a customized work space.

small to access easily. This mechanism yields a tool that allows a user to build a work bench setup with the main content in the middle and all other important features in an easily accessible location.

3.3 Macro Tool

Moreover, we included a way of automating often used actions that require a mouse click/drag, keyboard button press, or sequences of scriptable inputs. Users can create such scriptable actions, or macros, by programming a script, or by recording the actions directly in VR. The macros are represented inside the virtual world as a 3D widget (see Fig. 3). Once, the user presses the widget, the macro is executed. The macro tool can also be used to transfer common 2D widgets into 3D widgets. A button or checkbox widget uses a simple macro that simulates a mouse click at a specific location. A 2D slider or scroll bar can be represented by a lever in 3D, where the start and end location of the lever represent the start and end location of the slider in 2D. By moving the lever, a mouse click is simulated at the respective linearly interpolated location so that the 2D slider is set to the correct position. The macro tool allows an easy and quick access to frequently used features and extends the interaction with the 2D window into the 3D world.

Fig. 3. The user defined macros for often used features and is using a slider to change the zoom of the application.

4 Conclusion and Future Work

It is unlikely that existing 2D applications will be redesigned for 3D environments. Nevertheless, access to standard programs is necessary to avoid frequent changes between the real and virtual world. Using screen capturing, arbitrary

2D applications can be displayed within the VE without reimplementation. The tools presented in this paper extend the possibilities for interacting with virtual windows to provide easy and quick access to small menus or frequently used functions. Interaction with 2D applications will make VR and AR technology more economically viable and increase user productivity by giving them quicker access to valuable information.

For future work, it would be interesting to investigate whether automatic content or usage analysis can increase the usefulness of the implemented tools. The work bench tool could benefit from an automatic subdivision and arrangement of the sub-windows. Also, the macro tool could generate shortcuts for repeatedly used actions.

References

1. Ahlström, D., Hitz, M., Leitner, G.: An evaluation of sticky and force enhanced targets in multi target situations. In: Proceedings of the 4th Nordic Conference on Human-Computer Interaction: Changing Roles, NordiCHI 2006, pp. 58–67. Association for Computing Machinery, New York (2006). https://doi.org/10.1145/1182475.1182482
2. Andujar, C., Argelaguet, F.: Virtual pads: decoupling motor space and visual space for flexible manipulation of 2D windows within VEs. In: 2007 IEEE Symposium on 3D User Interfaces, March 2007. https://doi.org/10.1109/3DUI.2007.340781
3. Angus, I.G., Sowizral, H.A.: Embedding the 2D interaction metaphor in a real 3D virtual environment. In: Fisher, S.S., Merritt, J.O., Bolas, M.T. (eds.) Stereoscopic Displays and Virtual Reality Systems II, vol. 2409, pp. 282–293. International Society for Optics and Photonics, SPIE (1995). https://doi.org/10.1117/12.205875
4. Azuma, R.T.: A survey of augmented reality. Presence: Teleoperators Virtual Environ. **6**(4), 355–385 (1997). https://doi.org/10.1162/pres.1997.6.4.355
5. Barsoum, E., Kuester, F.: WebVR: an interactive web browser for virtual environments. In: Woods, A.J., Merritt, J.O., Bolas, M.T., McDowall, I.E. (eds.) Stereoscopic Displays and Virtual Reality Systems XII, vol. 5664, pp. 540–547. International Society for Optics and Photonics, SPIE (2005). https://doi.org/10.1117/12.582624
6. Bigscreen, inc.: Bigscreen (2020). https://www.bigscreenvr.com/
7. Bowman, D.A., Hodges, L.F.: An evaluation of techniques for grabbing and manipulating remote objects in immersive virtual environments. In: Proceedings of the 1997 Symposium on Interactive 3D Graphics, I3D 1997, p. 35-ff. Association for Computing Machinery, New York (1997). https://doi.org/10.1145/253284.253301
8. Bowman, D.A., Kruijff, E., LaViola, J.J., Poupyrev, I.: An introduction to 3-D user interface design. Presence: Teleoperators Virtual Environ. **10**(1), 96–108 (2001). https://doi.org/10.1162/105474601750182342
9. Facebook Technologies, LLC.: Oculus Dash (2020). https://developer.oculus.com/documentation/native/pc/dg-dash
10. hecomi: uDesktopDuplication (2016). https://github.com/hecomi/uDesktopDuplication
11. Hoppe, A.H., Marek, F., van de Camp, F., Stiefelhagen, R.: Virtualtablet: extending movable surfaces with touch interaction. In: 2019 IEEE Conference on Virtual Reality and 3D User Interfaces (VR), pp. 980–981, March 2019. https://doi.org/10.1109/VR.2019.8797993

12. Hoppe, A.H., Otto, L., van de Camp, F., Stiefelhagen, R., Unmüßig, G.: qVRty: virtual keyboard with a haptic, real-world representation. In: Stephanidis, C. (ed.) HCI 2018. CCIS, vol. 851, pp. 266–272. Springer, Cham (2018). https://doi.org/10.1007/978-3-319-92279-9_36

13. Jim and OBS Studio Contributors: Open Broadcaster Software (2020). https://obsproject.com/

14. Lindeman, R.W., Sibert, J.L., Hahn, J.K.: Hand-held windows: towards effective 2D interaction in immersive virtual environments. In: Proceedings IEEE Virtual Reality (Cat. No. 99CB36316), pp. 205–212, March 1999. https://doi.org/10.1109/VR.1999.756952

15. Mazuryk, T., Gervautz, M.: Virtual reality-history, applications, technology and future (1996)

16. Microsoft Corporation: Desktop Duplication API (2018). https://docs.microsoft.com/en-us/windows/win32/direct3ddxgi/desktop-dup-api

17. Microsoft Corporation: Windows GDI (2018). https://docs.microsoft.com/en-us/windows/win32/gdi/windows-gdi

18. Microsoft Corporation: Windows Mixed Reality home (2018). https://docs.microsoft.com/en-us/windows/mixed-reality/navigating-the-windows-mixed-reality-home

19. Microsoft Corporation: WindowsGraphicsCapture (2018). https://docs.microsoft.com/en-us/uwp/api/windows.graphics.capture

20. Mine, M.R., Brooks, F.P., Sequin, C.H.: Moving objects in space: exploiting proprioception in virtual-environment interaction. In: Proceedings of the 24th Annual Conference on Computer Graphics and Interactive Techniques, SIGGRAPH 1997, pp. 19–26. ACM Press/Addison-Wesley Publishing Co., USA (1997). https://doi.org/10.1145/258734.258747

21. Regenbrecht, H., Baratoff, G., Wagner, M.: A tangible AR desktop environment. Comput. Graph. **25**(5), 755–763 (2001). https://doi.org/10.1016/S0097-8493(01)00118-2. Mixed realities - beyond conventions

22. Steinicke, F., Ropinski, T., Hinrichs, K.: VR and laser-based interaction in virtual environments using a dual-purpose interaction metaphor. In: IEEE VR 2005 Workshop Proceedings on New Directions in 3D User Interfaces, pp. 61–64 (2005)

23. Toyama, S., Al Sada, M., Nakajima, T.: Vrowser: a virtual reality parallel web browser. In: Chen, J.Y., Fragomeni, G. (eds.) Virtual, Augmented and Mixed Reality: Interaction, Navigation, Visualization, Embodiment, and Simulation, pp. 230–244. Springer, Cham (2018)

24. Valve Corporation: Steam VR (2020). https://store.steampowered.com/app/250820/SteamVR

25. van de Camp, F., Stiefelhagen, R.: Applying force fields to black-box guls using computer vision. In: 2013 1st IEEE Workshop on User-Centered Computer Vision (UCCV), pp. 1–6, January 2013. https://doi.org/10.1109/UCCV.2013.6530799

26. Virtual Desktop Inc: vrdesktop (2019). https://www.vrdesktop.net

27. Wobbrock, J.O., Morris, M.R., Wilson, A.D.: User-defined gestures for surface computing. In: Proceedings of the SIGCHI Conference on Human Factors in Computing Systems, CHI 2009, pp. 1083–1092. Association for Computing Machinery, New York (2009). https://doi.org/10.1145/1518701.1518866

A Preliminary Study: Examining the Contribution of Neck Angles of a Virtual Dog to Its Realness

Satsuki Inoue[✉] and Iiji Ogawa

Teikyo University of Science,
2525 Yatsusawa, Uenohara, Yamanashi-Ken 409-0193, Japan
sl7ag014@st.ntu.ac.jp

Abstract. This study examined qualities of dog that allowed individuals to recognized virtual dog as a living dog. The contribution of shape and neck angles was focused as preliminary characteristics. To investigate the impact of change in the neck angles, two types of virtual dogs, one is dog-like and the other wolf-like, were developed and projected on a monitor with four kinds of neck angles (−45, 0, 45, and 90 degree). Twenty university students (female, n = 10; age range 19–23) participated in the experiments. Participants were asked following questions in random order: 'do you think this is definitely dog?' for virtual wolf-like dog, 'do you think this is definitely wolf?' for virtual dog-like dog. Participants filled out the evaluation sheet using 5-point scale after viewing each virtual dog. The experimental design was applied with the two levels of virtual dogs (dog-like and wolf-like), the four levels of neck angles, and 5 repetitions of each figure. As a result, it was found that the evaluation scores for two virtual dogs were significantly different ($p < 0.05$) and the neck angles were highly significant factor ($p < 0.01$). Also, the neck angle of 90 degree for virtual dog-like dog and the neck angle of 45 degree for virtual wolf-like dog were recognized as a dog the best. Those findings suggest that the neck angles would be one of the important factors to recognize a virtual dog to its realness.

Keywords: Neck angles · Virtual dog · Realness

1 Introduction

Virtual and Mixed Reality are increasingly attracting attention and have important role in real life. In Japan, Robot Assisted Activity/Therapy have recently been introduced into hospitals and nursing home facilities for therapeutic and recreational purposes; i.e., rehabilitation and mental support and have become increasingly popular. However, virtual animals' design (i.e., dog and wolf), were not fully investigated for their characteristics (i.e., ears, tail, size, color, and hair). It is well understood that there are features that are common and different between dog and wolf [1]. Furthermore, we are able to distinguish between dog and wolf based on observation of morphological and anatomical features [1]. However, in the field of Virtual and Mixed Reality, the virtual dogs seem to be very similar to wolves.

© Springer Nature Switzerland AG 2020
C. Stephanidis and M. Antona (Eds.): HCII 2020, CCIS 1225, pp. 37–42, 2020.
https://doi.org/10.1007/978-3-030-50729-9_5

While examining the similarities and differences between dogs and wolves, it is important to further examine into our visual intelligence which is defined as the ability to generate, store, retrieve, and transform visual images and sensations [2]. Hoffman [3] suggested that, after watching the face of human or animal, we, humans, are able to recognize who it is or what kind of animal it is; however, without function of visual intelligence, the recognition of an object/person is unrecognizable. Thus, to avoid misclassification, it is necessary to construct and validate key characteristics of animals that will be useful in developing animals in the visual world. Hoffman and Singh [4] suggested that many objects have component parts, and these parts often differ in their visual salience. Furthermore, authors presented evidence that the salience of a part depends on three factors: 1) its size relative to the whole object, 2) the degree to which it protrudes, and 3) the strength of its boundaries and that these three factors influence visual processes which determine the choice of figure and ground [3]. Given the complexity of virtual system, the key characteristics of virtual dog to its realness are unknown and warrant further examination.

Although there are many characteristics for dogs, in this study, the contribution of shape and neck angles was focused as preliminary characteristics. We examined whether the shape and neck angle contribute to virtual dog to its realness.

2   Method

The experiments were carried out in a shield room (W3.5 m × D2.6 m × H2.4 m). The Institutional Review Boards (IRB) of Teikyo University of Science approved all procedures and methods. All protocols for this study and consent procedures were also approved by the IRB. The description of experimental procedure including participants is described below.

2.1   Participants

Twenty university students (female, n = 10; age range 19–23), participated in the experiments. All participants had normal visual acuity.

2.2   Virtual Dogs

Two types of virtual dogs were developed using the 3D CG software Blender and used in this study: the virtual dog A is a 2D virtual dog depicted to be a dog with round body and the dog B is depicted to be a wolf with sharp looking as shown in Figs. 1 and 2, respectively. Each virtual dog was projected with four kinds of neck angles (−45, 0, +45, and +90 degree) as shown in Fig. 3.

2.3   Experimental Procedure

For each trial, participant viewed a question (3 s) and a virtual dog (3 s) on the monitor (40 V, 1,920 × 1,080 pixels), then filled out an evaluation sheet. The questions on the monitor differed by the virtual dogs. For example, for virtual dog A (dog-like), participants were asked 'do you think this is definitely wolf?' and for virtual dog B (wolf-like), participants were asked 'do you think this is definitely dog?' For each trial, participant fill out the evaluation sheet using a 5-point scale (1: disagree 2: slightly disagree 3: neutral 4: slightly agree 5: agree). In totally, each participant completed 40 trials (two types of virtual dogs, four kinds of neck angles, 5 repetitions of each figure). The sequence of the trial (virtual dogs, neck angles) was random and controlled by tablet PC (surface pro 7) outside of the shield room. Experimental procedure is depicted in Fig. 4. In addition, participants' personality was diagnosed using Yatabe-Guilford personality test which participants can be classified into 5 types: 1) average type, 2) black list type, 3) calm type, 4) director type, and 5) eccentric type.

2.4 Statistical Analysis

Two-factor repeated measure ANOVA was applied with two levels of virtual dogs (dog-like and wolf-like), the four levels of neck angles, and 5 repetitions of each figure. For each virtual dog, multiple comparison test (Steel-Dwass test) was applied to find out the difference between the neck angles.

Fig. 1. Virtual dog A (dog-like).

Fig. 2. Virtual dog B (wolf-like).

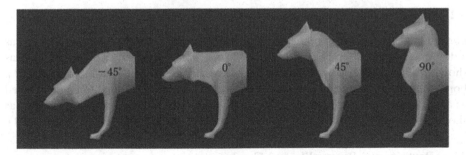

Fig. 3. Four kinds of neck angles for virtual dog B.

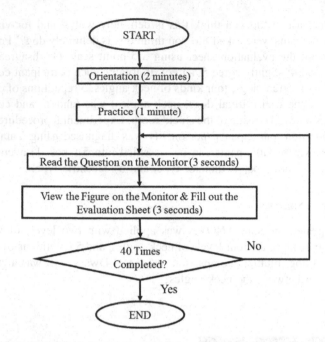

Fig. 4. Experimental procedure for each participant.

3   Results

3.1   The Effect of Virtual Dogs A (Dog-like) and B (Wolf-like)

Participants' response to virtual dogs A and B are shown in Figs. 5 and 6, respectively. Two type of virtual dogs were found to be significant factor ($p < 0.05$) on the evaluation scores. Also, the neck angles were found to be significant factors ($p < 0.01$) on the evaluation scores.

3.2   The Effect of Neck Angles on Virtual Dogs A and B

For virtual dog A (dog-like), the neck angle of 90 degree was found to be recognized as a dog the best and the neck angle of −45 degree was recognized as a dog the least as shown in Fig. 5. They were found to be statistically significantly different ($p < 0.01$). For virtual dog B (wolf-like), the neck angle of 45 degree was found to be recognized as a dog the best and the neck angle of −45 degree was recognized as a dog the least as shown in Fig. 6. They were found to be statistically significantly different ($p < 0.01$).

3.3   Participants' Personality and Gender

As a result of Y-G test, participants were classified into 5 groups: 4 participants for average type, 2 for black list, 6 for calm type, 2 for director type, 5 for eccentric type,

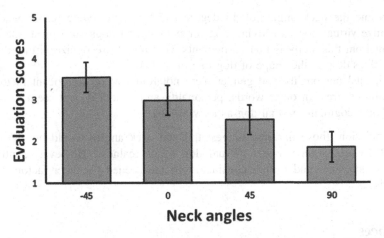

Fig. 5. Results of participants' evaluation scores for virtual dog A (N = 20).

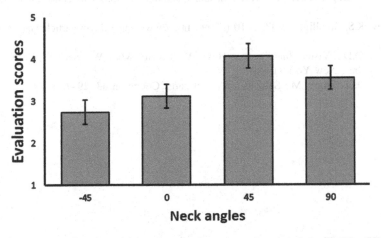

Fig. 6. Results of participants' evaluation scores for virtual dog B (N = 20).

and 1 for entry mistakes. Their personality was not found to be significant factor for the evaluation scores. Also, participants' gender difference was not found to be significant.

4   Discussion

Under the limited conditions, the following conclusion can be made:

1. We observed statistically significant difference between virtual dogs A and B ($p < 0.05$). This is due to the fact that the question for virtual dog A was different from the question for virtual dog B. For virtual dog A (dog-like), the question was about wolf. For virtual dog B (wolf-like), the question was about dog. However, the neck angles were found to be highly significant factor ($p < 0.01$) on the evaluation

scores and the neck angles of 45 degree and 90 degree were recommended to recognize virtual dog as a living dog for both virtual dogs. The most interesting finding from this study is that participants were able to recognize virtual dogs as living dogs despite the shape of dog-like or wolf-like.

2. Participants' personality and gender were not found to be significant factors for evaluation scores. In other words, personality and gender do not seem to be any effect on recognizing virtual dog as a living dog.

In conclusion, those findings suggest that the neck angles would be one of the important factors to recognize a virtual dog to its realness. However, continuous research is necessary and further considerations are needed for other factors of dog characteristics.

References

1. Miklósi, Á.: Dog Behaviour, Evolution, and Cognition. Oxford University Press, England (2007)
2. McGrew, K.S.: Intelligence 37, 1–10 (2009). http://www.iapsych.com/articles/mcgrew2009.pdf
3. Hoffman, D.D.: Visual Intelligence: How We Create What We See. W.W. Norton & Company, Inc., New York (1998)
4. Hoffman, D.D., Singh, M.: Salience of visual parts. Cognition 63, 29–78 (1997)

Authoring Interactions for Tangible Augmented Reality

Karan Jain[✉] and Young Mi Choi

Georgia Institute of Technology, Atlanta, GA 30332, USA
Kjain33@gatech.edu

Abstract. Tangible Augmented Reality (TAR) has been explored for creating design representation for usability testing of industrial products. Currently, the process of authoring complex interactions for TAR entails scripting or low-level programming. A review of existing AR authoring tools showed that visual programming and authoring in the augmented view can potentially improve the efficiency of authoring interactions for TAR. This paper presents a review of the abilities and features provided by current AR authoring tools in order to identify requirements and opportunities necessary for non-programmers to author interactions for TAR.

Keywords: Tangible Augmented Reality · Authoring interactions · Usability

1 Introduction

Tangible augmented reality (TAR) is an augmented reality (AR) related technology where virtual components are registered to physical components and virtual components can be manipulated by interacting with physical components in the real world [4, 5]. In the context of creating design representations for usability testing, a TAR design representation can be extremely valuable since these representations not only communicate product aesthetic and scale but also tangible interactions with the product. These capabilities of TAR design representations allow for an accurate communication of how the product functions and feels [6, 12]. Figure 1 shows the TAR design representation of a space heater where users interact with the physical representation of the heater and the results of the interaction are seen in the digital model of the heater through the iPad [10]. TAR design representations can be extremely useful in the early stages of the product development process where designers can test a greater number of product concepts and get more accurate feedback from users more efficiently.

Even though TAR provides benefits in representing designs in the product development process, developing TAR representations is extremely challenging and time consuming. As discussed by Jain, the development of a TAR representation entails creating 2D and 3D assets of product visuals, fabricating a physical representation of the product, and developing interactions between the physical and digital elements of an experience [10]. It can be assumed that designers are proficient with 2D and 3D asset creation, however, developing the response, in a virtual component, when a user manipulates a physical component is a challenging task with current existing tools and

C. Stephanidis and M. Antona (Eds.): HCII 2020, CCIS 1225, pp. 43–50, 2020.
https://doi.org/10.1007/978-3-030-50729-9_6

Fig. 1. TAR design representation of a space heater

technologies. A literature review of existing authoring tools for augmented reality (AR) applications showed that currently the most efficient way to author tangible interactions for AR applications is through scripting. However, visual programming can be a more efficient way of authoring tangible interactions for non-programmers. This paper presents a review of the abilities and features provided by current AR authoring tools in order to identify requirements and opportunities necessary for non-programmers to author interactions for TAR. An interaction for TAR entails a physical component and a digital component and this paper will focus on the process of developing the effect in the augmented visual that the physical manipulation has.

2   Related Work

Gimeno et al. describe AR authoring tools as tools that allow for easy and fast development of AR applications by not relying on time and cost computing recompilation steps [7]. Authoring tools can be programming tools that provide greater control over the development of the application or they could be tools that hide the low-level tasks and provide a graphical user interface (GUI) to author an application. In the latter case, the user has less control over the development of the application since there is a greater level of abstraction required. The review on AR authoring tools showed that low-level libraries, high level frameworks, plug-in tools, and stand-alone tools have a different process of authoring interactions and hence, tools from each of these categories is discussed in this paper.

2.1   Authoring Interactions with Low Level Programming

When low-level libraries like ARToolkit [15], Wikitude SDK [1], Vuforia SDK [16], etc. are used for developing AR applications, interactions need to be authored with the C++ programming language. These tools require a thin level of abstraction, which yields a high degree of performance and flexibility. However, the cost to this benefit of authoring applications is that these tools require the user to manually define interaction techniques, visualization, and simulation aspects [9]. Since, the main purpose of low-level tools is to provide core functionalities like image marker tracking, spatial registration of objects, and 3D rendering, they are often not used solely by themselves, but combined with other libraries and tools to make the process of authoring AR applications more efficient. These high level software frameworks or wrappers combine low-level libraries to provide core AR functionalities and other libraries for authoring of media content and interactions, allowing developers to worry about interactions between virtual objects rather than low- level tasks like tracking and object rendering. An example of a wrapper for AR development is osgART, which is a cross platform development library that combines computer vision based tracking libraries with the 3D graphics library OpenSceneGraph [17]. It provides functionalities like high level integration of video output, spatial registration, and photometric registration. Even with osgART, users have to author interactions with C++.

2.2 Authoring Interactions with Scripting

It is common for users to author interactions with a scripting language if they are using a plug-in or stand-alone authoring tool. Plug-in tools combine low-level libraries, which provide core AR functionalities like AR visualization, tracking, and rendering, into a wrapper that can be used with commonly used authoring platforms that a user may be familiar with [2, 3]. These tools do not require the user to have knowledge of low-level programming but be familiar with object oriented scripting if the user wants to develop complex interaction behaviors. DART (Designer's AR Toolkit) is an AR authoring tool that was developed as a plug in for Macromedia Director. DART was developed to aid early and often testing of AR experiential designs and it supported early design activities like the transition from story boards to working experiences [13]. The target user was a skilled multimedia designer who was familiar with Macromedia Director. It was built with the assumption that "designers can and will venture out "into the code" and they will continue to use their existing tools (e.g. Photoshop, Maya) for content creation.". DART was built on top of Director which included an object-oriented programming language called Lingo. Since, all of the behaviors in DART were written in Lingo, it allowed developers to modify standard behaviors as well as write their own scripts from scratch. Designers could also add scripts to objects through a drag and drop interaction.

Unity is one of the most popular commercially available game development platform that is used by professional game developers and indie game developers [18]. The Vuforia software development kit (SDK) can be used with Unity3D to provide AR functionalities like tracking and AR visualization to content that is authored in Unity. This has made the platform popular among virtual reality (VR) and AR developers and is used as a prototyping tool for AR and VR experiences by hobbyists and researchers. The Unity interface is a GUI, which allows users to use visual programming paradigms to author media content, like drag and drop 3D geometries into the Unity scene, click buttons and drag sliders in the inspector window to edit appearance or behaviors of virtual components. However, authoring complex interaction behaviors in Unity is not possible through visual programming but by scripting with C#, especially for TAR. Several C# libraries, developed by third party developers, can also be found on the Unity Asset Store to author interaction behaviors for virtual components. An example of such a library is Lean Touch [19]. Using such libraries does not require the user to write any scripts, however, the user still needs to have some understanding of object oriented scripting in order to understand how to use such libraries and slightly tweak the scripts to make them more applicable for their use case. Further, the workflow of Unity entails setting up the Unity scene and writing scripts for object behaviors in the desktop view and then exporting the application to the respective platform for testing the build or testing on the device through the Unity Editor. This flow makes the process of authoring and testing interactions slow since the user does not get immediate feedback to an action they perform.

2.3   Authoring Interactions with Visual Programming

Users who want to author AR applications without writing any code can use stand-alone AR authoring tools that provide a complete software to build end-to-end AR applications. These tools use low-level libraries to provide all the core AR function-alities and a GUI that allows for authoring interactions and media content. These tools can be extremely valuable for rapid prototyping of AR experiences, however, they may limit the functionalities of object behaviors since users can only work with function-alities offered by the software and not develop complex interactions though low-level programming or scripting. ComposAR is a GUI based tool for users with non or little programming knowledge to author AR applications [14]. It supports both visual pro-gramming (drag and drop interface) and interpretive scripting. The GUI consists of a tree layout, where a node in the tree structure can be activated with a click, highlighting the respective 3D object in the scene and showing manipulation handles. In the context of TAR, ComposAR provides basic interaction approaches based on fiducial proximity, occlusion, tilting, and shaking and also provides the functionality to interactively write live code and monitor the actual outcome (immediate mode for runtime testing). An additional benefit of ComposAR is that the software is built in Python which allows for third party modules to be incorporated into the authoring environment. It provides a GUI for authoring interactions, however, complex interactions with physical compo-nents can only be developed with Python scripts.

Similar to ComposAR, AMIRE (Authoring Mixed Reality) was another research project that focused on authoring interactions for AR experiences. AMIRE was a project whose goal was to "motivate people without programming skills (e.g. designers, artists, domain specific experts, etc.) to author mixed reality applications instead of coding them." [8]. The AMIRE authoring tools was based on a component-based framework, which supported an authoring environment for PDAs and Tablet PCs. CATOMIR was a visual programming interface that was built on top of AMIRE. The interface followed a three step approach where users had to find the right com-ponents for the application, tweak the components respectively, and connect the components through a drag-and-drop interaction to define logical behaviors. The drawback of CATOMIR was that AR applications could only have the functionality supported by the components, and it was difficult to add new components [2, 3]. This limited the type and number of interactions that users could develop for virtual com-ponents. A tool that focused on authoring tangible interactions for AR experiences, without requiring any programming, was developed by Lee et al. [11]. The goal of their study was to evaluate a tool for authoring AR content behavior and interactions from within the AR interface, which they called "immersive authoring". The development environment and the execution environment was the same in "immersive authoring" and the authoring environment provided the full experience of the building contents by itself. Just like AMIRE, Lee et al. proposed a component based application model for tangible AR applications to develop their framework. User interactions involved browsing through a list of components and properties for those components with a physical object that acted as a pointer. The user identified properties of different components and then connected the properties to author interactions. Such a component based framework allowed for easy direct manipulation of 3D virtual objects with immersive authoring AR environments. A drawback of this tool was that users could not author complex interaction behaviors because the component based framework allowed for matching the specified properties and did not allow the user to create new properties.

Other commercially available tools like Layar Creator allow for web based authoring and creating AR links on printed materials. This is commonly used for marketing purposes because it allows users to upload images to the Layar Creator website and add virtual buttons that have links to various services available on the mobile device, such as opening a webpage or a YouTube video, calling a specific number, or sharing information on social network services. The created content can be viewed through the Layar mobile AR browser [2, 3]. Wikitude Studio [20], which is built with the Wikitude SDK, is a more complete web based authoring tool that allows users to create mobile AR content and deploy either onto the Wikitude AR browser app or even create a custom mobile app [2, 3]. Wikitude provides a platform for target management and a platform for creating and editing AR content, without writing any code. Wikitude's studio editor supports simple drag-and-drop interface, an intuitive workflow, easy testing, and fast publishing. It allows a non-programmer to build a complete AR experience without writing any code as well as developing simple interactions for the virtual components. More recent authoring tools include Amazon Sumerian and Adobe Aero. Sumerian was developed with the goal of allowing users to build quick 3D and AR web experiences. These experiences can be accessed via simple browser URL and also run on popular AR/VR hardware. It also allows users to drag and drop assets, like a fbx 3D model, from their desktop into the scene view. Since this is a web based tool complex interactions can be developed with HTML, CSS, and Javascript [21]. Aero is developed by Adobe for quickly prototyping AR experiences for testing concepts or developing pitches for clients [22]. It is targeted towards designers who are well versed with the Adobe Creative Cloud, since it allows for importing files from other Adobe tools like Photoshop, Illustrator, Dimension, Substance, and third party apps like Cinema 4D. The workflow of Aero allows users to anchor virtual content to a physical space and then resize and reposition the objects. Further interactivity can be developed for virtual content using an event driven framework. Users can set a trigger, such as touch, that would set off an action from a list of specific behaviors (like jump, rotate, etc.). The shortcoming of this tool is that it does not allow for an input trigger to be from the physical world, but only from an interaction with the digital device the application is running on.

3 Conclusion – Gaps and Opportunities

Features that are essential in the design of an authoring tool for TAR can be identified from the review of existing tools and frameworks. All AR authoring tools provide the core functionalities of tracking and rendering by using low-level libraries and frameworks. Currently, to author tangible interactions for AR, designers use plug-in tools or stand-alone tools that allow for interaction authoring through scripting. However, visual programming can be a more efficient method for non-programmers to author tangible interactions while developing TAR design representations for usability testing. The review of existing GUI based tools showed that these tools cannot be used to develop complex interaction behaviors for TAR. An example of complex behavior can be seen in Fig. 1, where the virtual fan in the digital model of the heater spins when the knobs on the physical model of the heater are rotated. Currently, such an interaction can only be achieved through scripting or low-level programming, which may not be the most efficient method for designers to authoring interactions for TAR. Another feature that significantly influences the user experience of an AR authoring tool is discussed by Lee et al. Their study discussed the concept of what you see is what you get output (WYSIWYG), which is a crucial component of most 2D authoring systems like Microsoft PowerPoint, Adobe Illustrator, etc. Authoring interactions in the augmented view and getting immediate feedback to the action taken by a user is presumed to provide fast evaluation of the resulting content. This entails the authoring platform and execution or testing environment being the same [11]. Platforms like CATOMIR, ComposAR, Adobe Aero, and "Immersive Authoring", provide this functionality of authoring in the augmented view, however, they all do not give immediate feedback to a user's action.

Table 1 shows high level features that are recognized to be essential in the design of a tool for authoring interactions for TAR. It can be hypothesized that having these features in the tool will increase the efficiency of authoring interactions for TAR design representations for designers and content creators who currently author interactions with scripting in plug-in or stand-alone tools. "Authoring interactions" is defined as developing the response in the virtual component when a user manipulates a physical component in the real world.

Table 1. Identified high level features for an authoring tool for TAR interactions.

Authoring method	Authoring platform	Testing platform
Visual programming	Mobile device	Mobile device

In conclusion, designers can only author complex interaction behaviors for TAR with scripting or low-level programming. A review of current existing tools showed that visual programming and authoring in the augmented view can potentially improve the efficiency of authoring interactions. A tool for authoring the effect in a virtual component of a TAR design representation for a physical manipulation will be developed and investigated in a subsequent study.

References

1. Amin, D., Govilkar, S.: Comparative study of augmented reality SDK's. Int. J. Comput. Sci. Appl. **5**(1), 11–26 (2015)
2. Billinghurst, M., Clark, A., Lee, G.: A survey of augmented reality. Found. Trends Hum.-Comput. Interact. **8**(2–3), 73–272 (2014)
3. Anderson, R.E.: Social impacts of computing: codes of professional ethics. Soc. Sci. Comput. Rev. **10**(2), 453–469 (1992)
4. Billinghurst, M., Kato, H., Poupyrev, I.: Tangible augmented reality. In: ACM SIGGRAPH ASIA 2008 Courses (2008)
5. Heilig, M.L.: Sensorama Simulator. U.S. Patent 3,050,870, Filed 10 January 1961, issued 28 August 1962 (1962)
6. Choi, Y.M.: Applying tangible augmented reality for product usability assessment. J. Usability Stud. **14**(4), 187–200 (2019)
7. Gimeno, J., Morillo, P., Orduña, J.M., Fernández, M.: An easy-to-use AR authoring tool for industrial applications. In: Csurka, G., Kraus, M., Laramee, R.S., Richard, P., Braz, J. (eds.) VISIGRAPP 2012. CCIS, vol. 359, pp. 17–32. Springer, Heidelberg (2013). https://doi.org/10.1007/978-3-642-38241-3_2
8. Haller, M., Stauder, E., Zauner, J.: AMIRE-ES: authoring mixed reality once, run it anywhere. In: Proceedings of the 11th International Conference on Human-Computer Interaction, HCII 2005 (2005)
9. Hampshire, A., Seichter, H., Grasset, R., Billinghurst, M.: Augmented reality authoring: generic context from programmer to designer. In: Kjeldskov, J., Paay, J. (eds.) Proceedings of the 18th Australia Conference on Computer-Human Interaction: Design: Activities, Artefacts and Environments (OZCHI 2006), pp. 409–412. ACM, New York (2006). http://dx.doi.org/10.1145/1228175.1228259
10. Jain, K., Choi, Y.M.: Building tangible augmented reality models for use in product development. In: Proceedings of the Design Society: International Conference on Engineering Design, vol. 1, no. 1, pp. 1913–1922 (2019)
11. Lee, G.A., Kim, G.J.: Immersive authoring of Tangible Augmented Reality content: a user study. J. Vis. Lang. Comput. **20**(2), 61–79 (2009)
12. Lee, W., Park, J.: Augmented foam: a tangible augmented reality for product design. In: Proceedings of the Fourth IEEE and ACM International Symposium on Symposium on Mixed and Augmented Reality, ISMAR 2005, pp. 106–109 (2005)
13. MacIntyre, B., Gandy, M., Dow, S., Bolter, J.D.: DART: a toolkit for rapid design exploration of augmented reality experiences. In: Proceedings of the 17th Annual ACM Symposium on User Interface Software and Technology (UIST 2004), pp. 197–206. ACM, New York (2004). https://doi.org/10.1145/1029632.1029669
14. Seichter, H., Looser, J., Billinghurst, M.: ComposAR: an intuitive tool for authoring AR applications. In: Proceedings of the 7th IEEE/ACM International Symposium on Mixed and Augmented Reality (ISMAR 2008), pp. 177–178. IEEE Computer Society, Washington, DC (2008). https://doi.org/10.1109/ISMAR.2008.4637354
15. ARToolKit. http://www.hitl.washington.edu/artoolkit/. Accessed 20 Dec 2019
16. Vuforia Developer Portal. https://developer.vuforia.com/. Accessed 23 Dec 2019
17. osgART. https://osgart.org/. Accessed 23 Dec 2019
18. Unity Real-Time Development Platform: 3D, 2D VR & AR Visualizations. https://unity.com/. Accessed 23 Dec 2019
19. Lean Touch - Asset Store. https://assetstore.unity.com/packages/tools/input-management/lean-touch-30111. Accessed 23 Dec 2019

20. Wikitude Studio-Augmented Reality Creation & Management Tool. https://www.wikitude.com/products/studio/. Accessed 23 Dec 2019
21. Amazon Sumerian Overview. https://aws.amazon.com/sumerian/. Accessed 23 Dec 2019
22. Create augmented reality experiences: Adobe Aero. https://www.adobe.com/products/aero.html. Accessed 23 Dec 2019

A Method of Shape Deformation Using a Cage Considering Shape Features

Takayuki Kanaya[1(✉)], Naoyuki Awano[2(✉)], Yuta Muraki[3(✉)],
and Ken-ichi Kobori[3(✉)]

[1] Hiroshima International University, Higashihiroshima City, Hiroshima, Japan
t-kanaya@hirokoku-u.ac.jp
[2] Osaka University of Economics, Osaka City, Osaka, Japan
awano@osaka-ue.ac.jp
[3] Osaka Institute of Technology, Hirakata City, Osaka, Japan
{yuta.muraki,kenichi.kobori}@oit.ac.jp

Abstract. In computer graphics, cage-based deformation techniques have been relatively studied. The most time-consuming task in cage-based deformation is the construction of the cage which surrounds the model to be deformed. In this paper, we propose a method of cage-based deformation considering the shape features of its original model. In particular, we describe how to generate the cages. We first evaluate the features, such as curvature, the dihedral angles of the input model, and then voxelize it. We generate a triangular mesh from the surface voxels bounding them and transfer the features of input model to the triangular mesh. Finally, we apply a variational remeshing method to this triangular mesh. The variational remeshing method is a method minimizing the energy function resulting in good solution by global relaxation until convergence. An experiment result demonstrates that our method is effective.

Keywords: Cages generation · Voxels · Cage-based deformation

1 Introduction

Sorkine et al. [1] proposed a discrete deformation technique based on the Laplacian of the mesh. In this method, for every vertex and 1-ring neighborhood vertices connected to it, the shape is deformed so that all vertices are optimized. This approach is numerically stable, but is not able to compute in real-time, because it depends on the number of vertices. Therefore, Ju et al. [2] proposed a method to reduce computational cost. This is a way to build a similar but coarse structure with fewer vertices, and then deform the dense model through the coarser structure. This coarser structure, which surrounds the original dense model, is called a cage. However, the cage is constructed mainly by hand. It takes several hours, or even longer to construct it over the dense mesh model. So, automatic generation methods of the cage over the dense mesh model are needed.

There are many methods of automatic cage generation [3–9]. For example, Ben-Chen et al. [3] has proposed in a paper related to a deformation transfer method. The deformation transfer method receives as an input: a source reference pose, a deformed

© Springer Nature Switzerland AG 2020
C. Stephanidis and M. Antona (Eds.): HCII 2020, CCIS 1225, pp. 51–56, 2020.
https://doi.org/10.1007/978-3-030-50729-9_7

source pose and a target reference pose. The output of the deformation transfer is a deformed target pose. In this method, to apply the space deformation analysis and synthesis they need to envelopes the source and target reference shapes with polyhedral cages, they proposed an automatic cage generation using a simplification. Xian et al. [4] have proposed a method to generate the coarse bounding cage by uniform voxelization. However, the size of the voxels is uniform, the generated coarse bounding cage is usually too dense. Therefore, they have improved [4] using the improved OBB tree and the Boolean union operation to adjust and merge them into a whole entity [5]. In addition, they have developed another automatic method to generate the cage using voxelization based decomposition [6]. After voxelizing an input model, they decompose the model into broad regions and narrow regions by dilating the inner voxel groups. Then they construct partial cages using different strategies and unite them to get a cage. Zheng-Jie et al. [7] have proposed an automatic cage generation based on a simplification. When simplifying an input model with quadric error metrics and quadratic programming to build a coarse cage. Sacht et al. [8] have proposed an approach for nesting multiresolution mesh. This approach constructs and adds a coarser level to the hierarchy, using a sequence of decimation, flow, and contact-aware optimization steps. Huy et al. [9] have proposed a semi-automatic method to generate cages. Starting from user-specified cut slides, this method automatically optimizes the consistent, orthogonal orientations of cage cross sections. Then these cross sections together divide the whole cage into parts.

Our method is a kind of voxel-based method. The target shape is the initial shape of industrial products without skeletons. If there is a skeleton, the deformation that does not follow the skeleton becomes unnatural, and it is not suitable for the initial shape of industrial products. In addition, it is possible to be able to place many vertices at characteristic points of the shape using our method.

2   Cage Generation Algorithm

Since our algorithm is an extension of Alliez's algorithm [10] which is a kind of variational remeshing methods, we briefly explain the basic principles and the resulting base algorithm, as illustrated in Fig. 1. The first stage of this algorithm provides an initial geometry resampling by performing an error diffusion process directly over the original triangle mesh. The second stage computes a conformal parameterization of the original model over a planar domain, connects the samples using a constrained Delaunay triangulation built in parameter space, then optimizes the sampling by building a weighted centroidal Voronoi tessellation in parameter space. The final stage restores the embedding by locating every vertex in its associated triangle in parameter space and computing its barycentric coordinates.

Next, we explain the procedure of the cage generation method we propose. Our algorithm mainly includes the following steps:

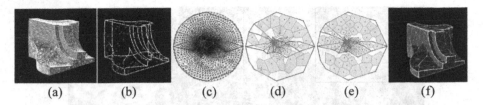

Fig. 1. An example of Alliez's algorithm. (a) An original mesh model. (b) Providing the initial geometry resampling. (c) Computing the conformal parameterization. (d) Connecting the samples by the constrained Delaunay triangulation. (e) Optimizing the sampling. (f) projecting back every sample onto its corresponding triangle in $\mathbb{R}^3$.

1. Evaluate the features of an original mesh model.
2. Voxelize the mesh model and create feature edge voxels.
3. Create the surfaced voxel model of the voxels and transfer the features of the original mesh model to the surfaced voxel model.
4. Apply Alliez's algorithm to the surfaced voxel model.

2.1   Evaluating the Features of an Original Mesh Model

The first step of the cage generation algorithm is to evaluate the features of an original mesh model M_o. The features we evaluate are curvatures and sharp edges. As the curvature d, we use the absolute value of the mean curvature and Gaussian curvature at each vertex as shown in Eq. (1).

$$d = \alpha d_m^p + \beta d_g^q \tag{1}$$

where, d_m is the absolute value of the mean curvature and d_g is the Gaussian curvature. α, β, p, q are factors, which are specified by a user. Currently, we chose $\alpha = 0.5$, $\beta = 0.5$, $p = 2$, $q = 1$ respectively on an empirical basis. Also, the sharp edges are mainly classified using dihedral angle thresholding specified by a user. We can further use a more sophisticated approach [11, 12]. We call edges extracted with the associated dihedral angle "Feature Edges" (*FE*).

2.2   Voxelization of the Mesh Model and Creation of Feature Edge Voxels

The M_o is voxelized. The purpose of this step is to generate a cage outside M_o. The length of the bounding box is the length of the M_o's bounding box plus 0 to half the voxel length of the M_o's bounding box depending on the gaps. The resolution of the voxels for this bounding box is specified by a user. Boundary voxels, which are the ones intersecting with the mesh surface, are identified.

Next, we compute Feature Edge Voxels (*FEV*) from voxels and *FE*s, as illustrated in Fig. 2. The *FEV* is generated from the voxel model and the feature edge information. This is created by testing the intersection of each voxel and the *FE*s. These red voxels in Fig. 2(c) represent voxels that contain the terminal points of the *FE*s. We call the red voxels "Feature Vertex Voxels" (*FVV*).

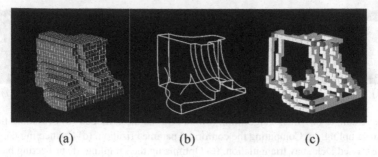

Fig. 2. Creation of feature edge voxels. (a) Voxels. (b) Feature Edges (*FE*). (c) The voxels are Feature Edge Voxels (*FEV*), especially, the red voxels are Feature Vertex Voxels (*FVV*). (Color figure online)

2.3 Create the Surfaced Voxel Model of the Voxels and Transfer the Features of M_o to the Surfaced Voxel Model

The adjacency of 6 neighbors for each boundary voxel is checked and then faces are created on the surfaces of the boundary voxel that are not adjacent to other boundaries and internal voxels. We call this creation "Surfaced Voxel Model" (*SVM*). Next, *FE*s are generated on the *SVM* based on the *FEV* using the Dijkstra method [13].

We first regard vertices and edges of the outer faces constructing to a piece of *FEV* as a graph. A source vertex and target vertex are decided in the graph. To decide the terminal vertices, the number of the outer faces constructing a voxel is taken into consideration as shown in Fig. 3. In the case of 3 faces, the vertex sharing 3 faces is selected. In the case of 2 faces, there are two candidate vertices sharing 2 faces. Therefore, the vertex sharing other feature edges is selected. Because the terminal vertices are also intersections of a few *FE*s. If there are two *FE*s, the vertex with the shorter *FE* is selected. In the case of 1 face, there are 4 candidate vertices per face. Therefore, the vertex that has the shortest *FE* is selected. Then, the distance on the graph is decided. We want *FE*s to pass through corners as much as possible. Therefore, the combination of 6-adjacent relationships between voxels is considered, so the length of each edge is adjusted so that the lengths of edges passing through corners are shorter than the lengths of edges passing through interiors. By applying the Dijkstra method with these settings, a *FE* that preferentially passes through the corners of the shape can be created.

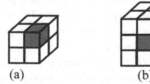

(a)   (b)   (c)

Fig. 3. The pattern of the terminal vertices. (a) Only one vertex sharing 3 faces. (b) The 2 candidate vertices of edge sharing 2 faces. (c) The 4 candidate vertices of 1 face.

Next, we describe the curvature at each vertex of the *SVM*. First, the curvature of each voxel is computed. The curvature of the vertices of the original model contained in a voxel is averaged and is used as the voxel curvature. Then the curvature of the vertex on the *SVM* is the average value of the 4 voxel curvatures adjacent to the vertex.

2.4 Apply Alliez's Algorithm to the Surfaced Voxel Model

Vertices that constitute a cage are distributed on the *SVM*. At this time, the number of vertices is specified by the user. In the same way as Alliez's method, samples are preferentially distributed over the terminal vertices of the *FE*s, the areas with large curvature on the *FE*s, and the areas with large curvature on the faces. The remainder of the procedures also is executed in the same way as Alliez's algorithm.

3 Result and Discussion

The automatic cage generation algorithm developed in this paper runs on PCs with Intel Core i7™ 3.6 GHz CPU and 16.0 GB memory. The generated cage and the deformed shape by the cage are illustrated in Fig. 4. We used Ju's algorithm [2] for the cage-based deformation. The number of faces of the original model is 12,946. The number of faces of the cage is 314 (Using 32 × 32 × 32 voxels).

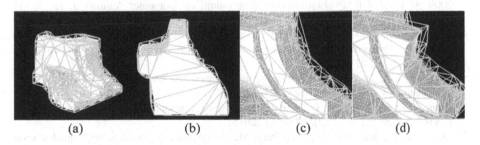

(a)   (b)   (c)   (d)

Fig. 4. Cage generation for the Fandisk and shape deformation by using our method. (a) The cage (The front view). (b) The cage (The bottom view). (c, d) The cage of original model before and after deformation.

As shown in Fig. 4, we can get the coarse cage which encloses the original model. Additionally, we generate the cage so that it depends on the curvature. As you can see in Fig. 4(a)–(c), there are many vertices in the areas with high curvatures but there are few vertices in flat areas. Also, as you can see in Fig. 4(c)–(d), the parts with high curvature can be flexibly deformed using the cage made by our method. With our method, it is possible to increase the number of cage vertices, which are control points, in the areas of high curvature where the user is interested. However, in many of the previous works described above, it is not possible to partially control the number of vertices that generate a cage depending on the shape features, such as curvature and dihedral angle.

4 Conclusions and Future Work

In this paper, we have proposed an automatic cage generation algorithm from a shape with a variational remeshing method and deformed the shape using the cage. The shape's feature are evaluated, and the shape is voxelized. Also feature edge voxels and the surfaced voxel model are created, and the features of the shape are transferred to the surfaced voxel model. Finally, Alliez's algorithm is applied to the surfaced voxel model and we can get a cage that considers shape features for the shape and deformed the shape using the cage.

For future work we plan to make a comprehensive evaluation of the cages with our method, when the cages are applied to collision detection, deformation transfer, physical simulation and so on.

References

1. Sorkine, O., Cohen-Or, D., Lipman, Y., Alexa, M., Rössl, C., Seidel, H.-P.: Laplacian surface editing. In: Proceedings of Symposium on Geometry Processing, pp. 179–188 (2004)
2. Ju, T., Schaefer, S., Warren, J.: Mean value coordinates for closed triangular meshes. In: ACM SIGGRAPH 2005, pp. 561–566 (2005)
3. Ben-Chen, M., Weber, O., Gotsman, C.: Spatial deformation transfer. In: Proceedings of the 2009 ACM SIGGRAPH/Eurographics Symposium on Computer Animation, pp. 67–74 (2009)
4. Xian, C., Lin, H., Gao, S.: Automatic generation of coarse bounding cages from dense meshes. In: Proceedings of 2009 IEEE International Conference on Shape Modeling and Applications, pp. 21–27 (2009)
5. Xian, C., Lin, H., Gao, S.: Automatic cage generation by improved OBBs for mesh deformation. Visual Comput. **28**(1), 21–33 (2012)
6. Xian, C., Li, G., Xiong, Y.: Efficient and effective cage generation by region decomposition. J. Vis. Comput. Anim. **26**(2), 173–184 (2015)
7. Zheng-Jie, D., Xiao-Nan, L., Xiao-Ping, M.: Automatic cage building with quadric error metrics. Comput. Sci. Technol. **26**(3), 538–547 (2011)
8. Sacht, L., Vouga, E., Jacobson, A.: Nested cages. ACM Trans. Graph. (TOG) **34**(6), 1–14 (2015)
9. Huy Le, B., Deng, Z.: Interactive cage generation for mesh deformation. In: Proceedings of the 21st ACM SIGGRAPH Symposium on Interactive 3D Graphics and Games (2017). Article No. 3
10. Alliez, P., de Verdire, E.C., Devillers, O., Isenburg, M.: Isotropic surface remeshing. In: Proceeding of 2003 Shape Modeling International, pp. 49–58 (2003)
11. Hubeli, A., Gross, M.: Multiresolution feature extraction from unstructured meshes. In: Proceedings of IEEE Visualization Conference, pp. 287–294 (2001)
12. Watanabe, K., Belyaev, A.: Detection of salient curvature features on polygonal surfaces. In: Proceedings of Computer Graphics Forum. Eurographics 2001, vol. 20(3), pp. 385–392 (2001)
13. Dijkstra, E.W.: A note on two problems in connexion with graphs. Numer. Math. **1**, 269–271 (1959)

Exposure Compensation from a Single Image

Keitaro Kawamori[1]([✉]), Ryo Akamatsu[1], Yuta Muraki[1],
Toshiaki Kondo[2], and Ken-ichi Kobori[1]

[1] Osaka Institute of Technology, 1-79-1 Kitayama, Hirakata City, Osaka, Japan
gurennnya@gmail.com
[2] Sirindhorn International Institute of Technology, 99 Moo 18,
Km. 41 on Paholyothin Highway Khlong Luang, Pathum Thani 12120, Thailand

Abstract. We propose a method to convert underexposed/overexposed images to appropriately exposed image from a single image. Digital cameras have a limited dynamic range which is smaller than one in the real world, so that it often takes overexposed/underexposed images. The HDR method synthesizes images with different exposures into an image to improve visibility of a narrow dynamic range image. However, HDR has several limitations to get good images. One of them is difficult to take the appropriate multiple exposed images. Because When taking the multiple exposed images, the camera and object must not move to avoid the ghost effect. The proposed method can improve the narrow dynamic range with a single image. In addition, it can avoid to generate ghost effect in the output image. Our method generates three of the pseudo multiple exposed images from a single image. In the process of generating pseudo high exposed and low exposed image, our method uses gamma correction to adjust luminance of input image. Moreover, gamma correction can enhance the difference between each color channel in the dark or bright area of the input image. Because of gamma correction, the contrast of the input image is properly improved. We utilize the Contrast Limited Adaptive Histogram Equalization (CLAHE) to make the pseudo middle exposed image. Three types of pseudo exposed images generated will be synthesized into an output image which is high quality image as same as HDR image.

Keywords: HDR · Pseudo exposure image · Synthesis

1 Introduction

Digital cameras have a limited dynamic range which is smaller than one in the real world, so that it often takes overexposed/underexposed images that have bad visibility.

The HDR method synthesizes images with different exposure images into an image to improve visibility of a narrow dynamic range image. However, HDR has several limitations to get good images. One of them is difficult to take the appropriate multiple exposed images. Because When taking the multiple exposed images, the camera and object must not move to avoid the ghost effect. Because of the limitation, HDR cannot be applied directly images which are taken under dynamic scenes. It isn't useful for users.

© Springer Nature Switzerland AG 2020
C. Stephanidis and M. Antona (Eds.): HCII 2020, CCIS 1225, pp. 57–63, 2020.
https://doi.org/10.1007/978-3-030-50729-9_8

In this study, we propose the method that can improve the narrow dynamic range with a single image. In addition, it can avoid to generate ghost effect in the output image. High quality photos can be obtained easily for users who take photos.

2 The Proposed Method

The proposed method generates three of the pseudo multiple exposed images from a single image. In the process of generating pseudo high exposed and low exposed image, our method uses gamma correction to adjust luminance of input image. Gamma correction can enhance the difference between each color channel in the dark or bright area of the input image. Because of gamma correction, the contrast of the input image is properly improved. We use the Contrast Limited Adaptive Histogram Equalization (CLAHE) [1] to make the pseudo middle exposed image. Three types of pseudo exposed images obtained will be synthesized into an output image. Figure 1 shows a flowchart of the proposed method.

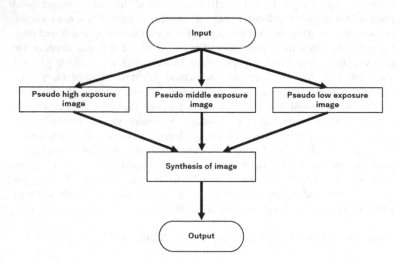

Fig. 1. A flowchart of the proposed method.

2.1 Generate Pseudo High Exposure Image

To obtain the pseudo high exposure image, we use gamma correction. Gamma correction is defined as follows:

$$f(x) = 255 \times \left(\frac{x}{255} \right)^{\left(\frac{1}{\gamma} \right)} \tag{1}$$

where x is a value of each color channel, and $\gamma (1 > \gamma)$ is value of gamma that adjusts correction strength. Pseudo high exposure image is generated by Gamma correction. Furthermore, determining the value of γ is important to generate an appropriate pseudo high exposure image. In general, best high exposure image has a lot of edges. Because an image including many edges has good visibility. Therefore, value of γ is determined by amount of edges. The flowchart for determining the appropriate γ value $(1 > \gamma)$ is illustrated in Fig. 2. First, Dark area image is extracted from input. Next, the gamma collection increases luminous of the dark area image. After that, amount of edges in the dark area image which has been adjusted by gamma collection is calculated using the edge detection [1], and compare it with amount of edges in the original dark area image. If edges of adjusted dark area image are bigger than original one, γ will be subtracted, and the procedure of gamma collection is repeated. From the second edge counting, make a comparison between edges in dark area image adjusted by added γ and edges in dark area image adjusted by before γ(no-added γ). If it shows decrease, previous γ will be determined as the appropriate γ to generate pseudo high exposure image.

And then, the gamma collection for input using determined γ gives pseudo high exposure image. Figure 3 shows an input and a pseudo high exposure image.

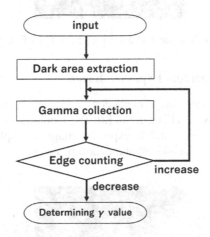

Fig. 2. A flowchart of determining γ value.

(a) Input image   (b) Pseudo high exposure image

Fig. 3. An input image and a pseudo high exposure image. (a) Input image, (b) Pseudo high exposure image

2.2   Generate Pseudo Low Exposure Image

The inverse gamma collection $(1 < \gamma)$ applies for input image to generate the low exposure image. Determining the appropriate value of γ is necessary. The procedure for determining the appropriate γ is similar to the one for making pseudo high exposure image. The generation of pseudo low exposure image extracts the bright area from the input image firstly. The appropriate $\gamma(1 < \gamma)$ is determined by same procedure for pseudo high exposure image. After that, input image is adjusted by inverse gamma collection using the determined γ to make pseudo low exposure image. The pseudo exposure image is shown in Fig. 4.

Fig. 4. Pseudo low exposure image from Fig. 3(a)

2.3   Generate Pseudo Middle Exposure Image

The pseudo middle exposure image is generated by using Contrast Limited Adaptive Histogram Equalization (CLAHE) method [2]. The method can equalize the luminance of image. We generate pseudo middle exposure image by applying this method. Figure 5 shows the generated pseudo middle exposure image.

Fig. 5. Pseudo middle exposure image from Fig. 3(a)

2.4   HDR Synthesis

The three of generated pseudo exposure images are synthesized into one pseudo HDR image by the HDR method [3]. A synthesized image is shown in Fig. 6.

Fig. 6. An output image of the proposed method from Fig. 3(a)

3   Experimental Result

Images by the proposed method and input images are shows in Fig. 7.

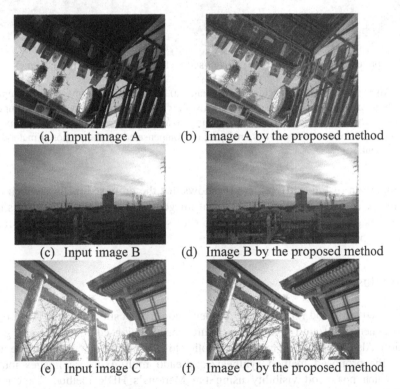

(a) Input image A   (b) Image A by the proposed method

(c) Input image B   (d) Image B by the proposed method

(e) Input image C   (f) Image C by the proposed method

Fig. 7. Input and Output of the proposed method. (a), (c), (e) Three test images and (b), (d), (f) compensated images by the proposed method.

Figure 7 shows experimental results by the proposed method on three test images. The left column shows the three test images that have underexposed or/and overexposed problems, while the right column exhibits compensated images by the proposed method. It is evident that the proposed method can improve the quality of the images. Figure 8 shows the differences between a common HDR method and the proposed method. An important feature of the proposed method is that it can be applied to a single image, whereas the HDR method is generally based on multiple images. Figure 8 also shows that the proposed method is free from the ghost effect.

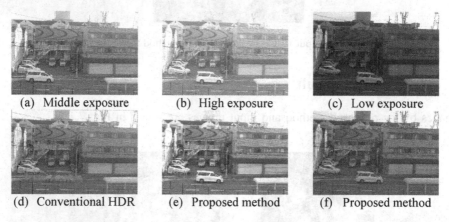

(a) Middle exposure   (b) High exposure   (c) Low exposure

(d) Conventional HDR   (e) Proposed method   (f) Proposed method

Fig. 8. An example of ghost effect on active scene. (a) Middle exposure image (one of inputs for (d)), (b) high exposure image (one of inputs for (d)), (c) Low exposure image (one of inputs for (d)), (d) synthesized by typical HDR method using (a) and (b) and (c) as inputs, (e) compensated by the proposed method using (b) as an input, (f) compensated by the proposed method using (c) as an input.

Comparison of Fig. 8(d), (e) and (f) shows that the proposed method which uses a single image is able to improve visibility of image as same as HDR which uses multi-exposure images. And the comparison also shows that the proposed method can avoid generating ghost effect.

4 Conclusion

We proposed a method for exposure compensation from a single image. The proposed method generates pseudo high/low exposure images using edge amount and gamma collection. Also, the CLAHE method is applied to generate the middle exposure image. Finally, the proposed method synthesizes pseudo multi-exposure images into one image which has good visibility using the Mertens's HDR method. Experimental results show that the proposed method can improve visibility as same as HDR without ghost effect. Therefore, users can take high quality images without taking multi-exposure photos. The proposed method gives the user an image similar to the HDR image in various scene.

References

1. Canny, J.: A computational approach to edge detection. IEEE Trans. Pattern Anal. Mach. Intell. **8**(6), 679–698 (1986)
2. Pizer, S.M., Amburn, E.P., Austin, J.D.: Adaptive histogram equalization and its variations. Comput. Vis. Graph. Image Process. **39**, 355–368 (1987)
3. Mertens, T., Kautz, J., Van Reeth, F.: Exposure fusion: a simple and practical alternative to high dynamic range photography. Comput. Graph. Forum **28**(1), 161–171 (2009)

Optimizing Virtual Reality Eye Tracking Fixation Algorithm Thresholds Based on Shopper Behavior and Age

Jaikishan Khatri[✉][iD], Masoud Moghaddasi[iD], Jose Llanes-Jurado,
Luciano Spinella, Javier Marín-Morales, Jaime Guixeres,
and Mariano Alcañiz

Instituto de Investigación e Innovación en Bioingeniería,
Universitat Politècnica de València, Valencia, Spain
jkhatri@i3b.upv.es

Abstract. Eye tracking (ET) is becoming a popular tool to study the consumer behavior. One of the significant problems that arise with ET integrated into 3D virtual reality is defining fixations and saccades, which are essential part of feature extraction in ET analysis and have a critical impact on higher level analysis. In this study, the ET data from 60 subjects, were recorded. To define the fixations, Dispersion Threshold Identification algorithm was used which requires to define several thresholds. Since there are multiple thresholds and extracted features, a Multi-Objective Reinforcement Learning (MORL) algorithm was implemented to solve this problem. The objective of the study was to optimize these thresholds in order to improve accuracy of classification of the age based on different visual patterns undertaken by the subject during shopping in a virtual store. Regarding the nature of the classification, the objective for this optimization problem was to maximize the differences between the averages of each feature in different classes and minimize the variances of the same feature within each class. For the current study, thresholds optimization has shown an improvement in results for the accuracies of classification between age groups after applying the MORL algorithm. In conclusion, the results suggest that the optimization of thresholds is an important factor to improve feature extraction methods and in turn improve the overall results of an ET study involving consumer behavior inside virtual reality. This method can be used to optimize thresholds in similar studies to provide improved accuracy of classification results.

Keywords: Multi-objective optimization · Reinforcement learning · Threshold · Optimization · Virtual reality · Eye tracking · Dispersion

1 Introduction

In recent years, with the increase in the number of consumer-grade eye trackers and the ability to be integrated with the Head Mounted Displays (HMD), Eye Tracking (ET) is becoming increasingly popular in retailing as a way to better understand consumers' visual attention and so gain insights as to how to stimulate sales of particular products

© Springer Nature Switzerland AG 2020
C. Stephanidis and M. Antona (Eds.): HCII 2020, CCIS 1225, pp. 64–69, 2020.
https://doi.org/10.1007/978-3-030-50729-9_9

or help consumers make better decisions [1]. Extracting meaningful features from such a complex process requires careful examination of the raw data received by the ET glasses. One of the significant problems that arise is the definition of fixations and saccades from this data. Cognitive process of a human starts after a visual fixation [2], but the eyes are never still, the rapid voluntary eye movements used to move from one fixation point to another are saccades [3]. According to the Eye Tracker System Manual [3] a fixation can be seen as "the mean X and Y position coordinates measured over a minimum period during which the eye does not move more than some maximum amount". In simpler words, "point-of-gaze must continuously remain within a small area for some minimum time". Since most of the literature is focused on eye fixations based on 2D screens, there is only a limited studies in defining and standardizing fixations in real and 3D VR environment [1]. Moreover, Rayner [4] indicated that the mean duration of a single fixation may depend on the nature of the task. Therefore, this study focusses on creating a methodology which can define fixations based on the task employed by consumers inside a virtual reality store (VS).

In this study, we propose a novel methodology capable of optimizing thresholds for the definition of fixations in classification problems. Regarding stimuli, a VS was designed to classify the behavior of shoppers based on their age and is presented using a portable HMD. The dispersion threshold algorithm for fixation identification (I-DT) of Salvucci and Goldberg [5] is implemented, and an attempt is made to determine the optimum thresholds (duration threshold, dispersion threshold) for different parameters of dispersion algorithm using a Multi-Objective Reinforcement Learning (MORL) algorithm [6]. For age classification, a binary classifier will be presented, which uses effective features extracted from ET data gathered from integrated ET of HMD and combined through a set of basic classifier algorithms.

2 Materials and Method

2.1 Participants

A group of 60 healthy volunteers was recruited to participate in the experiment. They were balanced in terms of age (25.36 ± 4.97) and gender (50% females). Inclusion criteria were as follows: age between 18 and 36 years; having normal or corrected-to-normal vision and hearing; having no previous experience of virtual reality. After a careful pre-examination of the dataset from all sources, 3 participants were removed due to corrupted data in ET signals. All methods and experimental protocols were performed in accordance with the guidelines and regulations of the local ethics committee of the Polytechnic University of Valencia.

2.2 Experiment

The experiment was conducted in a 6 M × 6 M VS developed using Unity 3D game engine based on a physical room of the same size. The VS was projected from the computer to – VIVE Pro VR Headset [7] developed by HTC (HTC Corporation,

Taiwan). Participants were familiarized with the technology in a neutral training room where they were informed about the HMD, controllers and their functioning.

The VR environment was made as a VS (Fig. 1), there were 7 different shelves each consisting of different products in each of three sections - upper, middle and bottom. Each product was priced differently and had a description of the product at the back of packaging. The freedom was given to the participant to move freely in the VS to get familiar with the environment and interact with the products as shows in Fig. 2.

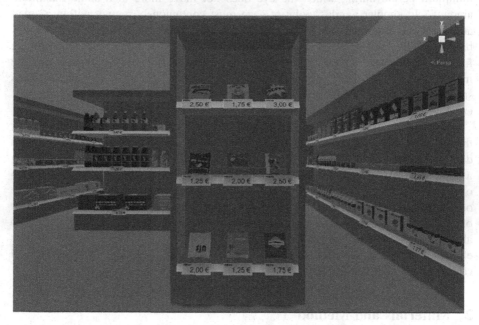

Fig. 1. Virtual store with products placed in three sections of shelves.

In the first section, they underwent a calibration of ET while getting instructions for the next section. After calibration, participants were asked to perform a forced search task in which they were instructed to search for potato chips (product). After finding the product, they were instructed to purchase some of them given the condition of a limited budget of 5 Euros. To end the task, they returned to the starting position. There was no mention in the instructions that the subject must use the complete amount of money allotted to them. Figure 1 shows the VS consisting of products in each section of the shelves with the focus on the potato chips which were used as the product in the study.

2.3 Optimizing Thresholds with Multi-Objective Reinforcement Learning

This study uses the I-DT algorithm which utilizes the fact that fixation points tend to cluster closely together [5]. I-DT identifies fixations as groups of consecutive points within a dispersion, calculated as maximum angle between the projection of the gaze

Fig. 2. Movement and interaction of subject inside physical environment.

and the eyes. To this extent, we implemented a 3D adaptation of I-DT algorithm which combines the projection of the gaze in the virtual space with the dynamic of the head during the task. The dispersion was computed using the maximum angle between the points candidates to be part of the fixation, and the mean of the position of the head during the time candidate to be a fixation as a vertex. Therefore, in order to calculate fixations the I-DT algorithm requires two threshold, the maximum dispersion and the minimum duration of fixation [5]. These thresholds values are set depending on the nature of the task performed. The objective of the optimization of these thresholds was to classify the shoppers based on two age groups: young (18–25) and adult (26–36).

Optimization of thresholds was done using MORL [6] which requires a cost function. The cost function used was a simple method to maximize the differences between the averages of each feature in different age groups and minimize the variances of the same feature within each age group. Multi-objective problems have usually no unique, perfect solution, but a set of non-inferior, alternative solutions, known as the Pareto optimal solutions, which represent the possible trade-off among conflicting objectives. The Pareto optimal objective vectors, i.e. vectors of cost values obtained by applying Pareto optimal solutions in objective functions, form a Pareto front in the objective space [6].

In MORL, a search is undertaken on individual dimension in a high dimensional space via a path selected by an estimated path value which represents the potential of finding a better solution. During the process of search, an elite list memorizes the previously found non-dominated Pareto solutions, and is used to construct the Pareto front finally [6].

To test the optimized thresholds, along with some arbitrary thresholds, a set of classic classifiers are used to classify shoppers based on the two groups (young and adult). This set includes Support Vector Machine (SVM), K-nearest Neighborhood (KNN), Decision Tree Classifier (DTC), and Gaussian Naïve Bayesian (GNB). Then the best results are reported. Data preprocessing and analysis was done using python version 3.7.3 in jupyter environment. The scripts were written using numpy, pandas, matplotlib, scikit-learn, and pickle libraries.

3 Results

The MORL optimizer suggested 6.36° and 891 ms for dispersion threshold and minimum duration threshold of fixation respectively, as optimum values. To examine these results, the features which were extracted using these thresholds and with several other arbitrary thresholds, were given to a set of classic classifiers and the best results are reported. In Table 1 the classification results confirm the optimizer results to be an improvement over others as it uses less features, while true positives for young group and true positive for adult group outperform other results. It shows the best combination of the dispersion threshold and duration threshold that was provided by the optimizer utilizing the minimum number of features to improve the accuracy for classification of the shopper based on age.

Table 1. Classification results for optimum thresholds and other thresholds.

Dispersion threshold (deg)	Duration threshold (ms)	Features number	Young group true positives	Adult group true positives	Accuracy
6.36	**891**	**2**	**0.72**	**0.77**	**0.75**
8.4	415	9	0.59	0.81	0.71
8.4	282	3	0.66	0.73	0.70
13	282	8	0.59	0.76	0.68
20	1000	8	0.65	0.52	0.58

4 Discussion and Conclusion

The aim of this study was to provide a novel methodology to define the fixations based on optimum thresholds for dispersion algorithm in order to improve the accuracy of classification of individuals based on any independent parameter. Previous studies have shown the definition of fixations based on 2D screens [8] and real world, whereas this study focused on 3D VR environment.

The results show that the dispersion and duration thresholds obtained by the optimizer improve the accuracy of the classification of the shopper behavior based on their age. Moreover, the optimized model has a more balanced confusion matrix and used a lower number of features, suggesting a better performance of the model. Since the optimized duration threshold is rather long (891 ms), it can be inferred that long fixations are better metrics to discriminate the age of the shoppers.

In this study, a simple variance method was used as a cost function for the sake of reducing complexity, other cost functions like Fischer criterion can be used and may show improved results based on the nature of the study. Moreover, it might be noted that dispersion uses the angle between the gaze projections and head as a threshold, and usual 2D algorithm does not consider the movement of the head since it is static. However, considering the nature of 3D VR the subject can freely navigate, and the dynamic of the head need to be considered to compute the dispersion.

This study was done using HTC Vive Pro HMD, since the scope of the study was to classify shopper behavior based on age in virtual reality. This method to optimize thresholds can be used in other eye tracking studies beyond virtual reality studies, using augmented reality/mixed reality glasses. Since, this study uses optimizer to define thresholds for fixation, this optimizer can be used to define thresholds for navigation, interaction, and definition of Areas of Interest (AOIs). This method can also be used to pre-test a calibration for fixation of individuals in order to customize fixation patterns based on every individual. Another interesting future study can be the comparison of thresholds optimized for 2D screen of physical recording and VR.

Acknowledgements.   This work was supported by the European Commission (Project RHUMBO H2020-MSCA-ITN-2018-813234 and HELIOS H2020-825585).

References

1. Meißner, M., Pfeiffer, J., Pfeiffer, T., Oppewal, H.: Combining virtual reality and mobile eye tracking to provide a naturalistic experimental environment for shopper research. J. Bus. Res. **100**, 445–458 (2019). https://doi.org/10.1016/j.jbusres.2017.09.028
2. Just, M.A., Carpenter, P.A.: Using eye fixations to study reading comprehension. In: New Methods in Reading Comprehension Research, pp. 151–182. Routledge (2019)
3. Eye Tracker System Manual ASL EyeTrac 6 EyeNal Analysis Software (2007)
4. Rayner, K.: Eye movements in reading and information processing: 20 years of research. Psychol. Bull. **124**, 372–422 (1998). https://doi.org/10.1037/0033-2909.124.3.372
5. Salvucci, D.D., Goldberg, J.H.: Identifying fixations and saccades in eye-tracking protocols. In: ETRA'00: Proceedings of the 2000 Symposium on Eye Tracking Research & Applications, pp. 71–78 (2000). https://doi.org/10.1145/355017.355028
6. Liao, H.L., Wu, Q.H., Jiang, L.: Multi-objective optimization by reinforcement learning for power system dispatch and voltage stability. In: 2010 IEEE PES Innovative Smart Grid Technologies Conference Europe (ISGT Europe), pp. 1–8 (2010). https://doi.org/10.1109/ISGTEUROPE.2010.5638914
7. VIVE Pro: The professional-grade VR headset. https://www.vive.com/eu/product/vive-pro/ Accessed 15 March 2020
8. Blignaut, P.: Fixation identification: the optimum threshold for a dispersion algorithm. Atten. Percept. Psychophys. **71**, 881–895 (2009). https://doi.org/10.3758/APP.71.4.881

On the Peripherals of Peripherals: Exploring a Holistic Augmented Reality Product System

Julian King[(✉)] and Ralf Schneider[(✉)]

Syracuse University, Syracuse, NY 13244, USA
{Jsking01, rosch100}@syr.edu

Abstract. Substantial advances in technology have consistently been developed alongside new methods of interaction. With the recent advances in the areas of both augmented and virtual reality (AR, VR), there exists a strong need to explore what new interaction paradigms should be implemented to ensure the best possible user experience for those engaging with these technologies. With VR having far more definition in this space then AR, the focus of this research is on defining types of functionality best suited for a product that can assist its user in better navigating an AR-based experience. Research areas were selected based upon the information most relevant to AR-wearable products, including: use-cases, wearable technology, and virtual reality. Each of these subjects occupied a distinct phase of research (1–3). Insight gained from the present study could serve as a useful guide for the design of a concept peripheral product with the goal of improving the user experience of those unfamiliar with AR systems. Results showed that there is certainly a potential opportunity for an AR product in the right environment, that the general public is ready and willing to adopt wearable technology so long as it supplies enough functionality to justify its use, and that adopting affordances of technology that users are familiar with such as touch screens and haptic vibrations greatly improves the comfort and ease of use of AR products.

Keywords: Augmented reality · Virtual reality · Wearables · Haptic vibration

1 Introduction

With rapid advances in the field of AR [1], there exists an increasing need to design intuitive 3D user interfaces that can coalesce effectively with new hardware products [2]. There does still exist a need to help facilitate a transition from current 2D interfaces to next generation spatial interfaces. Determining what features will most efficiently assist users in utilizing these new products will necessitate exploring areas of research that are tangentially related to AR such as wearables and virtual reality both of which have far more definition in the consumer marketplace.

Office spaces are one of the primary areas that AR is being implemented. Consequently, one of the aims of this study was to determine the effectiveness of AR systems implementation. Research into wearable technology, specifically smart-watches can help determine the factors contributing to consumers interest in their daily use [3]. The last area of research was VR, with the primary goal being to better understand what

© Springer Nature Switzerland AG 2020
C. Stephanidis and M. Antona (Eds.): HCII 2020, CCIS 1225, pp. 70–76, 2020.
https://doi.org/10.1007/978-3-030-50729-9_10

features have been implemented to improve user experience [4]. All collected data was synthesized and used to design a conceptual AR hardware product that would aid in bridging the gap between 2D and 3D user interfaces.

2 Phase I: Desk Space and Productivity Analysis

With several companies developing AR products aimed at productivity in the workspace, the decision was made to interview individuals who spent most of their work days in an office environment. Participants came from a wide range of industries and utilize diverse work-flows. Participants were asked about their personal organizational strategies. They were also asked to share their insights on the role of technology in their work, whether it helped or hindered their overall productivity.

2.1 Participants

A 24-year-old designer, 49-year-old doctor, 27-year-old software developer participated in this phase of the study.

2.2 Locations

Office environments included a clothing store office, hospital office, and a research office.

2.3 Workspace Findings

On average each participant used between 4–6 screens. All participants indicated an interest in consolidating their screen usage down to one or two systems. All three participants also relied on between 3–4 different screen-based systems to conduct various work throughout the day. This information supports the inclusion of an AR-based system which could reduce the number of physical screens.

3 Phase II: Wearables, Viability and Use

Phase two of the present study involved surveying public opinion on wearable technology, with an emphasis on smartwatch. This phase would involve two distinct approaches one for participants with no previous smartwatch experience and one for seasoned users.

3.1 New User Smartwatch Testing

The new user smartwatch testing was aimed at determining why an individual would or would not use a wearable by giving them a very basic smart-watch to use for a week. A tally of days that participants chose to wear their device was recorded along with any feedback about what they did or did not like about the device.

Participants. Three college students aged 21–22 (None of these participants had previously owned or used a smart-watch.) participated in this study.

Device. First Generation Pebble Smart-watch made by Pebble Technology Corporation.

Observations. Two of the participants felt the smart-watch they were using was functional enough to justify wearing it five to seven days of the week. The third participant only wore the watch two days.

3.2   Seasoned User Interviews

Participants with prior smart-watch experience were interviewed to assess what motivated them to purchase their device. Each participant had bought their watch with a different use-case in mind such as fitness or productivity. All were asked the same series of questions with the goal of gauging what features were successful, and which were not. For example, users were asked "Was your watch worth its price?"

Participants. Five seasoned smart-watch owners participated in this phase of the project. Three bought their device for improving productivity; two bought them for fitness.

Observations. Although all participants wore their watches daily, two of the productivity users did not find them completely enjoyable or worth the cost. In contrast both fitness users were satisfied with their devices. All five participants expressed a desire to see expanded functionality from their devices.

3.3   Wearable Findings

These finding suggest that individuals will wear technology products regardless of whether or not they feel they are completely useful, but it also suggests that there is still a decent amount of dissatisfaction regarding the functionality these devices offer. Users who owned devices for improving productivity reported feeling frustrated with the functionality of their smart-watch.

While productivity was also found to be one of the primary motivations for smart-watch use, as demonstrated in the office interviews (Phase 1) it did not help in the reduction of overall screen quantity. This confirms that while people are looking to use wearables to improve productivity, they are not necessarily satisfied with the functionality their devices provide. It suggests that a technology like augmented reality, which by provides a far more versatile and expansive display method might give users the utility they desire.

4   Phase III: Impact of Haptic Vibrations on a Virtual Reality Experience

The final phase of the project investigated user experience of virtual reality products. VR has become far more defined as a consumer facing product than AR and consequently its overall usability and comfort is much more refined.

One of the primary differences between most VR and AR products is VR's focus on immersion, which is partially achieved through the use of haptic technology integration in its hardware. Haptic technology has long been used as a way of improving users' ability to physically interact with technology and objects [5]. AR has typically tried to be more hands-free and this test would explore what impact haptics have on improving users' comfort.

4.1   Participants

Three college students aged 22–23 (None of these participants had previously experienced VR) participated in this study.

4.2   Testing Criteria

Each participant was instructed to use an Oculus CV1's touch controllers to type out a sentence in a VR application, once with haptic vibrations on and once with them off. Participants times and their feedback on the experience was recorded.

4.3   Findings

This study concluded that the addition of haptic vibration made an overwhelmingly positive improvement in both user comfort and efficacy. All participants doubled their typing speed in the haptics trial type and all users reported improved comfort. This test demonstrates the positive value haptic vibrations contribute to improving VR's user experience.

5   Research Conclusions

Findings from Phase I showed all participants felt overloaded by an excess of screens in their office environment. A consolidation of technology would maximize productivity while still being organization.

Findings from Phase II showed participants were using wearable technology to help with productivity but felt disappointed with the utility from these devices. Peripheral technology could supplement productivity by improving user experience.

Finding from Phase III showed users of VR systems experience vastly improved comfort with the addition of physical responses such as haptic vibrations. Applying the same affordances part of VR systems could significantly improve the transition to AR interfaces.

6   Concept Product Proposal

The synthesis of the research findings suggests that there is potential for developing a peripheral device for AR product systems for facilitating the transition from 2D to 3D interfaces. This product could be worn on the wrist like a smart-watch to provide a hands-free experience. This new device would work in tandem with a head mounted display to improve the usability of AR experiences. Lending enhanced feedback to the user in the form of haptic vibrations when interacting with digital objects, providing increased movement precision by tracking the watches movement in space, and giving users a physical interface to help transition information between 2D and 3D.

6.1   Use-Case

The proposed product would serve primarily as an intermediate device that will still provide users the familiarity they experience with their touch-screen based devices, while helping them navigate content in AR. Through its use office workers can eliminate the need for both computer monitors and make use of AR's spatial interface to multi-task between several different activities.

6.2   Technology

The proposed product would use a variety of brushless servo motors to deliver a variety of complex outputs to the user. Its wide touch screen gives the user plenty of space to transition content between 2D and 3D (Fig. 1). Through the use of a gyroscope and accelerometer the device will better communicate with the head-mounted display, which then delivers more precise inputs.

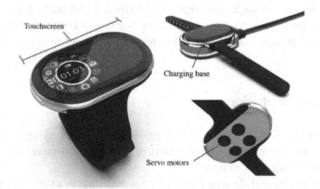

Fig. 1. Concept peripheral device for augmented reality

6.3   Functionality Test

To test one aspect of this concepts device functionality, a prototype of the device was constructed using basic components. Comprised of a physical device which would deliver haptic vibrations to the user and digital application of a 3D object. Participants would be tested on how the haptics impacted their interaction with the 3D object. Specifically their precision and comfort.

Procedure. Two motors connected to an Arduino board were fixed to a watch. This Arduino communicated with a basic Unity 3D program run on Metavisions Meta 2 AR headset. The program was a hollow virtual cube, which, when, touched or picked up would send different outputs to the participant through haptic vibrations (Fig. 2).

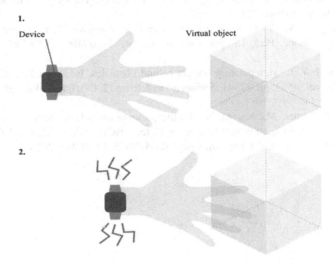

Fig. 2. Visual representation of augmented reality haptic test.

Participants. This final phase of the study had five participants, all of them college students who had not used VR or AR previously.

Results. Users were twice as likely to miss the collider on the cube when they did not have haptics on and therefore be unable to lift it. When haptic vibrations were on users lifted the cube within an accuracy threshold of 0.1 meters in Unity 3D.

7 Conclusions

The principle aim of this study was to establish a use-case for an AR system based on research gathered from tangential technologies such as virtual reality and wearable technology. The insights gathered were used to explore the potential for a conceptual product to supplement AR head-mounted displays. This conceptual product was tested using a prototype of the device which featured a software and hardware element. In conclusion, this study demonstrates the value of examining the user experience of future AR products. A device which would work in tandem with a head mounted display to improve the usability of AR experiences by lending enhanced feedback to the user in the form of haptic vibrations when interacting with digital objects, providing increased movement precision by tracking the watches movement in space, and giving users a physical interface to help transition information between 2D and 3D.

References

1. Schmalsteig, D., Hollerer, T.: Augmented Reality, Principles and Practice, 1st edn. Addison-Wesley, Boston (2016)
2. LaViola, J., Kruiff, E., McMahan, R.: 3D User Interfaces, Theory and Practice, 2nd edn. Addison-Wesley, Boston (2017)
3. Xu, Y., Wang, L., Xu, Y.: Cross-device task interaction framework between the smart watch and the smart phone. Pers. Ubiquit. Comput. (2019). https://doi.org/10.1007/s00779-019-01280-7
4. Flasar, J., Sochor, J.: Manipulating objects behind obstacles. In: Shumaker, R. (ed.) ICVR 2007. LNCS, vol. 4563, pp. 32–41. Springer, Heidelberg (2007). https://doi.org/10.1007/978-3-540-73335-5_4
5. Yamazaki, Y., Imura, M., Nagata, N.: Tactile presentation scheme based on physiological characteristics of the fingertip. In: Stephanidis, C. (ed.) HCII 2019. CCIS, vol. 1032, pp. 172–179. Springer, Cham (2019). https://doi.org/10.1007/978-3-030-23522-2_22

Building Cognitive Readiness and Resilience Skills for Situation Assessment and Diagnostic Reasoning in a VR CR

Jari Laarni[1], Marja Liinasuo[1(✉)], Satu Pakarinen[2],
Kristian Lukander[2], Tomi Passi[2], Ville Pitkänen[3], and Leena Salo[3]

[1] VTT Technical Research Centre of Finland Ltd, Espoo, Finland
marja.liinasuo@vtt.fi
[2] Finnish Institute of Occupational Health, Helsinki, Finland
[3] Fortum Power and Heat Ltd, Espoo, Finland

Abstract. We conducted a preliminary study to investigate how an immersive 3D environment based on novel technology can be used in simulator studies in nuclear domain. Our ultimate aim is to better understand the cognitive processes in achieving an overview of the nuclear process in a virtual reality control room (VR CR). The VR-environment was created by importing 3D-models into the Unity design environment. A novel headset was used offering a blend between the central high-resolution display and a larger lower-resolution context display. Two operator crews participated in the main test, and one crew for the pilot test. In brief simulated incidents and accidents the operators had to detect a fault and start to manage it; in a longer run, a sudden fire in the CR was simulated, forcing the crew to move to the Emergency CR. After each trial, the operators were interviewed and asked to describe what they had done during the trial, what information they had used and what hypothesis they had made about the cause of the fault. The results showed that the crews were able to successfully complete their tasks and manage the incident/accident, even though the development of the VR CR is still in progress.

Keywords: Virtual reality control room · Nuclear power plant · Cognitive processes

1 Introduction

Professionals in many domains have to meet demanding operational environments. For example, first-responders face deadly dangers in emergency situations and disasters. In order to be able manage accidents and save life of victims they have to be able to cope with acute stress and extreme fear. In short, they need resilience skills, such as adaptive expertise and problem solving, decision making, situation awareness and seamless teamwork. A big challenge is how to develop these skills for demanding situations and environments, if you are not able to gain first-hand experience and train them in real life settings. A training station for learning and evaluation of resilience skills in virtual reality will be a precise response to these challenges.

© Springer Nature Switzerland AG 2020
C. Stephanidis and M. Antona (Eds.): HCII 2020, CCIS 1225, pp. 77–84, 2020.
https://doi.org/10.1007/978-3-030-50729-9_11

The aim of the present study was to investigate the evaluation of cognitive readiness in nuclear domain with a new version of a virtual reality control room (VR CR) system. Our earlier studies suggest that a VR CR provides new opportunities for operator training and skills assessment. On the other hand, we found in the earlier studies some room for improvement, for example, the visual resolution of the VR system was not perfect, and therefore, operators encountered some problems in the acquisition of information, e.g., in reading text from a distance.

2   Methods

The study was conducted in accordance with the Declaration of Helsinki. The ethical statement was obtained from the ethical board of the Helsinki University Hospital, and the participants signed an informed consent before participating in the experiment.

2.1   Participants

Two operator crews (altogether six licensed operators, two shift supervisors (SS), two reactor (RO) and two turbine (TO) operators) were recruited for the main test. In addition, one crew participated in the pilot test. Its results are only included in evaluation of VR experience. Two of the operators had participated in one of the earlier VR CR tests, but the last four were not. The participants had limited experience in using VR applications.

2.2   Test Procedure

Three days were reserved for the test, one for the pilot and two for the actual test. The test day began with a short training session (about 30 min), during which the operators received instructions regarding the basic functionalities and ways of interaction in the VR CR. The operators also had time to individually explore and practice operator tasks in virtual reality.

The test session consisted of four brief simulated incidents or accidents (duration varied from about 10 to 20 min) and one longer one (duration about 40 min). The short incidents/accidents were: 1) failed sensor measurement, 2) anticipated transient without scram (ATWS), 3) combination of two incidents caused by a mechanical error of a control valve and a hydrogen leakage, and 4) loss of the BB bus bar. In the longer scenario run, a sudden fire in the CR was simulated, forcing the crew to execute both the reactor and turbine scram and move to the Emergency Control Room (ECR).

The operator stress and workload was quantified with measurements of cardiac (electrocardiography) and sudomotor (skin conductance) activity of the autonomic nervous system, but the results of psychophysiological measurements are not presented in this paper.

Immediately after the scenario run, the operators were asked to fill in several questionnaires (i.e., a workload, situation awareness (SA), spatial presence and simulator sickness questionnaire). After filling in the questionnaires, they were briefly interviewed. At the end of each test day, the operators filled in the Systems Usability questionnaire and participated in a debriefing session, during which they discussed their experiences and reflections on the VR CR.

After each test run, one simulator instructor evaluated the performance of the crew from perspectives such as process and alarm monitoring, process control, situational management, procedure usage and communication. In addition to that, the operators themselves evaluated their own performance after the loss of the MCR accident.

2.3   Technical Set-up

Apros®, a multifunctional software for modeling and dynamic simulation of nuclear and thermal power plant processes, was used in creation of the incident and accident scenarios, and the Unity™ cross-platform engine was used to create realistic CR environments. Each VR workstation included a computer with a high-end graphic card, a Varjo™ headset and Valve™ Index controllers. In the VR CR each operator was sitting in front of his workstation, with a free movement area of about 2 m * 2 m, wearing a headset and using the controllers to interact with the VR CR.

The VR CR was a high fidelity copy of a physical CR. Procedures were modelled in the environment in different folders with the name of each procedure written on its cover. The procedures could be picked up by squeezing the fingers into a fist with the controller; and page-turning was performed with the flick of one's fingers. A fire simulation included a realistic simulation of flame and smoke propagation in the VR CR.

Operators used the controllers to move inside the VR CR. Every operator had his or her own avatar. Animations inside of Unity represent the operators' movements and actions (e.g., walking forward, sitting and using a computer) in the VR CR. The animations also consist of headset movements and rotations so that an operator could see what other crew members were looking at and what human-system interfaces (HSIs) they were using. Data on operators' movements and on their interactions with various objects were transferred through a computer network to other users and represented in real time. Control panels and desks in the VR CR were virtual touch screens, indicating that the buttons, knobs and switches were operated differently than their analog counterparts. Otherwise the operation of different HSIs in the VR CR was as realistic as possible.

2.4   Test Facility and Data Recording

One physical room space was reserved for the test in which the VR workstations were located. An example image from the physical and virtual simulator environment are shown in Fig. 1. The test sessions were audio and video recorded. Two video cameras were set up for recording the operators' physical activities during the simulator runs.

Fig. 1. Example image from the physical (left) and virtual (right) simulator environment.

3 Results and Discussion

3.1 Task Performance

Both crews were able to complete successfully their tasks in the VR CR with one exception (see below). Especially, performance in the loss of the MCR accident was quite fluent, apparently because the crews had recent experience of training it.

According to the expert's evaluation, there were slight differences in performance between the crews, and one of them performed slightly better than the other one in most of the simulator runs. Since it can be assumed that licensed operators are nearly equally proficient in managing these incidents/accidents, the differences in performance might be caused by possible differences in skills and knowledge in VR use and/or possible differences in cognitive resilience: Some operators may be less frustrated with all the inconveniences encountered in VR, and may, thus, be better able to maintain their level of performance.

On the negative side, the crews had some problems in problem monitoring and process control because of the problems caused by the VR system or by deficiencies in the simulation model. The number of simulated process computer system (PCS) displays, panels and desks seemed to be too small for reliable monitoring of the nuclear process and for prompt process control, especially when the number of events was high, as in the loss of the BB bus bar incident. Some parts of the computer system crashed several times, and their response was also slightly slower than in the physical CR. Because of all these inconveniences, the operators had some problems to notice alarms and react to them promptly. This might be one of the reasons that one of the crews did not notice the hydrogen leakage. It was also found that communication and collaboration was poorer than in the physical CR, because operators did not wear an earphones/microphones set, and their voice was thus not heard in VR but in the physical environment.

According to the process expert's evaluation, overall crew performance was somewhat higher for the failed measurement and the loss of the MCR scenario. The former one was apparently more straightforward than the other incidents, and the latter one was considered quite easy, because it has been trained more frequently, and all operations were executed through one single panel in the ECR.

According to the operator interviews, all the operators seemed to have a good understanding of what had happened in each scenario and what they should have done. The problem that came about was that the operators were not always able to perform operations they would normally do in a physical CR.

3.2 Situation Awareness

Situation awareness was measured by the Mission Awareness Rating Scale (MARS). It was found that SA was highest in the failed measurement scenario (S1 in Fig. 2) and lowest in the combined incidents scenario (S3 in Fig. 2) for three dimensions of SA, Observing, Understanding and Anticipating. There were also small differences between the two crews in SA for all the four dimensions. Regarding Observing and Understanding, SA scores were somewhat lower for SS than the other two operators. This finding is consistent with the SSs' comments: the SSs complained that they could not properly see the panel information when they were sitting at their workstation. And since the PCS did not work smoothly enough, the SSs sometimes did not know what is going on, and their situation understanding was thus poorer than that of the other two operators.

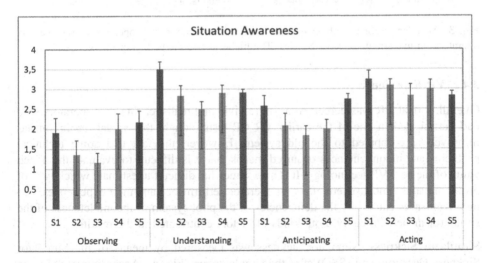

Fig. 2. SA scores with error bars (standard error) for two operator crews (i.e. six operators) in five scenarios (S1–S5). The higher the score the higher the SA is.

3.3 Workload and Stress

Scores of mental workload, measured by NASA-TLX, were at a quite low level, suggesting that the operators did not experienced high degrees of workload during the simulator runs (Fig. 3). The scores were highest for the ATWS scenario and lowest for the failed measurement scenario. This finding is understandable given that ATWS is a severe accident whose consequences are far-reaching and damaging, whereas the failed measurement scenario is a quite 'normal' incident without any dramatic outcomes.

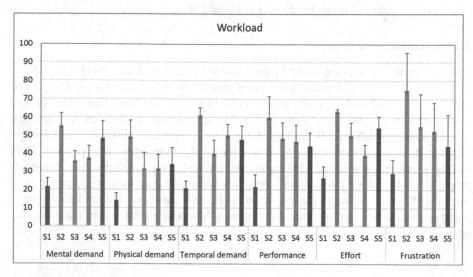

Fig. 3. Workload scores with error bars (standard error) for two operator crews (i.e. six operators) in five simulator runs (S1–S5). The higher the score the higher the workload is.

3.4   VR Experience

Overall, virtual CR was perceived as quite vivid and realistic. The two operators who had participated in one of the earlier VR CR tests thought that visual resolution has improved as compared to the old system. However, the fact that some technical problems and inconveniences occurred means that it is difficult to evaluate the added value of the new VR technology. It is also somewhat difficult to estimate which type of problem had the most severe effect on operator performance and their experiences, i.e., inconveniences caused by the deficiencies of the pilot system or incompleteness of the simulator model. Probably, both kinds of factors contributed to the results.

Simulator Sickness. Simulator sickness was measured by means of the Simulator Sickness Questionnaire (SSQ) after the simulator run (Fig. 4). According to SSQ, the signs of symptoms of simulator sickness were quite low. However, scores for Eye strain and Difficulty in focusing were somewhat higher, indicating that the operators had some problems in focusing at different distances. These troubles might, in turn, cause squinting of one's eyes which perhaps led to eye strain symptoms.

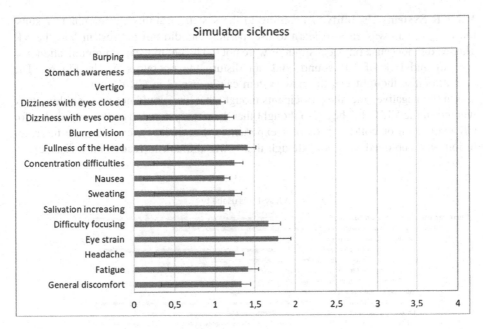

Fig. 4. Simulator sickness scores with error bars (standard error) for three operator crews (i.e. nine operators). The higher the score the higher the symptoms of simulator sickness are.

Spatial Presence. The Spatial Presence Scale was used to measure presence. This scale is based on a process model of presence according to which operators generate a mental presentation of the CR environment, and after that, they test perceptual hypotheses concerning the acceptance of the VR CR as their primary frame of reference. The questionnaire consists of two subscales, one for self-location and the other for perceived possible actions.

Overall, the Spatial Presence scores were at a moderate level (Fig. 5), and they were even somewhat lower than in our previous studies in which another VR system had been used. Apparently, improved resolution and the other novel features of the VR CR could not fully compensate the effects of the deficiencies of the pilot system.

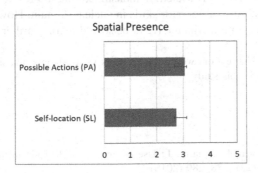

Fig. 5. Spatial presence scores with error bars (standard error) for three operator crews (i.e. nine operators). The higher the score the higher the sense of spatial presence is.

VR CR Systems Usability. According to the system usability questionnaire results, the new system was easy to learn to use, participants did not get lost in VR, the VR glasses did not cause physical strain or were not too heavy to wear, communication was smooth and lack of CR sounds did not disturb the operators much (Fig. 6). The operators also thought that the new system can be useful in CR design.

On the negative side, the participants thought that they could not do everything they wanted in the VR CR. They also thought that the new system was not very suitable for CR evaluation or collection of user experiences. Surprisingly, even though the resolution was improved, they still though that it was difficult to read from a distance.

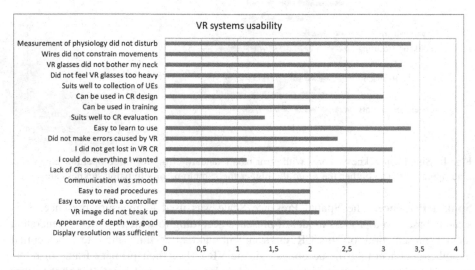

Fig. 6. Systems usability of a virtual CR. The higher the score the more the respondent agreed with the statement.

4 Conclusion

The pilot study with a new VR system demonstrated that a VR CR has great potential for evaluation and training of operator skills in nuclear domain. However, some targets for development were found, which have to be solved before further testing is initiated.

Acknowledgments.   The authors would like to thank the designers, the simulator trainers and the operators involved in this study.

Reference

1. Bergroth, J., Koskinen, H., Laarni, J.: Use of immersive 3-D virtual reality environments. Nucl. Technol. **202**(23), 278–289 (2018)

Multiuser Virtual Reality for Designing and Editing 3D Models

Noppasorn Larpkiattaworn, Pitijit Chareonwuttikajorn(✉),
Pattaraporn Punya(✉), and Siam Charoenseang(✉)

Institute of Field Robotics (FIBO), King Mongkut's University of Technology
Thonburi, Bangmod, Thungkru, Bangkok 10140, Thailand
{noppasorn.larp,pitijit.cha,
pattaraporn.fibo}@mail.kmutt.ac.th, siam@fibo.kmutt.ac.th

Abstract. This research proposes the development of a virtual reality system in which multiple users could collaboratively design and edit 3D models. In the virtual environment, users also obtained the rendered version of the actual environment using the Kinect's point clouds. The proposed system provides several features of model building, coloring, realistic dimensions of actual environment, user's collaboration, and STL file exporting for 3D printing.

Keywords: Virtual reality · Multiuser · 3D model · Unity3D

1 Introduction

Computer-aid design (CAD) software has played a crucial role in the material or product design process. However, due to the limitation of the software, the CAD software lacks clarity in the visualization of the 3D model and good collaborative features. In collaborative work, users need to share knowledge and idea and avoid misunderstanding problem. Also, there is a difficulty in collaborative designing and editing models if model designers are in different places. The users can collaborate on the system by using the multiplayer high-level API (HLAPI) with Unity technology which is a cross-platform game engine. The engine can be used to create two-dimensional, three-dimensional, virtual reality, and augmented reality for games and the other experiences [1]. Furthermore, the HLAPI is a set of networking for building multiplayer capabilities for Unity [2].

The virtual reality (VR) is a technology that simulates the environment and allows users to interact with the three-dimensional virtual environment by using the headset and controllers. This helps users to reduce risk and have more understanding and effective communication. The implementation of the application can present on the VR headset or head-mounted display (HMD), VR controllers, and LED display. The headset is responsible for mapping the display to a wide field of view [3].

This paper presents the development of the multiuser system for designing and editing three-dimensional models in virtual reality with HTC VIVE and Microsoft Kinect 2. The Kinect is a depth camera consists of an RGB camera, an IR emitter, an IR camera, and the depth measurements are using the speckle pattern technology [4]. The

C. Stephanidis and M. Antona (Eds.): HCII 2020, CCIS 1225, pp. 85–91, 2020.
https://doi.org/10.1007/978-3-030-50729-9_12

system has developed using Unity3D and C# language with Microsoft Visual Studio. The proposed system explored the development of a virtual reality for designing and editing 3D models. In addition, users can design and edit 3D models easily and more intuitively. The performance of the system was evaluated by using a 3D printer to make a realistic 3D model obtained from the proposed system.

2   Related Work

This section presents research works related to the proposed system that consists of virtual environment for collaboration system, designing and editing 3D model, and simulated 3D environment.

Virtual Environment for Collaboration
In virtual environment, the communication systems for collaboration mostly used avatar to represent the person and provided the clear voice to enhance the user's understanding. The collaboration system concerns about the point of view which users can see the object in the same position with the different views. Space time [5], the system of this paper supports users to see the same object even if users are in the different view. For example, users can request to see the same view as avatar's view by touching shoulder of avatar. Users can clone the other avatar, resize and place cloned avatar to any position. Then, the other avatar can see their cloned avatar and can choose to teleport to see the view. This method can be applied to change perspective of collaborative work.

Designing and Editing Model
To create the 3D objects with the virtual reality technology and Unity engine, most developers start by understanding meshes. The mesh manipulation is to draw the surface of the object [6]. The base of a mesh that developers should know is about vertices and lines because a mesh consists of lines that connect these vertices. Data of a mesh consists of four components including vertices, line or edges, triangle, and UV map. Triangle is formed when line is connected with three vertices in 3D space. UV map is about textures around the object's space. Furthermore, developers could bring mesh manipulation to create and edit 3D objects in Unity because it is easy to understand and can be developed in a variety of ways.

Simulated 3D Environment
There are many sensors for scanning 3D environment and generating point cloud data for rendering mesh in real-time. Kinect RGB-D camera is a sensor that can provide RGB, depth and body skeletal information. Virtualized Reality using Depth Camera Point Clouds [7] scanned real environment using the Kinect into VR and reconstructed mesh in real-time using Unity.

3 System Scenario

In the proposed system, two users are in the simulated environment scanned from the first user's environment. They could communicate with each other, see the user's avatar [8], and the first user's rendered environment. The user could design and edit the 3D model with another user in the virtual environment. Moreover, users could export the 3D model into an STL file for printing.

4 System Overview

As shown in Fig. 1, the system consisted of three main parts which are the simulated environment part, the designing and editing section, and the multiuser supporting function. The simulated environment part managed the connection between the Microsoft Kinect 2 and Unity. Microsoft Kinect 2 was used to collect the depth data from an infrared camera and colors data from RGB camera. Simulated environment system mapped the depth positions with positions of colors data, created the point cloud, and simulated the virtual environment through the Unity in Fig. 2. In the proposed system, as shown in Fig. 3 users must wear the VIVE headset to get into the virtual environment where they can work together and use controllers to perform the 3D model building. The designing and editing section managed the mapping the users' actions through the controllers into the model building commands while the multiuser support function acquired the users' action data to perform the avatar's movement.

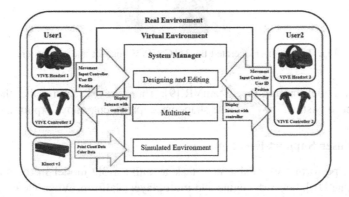

Fig. 1. System overview

4.1 The Designing and Editing Section

The designing and editing system flow is shown in Fig. 4. After the user performed an action, the action command was acquired though HTC VIVE controllers, which are connected to Unity engine through streamVR, a Unity plugin for VR development. Unity engine then performed corresponding actions based on the user's commands and sent the visualization data back to the HTC VIVE headset for the user in order to see

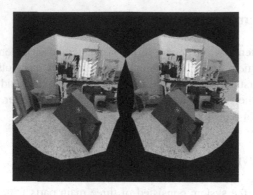

Fig. 2. Virtual environment in the user's viewports

Fig. 3. The user operated the HTC VIVE headset and controllers

the updated model through the streamVR [9]. There are 10 features that the software can perform consists of move, create shape, size, paint, cut, copy, export, and extrude.

4.2 Multiuser Support Function

Users could perform the collaborative task to build a 3D model in the VR through Photon engine [10], network engine and multiplayer platform. When the user connects the photon server successful then users will be a client in the system. Meanwhile, they can see each other's avatar and their actions as they were in the same virtual environment, and they can see environment scanned from Kinect via point cloud.

4.3 Simulated Environment

The simulated environment part obtained the depth and color data from the Microsoft Kinect 2 and used them to create the shader and point cloud through [11]. Users could

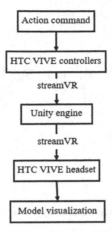

Fig. 4. The designing and editing system flow

build 3D models that were matched with the actual environment using the proposed virtual reality system.

5   System Evaluation

There are 3 system evaluations which cover system performance, usability, and value for specific task.

5.1   System Performance

Frame rates is the number of frames that are displayed per second used in photography, video, and game. FPS (Frames Per Second) is used to measure frame rate. The common frame rate used for creating a smooth appearance is 24 FPS and the acceptable frame rate in video games should be around 30 to 60 FPS. Frame rate depends on quantity of data in the system. After test the multiplayer system, the proposed system showed maximum frame rate of 75 FPS, minimum fame rate of 25 FPS, and the average of frame rate was equivalent to 55.46 FPS, which is greater than the common frame rates. The graph in Fig. 5 shows the changed frame rates in a 15-minute period.

5.2   Usability

Usability indicates that the users can use this system easily and more intuitively or not. Usability tests were performed with 10 participants by asking users to finish the task. There are 2 different type of participants. The first type covers participants who have experience about designing and editing 3D model and the second ones are participants who never have experience about designing and editing 3D model. Mission for user testing is to see a scanned puzzle sorter box by Kinect, to help each other to design and edit 3D model and compare it to a given box in virtual environment. Subsequently, 3D

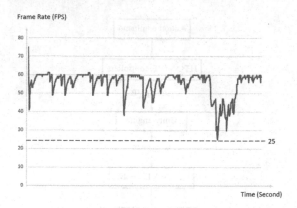

Fig. 5. The changed frame rates in a 15-minute period

model is printed and inserted to fit on a box in the actual environment. Furthermore, the hypothesis of this mission is that two users should spend less time than one user to complete the mission. After test the system, one user spent an average time of 7.27 min and two users spent an average of 4.32 min, subsequently, users were given the survey questionnaires call "USE Questionnaire" [12] to evaluate the usability of the system including ease of use, ease of learning, and satisfaction. In addition, The measurement criteria by having the option of Likert Scale, was divided into 5 options: strongly disagree (1), disagree (2), neutral (3), agree (4), and strongly agree (5). The result of a survey showed that the average of the ease of use is 3.125 (62.5%), of ease of learning is 3.5 (70%), and satisfaction is 3.875 (77.5%).

5.3   Value of Specific Task

The specific task of this system is to help users to design and edit 3D model together to complete the task. The system was evaluated by software and hardware testing. Software testing is about the completion of the given task. Hardware testing is to print 3D model from the virtual collaborative work to fit with the actual environment.

5.4   Discussions and Conclusions

From the result, this proposed system can help multi users to create, edit 3D models together, export file to .STL file for printing the 3D model to fit with the actual environment. The user can see and communicate with another one via the avatar by using virtual reality and can see the same 3D scanned environment in real-time. The result of the survey showed that users were satisfied with the system because the average of ease of use, ease of learning, and satisfaction were greater than 50%. However, most users who used VR for the first time needed some tutorials or examples of how to use this system. In addition, users could collaboratively apply the features within the proposed system to create a prototype-like object. The bottleneck of this system is the network. For the current version, the users cannot join the same room from the different network. In the future work, this system needs more features for users to support the design of more complicated models and better embedded tutorials.

References

1. Unity Engine. https://unity.com. Accessed 9 Dec 2019
2. The multiplayer high-level API. https://docs.unity3d.com. Accessed 9 Dec 2019
3. D'Orazio, D., Savov, V.: Valve's VR headset is called the Vive and it's made by HTC (2015). https://www.theverge.com. Accessed 9 Dec 2019
4. Shibo, L., Qing, Z.: A new approach to calibrate range image and color image from Kinect. In Proceeding 4. International Conference Intelligent Human-Machine Systems and Cybernetics (IHMSC), vol. 2, pp. 252–255, Nanchang, China. IEEE (2012)
5. Xia, H., Herscher, S., Perlin, K., Wigdor, D.: Spacetime: enabling fluid individual and collaborative editing in virtual reality. In: The 31st Annual ACM Symposium on User Interface Software and Technology, pp. 853–866 (2018)
6. Mesh manipulation – Sean Duffy. https://www.raywenderlich.com/3169311-runtime-mesh-manipulation-with-unity. Accessed 15 Feb 2020
7. Cazamias, J., Raj, A.S.: Virtualized Reality Using Depth Camera Point Clouds (2016)
8. Creating the Avatar. https://docs.unity3d.com/. Accessed 12 Dec 2019
9. SteamVR Plugin. https://assetstore.unity.com/. Accessed 15 Dec 2019
10. Photon Intro. https://doc.photonengine.com/en-us/pun/current/getting-started/pun-intro. Accessed 24 Jan 2020
11. Sugino, H.: Kinect Study Unity. https://github.com/sugi-cho/KinectStudy-Unity/. Accessed 20 Dec 2019
12. Measuring Usability with the USE Questionnaire. https://www.researchgate.net/publication/230786746_Measuring_Usability_with_the_USE_Questionnaire. Accessed 15 Dec 2019

Segmentation of Areas of Interest Inside a Virtual Reality Store

Masoud Moghaddasi(✉)📷, Jaikishan Khatri📷, Jose Llanes-Jurado,
Luciano Spinella, Javier Marín-Morales, Jaime Guixeres,
and Mariano Alcañiz

Instituto de Investigación e Innovación en Bioingeniería, Universidad Politécnica
de València, Valencia, Spain
mmoghaddasi@i3b.upv.es

Abstract. In consumer behavior studies, several signals like head position and eye-tracking, which are mostly unstructured, are recorded. Hence, the first step in these studies is to extract structured features. In feature extraction, segmenting the space into several Areas of Interests (AOI) can be beneficial. In this regard, these features are computed when the shopper is inside a specific zone or interacting with or looking at a specific area. One of the difficulties of this approach is defining AOIs. In this study, positional and eye-tracking data of 57 subjects were recorded in a virtual reality store using a Head Mounted Display. Each subject performed a free navigation task and the objective of the study was to classify the shoppers based on their genders. For this purpose, some AOI-based features were extracted from the behavioral data. The AOIs were cubic and defined with rectangles in zenithal perspective and the shelves levels in virtual store. Sizes of horizontal rectangles were then optimized using Genetic Algorithm (GA). In optimization, a cost function based on Fisher criterion is defined to maximize the linear separability between classes. After optimization, the features extracted with the optimized and several arbitrary AOIs are classified with Support Vector Machine method. The results show that gender classification accuracy with optimized AOIs is 85% and outperforms that of the other AOIs. Along with the outstanding results in this study, this methodology is capable of tuning other hyperparameters like navigational thresholds in classification problems.

Keywords: Virtual reality · Zone of interest · Area of interest · Genetic algorithm · Optimization

1 Introduction

Scientists have explored the limitations and benefits of virtual reality (VR) in multiple fields. In recent years, there has been a surge in usage of immersive virtual reality to study the consumer behavior inside a virtual store or shopping mall [1]. Many different tools are used including position tracking devices, eye, head, and hand tracking, etc. to track the behavior of a person inside a virtual environment [1]. These tools provide a

© Springer Nature Switzerland AG 2020
C. Stephanidis and M. Antona (Eds.): HCII 2020, CCIS 1225, pp. 92–98, 2020.
https://doi.org/10.1007/978-3-030-50729-9_13

different set of raw unstructured data. This leads to the question of extraction of structured features from these raw data. For feature extraction, two main approaches can be taken. First, extracting the metrics related to the whole shopping period. Second, computing the features related to some interesting periods such as, when the shopper is inside a specific zone on the floor plan, which is called Zones of Interest (ZOIs), or interacting or looking at a specific area at the shelf level, which is called Areas of Interest (AOIs). The major issue faced by the second approach is how to consider shape, place, and size of these ZOIs or AOIs [2].

In this study, the main objective is to define some ZOIs and AOIs so that the features extracted based on them from the behavioral signals of the shoppers discriminate the gender. In this regard, some rectangular ZOIs on the floor plan and cubic AOIs in front of the shelves' levels are defined. In this definition, the parameter of size in these ZOIs and AOIs plays a huge role on the classification results. Hence, these sizes are optimized using Genetic Algorithm (GA) [3, 4] which is one of the non-gradient-based evolutionary optimization methods. This algorithm tries to simulate the evolution in populations regarding genes and is a global random search method [5]. For implementation of GA, a fitness or cost function is required. Since the objective of the optimization is maximizing the gender prediction accuracy, current study uses modified Fischer criterion as cost function [6] which maximizes the linear separability of classes and subsequently, increases the accuracy of classification. In the final part of the study, the quantities which are suggested with the optimizer are examined using support vector machine (SVM) classifier.

2 Materials and Methods

2.1 Experiment

The experiment was conducted in the European Immersive Neurotechnology's Laboratory (LENI) of Polytechnic University of Valencia which is presented in Fig. 1. For this experiment, 57 healthy individuals (27 females and 30 males, mean age = 25.12, SD = 5.06 years) were recruited. All methods and experimental protocols were performed in accordance with the guidelines and regulations of the local ethics committee of the Polytechnic University of Valencia.

In the experiment, after a neutral familiarization with the virtual environment and calibration phase, the participants were instructed to navigate freely in the virtual store presented in Fig. 2(b) and interact with products arbitrarily under a time limit of 4 min. This task represents unplanned browsing behavior meaning that costumer does not have any specific goal for visiting the shop. Virtual Store of dimensions 6 M × 6 M was developed using Unity 3D game engine. Participant could move inside virtual environment walking in a natural way thanks to the special tracking zone of 6 × 6 m implemented just at the same dimensions of the virtual store generated Fig. 1.

Fig. 1. Physical environment of experiment. The facilities used in the experiment can be seen in the picture. A 6 × 6 m space from this room is dedicated to the virtual store.

The head and hand movement in 3D space as posture and eye-tracking data for each subject during the navigation in the virtual shop was recorded using HTC Vive pro Head Mounted Display (HMD) which is shown in Fig. 2(a).

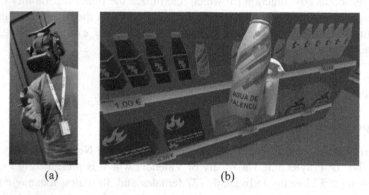

(a)   (b)

Fig. 2. (a) The shopper is interacting with the objects in the virtual store. (b) The virtual store which is shown through HMD.

2.2   ZOI and AOI Definition

In order to extract the features related to ZOIs or AOIs, the space was segmented. In zenithal view, the floor plan was divided into four different ZOIs namely Shelf, Adjacent, Near, and Far. These divisions are shown in Fig. 3(a). In this figure all the regions with the same color are in the same ZOI. The 3D space considering the shelves is divided into three levels namely Up, Middle, and Down as is shown in Fig. 3(b). AOIs are defined with the combination of the ZOIs and levels *i.e.* all the spaces in the ZOI Shelf and level Down are considered in the same AOI and named as "Shelf_-Down". In definition of these ZOIs and AOIs, widths and heights are constant and equal to the width of shelves and heights of the levels, but the lengths (L1 and L2) in Fig. 3(a) can be changed. Therefore, these two are considered for optimization. Note that, the levels in ZOI Far are not considered. Meaning that, in this ZOI all the space is considered as one AOI which is called "Far".

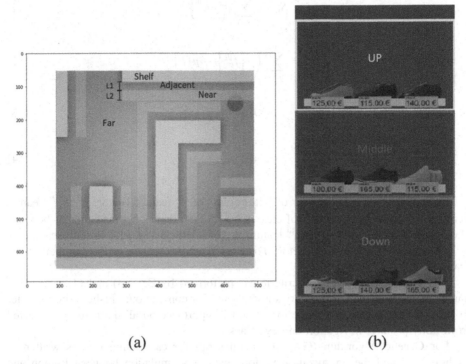

(a)   (b)

Fig. 3. (a) Floor plan with the divisions as Shelf, Adjacent, Near, and Far ZOIs. (b) Levels which are considered for AOIs.

2.3   GA Optimizer and Modified Fisher Criterion as Cost Function

In GA, the possible solutions are considered as chromosomes, and with crossover between chromosomes in a population it tries to generate other sets of solutions. With calculation of the fitness (cost) function, the algorithm removes some individuals created by crossovers and keeps the best solutions. For creation of non-existing chromosomes, the algorithm uses mutation. After a defined number of crossovers and mutations, a new generation will be created. This procedure leads to an optimal solution after a sufficient number of generations.

As it is mentioned, GA requires a fitness (cost) function for making decision about removing or keeping the individuals. This cost function should be defined based on the objective of an optimization problem. In this study, the objective is increasing the separability of the features extracted from shopper behavior to discriminate the gender by defining ZOIs and AOIs. Fisher criterion is used in linear discriminant analysis (LDA). LDA method tries to change the feature space in a way that they have the maximum linear separability, and the cost function is Fisher criterion. In this work, the modified Fisher criterion, as explained in Eqs. (1)–(4), is used as cost function.

$$S_{wi} = \sum_{j=1}^{n} \sigma^2 \left\{ f_i^{[j]} \right\} \tag{1}$$

$$S_{bi} = \sum_{j=1}^{n} \left(\mu \left\{ f_i^{[j]} \right\} - \mu \{ f_i \} \right)^2 \tag{2}$$

$$J_i = \frac{S_{wi}}{S_{bi}} \tag{3}$$

$$J = \frac{1}{\sum_{i=1}^{m} \frac{1}{J_i}} \tag{4}$$

In Eqs. (1)–(4), S_{wi} is scatter of within class of ith feature vector, $f_i^{[j]}$ is i^{th} feature vector of jth class, n is number of classes, $\sigma^2\{.\}$ is variance, S_{bi} is scatter of between classes of ith feature vector, f_i is i^{th} feature vector of all classes, $\mu\{.\}$ Is statistical mean, J_i is the cost for i^{th} feature vector, J is cost function, and m is the number of the features.

The modification of Fisher criterion is performed by Eqs. (3) and (4), i.e., using harmonic mean instead of ordinary summations. For conventional Fisher criterion refer to [6]. This modification is made to put equal importance on all the features extracted from body posture, navigation and eye-tracking.

For Genetic Algorithm (GA), the main script for calculating cost is written in Python V3.7 and the optimization is done using co-simulation between Python and MATLAB R2019b. The Population Size, Maximum Generations, Crossover Fraction, and Mutation Function are considered as 10, 20, 0.8, and "mutationgaussian" respectively.

2.4   Feature Selection and Classification

To examine the results of the optimization, ZOI and AOIs are used to extract some features from navigation, body posture and eye tracking data. Then, because of the plentiful number of the features extracted, an automatic feature selection (Forward Selection and then Backward Elimination) is utilized to obtain the best feature set for each classification. After feature selection, the classification is done using SVM classifier and the results of k-fold cross validation with 5 folds are reported.

3   Results and Discussion

After optimization, the optimizer selected 18 cm and 13 cm as optimal values for the L1 and L2, respectively. In order to examine the optimization results and show the improvement, optimal L1 and L2 and four other sets of L1 and L2 are tested with

SVM. The gender classification results are reported in Table 1. The optimal solution is reported in the first row of Table 1. Second to fourth rows represent ZOIs and AOIs with other quantities which are not optimal. The last row means the length of L1 and L2 are zero, in other word the ZOIs and AOIs Adjacent and Near are not considered for feature extraction.

Table 1. Classification results showing the accuracy of different combination of optimized and arbitrary length sizes. L1 and L2 are the length of ZOI Adjacent and Near respectively.

L1 (cm)	L2 (cm)	Features number	Males true positives	Females true positives	Accuracy
18	**13**	**15**	**0.87**	**0.85**	**0.86**
25	35	15	0.87	0.78	0.82
25	10	7	0.86	0.74	0.79
20	30	8	0.77	0.80	0.78
0	0	9	0.72	0.63	0.67

By comparison of the last row of Table 1, which means calculating the features without considering ZOI and AOIs, with the rest of the rows, it can be inferred that defining ZOIs and AOIs mainly can improve the classification results.

Table 1 shows adjusting of the sizes of the ZOIs and AOIs can have a huge impact on the improvement of the results. Also, it shows optimization could improve the classification accuracy.

4   Conclusion and Future Implications

In this study, Genetic Algorithm is used to optimize the ZOI and AOIs. These ZOI and AOIs are defined to extract features for classifying gender of the shopper based on the shopping behavior. After optimization, SVM classifier is applied on the features extracted with optimal sizes and some other arbitrary sizes of ZOIs and AOIs. The result showed optimal ZOI and AOIs with 85% accuracy outperformed the other sizes in classification of the shoppers' genders.

This study showed that extracting metrics related to segment the space of the store using ZOI and AOIs is beneficial for classification results. Also, by optimizing the sizes of these ZOI and AOIs, the results can improve. This method can be used to effectively optimize different types of segmentation with other classification methods. Besides, the approach can be used to adjust other thresholds and hyperparameters which emerge in feature extraction such as velocity and time thresholds for defining stops in navigation data.

As every other method, this methodology also has some limitations like, the cost function which was used in the study maximizes the linear separability, and obviously in some cases it does not lead to higher accuracy. As future work proposal, nonlinear kernels or another cost functions can be used to resolve this drawback. In addition, for future works other shapes for ZOIs and AOIs like circle and sphere, or other topologies can be considered.

Acknowledgements. This work was supported by the European Commission (Project RHUMBO H2020-MSCA-ITN-2018-813234 and HELIOS H2020-825585)

References

1. Xi, N., Hamari, J.: VR shopping: a review of literature. In: 25th Americas Conference on Information Systems (AMCIS 2019), pp. 1–10 (2019)
2. Hessels, R.S., Kemner, C., van den Boomen, C., Hooge, I.T.C.: The area-of-interest problem in eyetracking research: a noise-robust solution for face and sparse stimuli. Behav. Res. Methods **48**(4), 1694–1712 (2015). https://doi.org/10.3758/s13428-015-0676-y
3. Mitchell, M.: An Introduction to Genetic Algorithms. PHI Pvt Ltd., New Delhi (1996)
4. Gallagher, K., Sambridge, M.: Genetic algorithms: a powerful tool for large-scale nonlinear optimization problems. Comput. Geosci. **20**, 1229–1236 (1994). https://doi.org/10.1016/0098-3004(94)90072-8
5. Peck, C.C., Dhawan, A.P.: Genetic algorithms as global random search methods: an alternative perspective. Evol. Comput. **3**, 39–80 (1995)
6. Lin, Y.H., Tsai, M.S.: The integration of a genetic programming-based feature optimizer with fisher criterion and pattern recognition techniques to non-intrusive load monitoring for load identification. Int. J. Green Energy **12**, 279–290 (2015). https://doi.org/10.1080/15435075.2014.891511

An In-store Recommender System Leveraging the Microsoft HoloLens

Daniel Mora$^{(\boxtimes)}$, Shubham Jain, Oliver Nalbach, and Dirk Werth

AWS-Institute for Digitized Products and Processes gGmbH,
Campus Nord, 66123 Saarbrücken, Germany
{daniel.mora,shubham.jain,oliver.nalbach,dirk.werth}@aws-institut.de

Abstract. As the retail sector transitions into an omnichannel model, most brick and mortar stores are struggling to keep up with the competition by digital retail formats. Offline retail is still lacking the means to enrich the shopping experience in-store to make it more convenient, personalized and engaging. To this end, we introduce a novel in-store recommender system leveraging head-mounted mixed reality displays. The system enhances the shopping experience by introducing immersion and addressing the customer's desire to be treated on a personal level.

Keywords: Recommender system · Mixed reality · Omnichannel retail

1 Introduction

Traditional physical stores are closing down rapidly—the "retail apocalypse" [3]. Still, these stores remain the main pillar of the retail sector, accounting for 90% of worldwide sales [18]. Currently, physical stores are moving towards omnichannel retail [5] which aims to make customer experience the center of the business model and enhance it as much as possible. Hence, this omnichannel approach to retail differs from the traditional approaches (Brick and mortar and e-commerce) [14] in terms of deployment which poses a problem to retailer to transition. A promising approach is the deployment of novel digital technologies [13,15,27]. One of the mega-trends expected to revolutionize retail is mixed reality (MR) [5] as it offers a personalized hedonic experience using immersive holographic interfaces. However, little research has been done on concrete use cases of MR in omnichannel retail. In this paper, we aim to close this gap by providing a conceptual system that integrates the Microsoft HoloLens and an in-store recommender system for offline stores. We argue that the proposed system will have a positive impact on customers' path-to-purchase [29] and will accelerate both the search for information and the evaluation of alternatives [34].

We first discuss relevant previous work and the necessary theoretical and technological background in Sect. 2, before outlining the proposed system in Sect. 3. Finally, Sect. 4 offers an in-detail discussion which also takes into account limitations and future work and concludes the paper.

© Springer Nature Switzerland AG 2020
C. Stephanidis and M. Antona (Eds.): HCII 2020, CCIS 1225, pp. 99–107, 2020.
https://doi.org/10.1007/978-3-030-50729-9_14

2   Previous Work and Background

To justify the use of MR for in-store recommendations, we will review previous approaches to deploy recommender systems in physical retail but also investigate other use cases of MR in retail to identify their limitations and to draw inspiration for our recommender system (Sect. 3).

Researchers have experimented with a range of different technologies to integrate with recommender systems in brick and mortar stores. E.g., Fang et al. [9] created a smartphone-based store recommender system for shopping malls that implicitly captures customers' preferences by analyzing their positions using WiFi-RSS. Similarly, Silva et al. [30] provided recommendations of new or unseen stores in a mall to users via their mobile phones. By now, smartphones can also be used to check-out and pay [25]. Recently, [24] identified that resolving the complexity of the context data and creating more personalized advertisements as two of the directions where researchers need to contribute in order to improve mobile recommender systems and in the present article, we aim to work towards those directions. Another technology that has been integrated with recommender systems is computer vision which can be used to track customers in-store using surveillance cameras [22]. Other options include smart mirrors which detect RFID tags and recommend similar products [11].

In the recommender systems literature, collaborative filtering (CF) [12] is one of the most common approaches to generate recommendations. CF is often based on the idea of matrix factorization, e.g., using singular value decomposition (SVD) [4]. First, an initial matrix R that captures the preference of a set of users for a set of items is constructed based on known ratings of items by users. Then, using SVD, this user-item matrix is decomposed into a user-to-feature similarity matrix, an item-to-feature similarity matrix and a diagonal feature-weight matrix; this is used to predict users ratings to then generate the top-N most relevant items suggestions to the customers. To improve recommendation accuracy, additional information can be integrated, e.g., transactions of purchased products, or extensions of SVD like SVDFeature [7] can be used. Also, by capturing customers' movements inside the store and interactions with products, content-aware collaborative filtering approaches can be realized, which aim to use "contextual signals to become more human-centered" [10]. Methods to achieve context awareness can be categorized into pre-filtering, post-filtering and contextual modelling approaches. Their advantages and shortcomings have been discussed extensively in the literature [1].

Our proposed system will use MR technology. This term was defined to describe semi-virtual environments in which physical and digital objects coexist and interact with each other [21]. Possible advantages of this kind of virtual environment in retail have been discussed in the literature, concluding that they improve customer experience in terms of both utilitarian and hedonic values [20, 23] providing useful tools and making the shopping experience more enjoyable. One use case has been demonstrated in [31] where the authors evaluated augmented reality at the point of sales in retail stores to improve the assessment of information. Recently, recommender systems researchers have discovered

Table 1. Input and output channels provided by the Microsoft HoloLens.

Sensors	High-level input data	Output channels
Inertial measurement unit (1x)	3D Position	Holographic display
Front camera (1x)	Head orientation	Audio speakers
Depth camera (1x)	Eye gaze	Wi-Fi 802.11ac
Environment cameras (4x)	Gesture recognition	Bluetooth 4.1 LE
Ambient light sensor (4x)	Voice commands	
Microphone (4x)		

the technology, too, and first combinations have emerged [2,19] which promise to improve the item-exploration and decision-making stages of the shopping process.

The Microsoft HoloLens is a MR head-mounted display (HMD) which shows holographic content which are objects made of light and sound that appear in the world around the user, just as if they were real objects. Holograms respond to gaze, gestures and voice commands, and can interact with real-world surfaces. With holograms, digital objects can be created that are part of the real world. HoloLens enriches holograms with light and sound effects (Table 1, third column) and uses sensors to enable interaction. The same sensors (Table 1, first column) allow to extract different valuable inputs for a recommender system (Table 1, second col.): Position, head-gaze and eye-gaze of the user are determined by spatial mapping of the surrounding environment. Using the cameras and microphone, the HoloLens can recognize hand gestures and voice commands. Practitioners have added support for additional capabilities such as QR code and object recognition [32].

3   An In-store Mixed Reality Recommender System

Our MR recommender system proposes relevant products to customers throughout their shopping journey via an application running on a HoloLens, making product information search and comparison more efficient [34]. In this scenario, the device is owned by the customer, so it will contain personal information needed for the system to provide more personalized product suggestions. Recommendations are designed to take the customer's behavior in-store and other information, e.g., the history of purchases, into account to facilitate the search for relevant products. We first evaluate which of the input channels provided by the HoloLens (Table 1, second col.) can be used to extract information about the user (Sect. 3.1) and then conceptualize the recommender system using this information (Sect. 3.2).

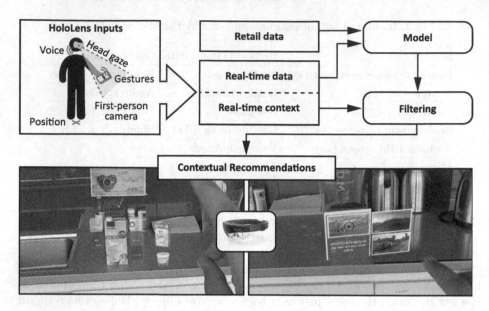

Fig. 1. Overview of our system. The bottom row shows two usage scenarios. In the left example, triggered by the examination of a package of milk, the user is presented with two product recommendations (milk drink and yogurt) shown as 3D holograms. In the second example, while looking at the box of a video game, the user is presented with additional information in the form of a video trailer, screenshots and prices.

3.1   Input Data

The top left corner of Fig. 1 shows the input channels provided by a HoloLens. Users can input information using the device's point-and-click interface, for example to maintain personal profiles with basic data such as age or interests but also dynamic information such as their current shopping list or wish list. The device itself provides the user's current and previous positions inside the store. By combining the raw positions with semantical information about the store layout, a list of encountered products, shelves and departments is computed. The inertial measurement unit provides information about the orientation of the user's head to determine an approximate gaze direction which can be refined employing the integrated cameras. The cameras are also responsible for image and object recognition tasks, e.g., of examined products. Finally, using gestures and voice commands, the customer can navigate the system's user interface in a natural way (Fig. 1, bottom) and provide feedback about products. Apart from these types of input data, the recommender system incorporates information maintained in the retail's IT systems, including product ratings by individual users, product information and the overall purchases of all customers.

3.2   Recommender System

We follow van Capelleveen et al.'s [6] Recommender Canvas methodology as a guidance framework. The design process is sub-divided into six areas—goal, domain characteristics, functional design, technical framework, interface design and evaluation—which we will describe in the following.

The *goal* of the proposed system is to support the product purchase decision by personalized products recommendations and to provide relevant information when making purchase decisions. Examples for such information include the location of a recommended product in the store and product information presented through a holographic interface (Fig. 1, bottom right).

The design of the system is influenced by several *characteristics of the target domain*, retail. One of the biggest challenges for the adaptation of recommender systems in offline retail is the availability of relevant data. By tapping the HoloLens inputs (Sect. 3.1) as a valuable source of additional data, we can overcome many of the limitations, e.g., the lack of contextual real-time information. In the proposed physical store system, data includes the customer's location and trajectory inside the store. This helps retailers to understand personal preferences and provide a purchase experience which is centered around individual customers. The integration of the additional inputs can be achieved using data hybridization through SVDFeature [8] which can leverage latent features and side information, such as visited departments.

The *functional design* of the system is driven by the question of what functionalities a user might expect from the system. Contemporary customers have a desire to be treated by retailers on a personal level (Sect. 1) which is facilitated by system's high level of context awareness and use of real time information [10].

The core *technical framework* for our recommender system follows a collaborative filtering approach. In this, the selection of the filtering method is critical. We propose to use SVDFeature [7] which is based on matrix factorization (Sect. 2) and provides a balanced trade-off between complexity and flexibility. This allows to incorporate all of the inputs provided by the HoloLens. Another important point of consideration is the training method to use. The model can be trained by minimizing the loss function using stochastic gradient descent [17]. As recommendations are known to be more relevant when customers are close to the recommended product [28], we propose to use the location of the user in post-context filtering [1].

The *interface design* takes into consideration how, when, what and where to present recommendations. They could be in the form of image, video, text overlays as well as three-dimensional holograms of recommended products. We devise two use cases. In the first one (Fig. 1, bottom left), the user sees a top-N list of recommended products. The second scenario is the automated presentation of additional information (Fig. 1, bottom right) that may help the user in making buying decisions. In both of these cases, users can use the interface of the system to receive recommendations and information effortlessly by clicking on the respective holographic buttons.

To *evaluate* the system performance, user-centric studies along the lines of [26] and [16] can be conducted to validate the claim that the system improves a customer's shopping experience. Common quantitative measures such as precision and recall can be used to measure the quality of the recommendations. Capelleveen's Recommender Canvas [6] also considers ways to optimize the recommender system further. However, given the prototypical nature of our system, optimization methods are not applicable yet.

4   Discussion

Both mixed reality and recommender systems have proven to be advantageous in retail [9, 23]. This paper proposes combining both to aid the transition of traditional retail into the omnichannel model. We leverage the capabilities of the Microsoft HoloLens using it as both a valuable source of input and an output channel for recommendations. The HoloLens can permanently monitor what shelves or products a customer is examining, collecting more information and allowing retailers to assist users better. The increased collection of input data reduces the problem of data sparsity resulting in more accurate recommendations for the customer.

An alternative approach to obtain similar real-time information is computer vision [22] which however has some limitations. For example, to infer which product a customer is seeing using standard surveillance cameras would require a large amount of cameras placed in different locations, powerful hardware and algorithms to analyze the video streams. In contrast, the HoloLens provides this information as a single integrated device which does not need any additional hardware or software to be set up. Furthermore, there are also evident advantages regarding the output. Perhaps the most important one is the immersive environment for the end user. This interaction is similar to that with real objects, making it more natural than in mobile phones and fully immersive environments. This immersion makes the shopping experience more pleasant to the user and more streamlined towards a buying decision.

In its current form, our system has some remaining limitations. The first is the accessibility and usability of its hardware. Also, the gesture-based interactions typically require some time for new users to get used to. Future work includes the deployment of our prototype in a lab or actual retail store for qualitative and quantitative user studies. There are multiple directions in which the system can be extended, for example a specialization for a specific type of retail. Regarding the hardware used, the next generation of the HoloLens has already been released. Some of its features are more precise position and eye gaze estimations which would improve the precision of the recommender system and reduce some of the current limitations. A challenge for retailers will be to understand the customers' perception regarding privacy. Customers usually express higher privacy concerns in personalized services than in non-personal ones [33]. Through user studies, it will be interesting to see to which extent immersion can aid the perception of the personalized recommender system.

Acknowledgments.

 This research is a part of the European Training Network project PERFORM that has received funding from the European Union's Horizon 2020 research and innovation programme under the Marie Skłodowska-Curie grant agreement No 765395. This research reflects only the authors' view, the European Commission is not responsible for any use that may be made of the information it contains.

References

1. Adomavicius, G., Tuzhilin, A.: Context-aware recommender systems. In: Ricci, F., Rokach, L., Shapira, B., Kantor, P.B. (eds.) Recommender Systems Handbook, pp. 217–253. Springer, Boston, MA (2011). https://doi.org/10.1007/978-0-387-85820-3_7

2. Álvarez Márquez, J.O., Ziegler, J.: Augmented reality based recommending in the physical world. In: Mensch und Computer 2018-Workshopband (2018)

3. Berman, B.: Flatlined: combatting the death of retail stores. Bus. Horiz. **62**(1), 75–82 (2019)

4. Billsus, D., Pazzani, M.J.: Learning collaborative information filters. In: ICML 1998, pp. 46–54 (1998)

5. von Briel, F.: The future of omnichannel retail: a four-stage delphi study. Technol. Forecast. Soc. Change **132**, 217–229 (2018)

6. van Capelleveen, G., Amrit, C., Yazan, D.M., Zijm, H.: The recommender canvas: a model for developing and documenting recommender system design. Expert Syst. Appl. **129**, 97–117 (2019)

7. Chen, T., Zhang, W., Lu, Q., Chen, K., Zheng, Z., Yu, Y.: SVDFeature: a toolkit for feature-based collaborative filtering. J. Mach. Learn. Res. **13**(Dec), 3619–3622 (2012)

8. Chen, T., Zheng, Z., Yong, Y., et al.: SVDFeature: user reference manual. Technical report. APEX-T R-2011-09-17 (2011)

9. Fang, B., Liao, S., Xu, K., Cheng, H., Zhu, C., Chen, H.: A novel mobile recommender system for indoor shopping. Expert Syst. Appl. **39**(15), 11992–12000 (2012)

10. Fischer, G.: Context-aware systems: the 'right' information, at the 'right' time, in the 'right' place, in the 'right' way, to the 'right' person. In: Proceedings of the International Working Conference on Advanced Visual Interfaces, pp. 287–294. ACM (2012)

11. Gao, G., Bai, C., Zheng, W., Liu, C.H.: The future of smart dressing mirror: an open innovation concept video. In: 2015 IEEE 12th International Conference on Ubiquitous Intelligence and Computing and 2015 IEEE 12th International Conference on Autonomic and Trusted Computing and 2015 IEEE 15th International Conference on Scalable Computing and Communications and Its Associated Workshops (UIC-ATC-ScalCom), p. 369. IEEE (2015)

12. Goldberg, D., Nichols, D., Oki, B.M., Terry, D.: Using collaborative filtering to weave an information tapestry. Commun. ACM **35**(12), 61–71 (1992)

13. Hagberg, J., Sundstrom, M., Egels-Zandén, N.: The digitalization of retailing: an exploratory framework. Int. J. Retail Distrib. Manag. **44**(7), 694–712 (2016)

14. Jain, S., Mora, D., Werth, D.: Retail customer experience: a comparative study between physical, online and omnichannel retail. In: 2019 9th International Conference of the Association Global Management Studies (ICAGMS), pp. 284–311 (2019)
15. Jain, S., Werth, D.: Current state of mixed reality technology for digital retail: a literature review. In: Nah, F.F.-H., Siau, K. (eds.) HCII 2019. LNCS, vol. 11588, pp. 22–37. Springer, Cham (2019). https://doi.org/10.1007/978-3-030-22335-9_2
16. Knijnenburg, B.P., Willemsen, M.C., Kobsa, A.: A pragmatic procedure to support the user-centric evaluation of recommender systems. In: Proceedings of the Fifth ACM Conference on Recommender Systems, pp. 321–324. ACM (2011)
17. Koren, Y., Bell, R., Volinsky, C.: Matrix factorization techniques for recommender systems. Computer **8**, 30–37 (2009)
18. Deloitte Touche Tohmatsu Limited: Global powers of retailing 2018 (2018). https://www2.deloitte.com/content/dam/Deloitte/at/Documents/about-deloitte/global-powers-of-retailing-2018.pdf
19. Márquez, J.O.Á., Ziegler, J.: Improving the shopping experience with an augmented reality-enhanced shelf. In: Mensch und Computer 2017-Workshopband (2017)
20. Meegahapola, L., Perera, I.: Enhanced in-store shopping experience through smart phone based mixed reality application. In: 2017 Seventeenth International Conference on Advances in ICT for Emerging Regions (ICTer), pp. 1–8. IEEE (2017)
21. Milgram, P., Kishino, F.: A taxonomy of mixed reality visual displays. IEICE Trans. Inf. Syst. **77**(12), 1321–1329 (1994)
22. Mora, D., Nalbach, O., Werth, D.: How computer vision provides physical retail with a better view on customers. In: 2019 IEEE 21st Conference on Business Informatics (CBI), vol. 1, pp. 462–471. IEEE (2019)
23. Papagiannidis, S., Pantano, E., See-To, E.W., Dennis, C., Bourlakis, M.: To immerse or not? Experimenting with two virtual retail environments. Inf. Technol. People **30**(1), 163–188 (2017)
24. Pimenidis, E., Polatidis, N., Mouratidis, H.: Mobile recommender systems: identifying the major concepts. J. Inf. Sci. **45**(3), 387–397 (2019)
25. Polacco, A., Backes, K.: The Amazon go concept: Implications, applications, and sustainability. J. Bus. Manag. **24**(1), 80–93 (2018)
26. Pu, P., Chen, L., Hu, R.: A user-centric evaluation framework for recommender systems. In: Proceedings of the Fifth ACM Conference on Recommender Systems, pp. 157–164. ACM (2011)
27. Rigby, D.: The future of shopping. Harvard Bus. Rev. **89**(12), 65–76 (2011)
28. Schrage, R., Hubert, M., Linzmajer, M.: Content is king? The effectiveness of message content, personalization, and location in mobile in-store advertising. In: Proceedings of the 52nd Hawaii International Conference on System Sciences (2019)
29. Shankar, V., Inman, J.J., Mantrala, M., Kelley, E., Rizley, R.: Innovations in shopper marketing: current insights and future research issues. J. Retail. **87**, S29–S42 (2011)
30. Silva, D.V.S., Silva, R.S., Durão, F.A.: RecStore: recommending stores for shopping mall customers. In: Proceedings of the 23rd Brazillian Symposium on Multimedia and the Web, pp. 117–124. ACM (2017)
31. Spreer, P., Kallweit, K.: Augmented reality in retail: assessing the acceptance and potential for multimedia product presentation at the PoS. Trans. Mark. Res. **1**(1), 20–35 (2014)
32. Vuforia: developing Vuforia engine apps for HoloLens (2019). https://library.vuforia.com/articles/Training/Developing-Vuforia-Apps-for-HoloLens

33. Wetzlinger, W., Auinger, A., Kindermann, H., Schönberger, W.: Acceptance of personalization in omnichannel retailing. In: Nah, F.F.-H., Tan, C.-H. (eds.) HCIBGO 2017. LNCS, vol. 10294, pp. 114–129. Springer, Cham (2017). https://doi.org/10.1007/978-3-319-58484-3_10

34. Willems, K., Smolders, A., Brengman, M., Luyten, K., Schöning, J.: The path-to-purchase is paved with digital opportunities: an inventory of shopper-oriented retail technologies. Technol. Forecast. Soc. Change **124**, 228–242 (2017)

Virtual Reality Body Exposure Therapy for Anorexia Nervosa. A Single Case Study

Bruno Porras-Garcia[1], Marta Ferrer-García[1],
Eduardo Serrano-Troncoso[2,3], Marta Carulla-Roig[2,3],
Pau Soto-Usera[2,3], Laura Fernández-Del Castillo Olivares[1],
Natalia Figueras-Puigderajols[1], and José Gutiérrez-Maldonado[1(✉)]

[1] Department of Clinical Psychology and Psychobiology,
University of Barcelona, Passeig de la Vall d'Hebron, 171,
08035 Barcelona, Spain
{brporras, jgutierrezm}@ub.edu
[2] Department of Child and Adolescent Psychiatry and Psychology,
Hospital Sant Joan de Déu of Barcelona, Passeig de Sant Joan de Déu, 2,
08950 Esplugues de Llobregat, Barcelona, Spain
[3] Children and Adolescent Mental Health Research Group,
Institut de Recerca Sant Joan de Déu, Passeig de Sant Joan de Déu, 2,
08950 Esplugues de Llobregat, Barcelona, Spain

Abstract. Exposure-based interventions have been proposed as an appropriate method for the treatment of fear of gaining weight (FGW) and body image disturbance (BID) in the treatment of anorexia nervosa (AN). However, exposure-based therapies have notable limitations (e.g., negative initial reaction in patients or higher risk of dropout). The use of virtual reality (VR)-based exposure techniques may overcome these limitations. This study provides initial evidence of the usefulness of a VR-based exposure therapy in the treatment of a 14-year-old female adolescent with AN. Over five exposure sessions, the patient was embodied in a virtual representation of her own silhouette whose weight was progressively increased. FGW, body anxiety, drive for thinness, BID, and Body Mass Index (BMI) were assessed before and after the intervention, and at 3-month follow-up. FGW, body anxiety and full body illusion (FBI) were also assessed at the beginning of each session. The patient was exposed to the immersive virtual scenario using a VR head mounted display (HMD-HTC-VIVE). After the intervention there was a clear reduction in FGW, drive for thinness, body-related anxiety, and BID. BMI rose slightly over the course of the intervention. FBI levels also rose progressively in each exposure session. However, these changes were not fully maintained at follow-up, when the improvement was lower than that achieved immediately post-treatment. This innovative VR-based exposure procedure achieved promising results for targeting FGW and AN symptoms in a short time. To pursue this study further, and to assess the effectiveness of this new VR software, a larger controlled clinical trial will be conducted.

Keywords: Anorexia nervosa · Virtual reality body exposure · Full body illusion · Fear of gaining weight · Body image

© Springer Nature Switzerland AG 2020
C. Stephanidis and M. Antona (Eds.): HCII 2020, CCIS 1225, pp. 108–115, 2020.
https://doi.org/10.1007/978-3-030-50729-9_15

1 Introduction

Anorexia nervosa (AN) is a severe eating disorder (ED) that usually begins during adolescence and often persists into adulthood. Previous studies have highlighted the need to address both fear of gaining weight [FGW; 1, 2] and body image disturbance [BID; 3, 4] in the treatment of anorexia nervosa (AN). Exposure-based interventions have been proposed as an appropriate method for the treatment of these disturbances [5]. However, in vivo-based exposure may present some limitations, such as high negative initial reaction in patients or higher risk of dropout [6]. This limitations may be overcome by VR interventions, since it is perceived as safer by participants and reduces withdrawal [7]. In addition, VR allow researchers to create real-size 3D simulations of participants' bodies with their own physical characteristics [7]. Real-size virtual bodies that participants can feel as their own, in an illusory feeling known as, full body illusion (FBI). Finally, VR offers the possibility of taking body exposure therapy one step further, allowing the patient to experience the FBI of a virtual body that progressively increases its weight until it reaches a healthy body mass index (BMI). The current study describes a technique involving VR body exposure to help a patient with AN to recover her healthy weight and reduce ED symptomatology.

This study provides initial evidence of the usefulness of a VR-based exposure therapy in the treatment of a 14-year-old female adolescent with AN (restrictive subtype). Over five VR exposure sessions, the patient was embodied in a virtual representation of her own silhouette whose weight was progressively increased until reaching a healthy Body Mass Index (BMI). Reductions in FGW, the body-related anxiety, BID and a return to a healthy-normative level for her BMI; finally, all these body-related changes were expected to be maintained after three months.

2 Method

2.1 Case Formulation

Patient A is a 14-year-old female adolescent that was diagnosed at the Eating Disorders Unit of Hospital Sant Joan de Déu of Barcelona. In the previous year, with a maximum BMI value of 23.17 kg/m^2, the patient started unhealthy diets without supervision and food-restrictive behaviors, such as counting calories and the progressive reduction or removal of some food perceived as unhealthy. Until there was the complete removal of solid food which lead to a significant lose weight (approximately 12 kg in the last twelve months). The patient also showed occasionally self-harming behaviors (e.g., scratching injuries in her forearms) with punitive purposes, and high anxiety levels in different daily situations (e.g., disputes with her family).

After reaching a minimum BMI of 17.67 kg/m^2, the patient was referred at the ED unit, where she was diagnosed with restrictive type AN according to the Diagnostic and Statistical Manual of Mental Disorders [8]. She also presented a high level of BID, with body concerns toward certain weight-related body areas (e.g., the stomach), high levels of FGW and body distortion.

She underwent day patient (DP) treatment for children and adolescents with ED. It was an intensive DP treatment program conducted at the ED Unit over 11-h periods, with permission to sleep at home. The treatment at the ED Unit consists of a multi-disciplinary protocol, including individual and group CBT, nutritional rehabilitation, a behavioral program aimed at improving eating patterns and weight, and individual and group parent counseling. The individual CBT consists of two sessions per week, each lasting 45 min. Finally, she also received a pharmacological treatment based on a single daily dose of Fluoxetine (10 mg) and Diazepam (5 mg).

2.2 Measures

Before starting the treatment (pre-evaluation), at the end of the treatment (post-evaluation) and after a follow-up of three months, the following measures were assessed:

- Evaluation of change in body weight: BMI.
- Eating Disorder Inventory (EDI-3; [9]). The EDI-3 is a self-report inventory consisting of 12 scales and 91 items, in which the answers are provided on a 6-point Likert scale. In the current study, the Spanish version of the body dissatisfaction scale (EDI-BD), and drive for thinness scale (ED-DT) were used.
- Physical Appearance State and Trait Anxiety Scale (PASTAS; [10]). The PASTAS comprise two self-report scales measuring weight-related and non-weight-related anxiety. In this study, the Weight Scale (W) was used.
- Silhouette Test for Adolescents (TSA; [11]). This Spanish instrument, adapted for the adolescent population, consists of eight male and eight female figures which progressively increase in body volume. The patient selected the one she perceived as their body size and the one she desired. Then, according to her BMI, the real silhouette is also selected. TSA-BD is assessed by calculating the discrepancy between the perceived and desired body sizes. Body distortion (TSA-D) is assessed by calculating the discrepancy between the perceived and real body sizes.
- Full-body Illusion (FBI), Fear of gaining weight (FGW) and Anxiety related to the whole body were assessed on Visual Analog Scales (VAS) from 0 to 100 at the beginning of each exposure session.

2.3 Instruments

The patient was exposed to immersive virtual scenario using a VR head mounted display (HTC-VIVE). In addition to the two controllers that HTC-VIVE usually provides, three additional body trackers were used to achieve full body motion tracking. Virtual avatars were created by Unity 3D and Blender 2.78, integrating all the components within the virtual environment. The virtual environment was a simple room without any furnishings, with a large mirror placed 1.5 m in front of the patient.

A young female avatar wearing a basic white t-shirt with blue jeans and black trainers was created. The avatar also wore a swim cap to avoid any influence of hairstyle.

2.4 Procedure

Prior to treatment, written informed consent was obtained from both the patient and her parents. The VR exposure intervention consisted of five sessions that were administered by two general health psychologist with clinical experience in the treatment of adolescents.

In the **pre-assessment session**, which lasted approximately one hour, the virtual avatar was generated by taking a frontal and lateral photo of the patient and creating an avatar whose silhouette matched the pictures by adjusting the different parts of its silhouette to the photographs. In the meantime, the other therapist administered the pre-assessment questionnaires and answered the patient's questions.

Next, the FBI was induced using two different procedures, a visuo-motor and visuo-tactile stimulation, both procedures lasted three minutes (for more details see Fig. 1). Once the FBI was induced, the three VAS examining intensity of the FBI, body-related anxiety and the FGW were assessed.

Visuo-motor stimulation
Synchronizing the movement of the participant and the avatar using motion capture sensors placed on hands, feet and waist.

Visuo-tactile stimulation
Synchronizing the patient's visual and tactile stimulation. While the patient was touched in different areas of the body (upper and lower limbs and stomach), she saw how her avatar was touched in the same areas and at the same time by a virtual controller.

Fig. 1. Brief description of visuo-motor and visuo-tactile stimulation procedures.

According to the **treatment sessions**, each of the five-exposure session, lasted approximately 1 h and took place once a week. All sessions began by inducing the FBI and assessing the VASs. The body exposure treatment was initiated with a virtual body with the same BMI as the patient. During the following sessions, the BMI of the avatar was progressively increased (0.35 BMI score/session) until the target weight (healthy BMI) was reached. During exposure to each avatar, the participant was asked to focus on different parts of the virtual body, by asking what they think and feel about them. In addition, the patient was asked about the level of anxiety experienced every 120 s throughout the exposure session (VAS-A). When her anxiety levels had decreased by

40% with respect to the initial measure, the session was terminated. At the end of each session, the patient was exposed to a relaxing VR environment (forest or garden) for 5 min.

Each of the following treatment sessions began with the next BMI increase. In cases where the initial whole-body anxiety had not fallen by 40% or if the exposure to various parts of the body had not been completed, exposure to the same avatar as the previous session was repeated.

3 Results

The results of the self-reported scales from the pre-post and follow-up assessment are detailed in Table 1. After the intervention there was a clear reduction in ED symptoms, including FGW, drive for thinness, body-related anxiety, and BID. BMI rose slightly over the course of the intervention. However, these changes were not fully maintained at follow-up, when the improvement was lower than that achieved immediately post-treatment.

Table 1. Pre, post-treatment and 3-month follow-up results.

Measures	Pre-treatment session	Post-treatment session	3 months follow-up
BMI	18.08	18.33	18.11
EDI-DT	27	8	21
EDI-BD	30	13	22
PASTAS	26	5	11
TSA-D	3	2	2
TSA-BD	2	−1	−1
BAS	22	43	37
VAS-A	70	30	50
VAS-FGW	100	30	50

Note: Body Mass Index (BMI), Eating Disorder Inventory (EDI-3) drive for thinness (DT) and body dissatisfaction (BD) scales, Physical Appearance State and Trait Anxiety Scale (PASTAS), Silhouette Test for Adolescents distortion (TSA-D) and body dissatisfaction (TSA-BD), Body Appreciation Scale (BAS), Visual analog scales (VAS) of Full-body ownership illusion (FBOI), anxiety and Fear of Gaining Weight (FGW).

As Fig. 2 shows, both measures VAS-A and VAS-FGW fell gradually across the five VR-body exposure sessions and the pre- and post-assessment sessions. FBI levels also rose progressively in each exposure session.

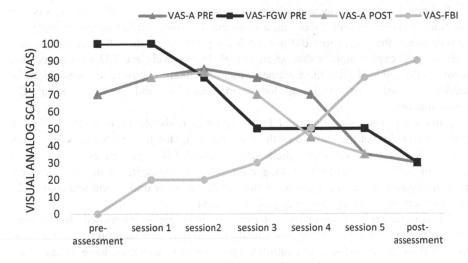

Fig. 2. First values for fear of gaining weight (VAS-FGW pre), body anxiety (VAS-A pre), full-body illusion (VAS-FBI) and the final value for body anxiety (VAS-A post) across the five VR-body exposure sessions and the pre- and post-assessment sessions.

4 Discussion

This innovative VR-based exposure procedure achieved promising results for enhancing CBT in ED. Before the intervention, the patient showed high to very high ED symptomatology, with both EDI-3 subscales scores within the high clinical ranges according to the original scales [9]. After a VR body exposure intervention, there were clear reductions in all ED symptomatology, including FGW, body anxiety levels, body dissatisfaction, drive for thinness and body distortion. In addition, BMI levels had slightly improved at the end of the intervention.

Our results provide further evidence that VR embodiment-based procedures can be successfully applied to modify BID, not only in healthy samples [e.g., 12, 13], but also to reduce body-related symptomatology in a patient with AN. These results are also in line with previous research that used in vivo exposure-based interventions (e.g., mirror-exposure techniques) to reduce body dissatisfaction in ED patients [14] and high body-dissatisfied women [4].

According FGW levels, after the intervention, there was a clear reduction of the scores. Our results are in line with those of a previous study [15] in which a decrease in AN symptomatology was observed after five sessions of imaginal exposure. However, the current study overcomes some of the typical limitations of imaginal exposure (e.g., such as the difficulty of achieving or maintaining visualization). Targeting the FGW seems a fundamental approach on AN treatment. Previous studies have found that FGW is one of the strongest predictor of ED symptomatology (e.g., dietary restraint) in AN patients [1]. Therefore, our results provide initial support for using VR embodiment-based procedures to help AN patients to confront their core fear, in a controlled and graded way.

Nevertheless, the reduction observed in the post-assessment session was not maintained at the 3-month follow-up assessment. In almost all ED measures there was an increase in the scores that did not reach the previous levels at the pre-assessment. One possible explanation is that, even though FGW levels and ED symptoms were substantially reduced after the treatment, more VR body exposure sessions might be needed in order to obtain a long-term reduction and stabilization in ED symptomatology.

This study has some important limitations which should be mentioned. First, it cannot conclude that the success of the intervention is due to the VR exposure per se, since it is based on a single patient who received VR treatment as an add-on to treatment as usual. In addition, a longer follow-up assessment, for instance one year after the assessment, would have been more useful to better understand and control the development of the symptomatology of the patient.

To confirm the efficacy of the VR exposure intervention controlled clinical trials should be conducted. Our group has already started one such study (clinicaltrials.gov, NCT 04028635), a randomized controlled clinical trial in which we have increased the sample size and compare CBT with added VR exposure to CBT alone.

Funding. This study was funded by the Spanish Ministry of Economy and Competitiveness (Project PSI2015-70389-R: Development of virtual reality-based exposure techniques for improving anorexia nervosa treatment) and by the AGAUR, Generalitat de Catalunya, 2017SGR1693.

References

1. Linardon, J., et al.: The relative associations of shape and weight over-evaluation, preoccupation, dissatisfaction, and fear of weight gain with measures of psychopathology: an extension study in individuals with anorexia nervosa. Eat. Behav. **29**, 54–58 (2018). https://doi.org/10.1016/j.eatbeh.2018.03.002
2. Murray, S.B., Loeb, K.L., Le Grange, D.: Dissecting the core fear in anorexia nervosa: can we optimize treatment mechanisms? JAMA Psychiatry **73**(9), 891–892 (2016). https://doi.org/10.1001/jamapsychiatry.2016.1623
3. Perpiñá, C., Botella, C., Baños, R., Marco, H., Alcañiz, M., Quero, S.: Body image and virtual reality in eating disorders: is exposure to virtual reality more effective than the classical body image treatment? CyberPsychology Behav. **2**(2), 149–155 (1999). https://doi.org/10.1089/cpb.1999.2.149
4. Delinsky, S.S., Wilson, G.T.: Mirror exposure for the treatment of body image disturbance. Int. J. Eat. Disord. **39**(2), 108–116 (2006). https://doi.org/10.1002/eat.20207
5. Reilly, E.E., Anderson, L.M., Gorrell, S., Schaumberg, K., Anderson, D.A.: Expanding exposure-based interventions for eating disorders. Int. J. Eat. Disord. **50**(10), 1137–1141 (2017). https://doi.org/10.1002/eat.22761
6. Vocks, S., Legenbauer, T., Wachter, A., Wucherer, M., Kosfelder, J.: What happens in the course of body exposure? Emotional, cognitive and physiological reactions to mirror confrontation in eating disorders. J. Psychosom. Res. **62**, 231–239 (2007). https://doi.org/10.1016/j.jpsychores.2006.08.007
7. Gutiérrez-Maldonado, J., Ferrer-García, M., Dakanalis, A., Riva, G.: Virtual reality: applications to eating disorders. In: Agras, W.S., Robinson, A.H. (eds.) The Oxford

Handbook of Eating Disorders, vol. 19, pp. 148–153. Oxford University Press, Oxford (2018). https://doi.org/10.1093/oxfordhb/9780190620998.013.26

8. American Psychiatric Association: Diagnostic and Statistical Manual of Mental Disorders, 5th edn. American Psychiatric Association, Arlington (2013)

9. Garner, D.M.: Eating Disorder Inventory-3. Professional Manual. Psychological Assessment Resources, Odessa (2004)

10. Reed, D.L., Thompson, J.K., Brannick, M.T., Sacoo, W.P.: Development and validation of the Physical Appearance State and Trait Anxiety Scale (PASTAS). J. Anxiety Disord. 5(4), 323–332 (1991). https://doi.org/10.1016/0887-6185(91)90032-O

11. Cruz, S., Maganto, C.: El test de las siluetas: un estudio exploratorio de la distorsión e insatisfacción con la imagen corporal en adolescentes. Revista del Instituto de Investigaciones de la Facultad de Psicología/UBA 8(1), 79–99 (2003)

12. Serino, S., et al.: Virtual reality body swapping: a tool for modifying the allocentric memory of the body. Cyberpsychology Behav. Soc. Network. 19(2), 127–133 (2016). https://doi.org/10.1089/cyber.2015.0229

13. Porras Garcia, B., et al.: Is this my own body? Changing the perceptual and affective body image experience among college students using a new virtual reality embodiment-based technique. J. Clin. Med. 8(7), 925 (2019). https://doi.org/10.3390/jcm8070925

14. Key, A., George, C.L., Beattie, D., Stammers, K., Lacey, H., Waller, G.: Body image treatment within an inpatient program for anorexia nervosa: the role of mirror exposure in the desensitization process. Int. J. Eat. Disord. 31(2), 185–190 (2002)

15. Levinson, C.A., Rapp, J., Riley, E.L.: Addressing the fear of fat: extending imaginal exposure therapy for anxiety disorders to anorexia nervosa. Eat. Weight Disord. 19(4), 521–524 (2014). https://doi.org/10.1007/s40519-014-0115-6

Implementation of Immersive Virtual Reality Through the Analysis of Diegetic User Interface

Gapyuel Seo[(⊠)]

Hongik University, Sejong 30016, South Korea
gapseo@hongik.ac.kr

Abstract. The primary factor in virtual reality is an interaction between user and system. To maximize the user's feeling of immersion, a user needs a user interface that can naturally interact with the system in virtual reality. In this paper, we introduce our VR learning program for the constellation that can enhance the user's sense of immersion using the diegetic UI in the VR environment. In order to utilize diegetic UI for immersion in VR learning content, we classified the diegetic UI that is mediated as an element in the VR environment into the following three types in our VR project. First, the diegetic UI mediated as a place can provide a realistic experience as a friendly place where we can visit easily even in ordinary times or a fantastic experience as an imaginary place that is hard to experience in reality. Second, the diegetic UI mediated as an agency plays a role in virtual reality in which the character becomes the subject of the story or helps the story progress in virtual reality. Third, the diegetic UI mediated as sensory is not limited to audiovisual as a means of interaction in virtual reality, but it enhances immersion by increasing interaction by utilizing all human senses.

Keywords: Virtual reality · User interface · Diegetic UI

1 Introduction

The rapid development of technology and the rapid growth of information society are changing the paradigm of education. Virtual reality (VR) is used in various fields such as games, education and training, and medical technology development [1]. The scope of use of VR education is increasing, and it is expanding to various fields used in our daily life. Virtual reality is widely used not only for general education, but also for job training in industrial fields, medical, military, and enterprises. In particular, it is attracting attention as an experiential content that provides a new learning experience by integrating virtual reality and artificial intelligence(AI) technology into educational content. It is possible to make an experiential education that can be experienced directly by moving to the place where it is difficult to escape from the limitations of space and observing the process of learning principles being executed. The learner actively participates in learning through critical thinking and imagination through experiential learning in virtual space [2, 3]. In the implementation of learning content, it will be necessary to provide a natural interaction between the user and the system by utilizing

© Springer Nature Switzerland AG 2020
C. Stephanidis and M. Antona (Eds.): HCII 2020, CCIS 1225, pp. 116–121, 2020.
https://doi.org/10.1007/978-3-030-50729-9_16

virtual reality to induce immersion in the learner and to lead a learning motivation and active learning effect.

Users interact with the system through the user interface (UI) and are crucial for systems that require intuitive interactions such as virtual reality. The primary purpose of UI design in the virtual reality will be to allow the user to naturally interact with the content and use it easily and conveniently. Virtual reality has the advantage of providing an immersive feeling through the realistic interaction between the user and the system and feeling the presence that can feel as if they are in the virtual world [4]. In particular, it maximizes the immersion of the user by supporting the user's natural interaction with the computer-generated environment. To induce the immersion of the user, a UI that can naturally be explored and interacted as in reality is required.

The purpose of this study is to analyze the components of the diegetic UI that can be applied to the VR environment and to suggest the utilization method of the VR content that can induce the sense of immersion. In this paper, we introduce our VR learning program for the constellation that can enhance the user's sense of immersion using the diegetic UI in VR environment.

2 Design Approach

In this project, we aim to expand students' curiosity about science and their scientific imagination by developing VR content that utilizes interesting space science materials that can be observed in everyday life. We implemented the exploration of space in the form of experience related to the constellations of the universe through the natural interaction with the user using virtual reality. We have made general scientific common sense about the universe and Greek myths related to constellations into interesting VR content in conjunction with storytelling. The player experiences the stories of the constellations by exploring the constellations of the universe, starting with an event that teleports into space from an astronomical observatory where he accidentally enters. Figure 1 shows the learning model of a constellation.

Fig. 1. The learning model of constellation

3 Diegetic User Interface

The diegetic user interface is the part of the scene and fiction of the virtual world [5]. Diegetic elements exist within the virtual world, and the player can directly manipulate the elements that make up the virtual world through the avatar's perspective. It is to configure the interface so that the player can interact with all of the internal elements such as characters, backgrounds, props, and sounds that exist in the virtual world that can be seen or heard. There are many virtual reality research results show that it is more efficient to create an interface with diegetic elements existing in the virtual world than a non-diegetic user interface represented by a typical GUI [6–8].

In this project, we classified the diegetic UI which is mediated as an element in the VR environment into the place, agency and sensory.

3.1 Place

A place is a diegetic UI element that creates new relationships and experiences between the player and the virtual world, and the realm can expand to serve as a role to create a new level of experience for the player. The astronomical observatory is the place where players start in this project and is a familiar place in reality. Players can interact and navigate by picking up, touching, and interacting with objects in space. From the moment the HMD is worn, the player is completely blocked from viewing and enters a virtual world different from that seen in reality. The player's first experience starts with a place that suggests how the story will unfold in the future. That is, it provides the user with a preparation step to immerse himself in the story. The universe is the second place where player can explore the constellations. By providing an experience of a fantastic place that is not commonly experienced in everyday life, it inspires players and allows them to become immersed in the real world. As a diegetic UI mediated as a place, it allows players to go beyond fantasy and reality to recognize that they have entered the virtual world rather than reality and become a subject in the virtual world. Besides, if we organize a place according to the progress of the story, we can make players experience dramatic inspiration. Figure 2 shows the diegetic UI mediated as a place in this project.

Fig. 2. Screenshots of diegetic UI mediated as a place

3.2   Agency

According to a locus of control, we classify an agency as an agent and an avatar [9]. The player controls the avatar to become the subject of the story, and also helps the story progress from the agent. The avatar gives the player the freedom to move around and observe the view and space from the first-person point of view so that the player becomes an imaginary person and feels immersed. It is essential to make the player immersive and interact in harmony with the virtual environment as if acting in reality. Through these experiences, you can make the player the subject of the story, experience the narrative structure, empathize with the situation, and induce empathy. Agent refers to a character or object controlled by a computer system, which means an animal, robot, or human in a virtual environment. An agent is the AI of the control panel in this project, and the player starts from the beginning by listening to the voice of the AI coming from the speaker of the control panel. Although it is the face and voice of the AI appearing on the screen attached to the controller, it makes the story smooth and improves the understanding of the situation. Even when moving from the observatory to outer space, the voice of AI continues to be heard and acts as an auditory medium connecting the real world with the fantasy world. Figure 3 shows the diegetic UI as an agent in this project.

Fig. 3.   Screenshot of diegetic UI mediated as an agent

3.3   Sensory

Sensory elements used to induce natural interaction and effective responses to the player. In virtual reality, players can refine their experiences by viewing, playing, and feeling perception cues related to their experiences. The main elements of perceptual immersion were visual and auditory. The visual and auditory elements focus the player's attention and provide clues. As a visual element in this project, a flickering effect was created on the button of the control panel to draw the attention of the player. It also provided clues for progress by faintly flashing the constellation shape when the player points to outer space. The visual elements generated effects on the objects that the player can interact with and drew the player's attention and provided clues to proceed with the story.

As the auditory element, the focus is on the moment of reaction that occurs in the direct interaction process between the user and the virtual environment, and it is produced with a diegetic sound existing in the virtual world so that heterogeneity does not occur. Perceptual immersion can improve through the synchronization of visual and auditory. When the player selects a constellation, the picture of the constellation overlaps and appears. Then, the agent told Greek myths related to the constellations to enhance the learning effect with interesting stories about the constellations. The agent that appears from the beginning of the story, although not visually expressed, accompanies the player and provides the necessary information. Also, the player can feel the social presence of interacting with a computer-generated agent and interacting with someone in the virtual world. Figure 4 shows the diegetic UI as a visual effect in this project.

Fig. 4. The visual effect of constellation display

The diegetic UI mediated as sensory induces direct interaction with the objects necessary for the story progression and conveys information to the player.

4   Conclusion and Future Work

In this study, we analyzed the diegetic UI that can be applied to the virtual reality environment and suggested a method to induce immersion. When we create a UI in virtual reality, we try to exclude the creation of a GUI that exists outside the virtual world and induce immersion as a diegetic UI that allows the user to interact naturally with all components in the virtual world. We classified the diegetic UI that is mediated as an element in the VR environment into the following three types. First, the diegetic UI mediated as a place can provide an immersion with a realistic experience as a friendly place where we can visit easily even in ordinary times or a fantastic experience as an imaginary place that is hard to experience in reality. Second, the diegetic UI mediated as an agency plays a role in virtual reality in which the character becomes the subject of the story or helps the story progress in events that occur in the narrative. Third, the diegetic UI mediated as sensory is not limited to audiovisual as a means of interaction in virtual reality, but it enhances immersion by increasing interaction by utilizing all human senses. As visual cues and auditory cues that exist in virtual reality, it serves as a clue to the player and helps the story progress.

As future work, we plan to utilize the tactile sense to maximize the user's immersion.

Acknowledgements. This work was supported by the Ministry of Education of the Republic of Korea and the National Research Foundation of Korea (NRF-2019S1A5A2A01047357).

References

1. Ahir, K., Govani, K., Gajera, R., Shah, M.: Application on virtual reality for enhanced education learning, military training and sports. Augmented Hum. Res. **5**(1), 1–7 (2019). https://doi.org/10.1007/s41133-019-0025-2
2. Chang, S.C., Hsu, T.C., Jong, M.S.Y.: Integration of the peer assessment approach with a virtual reality design system for learning earth science. Comput. Educ. **146**, 103758 (2020)
3. Taçgın, Z.: The perceived effectiveness regarding Immersive Virtual Reality learning environments changes by the prior knowledge of learners. Educ. Inf. Technol. 1–19 (2020). https://doi.org/10.1007/s10639-019-10088-0
4. Cummings, J.J., Bailenson, J.N.: How immersive is enough? A meta-analysis of the effect of immersive technology on user presence. Media Psychol. **19**(2), 272–309 (2016)
5. Fagerholt, E., Lorentzon, M.: Beyond the HUD - user interfaces for increased player immersion in FPS games. Master of Science Thesis, Chalmers University of Technology (2009)
6. Fragoso, S.: Interface design strategies and disruptions of gameplay: notes from a qualitative study with first-person gamers. In: Kurosu, M. (ed.) HCI 2014. LNCS, vol. 8512, pp. 593–603. Springer, Cham (2014). https://doi.org/10.1007/978-3-319-07227-2_56
7. Llanos, S.C., Jørgensen, K.: Do players prefer integrated user interfaces? A qualitative study of game UI design issues. In: Proceedings of the 2011 DiGRA International Conference: Think Design Play, Hilversum, Netherlands (2011)
8. Peacocke, M., Teather, R.J., Carette, J., MacKenzie, I.S.: Evaluating the effectiveness of HUDs and diegetic ammo displays in first-person shooter games. In: IEEE Games Entertainment Media Conference (GEM), p. 18 (2015)
9. Seo, G.: Study on the diegetic user interface mediated as illusion factor for virtual reality interactive storytelling. Doctoral Dissertation, Hongik University (2019)

Measurement of the Obstacle Avoidance Movement in an Augmented Reality Living Environment

Riku Toriyama[✉] and Hisaya Tanaka

Kogakuin University, 2665-1 Nakano-cho, Hachioji, Tokyo 192-0015, Japan
sodaclub.riku2910@me.com

Abstract. This study investigates if it is possible to avoid a virtual obstacle seen by a monocular head-mounted display (HMD) in an augmented reality (AR) living environment for the evaluation of motor function. The trajectory of a toe during obstacle avoidance was measured by optical motion capture. In four conditions consisting of an AR living environment or a real environment, movements to avoid obstacles were performed, and two points of toe clearance front (TCF) and toe clearance rear (TCR), the heights from the top of the obstacle to the toe tip, respectively, were evaluated. Obstacle heights were 2, 9, and 21 cm. The results verified that it was possible to avoid the virtual obstacle because both TCF and TCR were not less than 0 cm. In addition to TCF and TCR, the highest point of the toe tended to be higher as the living environment approached the AR living environment. Therefore, to verify the accuracy of the obstacle avoidance motion, the use of a binocular HMD is necessary as it offers a smaller effect on human perception of the obstacle and allows for the examination and an evaluation method that does not affect variations in gait.

Keywords: Augmented reality · Obstacle avoidance movement · Motion capture · Toe clearance

1 Introduction

The rate of adults living longer is progressing rapidly in developed countries. As a critical challenge of aging, falling by the elderly is often a concern. In Japan, more than 27000 elderly people died in accidents in 2016, of which 7116 fell, far exceeding the 3061 annual fatalities due to traffic accidents [1].

Even if a fall does not result in death, falling interferes with daily activities and increases the risk of requiring constant care, and it is a condition called locomotive syndrome. Fall factors are classified into internal factors from inside of the body and external factors from the surrounding living environment and can each cause falling incidents singly or together. Circumstances resulting in falls attributed to these factors include "slip," "totter," and "to loss." In addition, "stumble" instances with obstacles and from taking regular steps account for the largest proportion in the fall situations for elderly people [2–5]. The study by Saito et al. clarified that the cause of stumbling by the elderly is due to the difficulty in recognizing the perceived height of the feet, and the height of the feet is actually raised, so the drawing in of the feet becomes low [6].

© Springer Nature Switzerland AG 2020
C. Stephanidis and M. Antona (Eds.): HCII 2020, CCIS 1225, pp. 122–130, 2020.
https://doi.org/10.1007/978-3-030-50729-9_17

From this observation, measurements are necessary for these situations that are closer to actual living environments to clarify the cause of the "stumble" occurrence in which internal and external factors are independently or mutually related.

In recent years, augmented reality (AR) has become widespread in the industry with advanced developments in software and hardware. If an AR system can re-create a living environment, then it becomes possible to reproduce scenarios closer to that experienced by the elderly that is safe and inexpensive for analyzing falls caused by "stumbling" responses.

However, various behavioral responses are observed in "xR" environments (where "x" is a generic symbol representing multiple reality experiences, such as AR, virtual reality, and mixed reality) because AR can be inconsistent compared with real environments [7, 8]. Therefore, the purpose of this study is to verify if it is possible to "straddle" virtual obstacles reproduced by computer graphics (CG) in an AR living environment. Obstacle avoidance actions within an AR living environment and a real living environment are measured using optical motion capture, and differences between the resulting actions are compared.

1.1 Definition of Evaluation Points

To confirm if a virtual obstacle could be straddled in an AR environment, two evaluation points called the toe clearance front (TCF) and toe clearance rear (TCR) were configured following related research (Fig. 1) [9]. The height from the upper edge of the obstacle leading edge to the toe when the toe passes the upper part of the obstacle starting point is the TCF. The height from the upper end of the obstacle's leading edge to the toe as the toe passes over the obstacle's endpoint is referred to as the TCR. Because the toe follows an approximate parabolic path when straddling an obstacle, the obstacle is considered successfully straddled if both values of the TCF and TCR are not less than zero.

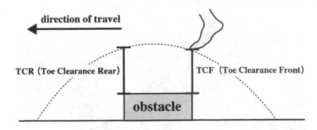

Fig. 1. The TCF and TCR evaluation points.

2 Methods

2.1 Development of the AR Living Environment

The AR living environment in this study is defined as a virtual obstacle generated by CG superimposed onto an image of the real surrounding space. An AR living environment is composed of AR devices, an AR engine, and a virtual obstacle.

The AR device was comprised of an iPhone XS Max manufactured by Apple Co. and an head-mounted display (HMD) from ELECOM Co., which is a monocular HMD for viewing images through a single lens. This HMD was selected because it enabled a straightforward creation of an AR living environment and was practical for the examinee to use during the evaluation.

The AR engine is the software for realizing the AR environment, and this study used the AR Kit from Apple. The optimized space recognition function available with this package was utilized, which enabled the detection of floors and walls without depending on specialized hardware or physical markers as well as three-dimensional (3D) processing of the space.

Three virtual obstacles with different dimensions were created of 2 cm (height) × 45 cm (width) × 15 cm (depth), 9 cm × 45 cm × 15 cm, and 21 cm × 45 cm × 15 cm in the AR environment. A People Occlusion function was incorporated to perform occlusion processing on a person to provide a better sense of reality when straddling virtual obstacles. Occlusion describes an object in consideration of the longitudinal relation between the object in front and the object behind. For a virtual obstacle that is intended to appear to be placed on the floor below, the front foot is then drawn on the front foot, which provides a sense of incongruity. However, after the virtual interaction, the obstacle is re-drawn in consideration of the anteroposterior relationship making it possible to perform obstacle avoidance movements without discomfort (Fig. 2). To compare avoidance actions of the virtual obstacle with a real environment, a similar obstacle was replicated in the real living environment for testing, as illustrated in Figs. 3, 4, and 5.

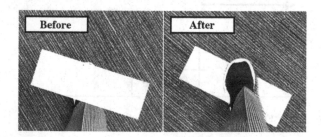

Fig. 2. The TCF and TCR as evaluation points.

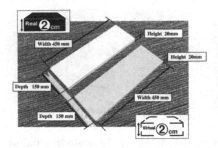
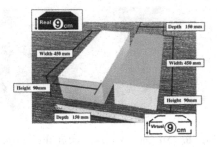

Fig. 3. 2 cm-tall real obstacle (left) and virtual obstacle (right).

Fig. 4. 9 cm-tall real obstacle (left) and virtual obstacle (right).

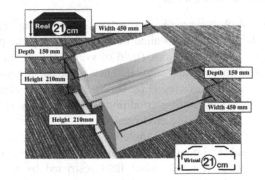

Fig. 5. 21 cm-tall real obstacle (top) and virtual obstacle (bottom).

2.2 Motion Capture

The obstacle avoidance motion was measured using an optical motion capture system, the "MAC 3D System," that is a method to calculate the 3D coordinates of a marker affixed to an object using an infrared camera in real time. The system consisted of 12 Kestrel measuring cameras and PCs installed with Cortex control software. The Kestrels were equipped with a sensor comprised of 2.2 million pixels that can photograph at 300 fps in full resolution. The Cortex software performed the setup of the Kestrels as well as provided analysis of the measured data.

Reflective markers were also attached to the subjects' feet to enable measurement of the obstacle avoidance movement. The application points were at the right and left toes (L_Toes, R_Toes), the left and right heels (L_Heel, R_Heel), and the right and left knees (L_Knee, R_Knee), as shown in Fig. 6.

Fig. 6. Attachment locations of the reflection markers for measuring the obstacle avoidance movement.

2.3   Conditions and Measurement

The subjects performed obstacle avoidance actions in virtual and real living environments defined as walking over an installed obstacle following the process outlined in Fig. 7. Three types of visual conditions (field of view unrestricted, mock HMD, and HMD) were configured to compare the difference in obstacle avoidance movements between virtual and actual obstacles (Fig. 8). Specifying the elements that can be improved is accomplished by setting conditions that gradually shift from an actual living environment to the AR living environment.

As outlined in Fig. 9, condition ① includes a real obstacle avoidance movement performed without visual field constraint. In condition ②, the real obstacle avoidance movement was performed with the visual field restricted by the mock HDM that imitates the head mount display to impose the constraint on the visual field. In condition ③, the real obstacle avoidance movement was performed with the visual field restricted by the HMD. In condition ④, the virtual obstacle avoidance movement was performed with the field of view restricted by the HMD. Twelve patterns were measured by changing the height of obstacles from 2, 9, and 21 cm for each condition using three healthy adult males as the subjects.

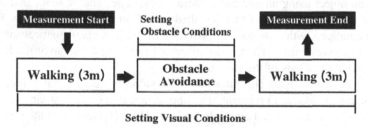

Fig. 7. The obstacle avoidance procedure.

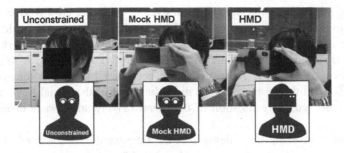

Fig. 8. Three visual conditions tested.

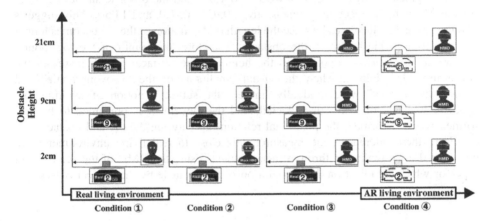

Fig. 9. Summary of the measurement patterns investigated.

3   Results and Discussion

3.1   Toe Trajectory

The trajectory of the toe during obstacle avoidance movements by one subject is shown in Fig. 10. Considering the graph for the obstacle height of 2 cm, the maximum point of the toe tends to increase gradually as the environment scenario shifted from real to AR, reaching 21, 23, 31, and 30 cm, respectively, in each condition. The difference between conditions ② and ③ at the highest point is a significant 8 cm. Even for the obstacle height of 9 cm, the difference between conditions ② and ③ at the highest point is 11 cm. For an obstacle height of 21 cm, the difference of the highest point between conditions ② and ③ is 6 cm. These differences are significant when binocular vision is shifted from possible to impossible.

These results suggest that as the cues for recognizing distance are gradually limited, it becomes difficult to raise the foot to an appropriate height. When a human recognizes an obstacle, the distance to the obstacle is obtained through stereoscopic vision by synthesizing images from the right and left eyes in the brain. However, as it becomes impossible to perform stereopsis through changing the condition to a single eye HMD, the distance to the object is inferred only to be obtained through an overlapping line perspective from the subject's experience. However, in condition ④ with an obstacle height of 2 cm, the highest point of the toe decreased by 1 cm compared with the condition ③. With this result, because the habituation of the visual field condition in the HMD is effected, the estimation of the comparatively appropriate distance is also affected.

The obstacle crossing time, defined as the time for the toes to land after initially lifting from the ground, for the obstacle height of 2 cm tended to gradually increase from 0.7, 0.75, 0.8, and 0.8 s. Obstacle straddling times for the 9 cm-high object also increased gradually from 0.85, 0.9, 0.95, and 1.0 s, and the obstacle straddling times for the 21 cm-high object also increase from 0.95, 1.0, 1.0, and 1.05 s. This suggests that the stride time increases because the length of the motion of the toe becomes longer in proportion to the height of the obstacle. Therefore, the length of the toe motion appears to increase in proportion to the height of the obstacle, which increases the stride time. In addition, when the visual conditions of the "viewing angle" and "binocular parallax" were gradually limited, the subject's notion of avoiding the obstacle without collision was reflected, and the movement is presumed to be performed while confirming the positional relationship between the toe and obstacle.

From these inferences, the measurements close to real living environments are considered to be replicable through measurements using the HMD of the see-through type for which the effect on the recognition of the obstacle by the subject is less.

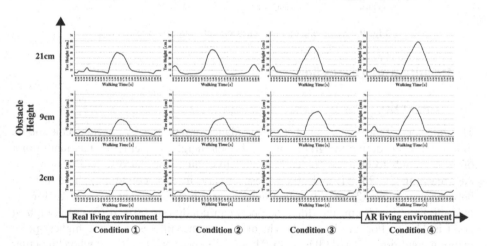

Fig. 10. The toe trajectory measurements.

3.2   TCF and TCR

Figure 11 indicates the TCF and TCR values for one subject. The result of condition ④ suggests that it is possible to cross the virtual obstacle because both values of TCF and TCR were not zero or negative. However, the values of TCF and TCR gradually increase as the living environment condition approaches that of the AR. When stepping over an obstacle in a parabolic motion, the TCF and TCR depend on the toe separation point, so its variation affects the TCF and TCR in each trial. In addition, because the evaluation site in this study is limited to the toe, the angles of the toe and the leg are considered to also influence the fluctuation of TCF and TCF values. Therefore, an analysis method that does not impact the variation of each trial must be performed.

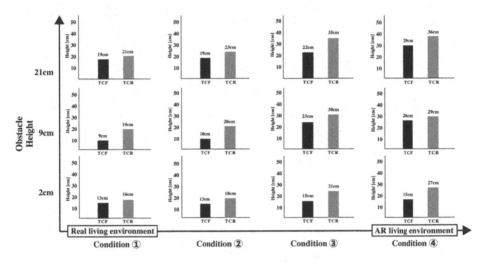

Fig. 11.   The resulting TCF and TCR values.

References

1. Consumer Affairs Agency. https://www.caa.go.jp/policies/policy/consumer_safety/caution/caution_009/pdf/caution_009_180912_0002.pdf. Accessed 20 Dec 2019
2. Blake, J., et al.: Fallsby elderly people at home: prevalence and associated factors. Age Ageing **17**, 365–372 (1988)
3. Rubenstein, L.Z., Robbins, A.S., Schulman, B.L., Rosado, J., Osterweil, D., Josephson, K.R.: Falls and instability in the elderly. J. Am. Geriatr Soc. **36**, 266–278 (1988)
4. Overstall, P.W., Exton-Smith, A.N., Imms, F.J., Johnson, A.L.: Falls in the elderly related to postural imbalance. Br. Med. J. **29**, 261–264 (1977)
5. Tinetti, M.E., Speechley, M., Ginter, S.F.: Risk factors for falls among elderly persons living in the community. N. Engl. J. Med. **320**, 1701–1707 (1989)
6. Saito, S., Muraki, S.: Study on tracks and sense of feet position while stepping over an obstacle in the elderly. Japan Hum. Factors Ergon. Soc. **46**, 172–179 (2010)
7. Mizuchi, Y., Inamura, T.: Difference evaluation of daily-life activities in physical and immersive VR environments. The Japanese Society for Artificial Intelligence (2018)

8. Kitamoto, E., Yamada, S., Munemoto, S., Oikawa, K.: A study on distance perception in architectural space. The Virtual Reality Society of Japan (2017). (Chapter 22)
9. Seki, Y., Kiriyama, Y.: Kinematic analysis of obstacle striding motion during walking, vol. 53. Japan Human Factors and Ergonomics Society (2017). (Supplement)

Visual Environment Design of VR Space for Sequential Reading in Web Browsing

Taisei Tsunajima[✉] and Nobuyuki Nishiuchi

Graduate School of Systems Design, Tokyo Metropolitan University, 6-6
Asahigaoka, Hino, Tokyo, Japan
tsunajima-taisei@ed.tmu.ac.jp, nnishiuc@tmu.ac.jp

Abstract. Recently, the use of VR is diversifying with the spread of the relatively cheap VR equipment. VR has been used in games, entertainment facilities, educational fields and so on. For example, web browsing in VR space is one of the focused fields. Some of its typical applications are Bigscreen and Virtual Desktop. Since these applications can create a big size screen for the web browser, users could easily browse the web in the VR space. Web browsing can be classified into information search and information acquisition (sequential reading). However, research on the information acquisition has not been conducted yet. Therefore, the purpose of this study is to verify the optimal visual environment for information acquisition task in the VR space. In the experiment, we created six conditions' web pages using Unity. They were consisted of two font size conditions and three screen size conditions. In the experimental task, the subjects were asked to loudly read the text on the screen, and they were asked to answer a questionnaire for subjective evaluation. In order to compare readability of each conditions, invisible area and reading time were measured. From the experimental results, we could verify the suitable visual environment for web browsing in VR space.

Keywords: Virtual reality · Web browsing · Sequential reading · Readability · Visual environment

1 Introduction

The year 2016 is called the first year of Virtual Reality (VR). The use of VR is diversifying with the spread of the relatively cheap VR equipment. The application area of VR has also been expanded to games, entertainment facilities and education. For example, some companies use VR for training employees in customer service and management. Some social VR applications can allow us to make online communication with others in the VR space. Moreover, web browsing in VR space is one of the focused fields. Some of its typical applications are Bigscreen and Virtual Desktop. Since these applications can create a big size screen for the web browser, users could easily browse the web in the VR space. However, it is not clarified that the big size screen is suitable for the web browsing, then it is necessary to verify the visual environment for comfortable web browsing in VR space [1–3].

© Springer Nature Switzerland AG 2020
C. Stephanidis and M. Antona (Eds.): HCII 2020, CCIS 1225, pp. 131–136, 2020.
https://doi.org/10.1007/978-3-030-50729-9_18

Web browsing can be classified into information search and information acquisition (sequential reading). However, research on the information acquisition has not been conducted yet. Therefore, the purpose of this study is to verify the optimal visual environment for information acquisition task in the VR space.

2   Experiment

2.1   Methodology

Twelve subjects (21 to 24 years old) participated in the experiment. We created six conditions' web pages using Unity. One of the experimental VR space is shown in Fig. 1. They were consisted of two font size conditions (standard: 12pt [80 mm], large: 16pt [100 mm]) and three screen size conditions (S: 2.36 × 7.20 m, M: 1.35 × 4.00 m, L: 0.81 × 2.40 m). MS Gothic was used and the distance between the subject and the screen in VR space was fixed at 1.0 m for all conditions. The three screen sizes was based on the previous study [4].

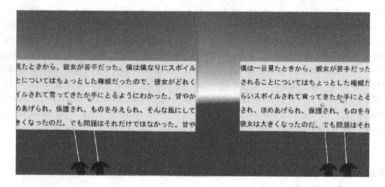

Fig. 1. Example of experimental VR space (Images for left and right eyes)

Six texts were extracted from Haruki Murakami's "Carousel Horse Dead Heat" for the experimental task. The six texts were unrelated to each other, and the number of characters of the six texts was arranged in 1,348. In the preliminary experiment, it has been confirmed that there was no significant difference between the six texts.

2.2   Procedure

Before starting the experiment, the subjects filled out the questionnaire about experience of VR equipment use, and performed the vision test to confirm that the subjects have more than 20/30 vision. After the explanation of the VR equipment operation, the subjects performed practice tasks as fully proficient in the experimental environment.

In the experimental task, the subjects were asked to loudly read the text displayed on the screen under each condition. And after each task, they were asked to answer a questionnaire on physical and cognitive fatigue for five-grade subjective evaluation.

Table 1 shows seven items of the questionnaire. A three-minute break was provided after each trial. As the evaluation indexes to compare readability, reading time and invisible area of the screen [5] were measured.

Table 1. Questionnaire items for subjective evaluation

	Questionnaire items
Physical fatigue	1. Fatigue on eyes
	2. Fatigue on head
	3. Fatigue on arms
	4. Overall fatigue
Cognitive fatigue	5. Information volume per one page
	6. Character size
	7. Comprehensive readability

3 Experimental Results

3.1 Reading Time

The experimental results of the average reading time for each condition were shown in Fig. 2. The horizontal axis shows the screen size, and the vertical axis shows the reading time, and each bar shows the font size. The asterisks *, ** indicate that the coefficients are statistically different from zero at the 5 and 1 percent level, respectively.

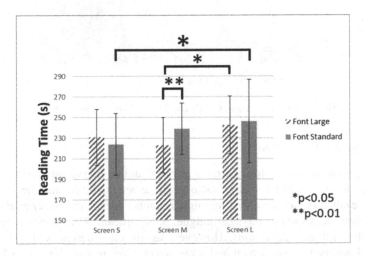

Fig. 2. Average reading time

As shown in Fig. 2, significant difference (p < 0.01) was recognized between standard size font and large size font at M size screen. Simultaneously, significant differences (p < 0.05) were also recognized between the screen conditions at standard size font and between the screen conditions at large size font.

3.2   Invisible Area

The results of the invisible area of the screen L, M, S are shown in Fig. 3. It shows the positions of character which the subjects could not read. In the experiment, the maximum number of subjects who couldn't read the character was 9 subjects at the same position, so nine color gradations from orange to red show the number of subjects. Only under the condition of the L size screen, the invisible areas appeared.

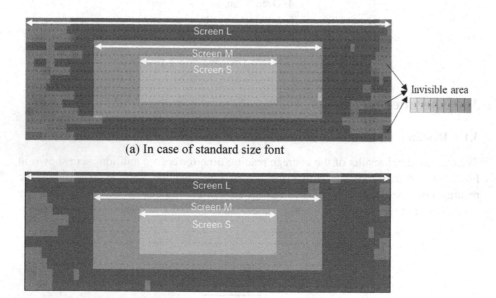

(a) In case of standard size font

(b) In case of large size font

Fig. 3. Invisible area of each condition. (Colour figure online)

3.3   Subjective Evaluation

The averages of the evaluation score on physical and cognitive fatigue are shown in Fig. 4 and Fig. 5. The horizontal axis shows the screen condition and the vertical axis shows the evaluation score so that the higher number means the better evaluation.

Regarding the results of physical fatigue, no significant difference was recognized between the font size conditions. However, significant differences (p < 0.05) were recognized between L size screen and other screen sizes in Fig. 4(a), (c), (d).

Regarding the results of cognitive fatigue, significant differences were mainly recognized between the condition of "standard size font using L size screen" and some other conditions in Fig. 5(a), (b), (c).

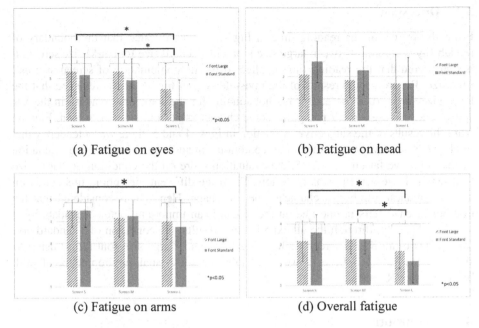

(a) Fatigue on eyes   (b) Fatigue on head

(c) Fatigue on arms   (d) Overall fatigue

Fig. 4. Results of subjective evaluation (physical fatigue)

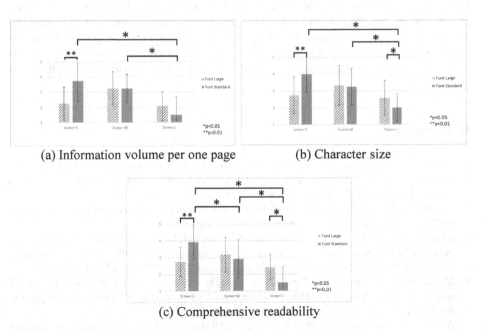

(a) Information volume per one page   (b) Character size

(c) Comprehensive readability

Fig. 5. Results of subjective evaluation (cognitive fatigue)

3.4   Discussion

From the results of the reading time in Fig. 2, it was revealed that the boundary of readability was found between large size font and standard size font at M size screen. It is considered that the reading time is affected by the combination of screen size and font size. Regarding the results of the invisible area in Fig. 3, it was revealed that the large size screen (0.81 × 2.40 m) is not suitable for the sequential reading in the VR space, because users can't recognize some characters at both sides of screen. Finally, from the results of the subjective evaluation in Figs. 4 and 5, there was a tendency that the L size screen was worse than other conditions. In addition, the subjective evaluation of the cognitive fatigue in Fig. 5, the evaluation score on the condition of "large size font using S size screen" was quite low. From the different viewpoint, this condition has the smallest number of characters per one page. Hence, it is considered that the number of characters in one line on the screen is an important factor of readability.

Consequently, through the all experimental results, the condition of "standard size font (12pt) using S size screen (2.36 × 7.20 m)" and "large size font (16pt) using M size screen (1.35 × 4.00 m)" were suitable for the visual environments of web browsing in VR space.

4   Conclusion

In this research, we verified the optimal visual environment for information acquisition task for web browsing in the VR space. In the experiment, the invisible area and reading time were measured by using the six conditions' web pages. From the experimental results, it is concluded that the number of characters in one line on the screen is an important factor and the combination of screen size and font size affects the readability.

References

1. Okada, T., Nishiuchi, N.: Research on web site design considering screen size, In: Proceedings of the 39th Conference on Annual Meeting of Kanto-Branch, pp. 94–95. Japan Human Factors and Ergonomics Society (2009)
2. Takano, K., Omura, K., Shibata, H.: Comparison between paper books and e-book readers in reading short stories. IPSJ. Res. Rep. **2011**(4), 1–8 (2011)
3. Brade, J., Lorenz, M., Busch, M., Hammer, N., Tscheligi, M., Klimant, P.: Being there again - presence in real and virtual environments and its relation to usability and user experience using a mobile navigation task. Int. J. Hum. Comput. Stud. **101**, 76–87 (2017)
4. Murakami, S., Nishiuchi, N.: Research on usability evaluation during web browsing in VR space. In: Proceedings of the 48th Conference on Annual Meeting of Kanto-Branch, pp. 48–49. Japan Human Factors and Ergonomics Society (2018)
5. Ayama, M., Ujike, H., Iwai, W., Funakawa, M., Okajima, K.: Effects of contrast and character size upon legibility of Japanese text stimuli presented on visual display terminal. Opt. Rev. **14** (1), 48–56 (2007)

Designing Virtual Equipment Systems for VR

Powen Yao[(⊠)], Tian Zhu, and Michael Zyda

GamePipe Laboratory, University of Southern California,
Los Angeles, CA, USA
{powenyao, tianzhu, zyda}@usc.edu

Abstract. Skeuomorphism in virtual reality can provide more than just visual cues for quick recognition, it can also provide spatial information. A Virtual Equipment System is a system that takes advantage of the spatial information from a user's body by equipping them with virtual counterparts of common wearables. It provides ways to quickly adjust a suite of functions that are conceptually related using spatial knowledge of human anatomy corresponding to the equipment. The system can also be used to provide shortcuts for interacting with properties of other objects related to the user's sensory channels. As a software solution, this Virtual Equipment System can be standardized and implemented across different devices and applied to different extended realities.

Keywords: 3DUI · Human-centered computing · Virtual reality

1 Introduction

In the current generation of virtual reality (VR) headsets, the user adjusts various audio-visual settings by using the menu button on the controller to bring up the system menu. Once the system menu appears, the process becomes much like using a mouse on traditional PCs. The controller is used as a pointer to interact with the menu and navigate to the desired option. This is a method that utilizes user knowledge that is easily transferable from traditional PC user interfaces, but it does not take advantage of the spatiality provided by VR or the user's own body awareness.

On certain VR devices such as Oculus Quest, users can adjust sound volume using buttons on the headset. Dedicated physical buttons enable quick access, but the positions and availability of these buttons are not universal across different VR devices. However, with a 6 Degree of Freedom (6DOF) Headset, we have spatial reference points for the headset. We can further associate the space around the headset to different conceptual areas of human anatomy such as eyes, ears, or mouth. We can then use the 6DOF Motion Controller to interact with these spatial reference areas.

Some VR games and experiences have explored using spatial reference points around the headset, but mostly for increased immersion. In games like Job Simulator [1], players can eat a food item by placing it near their mouth. In The Lab [2], players can bring a crystal sphere representing another world to their head to enter that world. An example of using spatial reference points for improved workflow and accessibility can be found in Fantastic Contraption [3]. As an advanced option, players can use the different areas around their head as shortcuts to grab different items (Fig. 1).

C. Stephanidis and M. Antona (Eds.): HCII 2020, CCIS 1225, pp. 137–144, 2020.
https://doi.org/10.1007/978-3-030-50729-9_19

Fig. 1. User grabbing a stick from the left ear area of the headset in Fantastic Contraption.

Lastly, we take inspiration from headphones with gesture control such as Sony's WH1000XM3 headphones [4] or the helmet touch interface by Takumi et al. [5]. Gesture Control increases the number of options that users have access to, given the same spatial reference point or area.

2 Proposed System

In most VR Setups, the user is equipped with a 6DOF Headset and two 6DOF Motion Controllers. With these physical devices, we have spatial reference points for the head and the hands. Virtual Equipment (VE) is a group of objects that are socketed to these spatial reference points. 6DOF Motion Controllers provide the means to interact with the VE.

VE provides an alternative to the traditional menu interface. Users can grab and put on different equipment. Furthermore, users can interact with their VE through controller gestures or body gestures (e.g. arm gestures or foot gestures). Lastly, the VE can be grabbed and used with other systems for additional interactions.

2.1 Location of VE

To determine the locations of VE, we need to have spatial reference points for the user's body. Here, we describe three approaches: Headset and Controller tracking, hardware tracker-based tracking, and camera-based tracking. With additional hardware, a Virtual Equipment System can be bolstered with full body tracking.

The latter two approaches involve full body tracking. Full body tracking provides additional spatial reference points that can then be outfitted with Virtual Equipment. Depending on the tracking, we may gain additional direct spatial reference points, but also indirect locations related to those points. Additionally, full body tracking will provide extra information that can help us improve our evaluation of the ergonomics of the Virtual Equipment System.

Headset and Controller Tracking. Headset & Controller Tracking is the most widely available and easiest method to utilize because it does not need any additional hardware. We utilize spatial reference points for the helmet directly to outfit the user with VE such as headphones, goggles, or microphones. We similarly utilize the controllers to outfit the user with arm bracers. These VE, as shown in Fig. 2, are displayed in addition to what the user is wearing and may be different than the physical objects (e.g. having virtual headphones while wearing earphones).

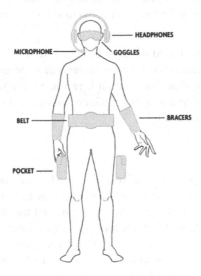

Fig. 2. Virtual Equipment available with Headset and Controller tracking that users can interact with using 6DOF Controllers in VR

For VE without a direct spatial reference point, we can estimate the associated location based on statistical data of the human body and the spatial reference points that we do have. For equipment such as a belt or pockets, we can use the height of the VR headset as the user's eye height and determine the user's waist height using anthropometry.

Advanced Tracking. One option for better tracking would be to use hardware trackers. Using hardware trackers such as the HTC's VIVE trackers, we can get direct spatial references for other body locations such as feet, knees, and elbows. The accuracy of the full body tracking will depend on the number of trackers we use.

At the time of this writing, the bulkiness and the inconvenience of the trackers makes it inconvenient to use many trackers. However, we can easily place two trackers on the user's left and right feet. Along with the existing headset and the two controllers, this gives us five points of reference. Using inverse kinematic solutions, we can perform inverse kinematics on a human body model to get an estimate of many more key points.

Another solution for better tracking would be camera-based tracking. Using two or more external cameras, we can track the human body using computer vision libraries

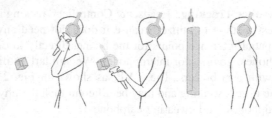

Fig. 3. From left to right: user moving controller to grab virtual headphones. User releasing a representation of headphones at the menu node. Audio settings menu is shown to the user.

such as OpenPose. Camera-based tracking has the benefit of being able to track more key points than trackers and does not require the user to wear additional hardware on the body. The downside is that this solution is restricted to a specific physical location and requires additional computing power, which can further tax a system that's already strained by enabling virtual reality.

2.2 Types of VE

VE can be grouped into two types: VE related to the human body and VE not related to the human body. The most straightforward example of the first type would be vision and hearing for the sensory systems as well as hands and feet for actuator systems. This category also includes VE that are conceptually associated with the respective body parts due to historic or cultural significance. These associations may not be as universal as the senses. Examples could include wristwatches for the wrist and a sword for the back or waist.

The second type includes anything else that does not fit the first category. This could be because the VE cannot be placed in its logical location due to other VE competing for the same space or because the VE cannot be functionally associated with any human body parts. For example, goggles with a snapshot functionality could be placed where the eyes are, but that location may be occupied by other goggles that allow the adjustment of brightness and enable alternate vision. The system or the user could choose to place the VE in a secondary spot, such as at the feet. However, the equipped VE would not be as intuitive as if they were the first type of VE, leading to more effort on the user's part to associate the VE with the body location.

Other functionalities in VR could take the form of VE and be placed on the user for quick access. For example, network settings could be made into a router that is equipped at the elbow. These VE move away from what is considered equipment in real life and cannot be easily associated with the body parts in which they are equipped, but they can be provided for the user's convenience within an existing VE system.

2.3 VE Interactions

VE such as a bow equipped on the back could allow the users to draw the bow and start firing arrows at targets like they could in real life. However, we envision three other types of VE interactions that are not commonly seen in real life: Drag & Drop, Controller Gesture, and Body Gesture.

VE Interaction – Menu Access via Drag and Drop. The user can use a 6DOF controller to quickly access the menus associated with VE using a special menu node or an "Alt Node". We envision this node to function like the alt key of the keyboard, enabling an object placed in the node to bring up its alternative function. Tentatively, we have attached this node to the controller.

This operation functions similarly to a drag-and-drop operation in PC systems. First, the user moves the motion controller to the location of the VE (e.g. headphones), receiving haptic feedback as it enters the equipment. Then, the user pushes and holds the trigger button to pick up the headphones, attaching the VE to the controller. The user can then move the VE headphones freely. If the trigger is released while the VE headphones are inside the Menu Node, the menu associated with the headphones will be opened. If the trigger button is released while the VE is anywhere else, the VE will return to its original position (Fig. 3).

Using this interaction with Type 1 VE, users will be able to access general sensory related menus. For example, vision and graphics menus through the VE at their eyes (goggles), the audio menu through the VE at their ears (headphones), and the voice menu through the VE at their mouths (microphones).

Since Type 1 VE also represents the sensory channels the users have, VE can also serve as a shortcut to open the settings menus related to the sensory channel for a specific object. Using the same drag and drop method described earlier, users can drag a Type 1 VE (headphones) from their body location (ear) to an object in the world to bring up that object's sensory menu (audio menu) as illustrated in Fig. 4.

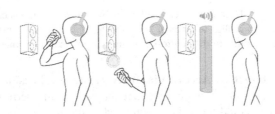

Fig. 4. From left to right: user grabbing virtual headphones with the controller. User placing the virtual headphones on an object in the world. Type 1 virtual headphones open the audio menu associated with the object.

VE Interaction Example - Function Access Via Controller Gestures. Some VE could include built-in motion gestures to allow quick access to different functions. Much like grabbing and moving the equipment to the menu node, users can perform gestures by moving the controller to the equipment (e.g. headphones). Instead of grabbing and releasing at the menu node, users would grab and release the headphones slightly away from their original position to perform a controller gesture. Depending on the direction and distance moved, the gesture could trigger different functions as detailed in Fig. 5.

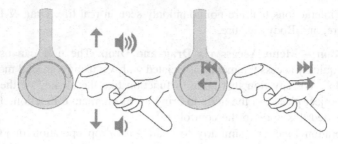

Fig. 5. On the left, using the controller to perform up and down gestures on the virtual headphones to increase and decrease volume. On the right, using the controller to perform a forward and backward gesture to go to the next song or previous song.

Like the object-specific sensory menu access, these controller gestures can also be expanded to target a specific object's audio or visual sensory channels. Users could select an object (grabbing with a controller or using a pointer) and perform the controller gesture to adjust that object's audio or visual properties as shown in Fig. 6.

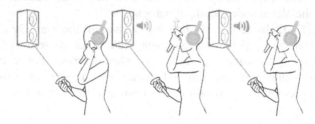

Fig. 6. From left to right. User uses the controller's pointer to select an object in the world. User uses the other hand's controller to interact with the headphones via controller gesture. The object's volume increases due to the controller gesture on the audio channel.

VE Interaction - Function Access Via Body Gestures. In addition to controller gestures, some VE are situated in places where the users could perform body gestures. For example, the user could have shoes equipped at the feet that can be triggered by tapping the heels together three times, like in the Wizard of Oz. Once the gesture is performed, it will trigger the associated functionality of the VE which could return to Home or bring up movement-related settings menus.

2.4   VE Customization

Since the VE is based on the user's body in 3D space, a user's physical characteristics affect our VE System. Improperly placed, the VE will be at best awkward to use, or at worst, inoperable. The ability to customize Virtual Equipment's positions becomes crucial for a good user experience. We outline two methods for user customization.

Tailored UI or Tracking-enabled Customization. We draw upon the clothing analogy to describe user interfaces that are modified by the system to work with a

Fig. 7. From left to right. User grabbing the virtual headphones on the mannequin using a controller. As the user moves the controller and thus the virtual headphones up, user's equipped virtual headphones also move up

user's physical characteristics such as height, arm length, etc. This is atypical in UI design as most user interfaces are designed for the average human in order to be accessible for the most people.

With the basic setup of a 6DOF headset and two controllers, we can utilize the headset to perform a user height calibration as well as utilize the controllers to get a user arm length calibration. With that information, we could then refer to anthropometry data to get estimates for the rest of the body. With full body tracking, we could have UI that's tailored or made-to-fit for the user. Aside from placing each VE in appropriate positions with respect to the user's body, we can adjust interactions based on the user's exact measurements.

For example, when the user performs an up gesture on the virtual headphones, the user's arm length and the rotation of the joints determine how easy it is for the user to move up and down. For people with longer arms, their hands might easily go out of bounds and end up moving the virtual headphones instead of performing an up gesture. It is critical that these interactions in 3d space take into consideration the user's physical attributes when determining the position and orientation in which users must move their controllers or body to interact.

Virtual Avatar Mannequin. The system can make its best prediction for what the user would want, but there are times when these predictions are insufficient. We need a way for the users to be able to adjust intuitively and easily. For that, we envision a mannequin that mirrors the user in terms of VE equipped. The mannequin provides a way for users to visualize and adjust the settings for their various VE.

When users interact with the VE that is equipped on themselves, it could either activate a gesture or move it for drag and drop interactions. When the user interacts with the VE that is equipped on the mannequin, it would adjust the position of the VE with respect to the body area they are equipped in. This is useful for situations where the user's VE cannot be interacted with due to it being stuck in a real-world object such as virtual headphones inside actual headphones or a virtual utility belt inside someone's belly.

Aside from adjusting the physical location of the VE, the mannequin can also provide feedback for performing controller gestures as well as adjusting controller gestures, something that's otherwise hard to visualize and see. With a mannequin mirroring the user's every action, the user can see how much they must move their controller to trigger a controller gesture. The user can also spatially adjust the parameters for what would be interpreted as a controller gesture (Fig. 7).

3   Evaluation

To evaluate the Virtual Equipment, we need to compare what it takes to perform a task using the different interaction methods in Virtual Equipment versus the traditional methods of using a menu button followed by pointers or dedicated hardware buttons.

Quantitative data that we can capture would be the time it takes, the user's accuracy, and the motion required to perform an action. If full body tracking is implemented, we would have more accurate quantitative data for the action required. We would also like to capture qualitative data to compare the effort and comfort. We will ask users about their experience with VE through user surveys with questions about areas such as difficulty, intuitiveness, comfort, and effort required.

Some basic tasks we want to compare would be adjusting the audio volume, adjusting the brightness of the display, opening the audio settings menu, and opening the visual settings menu. For each task, we will compare a VE system with the currently existing traditional interfaces.

4   Conclusion

There are many advantages to a Virtual Equipment System that utilizes the spatial reference points provided by a VR headset and its controllers. A user's spatial reference points can be utilized directly and indirectly, as well as bolstered through tracking. There are a variety of different ways to interact with the Virtual Equipment System, including how the Virtual Equipment can be tailored and customized, and how we can evaluate the performance of these Virtual Equipment.

References

1. Job Simulator (2016). Owlchemy Labs
2. The Lab (2016). Valve Corporation
3. Fantastic Contraption and why VR Menus Suck. http://www.youtube.com/watch?v=ASXST_iyhl4. Accessed 20 March 2020
4. Controlling the audio device (Bluetooth connection). https://helpguide.sony.net/mdr/wh1000xm3/v1/en/contents/TP0001703116.html. Accessed 20 March 2020
5. Kitagawa, T., Yamato, Y., Shizuki, B., Takahashi, S.A.: Viewpoint control method for 360° media using helmet touch interface. In: Symposium on Spatial User Interaction, pp. 1–2 (2019)

Virtual Humans and Motion Modelling and Tracking

Virtual Kayaking: A Study on the Effect of Low-Cost Passive Haptics on the User Experience While Exercising

Angelos Barmpoutis[1(⊠)], Randi Faris[1], Samantha Garcia[2],
Jingyao Li[1], Joshua Philoctete[1], Jason Puthusseril[2], Liam Wood[2],
and Menghan Zhang[1]

[1] Digital Worlds Institute, University of Florida, Gainesville, FL 32611, USA
angelos@digitalworlds.ufl.edu, {randi.faris,jingyaoli,
josh2497,zhangmenghan}@ufl.edu
[2] Computer and Information Science and Engineering, University of Florida,
Gainesville, FL 32611, USA
{sgarcia22,jasonputhusseril,liamwood}@ufl.edu

Abstract. This paper presents the results of a pilot study that assesses the effect of passive haptics on the user experience in virtual reality simulations of recreation and sports activities. A virtual reality kayaking environment with realistic physics simulation and water rendering was developed that allowed users to steer the kayak using natural motions. Within this environment the users experienced two different ways of paddling using: a) a pair of typical virtual reality controllers, and b) one custom-made "smart paddle" that provided the passive haptic feedback of a real paddle. The results of this pilot study indicate that the users learned faster how to steer the kayak using the paddle, which they found to be more intuitive to use and more appropriate for this application. The results also demonstrated an increase in the perceived level of enjoyment and realism of the virtual experience.

Keywords: Virtual reality · Passive haptics · Physical education · Kayaking

1 Introduction

Kayaking is an outdoor activity that can be enjoyed with easy motions and with minimal skill, and can be performed on equal terms by both people who are physically able and those with disabilities [1]. For this reason, it is an ideal exercise for physical therapy and its efficacy as a rehabilitation tool has been demonstrated in several studies [1–6]. Kayaking simulations offer a minimal-risk environment, which, in addition to rehabilitation, can be used in training and recreational applications [5]. The mechanics of boat simulation in general have been well-studied and led to the design of high-fidelity simulation systems in the past decades [3, 7]. These simulators immerse the users by rendering a virtual environment on a projector [1, 4, 6] or a computer screen that is mounted on the simulator system [2, 8]. Furthermore, the users can control the simulation by imitating kayaking motions using remote controls equipped with

© Springer Nature Switzerland AG 2020
C. Stephanidis and M. Antona (Eds.): HCII 2020, CCIS 1225, pp. 147–155, 2020.
https://doi.org/10.1007/978-3-030-50729-9_20

accelerometers (such as Wii controllers) [5] or by performing the same motions in front of a kinesthetic sensor (such as Kinect sensors) [4, 6].

The recent advances in virtual reality technologies and in particular the availability of head mounted displays as self-contained low-cost consumer devices led to the development of highly immersive virtual experiences compared to the conventional virtual reality experiences with wall projectors and computer displays. Kayaking simulations have been published as commercial game titles in these virtual reality platforms [13]. However, the use of head mounted displays in intensive physical therapy exercises bears the risk of serious injuries due to the lack of user contact with the real environment. These risks could potentially be reduced if the users maintained continuous contact with the surrounding objects such as the simulator hardware, the paddle(s), and the floor of the room, with the use of passive haptics. Additionally, the overall user experience can be improved through sensory-rich interaction with the key components of the simulated environment.

This paper assesses the role of passive haptics in virtual kayaking applications. Passive haptics can be implemented in virtual reality systems by tracking objects of interest in real-time and aligning them with identically shaped virtual objects, which results in a sensory-rich experience [9, 10]. This alignment between real and virtual objects allows users to hold and feel the main objects of interaction including hand-held objects, tables, walls, and various tools [11, 12].

In this paper we present a novel virtual reality kayaking application with passive haptic feedback on the key objects of interaction, namely the paddle and the kayak seat. These objects are being tracked in real-time with commercially available tracking sensors that are firmly attached to them. Although the users' real-world view is occluded by the head-mounted display, the users can see the virtual representation of these objects and naturally feel, hold, and interact with them. Subsequently, the users can perform natural maneuvers during the virtual kayaking experience by interacting with our "smart" paddle using the same range of motions as in real kayaking.

The proposed system was assessed with a pilot user study (n = 10) that tested the following hypotheses: a) The use of passive haptics helps users learn kayaking faster and operate the simulation better compared to the conventional controller-based interaction. b) The use of passive haptics improves the level of immersion while kayaking in virtual reality.

The study was undertaken at the Reality Lab of the Digital Worlds Institute at the University of Florida. The volunteers who participated in this experiment were randomly assigned to the study and control group and experienced the proposed virtual kayaking system with and without the use of passive haptics respectively. The data collection was performed with pre- and post-test surveys. In addition, the progress of each individual user during kayaking was recorded and the collected timestamps were analyzed.

The results from this study are presented in detail and indicate that the use of passive haptics in this application has a statistically significant impact on the user experience and affects their enjoyment, learning progress, as well as the perceived level of realism of the virtual reality simulation.

2 Methods

A virtual reality kayaking simulation was developed by imitating state-of-the-art kayaking simulations that are currently available in commercial virtual reality platforms [13]. The developed virtual environment featured realistic physics simulation and photorealistic water rendering with reflection, refraction, distortion and Fresnel effect. The user could steer the kayak by naturally moving a pair of typical virtual reality controllers that were visualized as two short paddles in the virtual environment (Fig. 3 top). This type of interaction was considered the baseline in our study as it represents the common way of interaction in modern virtual reality systems.

Additionally, our virtual kayaking simulation provided an alternative mode of interaction using a custom-made paddle controller. More specifically, two hand-held controllers (Oculus Rift) were rigidly attached to the blades of a real paddle as shown in Fig. 1. The placement of the controllers with the rings of LED markers around the paddle allowed continuous unobstructed 6 degree of freedom tracking. The physical paddle was aligned with a 3D model of a paddle in the virtual space (Fig. 3 bottom), so that the users could naturally hold and feel the paddle while being in the virtual environment. In both types of interaction, the controllers provided vibration cues when the corresponding virtual paddles were submerged in the virtual water.

Fig. 1. The proposed "smart" paddle with the two VR controllers rigidly affixed to the two blades for 6-DOF tracking and vibration feedback when submerged in the virtual water.

Furthermore, in our experimental setup the chair that was used during our study sessions was aligned to the 3D model of the kayak as shown in Fig. 2. More specifically, the flat arms of the armchair were aligned to the flat sides of the 3D model of the kayak so that the users could feel the size of the virtual kayak. This way the users could intuitively control the range of their motions while paddling in virtual reality and thus avoid hitting the armchair with the physical paddle. The position and orientation of the chair was tracked in the 3D space with respect to the virtual reality headset without requiring the attachment of any additional markers to the chair because its position was fixed within the real physical space.

A virtual environment with a river was designed and made long enough to allow 8–10 min of kayaking. The river was divided into 5 segments with checkpoints that were distributed along the river and served as progress indicators. Finally, the virtual environment included several other decorative as well as collectible objects that motivated the users to steer the kayak towards them in order to collect points (see Fig. 3 top). A virtual screen in the kayak displayed the time, progress/checkpoints, and score in the game as shown in Fig. 3.

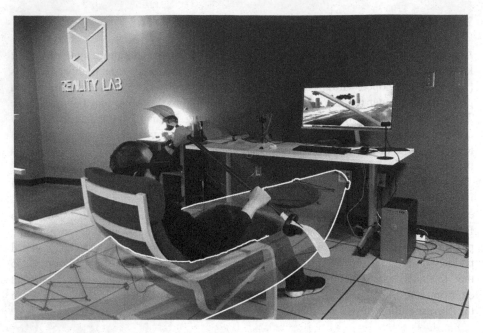

Fig. 2. The experimental setup in the Reality Lab of the Digital Worlds Institute. The virtual model of the kayak is superimposed to show the alignment between the real and virtual spaces.

3   User Study

A small-scale pilot study (n = 10) was conducted at the Reality Lab of the Digital Worlds Institute in order to test the two hypotheses stated in Sect. 1 (IRB 201902921). The study was structured as a randomly ordered A/B test. The data were collected through pre- and post-test questionnaires as well as through automatically recorded time-stamps during the kayaking simulation.

The variable in the A/B test was the mode of interaction, i.e. paddling using a pair of typical virtual reality controllers versus the proposed "smart" paddle. The order was randomly assigned to the subjects in order to minimize bias. At the end of the study the users responded to questions such as "Did you find the A or the B experience more enjoyable?" by selecting one of the 5 following responses: 1) clearly A, 2) slightly A, 3) about the same, 4) slightly B, 5) clearly B. Because of the randomization of the order of the A/B tests, after the end of the study the responses were transcribed so that they all have the same A/B reference. Table 1 presents the detailed list of metrics used in the survey.

Additional demographic, kayaking-specific, and open-ended feedback questions were included in the pre- and post-test questionnaires. It is worth mentioning that 60% of the participants had real kayaking experience at least once before this study and 30% of the participants stated that they used VR often.

Fig. 3. Screenshots from the virtual kayaking environment that demonstrate the two cases in our A/B tests: top) two short paddles controlled with the typical VR controllers, bottom) one long paddle controlled with the paddle of Fig. 1.

Table 1. The list of metrics used in our A/B test.

Metrics	Paddle %	χ^2	p
It was more appropriate for this application	100%	20	p < .001
It was clearer on how to operate	95%	16.2	p < .001
My virtual experience felt more real	95%	16.2	p < .001
My virtual experience was more enjoyable	90%	12.8	p < .001
I learned faster how to steer the kayak	90%	12.8	p < .001
It could help me improve my skills in kayaking	75%	5	p < .05
It could help me improve my fitness	75%	5	p < .05
It was more intense experience	70%	3.2	p < .1
I felt less dizzy	70%	3.2	p < .1
It was overall easier to kayak	60%	0.8	N/S
It was more comfortable to use	55%	0.2	N/S

4 Results

Table 1 lists the percentage of responses that favored the proposed "smart" paddle interaction for each metric/question in our survey. A chi-square test of independence was performed to examine the relation between each metric in this table and the type of interaction (virtual reality controllers vs. smart paddle). The probability of each test and the corresponding χ^2 values are shown in the last two columns of Table 1.

According to the results the users found that the proposed smart paddle was more appropriate for this application ($\chi^2 = 20$, p < .001), it was clearer on how to operate ($\chi^2 = 16.2$, p < .001), felt more real ($\chi^2 = 16.2$, p < .001), and kayaking was more enjoyable ($\chi^2 = 12.8$, p < .001) compared to the same experience with traditional VR controllers. These findings support our hypothesis that the use of passive haptics improves the level of immersion while kayaking in virtual reality.

Additionally, the results indicate that the users felt that they learned faster how to steer the kayak using the proposed paddle ($\chi^2 = 12.8$, p < .001), which is in agreement with the timestamps collected during their virtual kayaking experiences. More specifically, the plot in Fig. 4 shows the progress of the subjects during their experience "A". The subjects who used the proposed paddle in their first experience finished the level in 20% less time (585 s vs. 760 s), which corresponds to an overall 30% increase in their speed compared to those who used the typical VR controllers.

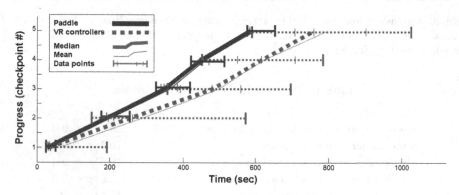

Fig. 4. The progress of the subjects in our kayaking simulation during case A of our A/B tests. The plot compares the subjects who used our paddle (solid blue line) with those who used two typical VR controllers (dashed red line). (Color figure online)

Similar observations can be made for experience "B". As expected, all users improved their performance during their second experience, which indicates that the skills acquired in our simulation are transferable between the two modes of interaction. The plot in Fig. 5 shows the time improvement from "A" to "B". The subjects who used our proposed paddle in their second experience improved their previous performance 3 times more (315%) compared to those who used the typical VR controllers (142 s vs. 45 s improvement). These findings support our hypothesis that passive haptics help users learn kayaking faster and operate the simulation better compared to the conventional controller-based interaction.

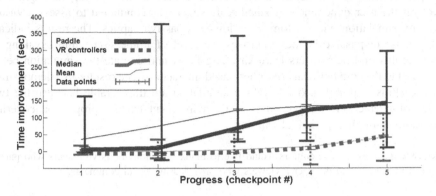

Fig. 5. The time improvement of the subjects during case B of our A/B tests with respect to their performance in A. The plot compares the subject based on the controller used in test B.

There was no significant association found between the order of the experiences in the A/B tests and the responses. However there was a small inclination towards "intensity" (the first experience felt more intense, $\chi^2 = 1.90$) and "dizziness" (the users felt more dizzy in the second experience, $\chi^2 = 1.90$). Although these findings are not statistically significant, they may indicate that: a) the longer the users experience kayaking in VR the more probable it is to feel dizzy, and b) the user's knowledge from the first experience influences their perception of the second experience as "less intense".

Furthermore, as part of our pre-test questionnaire we asked the users how to paddle in order to turn the kayak to the right and we provided them with 3 possible responses: a) paddle to the left, b) paddle to the right, c) I do not know. Half of the participants did not answer correctly this question in the pre-test questionnaire. However, all of them corrected their response in the post-test survey. This indicates that our kayaking simulation teaches proper maneuvering techniques through a risk-free experiential learning environment.

Finally, the users who provided feedback by responding to our open-ended question at the end of the study mentioned that the proposed paddle made the kayaking simulation "surprizingly more real than expected", and that the use of the paddle in combination with the vibration cues created the impression of "water resistance". One of the points of criticism was about the lack of hand tracking, which could improve the interaction with the paddle even more, according to the users.

5 Conclusions

This paper demonstrated that the use of passive haptics in virtual reality has significant effect on the user experience. A small-scale study was conducted to assess a virtual kayaking simulation with custom-made low-cost passive haptics. The results indicate that the use of passive haptics improves the level of immersion while kayaking in virtual reality and helps users learn kayaking faster and operate the simulation better compared to the conventional controller-based interaction. The results also demonstrate that the skills acquired in our kayaking simulation are transferable between the two modes of interaction and that our virtual environment teaches proper maneuvering techniques through experiential learning.

Acknowledgements. The authors would like to thank the anonymous volunteers who participated in this study and the peer reviewers who provided insightful comments.

References

1. Park, J., Yim, J.: A new approach to improve cognition, muscle strength, and postural balance in community-dwelling elderly with a 3-D virtual reality kayak program. Tohoku J. Exp. Med. **238**(1), 1–8 (2016)
2. Choi, W., Lee, S.: Virtual kayak paddling exercise improves postural balance, muscle performance, and cognitive function in older adults with mild cognitive impairment: a randomized controlled trial. J. Aging Phys. Act., 1–27 (2019). https://doi.org/10.1123/jap2018-0020
3. Recio, A.C., et al.: Use of a virtual reality physical ride-on sailing simulator as a rehabilitation tool for recreational sports and community reintegration: a pilot study. Am. J. Phys. Med. Rehabil. **92**(12), 1104–1109 (2013)
4. Ustinova, K.I., Perkins, J., Leonard, W.A., Hausbeck, C.J.: Virtual reality game-based therapy for treatment of postural and co-ordination abnormalities secondary to TBI: a pilot study. Brain Inj. **28**(4), 486–495 (2014)
5. Lee, M., Shin, D., Song, C.: Canoe game-based virtual reality training to improve trunk postural stability, balance, and upper limb motor function in subacute stroke patients: a randomized controlled pilot study. J. Phys. Ther. Sci. **28**(7), 2019–2024 (2016)
6. Shewaga, R., David, R., Bill, K., John, B.: Alpha testing of the rapid recovery kayaking-based exergame. In: 2015 IEEE Games Entertainment Media Conference (GEM), pp. 1–5. IEEE (2015)
7. Aranov, V.Y., Sergey, Y.B.: General approach to boat simulation in virtual reality systems. In: Fifth International Workshop on Nondestructive Testing and Computer Simulations in Science and Engineering, vol. 4627, pp. 322–326. International Society for Optics and Photonics (2002)
8. Ning, T., Hai-bo, M., Li, H., Fang, Z.: Virtual environment interactive system of treadmill. In: 2011 Fourth International Conference on Information and Computing, pp. 310–313. IEEE (2011)
9. Han, D.T., Suhail, M., Ragan, E.D.: Evaluating remapped physical reach for hand interactions with passive haptics in virtual reality. IEEE. Trans. Visual. Comput. Graph. **24**(4), 1467–1476 (2018)

10. Harley, D., Alexander, V., Mackenzie, W., Ashley, N., Lucas, B., Ali, M..: Sensory VR: smelling, touching, and eating virtual reality. In: Proceedings of the Twelfth International Conference on Tangible, Embedded, and Embodied Interaction, pp. 386–397. ACM (2018)
11. Harley, D., Aneesh, P., Tarun, D.G., Ali, M.: Tangible VR: diegetic tangible objects for virtual reality narratives. In: Proceedings of the 2017 Conference on Designing Interactive Systems, pp. 1253–1263. ACM (2017)
12. de Siqueira, A.G., Ayush, B.: Tangibles within VR: tracking, augmenting, and combining fabricated and commercially available commodity devices. In: IEEE Conference on Virtual Reality and 3D User Interfaces, Reutlingen, Germany, March (2018)
13. DownStream: VR Whitewater Kayaking. https://store.steampowered.com/app/1004510/DownStream_VR_Whitewater_Kayaking/ Accessed 20 March 2020

Extending the Robotic Workspace by Motion Tracking Large Workpieces

Mirco Becker$^{(\boxtimes)}$, Victor Sardenberg, and Marco Schacht

Leibniz Hannover Universität, Herrenhausen Straße 8, Hannover, Germany
becker@iat.uni-hannover.de

Abstract. The work explores coupling an affordable motion tracking system (HTC Vive Lighthouse and Trackers) with a collaborative robotic arm (Universal Robot UR 5) in order to machine workpieces a few times larger than the robotic workspace itself. The aim of that project is to demonstrate that such coupling would allow a human operator to manually push the workpiece through the robotic workspace without the need of additional numerically controlled motion axes.

In the test scenario, full scale architectural columns are cut with a hot-wire effector out of extruded polystyrene foam (XPS) blocks. The paper lays out the workflow of an integrated design-fabrication process and discusses its use for crafts based robotic practice.

Keywords: Motion tracking · Collaborative robot · Digital crafting

1 Introduction

1.1 Problem Definition

Every stationary robotic system has a limited workspace, the zone that can be reached by the end effector, which consequently defines the maximum size of the workpiece. The automotive industry traditionally addresses this constraint by having multiple robots working in sync with on overlapping reach to form a larger networked workspace and/or by having the workpiece travel through the workspace on an additional numerically controlled axis. This approach is firstly costly as it relies on additional machinery and secondly time-consuming as it requires system integration and task specific reprogramming. These factors have limited to use of robots in other industries for a long time. It is particular problematic where larger workpieces are the norm i.e. architectural prefabrication and construction.

There are good examples where large workpieces of architectural scale have been robotically fabricated using the traditional industrial robot integration strategies. The Landesgartenschau Pavilion 2014 Schwäbisch Gemünd is a great case of integrating a rotary table in order to robotically mill the flank joints of large hexagonal timber panels [1]. Similarly have linear drives been used in industry and research environments alike. A prominent example of linear axis integration at architectural scale is the research facility at TU Braunschweig Institute for Structural Design that consists of two portals, one for a concrete spaying robot and another one for formwork [2].

© Springer Nature Switzerland AG 2020
C. Stephanidis and M. Antona (Eds.): HCII 2020, CCIS 1225, pp. 156–162, 2020.
https://doi.org/10.1007/978-3-030-50729-9_21

Robotic automation is undergoing a paradigm shift from industrial robots where humans and machines are physically separated by safety systems towards collaborative robots where safety systems are integrated into the robotic actuators. Contemporary collaborative robots like the UR Series from Universal Robots or the LBR iiwa Series from KUKA have paved the way for novel ways of human-robot collaboration by providing a safe robotic work environment. While way more agile than industrial robots these collaborative robots still have the same size to workspace ratio and thus the same limitations in handling larger workpieces. A first experiments on full AR/VR and collaborative robot design work environments was initiated with Robo-Stim in 2018 [3].

1.2 Knowledge Gap

There have been several research projects dedicated to integrating motion tracking into a robotic process. From optical systems like OptiTrack such as the Quipt research project by Madeline Gannon to Vive Lighthouse system such as the Master Thesis by Kristian Sletten.

Quipt explores in an artistic as well as technological level novel direct human-robot interaction and ultimately "taming" industrial robots by providing an entirely different safety concept, one where the robot is always sensing, respecting, and prioritizing the human around [4].

Kristian Sletten looks at the technicalities driving a robot remotely via Vive controller movements and provides a software framework for real-time path test and correction [5]. Although both precedent projects make significant advances in direct human robot interaction they are both missing an integration into a full design and fabrication sequence.

1.3 Objective

The work presented here aims to support a wider use of robots in fabrication. It seeks to expand the use of robots to fields where they are hardly present yet due to their workspace constraints. The authors see a specifically suitable niche in areas which are working with collaborative robots such as small businesses in manufacturing but also, creatives like photographers. The available range of collaborative robots comes with an even smaller work area than industrial robots, making it even valuable to find way of working with larger workpieces.

2 Methods

We suggest a solution where a low-cost motion tracking system, HTC Vive Lighthouse, is installed in the robotic work environment trackers and HTC Vive Trackers are attached to the workpiece. The location of the trackers and thus the workpiece position and orientation are used to update the robotic toolpath in real-time. This would allow an operator to manually move large pieces of material through the stationary robotic workspace. The robot would then perform local manipulations in the area of the workpiece which is at that time slice in reach of the robot's end-effector. It requires a precise 3-dimensional representation of the workpiece in a design environment as the motion tracking only updates it location and orientation in space. The human operator is solely responsible for moving the workpiece similar to operating a table saw.

This approach of human-robot interaction is particularly suited for collaborative robots as their safety system relies on measuring torque abnormalities. Such a scenario would widen the application of robots in the realm of fabricating architectural components as well as brining traditional craftsmanship and robots closer together.

3   Proof of Concept

3.1   Robot, End-Effector, Tracking

To test this concept, we defined a scenario of fabricating a series of 2 m tall architectural columns by means of robotic hot-wire cutting large XPS-foam workpieces using a Universal Robots UR 5 robot (approx. 850 mm sphere diameter workspace) (see Fig. 1). Each column was cut out of a single block of 2000 mm × 400 mm 400 mm material. The workpiece was equipped with two 2017 Vive Trackers which sense orientation and position at 1 kHz and a theoretical tolerance in the millimeter range. The material was manually pushed with a linear guide (see Fig. 2). The speed by which the material was moving had to be manually adjust. It is limited by three physical factors: temperature of the hot-wire, XPS melting point, and wire tension. In our set-up this resulted in a approx. speed of 0.02 m/s. The operation of pushing the column through the robots working area was performed multiple times, each run with a different axial rotation of the column.

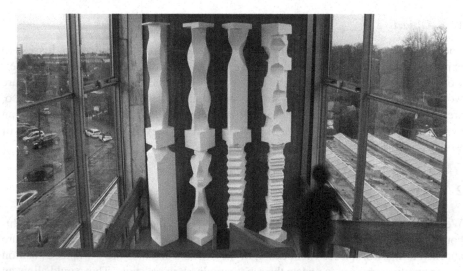

Fig. 1. Robotically hot-wire cut columns

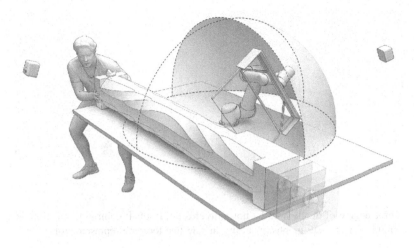

Fig. 2. UR5 robot with hot-wire effector and dashed work area, Vive Lighthouse base stations, XPS foam workpiece with Vive Trackers at either end.

3.2   Integrated Design

The technical set-up for this proof of concept scenario is implemented in the parametric design software Rhino Grasshopper (GH) and the Robots plug-in [6] for generating UR-Script code and sending it to the controller via a socket connection. The design of the columns was developed around the 3 DOF of the hot-wire tool, namely the in-plane rotation, the axial rotation and the cutting depth. (see Fig. 3) The different columns were designed by manipulation the 3 DOF graph directly thus generating a valid toolpath implicitly (see Fig. 4).

Fig. 3. Variation of column designs, all within the fabrication constraints.

The position and orientation of the 2 Vive Tracker is acquired via a VIVE Lighthouses and then fed via the Steam VR API into a custom GH-component. In GH the current tool position along the columns central axis is calculated as t-value. The t-value in consequence is used to retrieve the current pose for the robot and thus match hot-wire to the respective rule line (see Fig. 6).

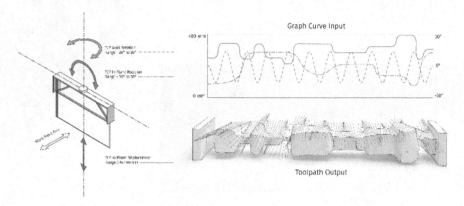

Fig. 4. Three degree of freedom at the hot-wire effector, implicit column fabrication design by direct manipulation of DOF graphs, resulting in rule line toolpath representation.

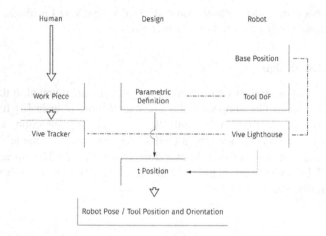

Fig. 5. Flow chart of the TCP position computation framework.

3.3 Fabrication

The process worked well in the test scenario and the speed of production was mainly determined by the hot-wire. The cutting time for one side of a column was between 15 and 30 min. The sensual force feedback the operator gets when pushing the XPS foam against the hot-wire is a good indicator for manually controlling the speed (see Fig. 5). Moving the workpiece too slowly leads to a ticker cut where a fast push of the workpiece ultimately snaps the wire. The job of interacting with the robot by moving the workpiece along its designated axis and rotating it after each pass could be done by a worker with minimum training. In our test scenario students who had no prior experience in robotics nor large scale hot-wire foam cutting. A second limiting factor is the shading of the VIVE Trackers. Our scenario included 2 trackers, one at either end of the column. The signal was "jumpy" at times which was fixed by smoothing but should be eliminated at the source in the next test scenario. The different columns produced were designed to showcase the variability of the process. Further test on repeatability will follow but only make sense when the system is tuned for better accuracy by additional trackers and possibly upgrading to current Vive Pro Lighthouse and Trackers.

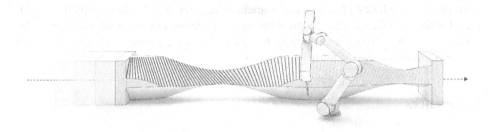

Fig. 6. Column fabrication, movement along central axis and rule line indicated.

4   Evaluation

The scenario shows that it is well possible to extend the workspace of a small collaborative robot like the UR 5 easily by factor 4 for the price of a Vive Lighthouse set and two Vive Trackers. This is at least an order of magnitude cheaper than a mechanical solution such as an additional liner or rotary robotic axis. It is also significantly cheaper than an optical tracking solution like an OptiTrack system.

5   Discussion

5.1   Outlook and Impact of Findings on Design

The set-up proposed in our scenario shows "quick and dirty" way of scaling work-area of a collaborative robot significantly. This is particularly interesting for a makers and creatives who already use collaborative robots in their workflows but are limited by the robot reach. It is suited for processes which don't require CNC accuracy but exhibit great variability within an algorithmic design and production approach. Interestingly, some control over the tolerances is given back to the human operator.

5.2   Further Development

Future work would include progressive local 3d-scanning in addition to global localization of the workpiece. This would allow to work with material which does not have a complete 3d- represented form at the start. We also see a great potential for designing with robots rather than having them to only execute the fabrication of a given design. Other fast and cheap in-line sensing methods such as 2d shape recognition could also contribute to build an even richer framework for smart collaborative robots.

5.3   Possible Products

The process developed for this scenario is to a certain degree independent of the hot-wire effector. More generally it is suitable for subtractive fabrication methods of hard materials and processes which don't require repeated evaluation of the formfactor by means of 3D-scanning. It could also be used for photography and video studios where a non-linear dependency of object and camera is required and hardcoded path to rigid. Besides these application in the creative sector, traditional craft could also benefit by seeing such an approach of coupling human and robotic action as a suitable digital transformation strategy.

References

1. Schwinn, T., Menges, A.: Fabrication agency: Landesgartenschau exhibition hall. Archit. Des. **85**, 92–99 (2015)
2. Neudecker, S., et al.: A new robotic spray technology for generative manufacturing of complex concrete structures without formwork. Proc. CIRP **43**, 333–338 (2016)
3. Johns, R.L., Anderson, J., Kilian, A.: Robo-Stim: modes of human robot collaboration for design exploration. In: Gengnagel, C., Baverel, O., Burry, J., Ramsgaard Thomsen, M., Weinzierl, S. (eds.) DMSB 2019, pp. 671–684. Springer, Cham (2020). https://doi.org/10.1007/978-3-030-29829-6_52
4. QUIPT: Taming Industrial Robotics. https://atonaton.com/quipt. Accessed 27 March 2020
5. Sletten, K.: Automated testing of industrial robots using HTC Vive for motion tracking. Master Thesis, Universitetet i Stavanger, Stavanger (2017)
6. Visose Robots GitHub. https://github.com/visose/Robots. Accessed 27 March 2020

A Robot Agent that Learns Group Interaction Through a Team-Based Virtual Reality Game Using Affective Reward Reinforcement Learning

Chawakorn Chaichanawirote[1]([⊠]), Masataka Tokumaru[2],
and Siam Charoenseang[1]

[1] Institute of Field Robotics (FIBO), King Mongkut's University of Technology
Thonburi, Bangmod, Thungkru, Bangkok 10140, Thailand
chawakorn.c@mail.kmutt.ac.th, siam@fibo.kmutt.ac.th
[2] Kansai University, Osaka, Japan
toku@kansai-u.ac.jp

Abstract. In the near future, robots are expected to be integrated into people's lives, interacting with them. To develop better robotics and artificial intelligence, this research focuses on the concept of teamwork. A robot agent was implemented in a virtual reality(VR) game to play the sport roundnet, a team-based sport similar to table tennis and volleyball [2]. The agent is trained with reinforcement learning with EDA skin sensor data [6] of players. The system is evaluated using a questionnaire on the player's feeling during the experiment and compared with agents not trained with affective data. The system is implemented in Unity3D's ML-Agents Toolkit.

Keywords: Virtual reality · Reinforcement learning · Unity3D

1 Introduction

Robots are soon to become a part of human life, integrating themselves into our homes. It is important to study social interactions between robots and humans [8]. One interaction they are expected to have with us is through entertainment, such as games. Since the purpose a game is to entertain, a game's difficulty must be adjusted to help the players better enjoy the game. The field of affective gaming then arises to answer the question: how do we improve the experience of games for players? Most games in this field focus on a single player, often changing the environment of the game itself according to the player's emotional state, such as increasing obstacles and decreasing helping items to challenge the player or doing the opposite to aid them. When it turns into a multiplayer environment, it becomes more difficult to adjust the game to suit every player, since there can be skill gaps between the players. We propose a robot that learns, using reinforcement learning, to play with other human players on a team.

© Springer Nature Switzerland AG 2020
C. Stephanidis and M. Antona (Eds.): HCII 2020, CCIS 1225, pp. 163–168, 2020.
https://doi.org/10.1007/978-3-030-50729-9_22

Cooperative robots are difficult and costly to develop, due to them being a hazard for human users within a game environment. However, in recent years, virtual reality has achieved significant progress, giving us an option to simulate the robot in a virtual game world, with a certain degree of realism and immersion. This research proposes a multiplayer virtual reality game with reinforcement learning-driven AI. The game we choose to develop is roundnet [2], since it is contained in a small area, has simple rules, and allows some interaction between players of the same team. The system will then be evaluated on the interaction within the human-robot team, as well as the performance of the group with the agent trained on affective rewards versus a group with a regular performance-based rewards model.

2   Methodology

2.1   System Overview

The system in Fig. 1 consists of an HTC VIVE virtual reality system [3], which is connected to a personal computer. While playing, the player's skin conductance is recorded by an Arduino Nano [1] using the Grove GSR Sensor. The skin data is then sent to PC via USB connection.

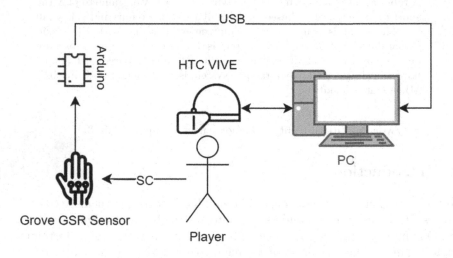

Fig. 1. The system data flow.

2.2   Game Scenario

Roundnet is a game played with 4 players, with 2 on each team. Its rules are a combination of volleyball and table tennis. Teams take turn spiking the ball onto a net. If a team fails to return the ball to the net, the other team scores.

2.3   Machine Learning

Using Unity's ML-Agents toolkit [10], the agents are trained using proximal policy optimization in 4 tasks:

1. Service: Each agent learns to serve the ball onto the net.
2. Competitive: 2 agents compete in a game of roundnet. Agents are rated on an Elo rating system [7].
3. Multi-agent competitive: 4 agents compete with 2 on each team.
4. Affective reward: Each agent is given skin sensor data-based observation and reward values.

Figure 2 and 3 show the agents during training. Currently the agents have been trained on Task 1.

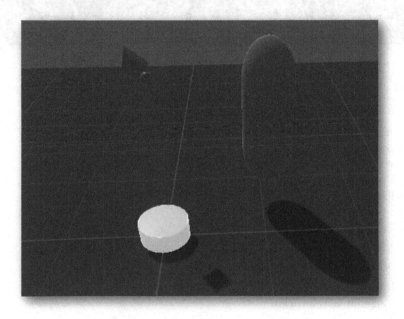

Fig. 2. The single-player roundnet agent.

2.4   Task 1: Service

An agent is trained to serve the ball onto the net. To aid in training, the agent is rewarded once if it hits the ball with its hand, and once if the ball hits the net. If the ball hits the ground or the agent torso, the episode ends, and the agent is given a negative reward.

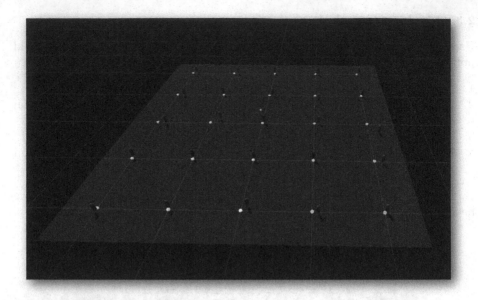

Fig. 3. The training scenario of Task 1 is composed of 25 agents in separate areas.

Observations:
- Ball position
- Ball velocity
- Hand position
- Hand rotation
- Hand velocity
- Hand angular velocity
- Torso position

Action Space:
- Hand acceleration
- Hand angular acceleration
- Torso acceleration

Rewards:
- (-1) if the ball hits the floor, episode ends
- (-1) if the ball hits the hand a second time, episode ends
- (-1) if the ball goes out of bounds(a 5 m radius), episode ends
- $(+1)$ if the hand hits the ball
- $(+2)$ if the ball hits the net(if the hand already hit the ball), episode ends.

Note that in a successful episode, the agent will get a cumulative reward of 3, and allowing the ball to fall results in a reward of -1.

2.5   Curriculum Learning

To counteract sparse rewards, we use curriculum learning [5] implemented in ML-Agents on Task 1. The results in the next section reflect the agent perfomance using these methods.

3   Task 1 Results

Figure 4 shows the mean cumulative reward for Task 1 agents trained with a curriculum (orange) and without curriculum (blue). When examining the agent results, we found that the agent without curriculum learning tended to hit the ball more than once, hence ending the episode. The agent with curriculum learning has already learned the objective in easier tasks, which enables it to perform better.

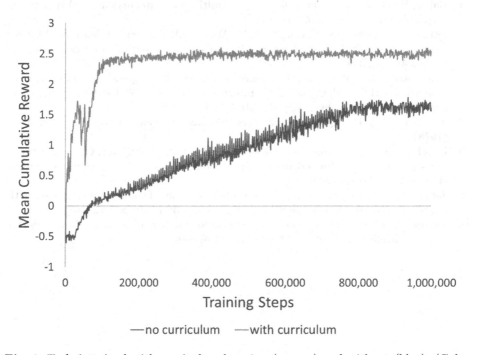

Fig. 4. Task 1 trained with curriculum learning (orange) and without (blue). (Color figure online)

4   Discussion

In Task 1 we used the methods provided by Unity's ML–Agents Toolkit to develop agents capable of performing a service or returning the ball to the net successfully. It became clear that using curriculum learning would help the agent greatly to learn the objective of the game.

However, for further work, the utility of such measures are questionable. Tasks 2–4 compose of more than 1 agent in a competitive setting, which has been demonstrated to stimulate learning, often helping agents find novel ways to compete with each other [4]. Sometimes teamwork can emerge between humans and robots that can even outperform pure robot teams [9]. We are working to implement our own agents in VR to then study these interactions, and their effects on human players.

References

1. Arduino nano (2019). https://store.arduino.cc/usa/arduino-nano
2. How to play (2019). https://spikeball.com/pages/how-to-play-1
3. Vive^{TM} Thailand: buy vive hardware (2019). https://www.vive.com/th/product
4. Baker, B., et al.: Emergent tool use from multi-agent autocurricula. arXiv preprint https://arxiv.org/abs/1909.07528
5. Bengio, Y., Louradour, J., Collobert, R., Weston, J.: Curriculum learning. In: Proceedings of the 26th Annual International Conference on Machine Learning, pp. 41–48. ACM (2009)
6. Braithwaite, J.J., Watson, D.G., Jones, R., Rowe, M.: A guide for analysing electrodermal activity (EDA) & skin conductance responses (SCRs) for psychological experiments. Psychophysiology **49**, 1017–1034 (2013)
7. Elo, A.E.: The Rating of Chessplayers, Past and Present. Arco Pub., New York (1978)
8. Hegel, F., Muhl, C., Wrede, B., Hielscher-Fastabend, M., Sagerer, G.: Understanding social robots. In: Second International Conferences on Advances in Computer-Human Interactions (2009)
9. Jaderberg, M., et al.: Human-level performance in 3D multiplayer games with population-based reinforcement learning. Science **364**, 859–865 (2019)
10. Juliani, A., et al.: Unity: a general platform for intelligent agents. arXive preprint https://github.com/Unity-Technologies/ml-agents

An Interactive Model of Physical Fitness Activity for the Elderly

Chen-Fu Chen[1(✉)] and Hung-Ken Lee[2]

[1] Department of Product Design, Ming Chuan University, Taoyuan 333, Taiwan
chenfu@mail.mcu.edu.tw
[2] Department of Digital Media Design, Ming Chuan University,
Taoyuan 333, Taiwan

Abstract. Taiwan has been an aged society since late 2007 and a "Long-term Care Services Act" is passed in 2015, which implicates an imperative to discover the needs for the elderly and provide products or services for the elderly's physical and mental demands. This research investigates the elderly's health maintenance and rehabilitation in terms of physical fitness mainly from the professional viewpoint of recreation therapy. This research explores the elderly's lifestyle and aerobic physical fitness approach (for example, walking, dancing, hiking, cycling, sports or planned exercises) in Taiwan. After conducting interviews to the elderly, physical therapists, and physical fitness trainers, this research has applied the Kinect system and created the 3D animation with physical fitness models. In addition, this research has discussed the applicability and usability of information technology devices, such as Kinect system and related devices, for the elderly in the current highly developed information technology society. Eventually, this research conducts an experiment combining 3D animation models and Kinect motion capture technology for assessing the fitness posture of the elderly, which has shown the potential application based on recreational therapy. However, more usability tests for the system stability and more advanced interactive technology are needed for improving the interactivity.

Keywords: Aged society · Fitness assessment · Interaction design

1 Introduction

The World Health Organization (WHO, 2016) recommends that the elderly should have planned physical activities every week to improve cardiopulmonary function and muscular fitness to adjust the pressure of life, depression and cognitive decline through leisure activities and sports [1]. However, the general pattern of physical activity is repetitive movements, which lacks psychological incentives and target stimulation. Moreover, the elderly often need to go to the hospital or clinic after a long-term rehabilitation treatment, which usually consumes time on both transportation and queuing. Therefore, the rehabilitation practitioner recommends that the elderly can be instructed and supervised by the rehabilitation practitioner through the internet transmission while recording the rehabilitation situation of the elderly at home.

© Springer Nature Switzerland AG 2020
C. Stephanidis and M. Antona (Eds.): HCII 2020, CCIS 1225, pp. 169–173, 2020.
https://doi.org/10.1007/978-3-030-50729-9_23

This study conducts in-depth interviews with rehabilitation therapists and fitness practitioners for understanding the behavior and living need of the elderly as well as the functionality of current recreational therapy products and services. Moreover, this study has created a 3D animation model for physical and mental health as an interactive physical fitness content with simple operation interface design to enable the elderly to follow. This study has explored a new approach by applying 3D animation technique and information technology hardware.

2 Literature Review

The weekly aerobic physical activity of the elderly also depends on the limitations of their surroundings. An important principle is to engage in activities they like. If the elderly who is continuously engaged in aerobic activities, he/she can reduce falls and cognitive degradation. Figure 1 shows the video of physical fitness for the elderly in Taiwan. Four users demonstrate different physical fitness types for the elderly [2].

Fig. 1. An example of the physical fitness demonstration video in Taiwan. (Sources: https://www.youtube.com/watch?v=_w50TfdCmKU)

3 Research Methods

This study explores the integration of information technology and 3D animation physical fitness after the literature review regarding the recreational therapy for the elderly. Interviews with 4 experts from the area of health care, information technology, multimedia and physical fitness are conducted for providing more comprehensive fitness-related research for the elderly.

The fitness simulation information system is established with two parts: the interaction between the manipulation model and the multimedia modeling. For the manipulation model, this research first builds a 3D model (Fig. 2) and skeleton (Fig. 3) into Unity with Maya. In addition, Kinect is used to detect the joint points of the human skeleton. The relative positions of the detected joint points are used to achieve the purpose of scene switching and option conversion.

This study plans the operation process, interface functions, and interaction modes of the fitness simulation system for the elderly, and then clarifies the integration mode of 3D modeling and Kinect system. The process is shown in Fig. 4.

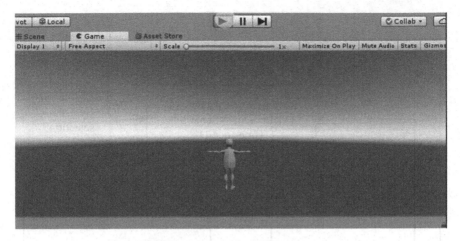

Fig. 2. Maya 3D modeling.

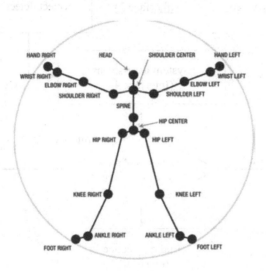

Fig. 3. Human skeleton node diagram.

Taking into account the physical strength, physical coordination, and vision of the elderly, as well as interviewing physicians and therapists, the proposed concept roughly achieves recreational and rehabilitation effects for the elderly. Moreover, this study revises the concept based on the discussion with experts. Figure 5 shows the roles and pages in 3D animation system.

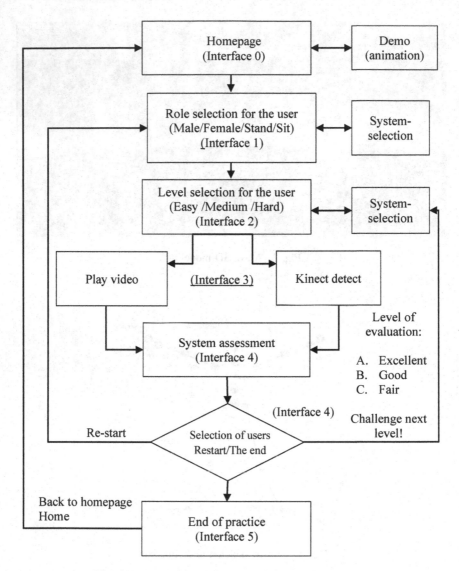

Fig. 4. Process for creating a 3D animation interaction.

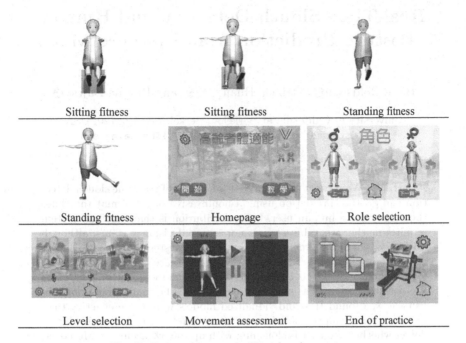

Sitting fitness	Sitting fitness	Standing fitness
Standing fitness	Homepage	Role selection
Level selection	Movement assessment	End of practice

Fig. 5. Roles and pages in 3D animation system.

4   Conclusion

"Aging at home" and "aging in the community" are part of governmental policies established by Taiwan government for the elderly. As physical fitness is one of popular lightweight activities for the elderly, the government has produced relevant physical fitness videos and apply real people as models. However, in addition to the function of motion, the videos may lack interaction and motivation to the elderly. This study tries to construct a 3D human body model and incorporates up-to-date information technology. It is mainly able to detect the physical fitness of the elderly and assess whether their movements meet physical fitness requirements. Encouragement is provided through evaluation. Hope it can improve the motivation of the elderly for physical fitness. Eventually, some results have been obtained and discussed.

Acknowledgement. The author would like to express gratefulness to Ministry of Science and Technology of Taiwan for funding this research with the grant of MOST 108-2410-H-130-013.

References

1. World Health Organization. Physical Activity and Older Adults (2016). http://www.who.int/dietphysicalactivity/factsheet_olderadults/en/. Accessed 8 Jan 2019
2. Physical Fitness for the Elderly. https://www.youtube.com/watch?v=_w50TfdCmKU. Accessed 20 Feb 2019

Real-Time Slouch Detection and Human Posture Prediction from Pressure Mat

Blaze Goldstein⑩, Isabella Huang$^{(\boxtimes)}$⑩, and Ruzena Bajcsy⑩

University of California at Berkeley, Berkeley, CA 94720, USA
{bgoldstein20,isabella.huang,bajcsy}@berkeley.edu

Abstract. We present a system that is capable of real time slouch detection and posture prediction using a noninvasive pressure mat that lines the seat under a human user. Our contribution is that our final system requires neither wearable sensors nor external vision systems, although during system development, a motion capture system was used to collect ground truth data. We collected systematic seated posture data from four women aged 18 to 54 in order to build data-driven models using the seat pressure mat as sensory input. Due to the small number of subjects, it was found that individualized models were more effective than training one universal model for all participants. Our system is able to detect whether the user is slouching with up to 95% accuracy. Moreover, using just the pressure mat sensor readings as input, we successfully built models that could predict the positions of nine points on the body with an average position error of 8.84 cm. As long as one has access to a real-time stream of data from such a pressure mat, it is possible to perform real-time slouch detection and posture prediction with the pre-trained models investigated here.

Keywords: Posture detection · Human modeling · Ergonomics

1 Introduction and Related Works

The average adult spends 6.5 h sitting down per day. Too much sitting, even when one is physically active otherwise, is shown to have negative effects on cardio-metabolic risk, type 2 diabetes, and overall premature mortality [3]. The health risks of prolonged sitting are further exacerbated when slouching, which adversely impacts spinal health, circulation, mood, and muscle pain [6]. While to eliminate sitting altogether is unrealistic, we strive to engineer a system that enables users to sit with good posture, and to encourage a happier and healthier society overall.

To constantly monitor one's own posture is cognitively laborious, and existing sensing systems have been built to alleviate this responsibility from the human. Existing sensing systems often require intrusive wearable devices or unwieldy surveillance systems. One possible method is to attach inertial measurement

This work was supported by NSF Award #1545126.

units to the body, such as along the spine [4] or along the head and neck to measure head posture [5]. Another popular slouch detection method is via use of vision systems such as mounting a Microsoft Kinect facing the human [7], or proximity sensors measuring the distance of the user's head to the computer screen [2]. We seek to improve on the shortcomings of both methods, noting that wearable sensors are inconvenient, and that externally mounted vision systems require additional setup and placement calibration. In this work, we introduce a reliable and non-invasive framework to monitor human posture and detect slouching in real-time which helps improve the ergonomics of sitting for the everyday user. To this end, we utilize a thin pressure mat that lines the seat, which is flexible in that it can be easily removed and placed on different chairs as required. From the seat pressure measurements, we build a data-driven model that predicts the state of the user's posture, and thus can detect immediately whether the user is in a slouch state. Moreover, we use this pressure mat not only to classify the slouch state, but also predict the entire configuration of the human upper body.

2   Experiments

2.1   Experimental Setup

The pressure mat used was a TekScan Body Pressure Measurement System mat, which is 2.5×2.5 ft in size with a density of 1 Sensel^{TM}/cm^2, pictured in Fig. 1. This mat was fixed atop a flat backless bench on which the subjects sat. To measure the ground truth body configuration, we used a PhaseSpace motion capture system that synchronously tracks the position of 9 markers attached to the body. These markers were placed on the left shoulder, right shoulder, left hip, right hip, left kneecap, right kneecap, collarbone, C2 vertebrate, middle of collarbones, and the coccyx. The front and back views of these marker placements are shown in Fig. 2.

2.2   Data Collection

Posture data was collected for four women aged 18 to 54. While seated, the configuration of the torso can be characterized by the segment connecting the torso endpoints in spherical coordinates with polar angle θ and azimuthal angle ϕ. Figures 3 and 4 illustrate how the θ and ϕ angles are defined respectively. During each data collection trial, the participant began at a neutral seated position, and then systematically explored the reachable workspace by lowering their torso (ie. increasing θ) as far as possible, and then returning to the neutral seated position. For each of these cycles, the subject was instructed to keep the azimuthal angle ϕ as constant as they could. For each trial, 12 cycles were performed, each at a different ϕ angle in the set $\phi = \frac{\pi k}{6}, k \in [0..11]$. The accuracy of the desired ϕ was never enforced by the researchers. Rather, each participant attempted to maintain the desired ϕ through proprioception. Regardless, the purpose of

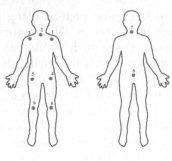

Front view.   Back view.

Fig. 1. TekScam BPMS mat [1].

Fig. 2. Motion capture marker placements.

diversifying the ϕ angles measured was purely for the sake of fully exploring the body workspace. Each participant performed five trials for each of three slouch conditions (straight back, slouch, and heavy slouch). Between each trial, the subject was instructed to stand up and sit back down again, increasing the variance in where they sat on the mat to encourage model generalization. The degree of slouching was not enforced quantitatively, but was performed according to each subject's interpretation of how to sit in the three slouch conditions. Example images of a subject in the three slouch conditions is depicted in Fig. 5, and example pressure mat data under different conditions and lean angles is in Fig. 6. In this work, we investigated only seated leaning, and no twisting data was collected. This is because the torso twisting in the z-direction was found to induce minimal changes in the seat pressure distribution. All data was collected at a rate of 10 Hz.

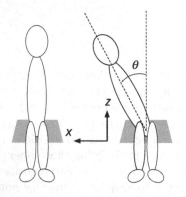

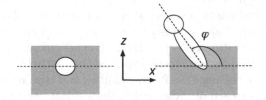

Fig. 3. Front view of seated subject.

Fig. 4. Top view of seated subject.

| Straight back. | Slouch. | Heavy slouch. |

Fig. 5. Subject sitting under the three different slouch conditions.

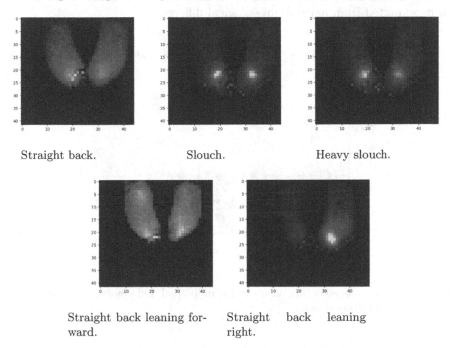

Fig. 6. Example pressure mat measurement visualizations for the three slouch conditions.

3   Classification Results

Using the mat image, we wanted to see whether it was possible to distinguish between the three different slouch states. To this end, we trained individual convolutional neural network models for each of the 4 subjects, as well as one combined network for all of the subject data. Each pressure mat reading, a 42×48 matrix, is passed through a series of two convolutional and max-pooling layers, and then through a softmax classification layer to yield the resultant predicted slouch class. We used the Adam optimizer with categorical cross-entropy loss and 7 training epochs. To train the model, we used the full data from 12 of the data collection trials, and validated the model on the remaining three. The results of the individually trained models as well as the combined model are shown in Fig. 7. We found that the accuracy for distinguishing between the three slouch classes was very low, but when we grouped the slouch and heavy slouch classes together, the models were generally able to distinguish them from the straight back condition extremely well. This is likely due to the two slouch classes being too similar, leading to many overlapping measurements during data collection across these two classes. Finally, with only 4 subjects tested, we were unable to build a collective combined model that performed better than random. This provides insight into how individual customized models are more effective, which can be expected from natural physiological differences.

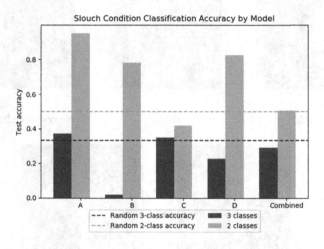

Fig. 7. Validation classification accuracy for individual and combined modes across 2 and 3 slouch condition classes.

4   Posture Prediction Results

With promising classification results, we wanted to further explore whether we could reconstruct the motion capture marker positions purely from the mat image. To this end, we repurposed the classification CNN model with a fully connected final layer to perform regression on the 27-dimensional target of the nine markers' 3D positions. With the same 80–20 train-test split and 30 training epochs, we achieved an average marker position error of 8.84 cm across all individual models and slouch conditions. It was found that the model consistently produced qualitatively accurate predictions, as can be visualized in Fig. 8 comparing the ground truth readings and predictions for several different validation points. This is a promising result in that rough posture prediction from only the pressure mat is feasible.

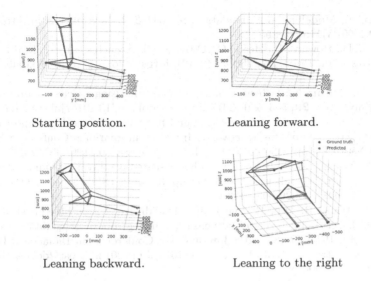

Starting position.   Leaning forward.

Leaning backward.   Leaning to the right

Fig. 8. Example predictions and ground truths for different validation datapoints from subject A's individual model.

5   Conclusion and Future Work

We have shown that is possible to train data-driven models that take seat pressure as input and detects the presence of slouching, as well as predicts the location of nine different body parts. The models that we have generated are not universal, and have some limitations. In both our classification models and posture prediction models, we generated customized models on a per person basis for each of our participants. We did not collect enough data with four participants to be able to generalize our models to be universal for diverse individuals. We also only tested on female participants from the ages of 18–54, so a potential future step would be to collect data on a larger and more diverse group of people to generalize our models. Although we did not fully implement a real-time response system, as long as there is access to a real-time stream of pressure mat data, this can be done using pre-trained models, or even models that are constantly updated online. In the future, we could investigate the effects of different types of slouching, for example by making distinction between neck slouching, shoulders hunching, and lower back bending.

References

1. TekScan body pressure measurement system. https://www.tekscan.com/products-solutions/systems/body-pressure-measurement-system-bpms-research. Accessed 30 Sept 2010
2. Alattas, R., Elleithy, K.: Detecting and minimizing bad posture using postuino among engineering students. In: 2014 2nd International Conference on Artificial

Intelligence, Modelling and Simulation, pp. 344–349, November 2014. https://doi.org/10.1109/AIMS.2014.55

3. Dunstan, D., Howard, B., Healy, G., Owen, N.: Too much sitting - a health hazard. Diab. Res. Clin. Pract. **97**, 368–76 (2012). https://doi.org/10.1016/j.diabres.2012.05.020

4. Fathi, A., Curran, K.: Detection of spine curvature using wireless sensors. J. King Saud Univ. - Sci. **29**, 553–560 (2017). https://doi.org/10.1016/j.jksus.2017.09.014

5. Kim, T., Chen, S., Lach, J.: Detecting and preventing forward head posture with wireless inertial body sensor networks. In: 2011 International Conference on Body Sensor Networks, pp. 125–126 (2011). https://doi.org/10.1109/BSN.2011.41

6. Pynt, J., Mackey, M.G., Higgs, J.: Kyphosed seated postures: extending concepts of postural health beyond the office. J. Occup. Rehabil. **18**(1), 35–45 (2008). https://doi.org/10.1007/s10926-008-9123-6

7. Taati, B., Wang, R., Huq, R., Snoek, J., Mihailidis, A.: Vision-based posture assessment to detect and categorize compensation during robotic rehabilitation therapy. In: 2012 4th IEEE RAS EMBS International Conference on Biomedical Robotics and Biomechatronics (BioRob), pp. 1607–1613, June 2012. https://doi.org/10.1109/BioRob.2012.6290668

A Novel Snowboard Training System Using Visual and Auditory Feedback

Takashi Kuwahara[1], Itsuki Takahashi[2(✉)], and Shintaro Harikae[2(✉)]

[1] Program in Empowerment Informatics, School of Integrative and Global Majors, University of Tsukuba, Tsukuba, Japan
kuwahara@golem.iit.tsukuba.ac.jp
[2] Graduate School of Systems and Information Engineering, University of Tsukuba, Tsukuba, Japan
{takahashi,harikae}@golem.iit.tsukuba.ac.jp

Abstract. In snowboard training, it is very important to perceive a gap between the perceived movement and the actual body movement. Previous training systems don't have sufficient function in that they only use either visual or auditory feedback, or only display value such as velocity. In this paper, we propose and develop a novel snowboard training system that assists snowboard training using visual feedback that has immediate effect and auditory feedback that has long-term effect. This system consists of four components: (1) a center of pressure detection (COP) device that detects weight shift using pressure sensors, (2) a posture estimation device that calculates orientation of a board using an IMU sensor, (3) a visual feedback device that displays the current position and the ideal position on the smart glasses, (4) an auditory feedback device that indicates direction and a gap between the current position and the ideal position using pitch and volume of sound. We conducted an experiment to verify feasibility to enhance motor learning using the system. As the results of experiment with three participants, we confirmed that our system could decrease the gap and standard deviation between the perceived movement and the actual body movement even after removing the system, and could assist the proper body control. In conclusion, we developed a novel snowboard training system and confirmed our system has a feasibility to enhance motor learning using visual and auditory feedback.

Keywords: Sports training · Snowboard · Visual and auditory feedback · Body control

1 Introduction

Small change in the snowboarder's balance or a simple body movement of snowboarders effects on the snowboarding. Therefore, it is very important to perceive a gap between the perceived movement and the actual body movement, and to improve the skills by imitating the motion of experts in snowboard training [1]. However, the degree of the gap between the perceived movement and the actual body movement might differ depending on the person, it is difficult to perceive the gap yourself. Hence, in the case of novice snowboarder's training, it is desirable that the instructors always

© Springer Nature Switzerland AG 2020
C. Stephanidis and M. Antona (Eds.): HCII 2020, CCIS 1225, pp. 181–187, 2020.
https://doi.org/10.1007/978-3-030-50729-9_25

be with you and can take advice from them, but such a situation is not commonplace. In addition, even in the ideal training situation, instructors cannot give novice proper advice based on one's experience quantitatively without subjective expressions. Therefore, there is also another gap between the actual body movement and the observed body movement. From the following reasons, a system that can quantitatively teach how to move the body is necessary in snowboard training (especially for novices) so that even one person can do snowboard training. Various snowboard training system such as XON SNOW-1 (CEREVO) [2], Oakley Airwave (Oakley) [3], or Motion Echo snowboard [1] and so on have been proposed and developed thus far. However, they don't have sufficient function in that they only display value such as velocity, or only use either visual or auditory feedback. In addition, since the system is attached to the snowboard, it does not have sufficient function in that it will be hidden by snow.

In this paper, we propose and develop a novel snowboard training system that assists snowboard training using visual feedback that has immediate effect and auditory feedback that has long-term effect [4].

2   Methods

We propose and develop a novel snowboard training system using visual and auditory feedback. Figure 1 shows system configuration of a developed snowboard training system. This system mainly consists of four components: (1) a COP detection device, (2) a posture estimation device, (3) a visual feedback device, (4) an auditory feedback device. Figure 2 shows schematic diagram of the system. The developed system calculates differences between the expert's motion data and user's motion data, and give the visual and auditory feedback to users.

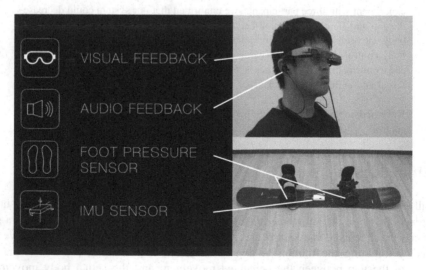

Fig. 1. System configuration of a developed snowboard training system

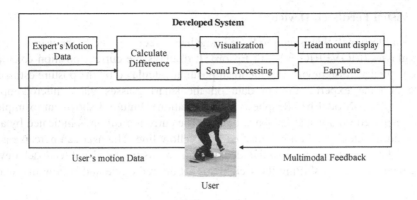

Fig. 2. Schematic diagram of the system

2.1 COP Detection Device

To detect weight shift, a COP detection device consists of eight pressure sensors (Flexiforce Pressure Sensor 100 lbs, SparkFun Electronics), and four pressure sensors are located on the bindings for each foot. The sensor values were filtered with a digital low-pass filter. In this study, the COP can be detected only in the front-back direction. The COP of user is calculated as follows:

$$COP = \frac{a_1 + a_2 + a_3 + a_4 - b_1 - b_2 - b_3 - b_4}{a_1 + a_2 + a_3 + a_4 + b_1 + b_2 + b_3 + b_4} \tag{1}$$

where $a_1 - a_4$ are sensor value of the pressure sensors on the toe side, $b_1 - b_4$ are sensor values of the pressure sensors on the heel side. From (1), it is possible to calculate the COP from -1 to 1.

2.2 Posture Estimation Device

A posture estimation device consists of a 9-axis IMU sensor (MPU-9250, InvenSense). It calculates orientation of a snowboard to decide the ideal position. The orientation of a snowboard can be calculated by integrating the angular velocity. However, it is inappropriate as a posture estimation method due to gyro drift which accumulates measurement errors and noise and so on. To solve this problem, there are some methods to estimate posture such as kalman filter, madwick filter, complementary filter. Although each method has some advantages and disadvantages, we used complementary filters in the posture estimation device because of the low computational cost and ease of implementation. The orientation of a snowboard is calculated as follows:

$$\theta_n = \alpha(\theta_{n-1} + \omega\Delta t) + (1 - \alpha)a \tag{2}$$

where θ_n, θ_{n-1} is the angle (such as roll, pitch, yaw) to estimate posture, ω is angular velocity, a is acceleration, Δt is a sampling time, α is a filter coefficient with a value from 0 to 1.

2.3 Visual Feedback Device

The visual feedback that is said to have immediate effect is given to the user through a smart glasses (MOVERIO BT30E, Epson). It displays the current position calculated by the COP detection device and the ideal position calculated by the posture estimation device and the expert's motion data on the smart glasses via a microcomputer (Raspberry pi 3 Model b+, Raspberry Pi Foundation). Figure 3 shows an example of image displayed on a visual feedback device. The current position is indicated by a red circle, and the ideal position is indicated by a yellow line. The user can perceive a gap between the current position and the ideal position by using the visual feedback device, and reduce the gap by shifting the weight so that the red circle and yellow line match.

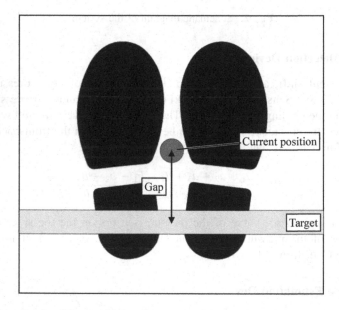

Fig. 3. An example of image displayed on a visual feedback device (Color figure online)

2.4 Auditory Feedback Device

The auditory feedback that is said to have long-term effect is given to the user through a Bluetooth earphone (WI-1000X, SONY). It indicates direction and a gap between the current position and the ideal position using pitch and volume of sound. The sound volume changes in proportion to the gap. When the current position is ahead of the ideal position as shown in Fig. 3, the sound is higher-pitched (800 Hz). On the other hand, when the current position is behind of the ideal position, the sound is lower-pitched (200 Hz). The user can perceive a gap between the current position and the ideal position by using the auditory feedback device, and reduce the gap by shifting the weight so that the sound is lowered.

3 Experiment

We conducted an experiment to verify feasibility to enhance motor learning using the system to three healthy young adults. Figure 4 shows experimental protocol. The participants performed three sessions: (1) pre-test session, (2) training session, (3) post-test session. The pre-test session and the pose-test session consists of three trials without systems. The training session consists of ten trials with system. One trial's time had about 60 s, and the target moved in nine cycles of sine curves at 0.14 Hz in the vertical direction on the monitor. Five cycles were analyzed, excluding the first, second, eighth and ninth sine curves for each person.

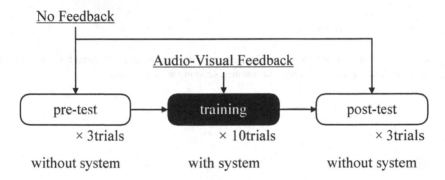

Fig. 4. Experimental protocol

As the results of experiment, Fig. 5 shows a comparison of root mean square error (RMSE) between the perceived movement and the actual body movement in pre-test session (without system) and training session (with system). The average value of RMSE in pre-test session was 74.3 [px] and the standard deviation in pre-test session was 12.3 [px]. The average value of RMSE in training session was 37.1 [px] and the standard deviation in training session was 4.3 [px]. In addition, Fig. 6 shows a comparison of RMSE between the perceived movement and the actual body movement in pre-test session (without system) and post-test (without system). The average value of RMSE in pre-test session was 74.3 [px] and the standard deviation in pre-test session was 12.3 [px]. The average value of RMSE in post-test session was 63.9 [px] and the standard deviation in post-test session was 0.6 [px].

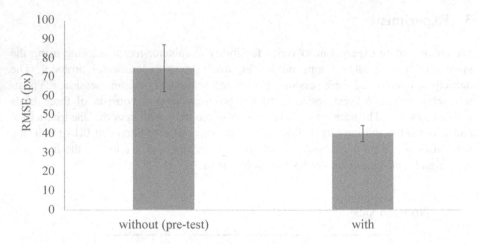

Fig. 5. Comparison of RMSE between the perceived movement and the actual body movement in pre-test session (without system) and training session (with system)

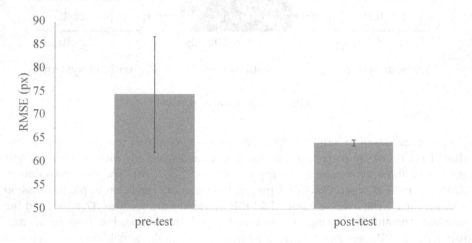

Fig. 6. Comparison of RMSE between the perceived movement and the actual body movement in pre-test session (without system) and pose-test session (without system)

4 Discussion

In the experiment to verify a feasibility to enhance motor learning using the system, we confirmed the RMSE between the perceived movement and the actual body movement in pre-test session (without system) and training session (with system). The average value of RMSE in pre-test session was 74.3 [px] and the standard deviation in pre-test session was 12.3 [px]. The average value of RMSE in training session was 37.1 [px] and the standard deviation in training session was 4.3 [px]. Hence, it is estimated that our system could decrease the gap between the perceived movement and the actual body movement, and could assist the proper body control. In addition, we confirmed the RMSE between the perceived movement and the actual body movement in pre-test session (without system) and post-test session (without system). The average value of RMSE in pre-test session was 74.3 [px] and the standard deviation in pre-test session was 12.3 [px]. The average value of RMSE in post-test session was 63.9 [px] and the standard deviation in post-test session was 0.6 [px]. Hence, it is considered that our system could decrease the error and standard deviation between the perceived movement and the actual body movement even after removing the system.

In this study, we confirmed a feasibility to enhance motor learning using visual and auditory feedback through an experiment. However, the experiment was conducted on a flat floor and conducted under the limited conditions where target moved back and forward at regular intervals. Hence, in the future, we will confirm the effect of the system under the condition when the ideal position changes randomly on snow. In addition, the experiment was conducted only one day, and we had not confirmed the long-term effect yet. Hence, we will conduct the experiment to confirm and maximize the effects of visual feedback and auditory feedback by repeating the experimental protocol conducted in this study for several days.

5 Conclusion

In this study, we developed a novel snowboard training system using visual and auditory feedback. In addition, we confirmed that our system could decrease the gap and standard deviation between the perceived movement and the actual body movement even after removing the system, and could assist the proper body control. It is considered that our system has a feasibility to enhance motor learning using visual and auditory feedback, and could assist snowboard training efficiently.

References

1. Park, H.K., Lee, W.: Motion echo snowboard: enhancing body movement perception in sport via visually augmented feedback. In: Proceedings of the 2016 ACM Conference on Designing Interactive Systems, pp. 192–203 (2016)
2. CEREVO, XON snow-1. https://xon.cerevo.com/ja/snow-1/
3. Oakley, Oakley Airwave. http://touchlab.jp/2012/10/oakley-airwave-iphone/
4. Hasegawa, N., Takeda, K., Sakuma, M., Mani, H., Maejima, H., Asaka, T.: Learning effects of dynamic postural control by auditory biofeedback versus visual biofeedback training. Gait Posture **58**, 188–193 (2017)

Developing Autonomous Adaptive Behavior for Human Behavior Simulation of an Atypical Architectural Space

Yun Gil Lee[✉]

Hoseo University, 20, Hoseo-ro, 79 beon-gil, Baebang-eup,
Asan-si, Chungcheongnam-do 31499, Korea
yglee@hoseo.edu

Abstract. Atypical buildings are growing in number daily, and the social demands on them are increasing. The atypical building design process is very different from existing building design processes because the generation and transformation of shapes occupies a large part of that process. In the process of designing atypical buildings, it is possible to overlook this safety and convenience while being immersed in form values. Ultimately, this study aims to develop a technology for architects to grasp the dwelling performance in a design in real time and to reflect it in the design. To do this, we developed a simulation module embedded in a commercial atypical design tool (Rhino and Grasshopper), named ActoViz. It transforms the designed plan into a 3D game-based virtual environment in real time and allows intelligent human figures to freely flow through the plan to evaluate it as including module. This study seeks to advance the development of ActoViz. There is a limit to the accuracy of user behavior simulations in which predetermined behavior models are simply repeated, because the physical forms of atypical buildings are so diverse. Since the realism of human-figured agents has a positive effect on the simulation, advanced and precise interactions between agent and space are very important. In this study, ragdoll physics and model predictive control techniques are applied to achieve more adaptive behavior for the virtual users. Through the use of such technologies, inconsistencies in the virtual users' behaviors and the physical space can be minimized, and more natural reactions can be achieved.

Keywords: Adaptive behavior · Virtual user · Atypical architectural space · Behavior simulation · Architectural design

1 Introduction

Atypical buildings are growing in number daily, and the social demands on them are increasing. The atypical building design process is very different from existing building design processes because the generation and transformation of shapes occupies a large part of it. While this may meet contemporary demands for new architectural forms, it also introduces risks to the safety and convenience of users that could be overlooked. Architecture is a machine for life, and the safety and convenience of the human users of a building determine the highest standards for determining its value. In the process of

© Springer Nature Switzerland AG 2020
C. Stephanidis and M. Antona (Eds.): HCII 2020, CCIS 1225, pp. 188–192, 2020.
https://doi.org/10.1007/978-3-030-50729-9_26

designing atypical buildings, when immersed in form values, it is possible to overlook this requirement for safety and convenience.

Ultimately, the present line of investigation aims to develop a technology for architects to grasp the dwelling performance in a design in real time and reflect it in the design. To this end, we previously developed a simulation module embedded in a commercial atypical design tool (Rhino and Grasshopper), named ActoViz. This transforms the designed plan into a 3D game-based virtual environment in real time and allows intelligent human figures to flow freely through the plan in order for it to be evaluated, including the module.

The present study seeks to further advance the development of ActoViz. There is a limit to the accuracy of user behavior simulations in which predetermined behavior models are simply repeated because the physical forms of atypical buildings are so diverse. Since the realism of human-figured agents has a positive effect on the simulation, advanced and precise interactions between agent and space are very important. In this study, ragdoll physics and model predictive control (MPC) techniques are applied to achieve more adaptive behavior for the virtual users. Through the use of such technologies, inconsistencies in the virtual user behaviors and the physical space can be minimized, and more natural reactions can be achieved.

2   Adaptive Behavior and Human Behavior Simulation

According to Hong and Lee (2019), when students design architectural spaces, the existence of a virtual user is of greater utility in designing a more creative and unexpected form than is its absence. In addition, the existence of virtual users adds to the discovery of various functions of the design results, confidence in their usefulness, and confidence in the safety and convenience of the user. Also, it is said that the virtual user responding to the physical form of the space is preferable for the discovery of new forms and functions and ascertaining the safety and convenience of the design result [6]. The behavior of the virtual user has a great influence on the design process and results, because through the proper interaction between the physical space and the virtual user, the architect can come up with novel ideas. In other words, the adaptive behavior of virtual users is an important requirement for determining the value of human behavior simulation. Figure 1 shows the human behavior simulation system (ActoViz) developed through the previous research. This study aims to enable enhanced human behavior simulation by adding functions for adaptive behavior to ActoViz.

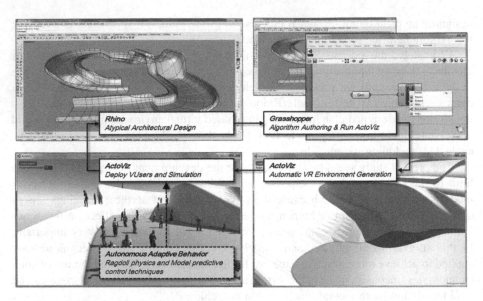

Fig. 1. The process of human behavior simulation based on autonomous adaptive behavior.

3 Autonomous Adaptive Behavior for Human Behavior Simulation of an Atypical Architectural Space

In order to overcome the limitations of current simulation and realize the adaptive behavior of virtual users in ActoViz, we wanted to introduce ragdoll physics and MPC methods.

Ragdoll physics is a type of physics engine procedural animation that is often used as a replacement for traditional static death animations in video games and animated films. When Ragdoll physics is applied to ActoViz, VUser reacts variously to irregular shapes of atypical geometry, enabling more natural user behavior simulation. Figure 2 shows a comparison of human behaviors between with and without Ragdoll physics in ActoViz. As shown in Fig. 2, using Ragdoll physics can solve the problem of a part of VUser being buried in atypical geometry.

Fig. 2. Comparison of ActoViz with Ragdoll physics (left) and without (right)

MPC is a process control method used to control a process while satisfying a set of constraints. The concept of MPC has traditionally been used in chemical plants, refineries, and power systems, but it is also used as a method of character animation. In ActoViz, MPC is used for VUser to properly interact with various types of atypical geometry. For example, when VUser climbs a steep slope, it reacts to balance, or when a fall occurs, it takes appropriate action using atypical geometry.

Fig. 3. An example of motion predictive control used in ActoViz (Falling down situation)

Fig. 4. Autonomous adaptive behaviors for human behavior simulation of an atypical architectural space in ActoViz

4 Conclusion and Discussion

This study aims to realize the autonomous adaptive behavior simulation of VUser in ActoViz. To do this, we applied ragdoll physics and MPC methods to ActoViz. As shown in Fig. 3, Using ragdoll physics and MPC methods, VUsers are able to take more nature behavior in ActoViz. However, as VUsers sometimes experience unexpected and inappropriate behavior, additional technology development is needed. In addition, it will be furthermore implemented for the simulation effect of autonomous adaptive behavior for architects (Fig. 4).

Acknowledgement. This work was supported by the National Research Foundation of Korea (NRF) grant funded by the Korea government (MSIT) (NRF-2018R1A2B6005827).

References

1. Steinfeld, E., Kalay, Y.E.: The impact of computer-aided design on representation in architecture. In: Proceedings of ARCC Conference on Representation and Simulation in Architectural Research and Design (1990)
2. Lee, Y.G.: ActoViz: a human behavior simulator for the evaluation of the dwelling performance of an atypical architectural space. In: Stephanidis, C. (ed.) HCII 2019. CCIS, vol. 1034, pp. 361–365. Springer, Cham (2019). https://doi.org/10.1007/978-3-030-23525-3_48
3. Lee, Y.L., Lee, Y.G.: Developing an autonomous behavior of virtual users based on psychological interpretation of human behavior to an atypical architectural shape. Int. J. ICT-Aid. Archit. Civil Eng. **6**(1), 1–6 (2019)
4. Watkinson, M.: Real time character animation: a generic approach to ragdoll physics. MSc Dissertation, Coventry University (2009)
5. Garcia, C.E., Prett, D.M., Morari, M.: Model predictive control: theory and practice a survey. Automatica **25**(3), 335–348 (1989)
6. Hong, S.W., Lee, Y.G.: Behavioural responsiveness of virtual users for students creative problem finding in architectural design. Archit. Sci. Rev. **62**(3), 238–247 (2019)

Bowing Detection for Erhu Learners Using YOLO Deep Learning Techniques

Bonnie Lu$^{(\boxtimes)}$, Chyi-Ren Dow, and Chang-Jan Peng

Department of Information Engineering and Computer Science,
Feng Chia University, Taichung, Taiwan
yelubonnie@gmail.com, crdow@fcu.edu.tw, jacky840327@gmail.com

Abstract. The traditional ways to learn musical instruments are having lessons with teachers, or self-paced by teaching videos and books. Nowadays, the musical instrument self-learning systems are in the ascendant. However, it is difficult for a musical instrument learner to know if his playing posture is correct unless the teacher provides guidance in person and corrects it immediately. Due to the breakthrough development of computer vision technology, computers with camera lenses can act as teachers' eyes to detect the learners' movements and give some assistance for their self-learning. Erhu, a kind of Chinese traditional stringed instrument, is getting popular worldwide. In this research, taking the erhu bowing method as an example, we use YOLO object detection technology to track the trajectory of the bow in the video and evaluate whether it meets the level and straightness requirements. For the purpose, we first define the measurement methods of level and straightness and design a system to record the progress. In 2016, Joseph Redmon et al. proposed a real-time object detection method called YOLO, "You Only Look Once". The multi-layer CNN architecture is executed only once, which greatly improves the detection speed. To track the movement of erhu's bow, we must at least detect the coordinates of two objects, the erhu bow and the right hand of the player who holding the bow. Our images data set to train the object detection model came from several Chinese music society in Taiwan. The experimental results show that the model can successfully mark the desired objects. Finally, the study found that even senior erhu players still have some deviations, but they are more stable than beginners. Self-correction through system prompts would help learners to reduce the bias problem.

Keywords: Computer vision · Convolutional neural networks · Object detection · Transfer learning · Self-learning system

1 Introduction

Practicing much more makes perfect skills when people learning musical instruments. In recent years, the musical instrument self-learning systems are in the ascendant [1,2]. Some researchers attempted to use sensor systems to assist learners, such as webcams can be used to capture images and record them for further

© Springer Nature Switzerland AG 2020
C. Stephanidis and M. Antona (Eds.): HCII 2020, CCIS 1225, pp. 193–198, 2020.
https://doi.org/10.1007/978-3-030-50729-9_27

computer analysis. The convolutional neural network is an effective method to classify objects in images, which can be used in object detection.

In 2015, Joseph Redmon et al. proposed the method of object detection called YOLO [3], "You Only Look Once". YOLO only does once CNN from the image input to the output prediction, thus greatly increasing the speed of detection. When training YOLO, the whole picture is directly trained in the neural network, so this End-to-End network design algorithm can avoid the disadvantage that traditional object recognition must be separately trained.

This research takes the stringed instrument erhu as an example and uses YOLO technology to detect and record the positions of the bow in the video for analysis. Erhu is one kind of the most popular musical instruments in Chinese society and its performing style just right for the front two-dimensional identification of the webcam. First, we focus on the correctness analysis of "Level and Straight" [4] and propose the measurement methods. Finally, a demonstration system is designed to assists erhu learners gradually reach the requirements.

2   Related Work

2.1   Convolutional Neural Network and Deep Learning

In 2012, Alex Krizhesky and others proposed "AlexNet" to win the championship in the ImageNet Large-Scale Image Classification Competition (ILSVRC) [5]. Before that, the focus of CNN always been covered by the hierarchical structure of "manual design features plus Support Vector Machine (SVM) classifiers". Three years later, Residual Network (ResNet) was proposed [6] and also won the classification task at ImageNet ILSVRC 2015. ResNet makes it possible to train hundreds or even thousands of network layers with superior performance. Many methods and related applications have used ResNet.

2.2   Object Detection and Transfer Learning

Object detection is a core issue in computer vision. The classic Deformable Parts Models (DPM) methods scan each image many times to determine all possible candidates, which consume a lot of computing resources. R-CNN [7] was the first successful introduction of CNN's method into the field of object detection, but it is still a slow step.

In 2015, Joseph Redmon et al. proposed the YOLO Model, a fast and efficient method of object detection. The current YOLOv3 provides the 53-layers Darknet-53 as base network [8]. YOLO uses the ResNet structure to solve the gradient weakening problem and the Feature Pyramid Networks (FPN) to improve the prediction of small objects. Instead of taking time to build a brand-new model, we can perform Transfer Learning from a pre-trained model [9] with a small amount of data.

2.3 Computer Assisted Learning System for Bowed Instruments

There are two main methods to learn musical instruments: finding professional teachers to give instructions, or self-learning by teaching materials, such as books and videos. With the advent of the Internet of Things (IoT) era, the ubiquitous sensor systems, another method of learning musical instrument online has gradually emerged [1,10]. The first principle of erhu bowing technique is to control the movement of bow to be level and straight by right hand. In recent years, a study used magnetic position sensors to measure the posture of bow [11], but there is still few mentions of tracking the bow movement.

3 Erhu Bowing Detection System

3.1 Measurement Method

Moving erhu's bow to be "Level and Straight" is conceptual technique. In order to assess the performance, we redefine the concept as follows:

Level. The bow's hair should be level and closed to the sound barrel of the erhu. When the movement goes flat, the right hand must be very closed to the horizon middle line of the bow's bounding box.

Straight. Some bowing methods are not kept in level, such as Jing-Hu style, but they must still move straight along a slash line. We can calculate the slope of the bow as the straightness indicator.

3.2 Model Development

For the purpose, an object detection model is required to catch the locations of the desired two objects, the bow and right hand in the video frames. Our images dataset came from several Chinese music society in Taiwan. We used an image annotation software which support the YOLO format to label these two objects in the image dataset.

This dataset with about two thousand images was separated to two parts, 80% as the training dataset and 20% as the testing dataset. We simply used the Darknet open source neural network framework [12] and the pre-trained darknet53.conv.74 weight file, provided by Joseph Redmon, to accelerate the training progress by Transfer Learning. Figure 1 shows the iterations of the training phase.

3.3 Bowing Detection

When the YOLO model was ready, we modified the python call Darknet function sample program provided by Joseph Redmon to detect and record the coordinates, width and length of the two objects to a csv file for further analysis. If the camera is used, these analysis results can be displayed real time. Figure 3 is an example of the bowing detection results and analysis outcome.

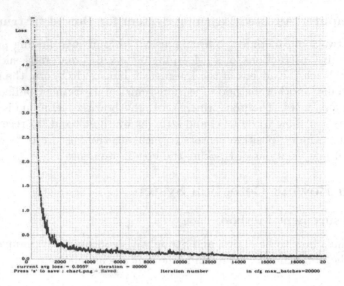

Fig. 1. The iterations of the training phase.

Fig. 2. An example of the bowing detection results and analysis outcome.

4   Performance Assessment

We define the performance metric as the correct number of times and the minimum slope range in all frames captured in the video. For each frame, the correct number of times is counted when the center point of the right-hand area reaches the level target within an accepted tolerance. The "Level" score will be the correct counts divided by the total number of captures. We show the "Level" score on the left top of video as Fig. 2.

The origin of the picture coordinates is located in the upper left corner. For the learner to see the inclination intuitively, the coordinate origin must be converted to the lower left corner before calculating the slope. Thus, when the bow is above the horizontal line, we will get a negative slope, otherwise we

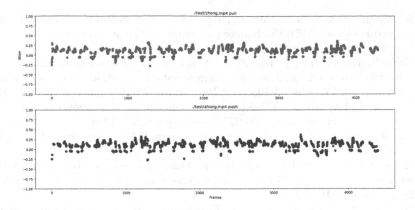

Fig. 3. An example of the "Straight" performance.

will get a positive slope. This representation would confuse the learner, so we convert the slope to its negative value. Figure 3 is an example of the "Straight" performance.

5 Conclusion

The traditional methods of learning musical instruments cannot record the information of the learner's practice as data. Computer assisted learning through sensing technology and computer vision can help learners analyze the progress. This study takes erhu as an example. It not only successfully identified the direction of bow movement in the video, but also gave a computational definition to the "Level and Straight" methods of erhu's bowing technique.

References

1. Kikukawa, F., Ishihara, S., Soga, M., Taki, H.: Development of a learning environment for playing erhu by diagnosis and advice regarding finger position on strings. In: Proceedings of the Conference on New Instruments for Musical Expression, pp. 271–276 (2013)
2. Hsiao, C.P., Li, R., Yan, X., Do, E.Y.: Tactile teacher: sensing finger tapping in piano playing. In: Proceedings of the Ninth International Conference on Tangible, Embedded, and Embodied Interaction, pp. 257–260 (2015). https://doi.org/10.1145/2677199.2680554
3. Redmon, J., Divvala, S., Girshick, R., Farhadi, A.: You only look once: unified, real-time object detection. In: Proceedings of the IEEE Conference on Computer Vision and Pattern Recognition (CVPR), pp. 779–788 (2016)
4. Yao, W.: Follow Me to Learn the Erhu. Anhui literature and Art Publishing House, Ch. 2, pp. 13–16 (2011)
5. Krizhevsky, A., Sutskever, I., Hinton, G.E.: ImageNet classification with deep convolutional neural networks. In: Proceedings of the 25th International Conference on Neural Information Processing System, pp. 1097–1105 (2012)

6. He, K., Zhang, X., Ren, S., Sun, J.: Deep residual learning for image recognition. In: Proceedings of the IEEE Conference on Computer Vision and Pattern Recognition (CVPR), pp. 770–778 (2016)
7. Girshick, R., Donahue, J., Darrell, T., Malik, J.: Rich feature hierarchies for accurate object detection and semantic segmentation. In: Proceedings of the IEEE Conference on Computer Vision and Pattern Recognition, pp. 580–587 (2014)
8. Redmon, J., Farhadi, A.: YOLOv3: an incremental improvement. Cornell University. https://arxiv.org/abs/1804.02767. Accessed 8 Apr 2018
9. Pan, J., Yang, Q.: A survey on transfer learning. IEEE Trans. Knowl. Data Eng. **22**(10), 1345–1359 (2010)
10. Young, D.: The hyperbow controller: real-time dynamics measurement of violin performance. In: Proceedings of the Conference on New Instruments for Musical Expression (NIME) (2002)
11. Kikukawa, F., Soga, M., Taki, H.: Development of a gesture learning environment for novices' erhu bow strokes. Procedia Comput. Sci. **35**, 1323–1332 (2014). https://doi.org/10.1016/j.procs.2014.08.171
12. Redmon, J.: Darknet: open source neural networks in C (2013–2016). https://pjreddie.com/darknet/

Archery Form Guidance System Using Acceleration Sensors and Foot Pressure Sensors

Ibuki Meguro[(✉)] and Eiichi Hayakawa

Takushoku University, Tatemachi Hatioji City, Tokyo 815-1, Japan
r78471@st.takushoku-u.ac.jp,
hayakawa@cs.takushoku-u.ac.jp

Abstract. Archery can improve its score by keeping the form constant. Therefore, the position where the center of gravity is arranged becomes important. It is also difficult for the center of gravity to be judged by human eyes and for players to always be conscious. The movement of the center of gravity can be estimated from the head movement and the foot pressure. This system uses an acceleration sensor and a foot pressure sensor to support the form. Since archery forms vary by skeleton, the system determines the optimal form for the individual from the accumulated data.

The center of gravity of the form is measured using the acceleration sensor and the foot pressure sensor, and the data, the moving image of the form, and the score are stored. The acceleration sensor is attached to the head and measures the acceleration on the x-axis, y-axis, and z-axis. The system obtains ideal shooting data from past shooting data and displays improvement methods based on the difference between the ideal and the current shooting data.

This system is aimed at players with a score of 500–600 points at 70 mW and the aim is to be able to exceed 600 points.

By performing repetitive exercises using this system, the relationship between the center of gravity and the score can be measured, which can help to stabilize the form.

Keywords: Archery · Sensor · Center of gravity · Data visualization

1 Introduction

1.1 Background

Archery is a sport that shoots a fixed number of arrows and competes for points. Competitors must practice using bows that match their skeletal and muscular strength in order to achieve high scores in matches and competitions. Practice includes strength training, repetitive exercises to help your body remember the best form. The most important of these is the practice of learning forms. If you understand your best form and repeat that form, you will get a higher score. However, even if the user learns the optimal form, the form will shift due to physical condition and motivation at that time

© Springer Nature Switzerland AG 2020
C. Stephanidis and M. Antona (Eds.): HCII 2020, CCIS 1225, pp. 199–203, 2020.
https://doi.org/10.1007/978-3-030-50729-9_28

in daily repetitive practice. The center of gravity is important in the form, but it is also difficult for human eyes to judge this and for the competitor to recognize it.

1.2   Related Work

Existing research [1] indicates that the distribution of the center of gravity is highly related to the archery score, but we thought it would be difficult to know the current state of the form and improve it using this information alone.

1.3   Archery Forms

The archery form is divided into six stages: set, setup, drawing, anchoring, aiming and release. The set stage is ready to fire fit an arrow to the string. The setup stage is to raise the bow and the puller to the height of the competitor's head. In the drawing stage, pulling the bow while lowering the lifted bow. The anchoring stage is placing the index finger side of the hand holding the string under the chin. The aiming stage is to aim while maintaining the anchoring posture. During this time, he is slightly draw a bow. The release stage means releasing your finger from the string and releasing the arrow.

2   Research Objectives

The purpose of this research is to develop a system that can confirm changes in form that occur over time and changes that are difficult for athletes to recognize, and that propose improvement methods. For beginners, because the form is not stable, the system is designed for use by intermediate and higher level competitors with a stable form.

3   Research Goal

There is a way for competitors to take a video to check their form, but it is difficult to see small changes. Also, even if you ask a third party to confirm, it is not always possible to get useful advice because the optimal form differs depending on the skeletal and muscular strength of the competitor. Even when measuring the center of gravity, electronic equipment is not allowed in the tournament, so use sensors that do not change the form when the system is not used and when it is used.

4   System Design

4.1   Overall System

The center of gravity can be inferred from the foot pressure where the weight is applied directly or the movement of the head which is the heaviest part in the body. The foot pressure sensor is thin, and the eyeglass-type acceleration sensor can communicate wirelessly, so there is no effect on the athlete. Figure 1 shows the system configuration.

The data of the foot pressure sensor and the acceleration sensor and the moving image of the form are associated and stored. The data to be used as teacher data is selected from the stored and accumulated data. The result and improvement method are fed back from the difference between the teacher data and the shooting data. Also, by saving the video of the form, you can check the optimal form.

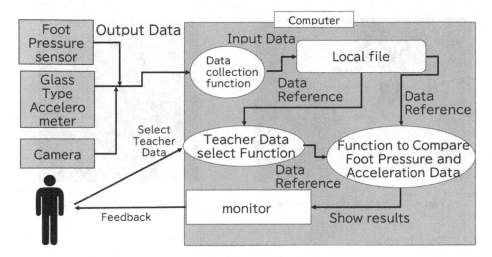

Fig. 1. The structure of overall system

4.2 Devices

Glass Type Accelerometer. Eyeglass-type acceleration sensors are used to measure head movement. It is worn on the head as shown in Fig. 2 and the acceleration is measured. The axes to be measured are the three axes of the x axis, the y axis, and the z axis as shown in Fig. 3. The acquired data is saved as a csv file. Based on this, Players can check their head movements that cannot be perceived by looking at the graph.

Fig. 2. Using eyeglass type sensor

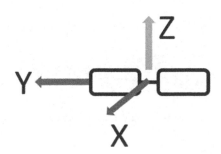

Fig. 3. Axis to measure

Foot Pressure Sensor. The foot pressure sensor is placed at the foot as shown in Fig. 4 to measure the center of gravity. Displayed on a 2D map as shown in Fig. 5, the white point is the center of gravity, and its position is stored. The weighted part is displayed on the 2Dmap by color, so you can easily grasp the foot pressure distribution. By combining multiple foot pressure sensor plates and synchronizing data, the width of each player's stance can be adjusted.

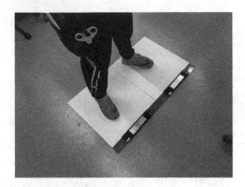

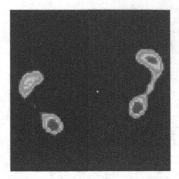

Fig. 4. Using foot pressure sensor   **Fig. 5.** 2D map of foot pressure

4.3 User Interface

Figure 6 shows the graph that visualizes acceleration sensor data. The feedback to the competitor is displayed on the PC screen, showing the difference between the measured data graph, the teacher data and the improvement method. Identify the deviation from

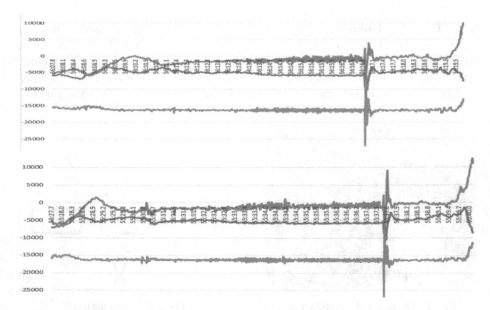

Fig. 6. Acceleration graph visualization

the time of aiming and the magnitude of the movement of the graph, and display advice on how to move the body to approach the optimal form. In addition, moving images of the graph and the form are displayed so that the deviation can be easily checked. As shown in Fig. 6, the graph of the measured acceleration shifts even when the competitor shoots several shots.

5   Conclusion and Future Work

As a prototype, a system for acquiring and analyzing data with an eyeglass-type acceleration sensor was developed. By graphing the movement of the head, the players can easily understand their habit and deviation of the head movement. In addition, they can confirm the movement of the center of gravity, and the relationship with the score. We will be able to acquire and analyze foot pressure sensor data the ability to automatically compare data.

Reference

1. Ahmad, Z., et al.: Biomechanics measurements in archery. In: Ahmad, Z. (ed.) ICMER (2013)

Generation of Brass Band Animation Synchronized with the Motion of Conductor's Hand

Yuta Muraki[(⊠)], Katsuki Kobayashi, Koji Nishio,
and Ken-ichi Kobori

Osaka Institute of Technology, 1-79-1 Kitayama, Hirakata City, Osaka, Japan
yuta.muraki@oit.ac.jp

Abstract. In recent years, VR devices such as PlayStation VR, HTC Vive, and Oculus Rift have become widespread, making it possible to easily experience Virtual Reality. There are contents that can get a high immersive feeling by synchronizing the motion of the user with the CG and music in the virtual space. Research on automatic generation of musical instrument performance animations using MIDI data, which is a type of music data, has been conducted. However, there is a problem that the motion and the sound during the performance are shifted, giving the viewer a sense of incongruity.

In this research, we propose a generation system of brass band animation synchronized with the motion of conductor's hand using VR devices. The user uses the VR controller as a baton. The user can control music and animation by performing the action of the conductor. In our system, the motion of the conductor's hand is acquired, and the motion speed and amount of motion are calculated. After that, animation and music are controlled using the acquired data. Specifically, the point at which the direction of the acquired velocity vector changes is set as the beat start point. Then, the music speed and animation are controlled using the estimated tempo. In addition, the music volume is changed using the calculated amount of motion. Furthermore, by generating CG animation in the virtual space, it gives the user a sense of immersion. As an experiment, 12 people used this system and verified the usefulness of the method.

Keywords: VR · Automatic performance · Synchronization

1 Introduction

The way in which the conductor gives instructions to the performer is not only by shaking the conductor but also by gaze and gestures. The conductor controls the ensemble by using various expressions to control the performer. In general, it is not easy to become a conductor, and requires a vast and wide knowledge and ability to music. In addition, it is very difficult to actually experience the conductor because instruments and players must be prepared.

In this research, we focus on the motion of the conductor's baton and develop a system that allows anyone to easily experience the conductor. In addition, we focused

C. Stephanidis and M. Antona (Eds.): HCII 2020, CCIS 1225, pp. 204–211, 2020.
https://doi.org/10.1007/978-3-030-50729-9_29

on two points: the volume of the music that changes depending on the magnitude of the motion of the baton, and the speed of the music and the speed of the movement that increases the speed of the motion of the baton. In order to realize this system, the magnitude and speed of the motion are estimated from the user's motion of the baton. Then, the volume of the music is changed according to the estimated magnitude. Also, the speed of music and the CG character playing are changed using the estimated speed. The motion of swinging the baton of the user is obtained in real time by using the controller of HTC Vive [1], a kind of VR device. Furthermore, by displaying the performers in a virtual space using Vive's head mounted display (HMD), it is expected that the user will be obtained immersion feeling. In addition, in estimating the speed of the movement, the tempo is corrected to reduce the gap between the conductor's motion and the music.

2 Related Works

By synchronizing the motion of the user with the animation of the CG character, the user can enjoy it as a content in a virtual space or show it as a performance, and the field of practical application is expanding.

Goto et al. proposed a method of making a virtual dancer "Cindy" dance according to the sound of an instrument played by multiple people [2]. This technique is realized by making a virtual dancer pause by using the strength of the sound, the pitch of the sound, and the number of sounds produced simultaneously. The performance of each player is input and those performances are output as sounds. Then, the performance of one player is analyzed, and the CG dancer is displayed according to the performance. By running these processes on multiple computers distributed on a network, the computation cost is distributed.

Ishizuka et al. proposed a performance synchronization method with a multi-agent system based on the user's performance and baton motion [3]. In this method, score tracking is used for performance synchronization between user and agent. The order of the notes played by the user is stored as a note sequence template, and the performance is tracked by searching the score for the note sequence that best matches the template. In addition, when the user inputs a performance using a MIDI controller, it becomes possible to synchronize the user's performance with the group of agents playing other instruments.

Lim et al. proposed a performance synchronization method using the gesture of the user playing the flute [4]. In the proposed method, the performance robot HRP-2 is operated using the gesture at the end of the flute opposite to the mouth. Using the gesture of the user playing the flute, it is possible to change the tempo and start and stop the performance. The gesture of the flute is limited to moving the edge up and down. Gesture detection is realized by detecting the inclination of the flute using Hough transform line detection. The only instrument that this method supports is the flute.

3   Proposed System

In this section, we describe a method for realizing a conductor system synchronized with the user's motion proposed in this research. In this study, speed and magnitude are estimated from user's motion. Using the estimated speed and magnitude, we control the music and performance animation to realize a system synchronized with the user's motion.

3.1   System Overview

Figure 1 shows the flowchart of the proposed system. In this system, the HMD is put on the head, and a VR controller is held in the right hand, and the conductor action is performed. The controller is displayed in the virtual space in the shape of a baton.

In this system, music data (MIDI) is first read using "Midi Tool Kit Pro" [5]. "Midi Tool Kit Pro" is suitable for the construction of this system because the speed and volume of the played music can be easily changed.

Then, according to the conductor action of the user, the CG player displayed on the HMD and the music being played are changed. The instruments used in this system are piano, guitar, drum, trumpet, clarinet and flute. The instrument information to be used is acquired using the information of MIDI data, and the performer is displayed. Figure 2 shows the arrangement when all players are displayed.

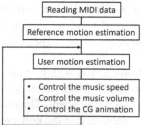

Fig. 1. Outline of the proposed system

Fig. 2. Performance scene of the proposed system

3.2   User Motion Estimation

In this research, we focused on the quadruple rhythm music with the largest number of music, and defined the user's conductor actions as the actions shown in Fig. 3. The position of the controller shown in the figure is the start position of each operation. The magnitude and speed are estimated from these operations shown in the figure.

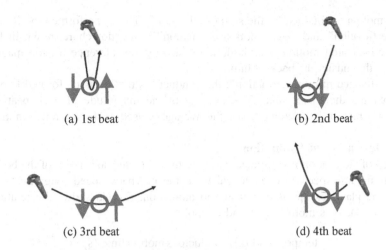

(a) 1st beat   (b) 2nd beat

(c) 3rd beat   (d) 4th beat

Fig. 3. Motion of each beat (Color figure online)

3.2.1 Motion Start Position Estimation

In order to estimate the magnitude and speed of the conductor's motion, it is necessary to find the start point of each beat. The start point of each beat has the following features.

- Point where the direction of the velocity vector of the controller changes from top to bottom
- Point where the direction of the controller's velocity vector changes from left to right
- Point where the direction of the velocity vector of the controller changes from right to left

The velocity vector is a vector that indicates the direction and how far the controller has moved. The start point can be estimated by obtaining the velocity vector. The velocity vector is calculated using the position that can be obtained from the controller. In addition, in order to prevent erroneous estimation for small movements, a change in the velocity vector size of 0.2 mm/s or more is detected. This value was determined by conducting preliminary experiments.

3.2.2 Motion Magnitude Estimation

The magnitude of the motion is estimated using the estimated start point of the motion of the beat. The magnitude of the estimated beat motion is used to change the playback volume.

In order to estimate the magnitude of the motion, the midway point is used in addition to the start point of each beat. The midway point is the point where the direction of the velocity vector changes from bottom to top. The midway points of each beat are shown in red circles in Fig. 3.

Assuming that the distance from the start point to the midway point is L1 and the distance from the midway point to the start point of the next beat is L2, the magnitude

L of the motion is obtained by the sum of L1 and L2. This is performed in "Reference motion estimation" and "User motion estimation" in the flowchart shown in Fig. 1. Then, the estimated motion magnitude is divided by the reference motion magnitude determine the music playback volume.

In "Reference motion estimation", the conductor's motion is performed five times before playing the music data. The average of the magnitude of each beat of the conductor's motion is calculated, and the average is used as the reference motion.

3.2.3 Motion Speed Estimation

The speed of the motion is estimated by using the estimated start point of the beat. The estimated motion speed is used to calculate the playback speed magnification that changes the playback speed of music and animation. Eq. (1) shows the relationship between conductor's motion time and tempo.

$$tempo = 60 \text{ (s)}/conductor's motion time \text{ (s)} \tag{1}$$

where conductor's motion time is obtained by measuring the time from the start point to the start point of the next beat. The playback speed magnification is calculated by dividing the obtained tempo by the original tempo read from the MIDI data. In this system, the minimum value of the playback speed magnification is 0.1, the maximum value is 5.0, and the maximum value of the estimated tempo is 240. (The reason why the maximum value of tempo is 240 is that when the tempo is 240, the conductor's motion time is 0.25 s, and when it is larger than that, it is not realistic.)

3.3 Optimization of Playback Speed Magnification

Using the motion magnitude and playback speed magnification obtained in Sects. 3.2.2 and 3.2.3, change the playback volume, playback speed, and animation of the music when the user's motion reached the start point of the next beat. However, if the music playback speed is changed at the start point of the next beat, there is a possibility that a large gap may occur between the actual beat position of the music and the start point of the beat motion. (For example, if you change the conductor's motion very slowly.)

Therefore, when the time of the previous beat has passed while conducting motion, the playback speed magnification is reduced. The amount of decrease in the reproduction speed magnification M is as shown in the following Eqs. (2) and (3).

$$M = 1/(ax+b)$$
$$a = (1 - 10v)/(t - t_{min})v$$
$$b = 10 - t_{min} \times a \tag{2}$$
$$t_{min} = 60/(0.1 \times def)$$

$$M_n = M_{n-1} - 1.2 / def \tag{3}$$

In Eq. (2), where t is the time of the previous beat, v is the playback speed magnification of the previous beat, x is the current time, t_min is the time at which the reproduction speed magnification becomes the minimum value, and *def* is the tempo obtained from the MIDI data.

Up to *t* sec., playback is performed using the playback speed magnification *v*. After the elapse of *t* seconds, if the midway point shown in Sect. 3.2.2 has been acquired, the degree of change in the playback speed magnification is reduced using Eq. (2). On the other hand, if the midway point has not been acquired, the degree of the change in the reproduction speed magnification is reduced constantly for each frame using Eq. (3) until the midway point is acquired. Then, after the midway point is obtained, the degree of change in the reproduction speed magnification is reduced using Eq. (2).

Figure 4 shows the change in the reproduction speed magnification when *def* = 120 and *t* = 0.5. Figure 4(a) shows the case where the midway point has already been acquired in 0.5 s. Figure 4(b) shows the case where the elapsed point was acquired in 0.7 s.

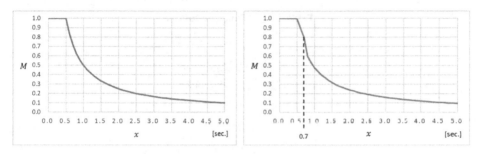

Fig. 4. Change in playback speed magnification

3.4 Performance Animation Generation

In this system, the musician performs the performance animation corresponding to each instrument. The performance animation was generated by "Mixamo" [6] and "EasyMotionRecorder".

"Mixamo" is a web service provided by Adobe that allows you to customize and animate 3D characters. Using this system, we generated animations of pianos, guitars, and drums with large movements.

For motion tracking using Vive, we used the "FinalIK" [7] asset that runs on Unity and the "EasyMotionRecorder" script [8]. "FinalIK" is an asset that allows users to freely move CG characters within Unity. It is also possible to move CG characters using VR device such as Vive used in this system. Therefore, it is possible to generate a performance animation of a CG character that actually performs a performance animation using this asset and Vive. "EasyMotionRecorder" is a script that records and plays back an animation of a CG character that has been motion-captured by the above method. The animation is recorded using this, and the animation is played back while the system is actually running.

4 Experimental Result

In order to verify the effectiveness of the proposed system, we asked 12 people, including men and women, to use this system and conducted a questionnaire on the following items. Items (1) and (2) were evaluated on a 5-point scale, and item (3) was freely answered by the subject.

1. Is the music or animation changing according to the motion speed?
2. Is the music or animation changing according to the magnitude of the motion?
3. Are there any parts of the music that cause discomfort?

Table 1 shows the results of the questionnaire. Since both items (1) and (2) received a high rating of 4.5 or more, it is considered that the tempo and volume were correctly estimated from the user's conductor's motion us ing the proposed method.

Table 1 Questionnaire results

In item (3), the following opinions were obtained from the subjects.

- There is a gap between the beat position of the music and the start position of the conductor.
- I intend to move the controller at the same speed, but I feel that the playback speed is uneven.

Even after optimizing the playback speed magnification, there is a slight gap between the music and the conductor's action. It is thought that this problem can be improved by performing motion prediction using deep learning.

In addition, since the distance of the motion defined for each beat is different, even if the conductor's motion is performed at the same speed, the estimated playback speed will change slightly. It is thought that this problem can be improved by normalizing the estimated tempo according to the motion of each beat with the distance.

5 Conclusion

In this paper, we proposed a method of synchronizing conductor's motion with music and CG characters. The motion of the user was acquired using the controller of the VR device, and the magnitude and speed were estimated from the motion. The music playback volume was controlled from the estimated magnitude, and the music speed and animation were controlled from the speed. In addition, by adjusting the playback speed magnification, the gap between the beat of the music and the start point of the conductor's motion was reduced.

From the experimental results, it was confirmed that the magnitude and speed of the motion could be estimated using the proposed method. It was also confirmed that the motion of the user was reflected in music and animation of CG characters.

As a future work, there is a study on the adjustment of the reproduction speed magnification using a mathematical stochastic model with the arm motion as learning data. In this paper, we focus on quadruple rhythm music as future developments. Furthermore, in this paper, we focused on quadruple rhythm music, but as a future perspective, we will also focus on music with other rhythms.

References

1. VIVE™. https://www.vive.com/
2. Goto, M., Muraoka, Y.: Interactive performance of music danced CG dancer. In: Proceedings on Workshop on Interactive Systems and Softwares, vol. 95, pp. 18–19 (1995)
3. Ishizuka, K., Nakamura, R., Gotoh, T., Tamura, N., Shimada, H.: Multiple agent simulation of joint performance with virtual orchestral and real player. ITE Tech. Rep. **37**, 99–102 (2013)
4. Angelica, L., et al.: Musical robot co-player: real-time synchronization with a human flutist recognizing visual start and end cues. IPSJ J. **52**(12), 3599–3610 (2011)
5. Midi Tool Kit Pro - Asset Store. https://assetstore.unity.com/packages/tools/audio/midi tool-kit-pro-115331
6. Mixamo. https://www.mixamo.com/
7. Final IK - Asset Store. https://assetstore.unity.com/packages/tools/animation/final-ik-14290
8. GitHub - duo-inc/EasyMotionRecorder. https://github.com/duo-inc/EasyMotionRecorder

Development of a Quantification Method for Tendon Vibration Inducing Motion Illusion

Hiroyuki Ohshima[✉], Hitoshi Ishido, Yusuke Iwata,
and Shigenobu Shimada

Tokyo Metropolitan Industrial Technology Research Institute (TIRI),
Sumida-Ku, Tokyo 130-0015, Japan
ohshima.hiroyuki@iri-tokyo.jp

Abstract. This study aims to establish a new method for quantifying tendon vibration during motion illusion by measuring the acceleration of a 3D-printed contact head attached to the vibration device. This contact head was designed with a hole in the center in which a single-axis accelerometer was fixed. Moreover, the upper end of the head was designed to be bolted to the vibrator. This aids in investigating whether the contact area influences perceptual parameters such as strength of motion illusion. A second accelerometer was attached to the exterior of the vibrator. For five participants, the biceps brachii tendon of the right arm (the dominant side for all participants) was stimulated for 30 s at 100 Hz. The accelerations measured inside and outside the contact head were recorded at 1000 Hz, and the ratio of root-mean-square (RMS) values of the two accelerations was calculated. The results showed a maximum ratio of 1.02 and a minimum of 0.97. We conclude that the proposed method can quantify tendon vibration during motion illusion to within ±3%. The use of a 3D printer to produce the contact head provides a convenient means of varying some parameters in these investigations. In future work, the size of the contact area could be changed by modifying this design, and we will examine the effect of the contact area in motion illusion. This is expected to be an extremely useful technique to provide a kinesthetic sensation in virtual reality.

Keywords: Kinesthetic sensation · Sensorimotor system · 3D printing

1 Introduction

Previous studies have reported that vibrating tendons on human limbs evokes motion illusion, a kinesthetic sensation experienced without joint movement [1]. Prior to our previous work [2, 3], there had been no reports on the influence of the angles of joints in motion illusion. The gravitational torque depends on the angle of the joint, so the angle could influence perceptual parameters, such as the strength of motion illusion. We compared motion illusion for two different angles of the elbow joint by subjective assessment in three aspects: strength of illusion, range of extension, and velocity of extension [2], and quantitative assessment in two further aspects: latency and duration [3]. The results showed that the three aspects of subjective assessment were affected by limb position, but the two quantitative aspects were not affected by the joint angle.

C. Stephanidis and M. Antona (Eds.): HCII 2020, CCIS 1225, pp. 212–216, 2020.
https://doi.org/10.1007/978-3-030-50729-9_30

Conversely, it is known that the area of contact affects vibrotactile thresholds and is a more important stimulus parameter than the gradient or curvature of displacement [4]. This is due to "spatial summation". Based on this, we proposed the following hypothesis: contact area influences perceptual parameters such as strength of motion illusion elicited by tendon vibration. To investigate this, we first needed to develop a convenient experimental setup and method.

In our previous studies, an accelerometer was attached to the exterior of the vibrator contact head to record tendon vibration. With this setup, it was difficult to change the area of contact. The present study aims to establish a new method for quantifying tendon vibration during motion illusion by mounting an accelerometer inside a 3D-printed contact head. To verify the validity of our proposed method, accelerometers were attached inside and outside the contact head, and the ratio of the root-mean-square (RMS) values of the two accelerations was calculated. If the ratio is close to unity, our proposed method will be viable, because the more convenient internal accelerometer can then be used instead of the previous external pickup.

2 Methods

2.1 Participants

Two males (aged 28 and 36 years) and three females (aged 42–46 years) volunteered as participants in this study. All provided prior written informed consent according to institutional requirements. The experimental procedure was approved by the Tokyo Metropolitan Industrial Technology Research Institute ethics committee.

2.2 Apparatus and Experimental Setup

A palm-sized vibration device (WaveMaker-Mobile, Asahi Seisakusho, Japan) was fixed to a fixing base (Fig. 1) [5]. The participant sat in front of the fixing base wearing a protective eye mask and earmuffs (Fig. 2 left). The arm was positioned on the horizontal armrest, so that the shoulder was held stationary at 90° flexion and the elbow was at 0° flexion in an anatomical position, with the palm of the hand upwards. The vibrator was positioned over the biceps tendon just above the elbow.

The contact head was designed with a hole in the center in which to fix a single-axis accelerometer (710-D, EMIC, Japan). The upper end of the contact head was bolted onto the vibrator (Fig. 3). This contact head was 3D printed using a commercial 3D printer (Objet500 Connex3, Stratasys, USA). Figure 2 right shows the positions of the two identical accelerometers, one bolted inside the contact head and the other was attached externally. The accelerometers were connected to a PC (VJ27M/C-M, NEC, Japan) through a vibration meter (UV-16, Rion, Japan) and multifunction I/O Device (USB-6000, National Instruments, USA). LabVIEW 2014 (National Instruments, USA) was used to record the output of both accelerometers.

Fig. 1. Vibration device fixing base and armrest.

Fig. 2. Experimental setup. Left: arm position. Right: vibrator contact head and accelerometers.

Fig. 3. 3D model of the contact head.

2.3   Procedure

Before the experiment, the participants were informed that they would experience a sensation of elbow joint extension without real movement. In a preliminary experiment, we determined the appropriate amplitude and location to consistently elicit the kinesthetic sensation. The stimulus location was marked on the participant's skin with a felt-tipped marker. The right arm was used, which was the dominant arm for all five participants.

The biceps brachii tendon of each participant was stimulated with a vibration frequency of 100 Hz for 30 s. The accelerations measured by the internal and external accelerometers were recorded at 1000 Hz, and the RMS value of each acceleration was calculated using the following equation

$$\text{RMS} = \sqrt{\frac{1}{n}\sum_{i=1}^{n}(x_i)^2} \tag{1}$$

where xi is an acceleration sample and n is the total number of samples. The ratio of the two RMS values was then determined.

After the experiment, participants were asked whether the illusion of motion was evoked.

3   Results

All five participants described consistent sensations of movement. Table 1 shows the results for the ratio of RMS values of acceleration measured internal and external to the contact head. A ratio of 1.00 corresponds to perfect agreement between the two measurements. The values obtained were in the range 0.97–1.02, indicating close agreement, within 3%, for all participants experiencing motion illusion.

Table 1. Maximum accelerations and ratio of RMS values of acceleration measured inside and outside the contact head for each participant.

Participant	Maximum acceleration inside (m/s^2)	Maximum acceleration outside (m/s^2)	Ratio of RMS value
#1	99.3	95.9	0.97
#2	104.5	103.7	0.99
#3	100.5	98.9	0.98
#4	119.1	121.5	1.02
#5	142.3	144.0	1.01

4 Discussion and Conclusion

The purpose of this study was to establish a new method for quantifying tendon vibration during motion illusion. An accelerometer was placed inside a specially designed 3D-printed contact head. To verify the validity of the proposed method, the measured acceleration was compared with that measured by an identical accelerometer attached externally. The ratio of the RMS values of the two accelerations was found to have a maximum value of 1.02 and minimum of 0.97. We conclude that the proposed method can consistently quantify tendon vibration during motion illusion to within a range of ±3%.

Kinesthesia is as important as the visual and auditory senses for safety, comfort and entertainment quality in immersive (VR) environments. However, the presentation methods of kinesthesia have not kept up with the presentation methods of the visual and auditory senses. This is because the mechanisms of kinesthesia have not been clarified, in contrast with the mechanisms of the visual and auditory senses.

In our previous study, we focused on the joint angle in motion illusion. [2, 3] Then, we focused on the contact area in motion illusion. The results of the present study suggest that the 3D-printing of the contact head will enable us to vary the contact area relatively easily. The internal dimensions of the head remain constant to enable attachment to the vibrator and accommodate the accelerometer, but the external dimensions can be changed to vary the contact area. In our future study, we are planning to examine the effects of the contact area in motion illusion. To organize knowledge about stimulus in motion illusion systematically will enable us to control kinesthesia and perhaps to simulate the experience of an Olympian or Paralympian.

Acknowledgements.   This work was supported by JSPS KAKENHI Grant Numbers JP16K21693 and JP19K20105.

References

1. Goodwin, G.M., McCloskey, D.I., Matthews, P.B.: Proprioceptive illusions induced by muscle vibration: contribution by muscle spindles to perception? Science **175**(4028), 1382–1384 (1972)
2. Ohshima, H., Shimada, S.: Does the limb position influence the motion illusion evoked by tendon vibration? In: 40th Annual International Conference on IEEE Engineering in Medicine and Biology Society, Honolulu, ThPoS-22.6 (2018)
3. Ohshima, H., Shimada, S.: The effects of the angle of an elbow joint on the latency and duration when tendon vibration evoke the motion illusion. In: 41st Annual International Conference on IEEE Engineering in Medicine and Biology Society, Berlin, WePOS-34.27 (2019)
4. Verrillo, R.T.: Effect of contactor area on the vibrotactile threshold. J. Acoust. Soc. Am. **35**(12), 1962–1966 (1963)
5. Ohshima, H., Shimada, S.: Development of a system to quantify the depth of tendon stimulus for the illusion of motion achieved by a vibrator. In: IUPESM World Congress on Medical Physics & Biomedical Engineering, Prague, T10-064 (2018)

Developing a Deployment Technology for Virtual Users with an Autonomous Psychological Behavioral Simulation in Atypical Architectural Space

Jimin Park, Hyangsun Lee, Sujin Kim, and Yun Gil Lee[✉]

Hoseo University, 20, Hoseo-ro, 79beon-gil, Baebang-eup,
Asan-si, Chungcheongnam-do 31499, Korea
{pml934,tjsgid15293,kimtnwls1797}@naver.com,
yglee@hoseo.edu

Abstract. The design of atypical buildings differs notably from traditional architectural design methods. If the traditional building design process is centered on problem solving, the design process of atypical buildings is concentrated on the creation of new forms. Thus, in such a process, it is sometimes possible to overlook elements of human safety and convenience, which are the most important factors to evaluate the value of buildings. One of the efforts required to solve this problem is the development of tools to support to evaluate the dwelling performance with virtual users. In a preliminary study, we developed a platform called ActoViz, which uses commercial atypical building design tools (Rhino and Grasshopper) to perform user simulations during the design process. And also, we surveyed users' behaviors interacting with atypical buildings and interpreted these behaviors psychologically, because we intended to realize the more natural simulation platform (ActoViz) based on intelligent virtual users (VUsers) which conduct psychologically-appropriate behaviors. This paper is to describe how to apply this idea to ActoViz systemically. The result of this study shows the technologies for deploying VUsers in a virtual place using the idea of trigger spot, trigger viewpoint, and behavioral area.

Keywords: Psychological behavior · Virtual user · Simulation · Atypical architectural space

1 Introduction

The social demand for atypical buildings is increasing, and such buildings are often found around cities. Accordingly, each university's architectural department needs to teach methods for designing atypical buildings. However, the design methods of atypical buildings differ notably from those of traditional architectural design. While the traditional building design process is centered on problem solving, the design process of atypical buildings is concentrated on the creation of new forms. In such a

© Springer Nature Switzerland AG 2020
C. Stephanidis and M. Antona (Eds.): HCII 2020, CCIS 1225, pp. 217–222, 2020.
https://doi.org/10.1007/978-3-030-50729-9_31

process, however, it is sometimes possible to overlook elements of human safety and convenience, which are the most important factors when evaluating the value of buildings. In particular, it is easy for students concentrating on creating new forms to ignore aspects related to user behavior. One of the efforts required to solve this problem is the development of tools to support the evaluation of dwelling performance with virtual users [1, 2].

In a preliminary study, we developed a platform called ActoViz, which uses commercial atypical building design tools (Rhino and Grasshopper) to perform user simulations during the design process [6]. Also in that study, we surveyed user behaviors when interacting with atypical buildings and interpreted these behaviors psychologically. This was because we intended to realize the more "natural" simulation platform ActoViz, which is based on intelligent virtual users (VUsers), who engage in psychologically appropriate behaviors. This paper describes how to work with this idea in ActoViz systemically. The result of the study is to depict the technologies for deploying VUsers in a virtual place employing the ideas of trigger spot, trigger viewpoint, and behavioral area.

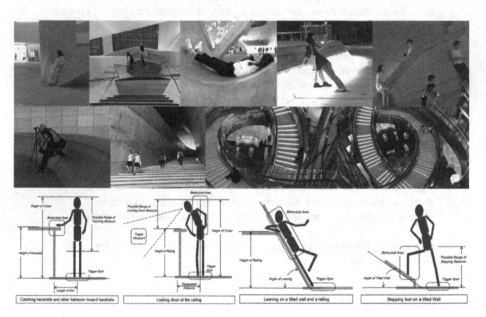

Fig. 1. User behavior in the atypical space and their computerized analysis [7].

2 How to Realize Autonomous Psychological Behavioral Simulation in a Designed Atypical Architectural Space

Figure 1 shows representative examples of user behaviors in the atypical space and their computational analysis. In the previous study, we found that these behaviors involve psychological reasoning. We determined that users in this atypical space can be organized based on specific information, such as on trigger spots, trigger viewpoints, and behavioral areas. If trigger spots, trigger viewpoints, and behavioral areas can be automatically detected from the geometrical properties of the atypical space designed by the architect, this will allow the VUser to act appropriately in the atypical space. Figure 2 shows how trigger spots, trigger viewpoints, and behavioral areas can be specified in a designed, atypical physical environment [3, 4].

3 Deployment Technology for Virtual Users Performing Autonomous Psychological Behaviors

This study looks at the technologies for deploying VUsers in a virtual place using the ideas of trigger spot, trigger viewpoint, and behavioral area. Figure 4 shows the algorithm for automatic placement of trigger spots, trigger viewpoints, and behavioral areas. The algorithm shows how to automatically calculate trigger spots, trigger viewpoints, and behavioral areas by computing the geometrical and topological information of designed spaces. In other words, ActoViz imports the geometries of atypical space into a list and classifies each face type by using their normal vector and linkage information. It also assigns appropriate behavioral information to each type and specifies the appropriate trigger spots and behavioral areas according to their types. Trigger viewpoints are specified by considering the visual openness and the position of a particular object [5].

Figure 3 shows the application of the algorithm in Fig. 2 to ActoViz. When one loads the atypical space designed in Rhino into ActoViz, it automatically classifies each face type as shown in Fig. 4 and calculates the places where psychological behavior can occur. The yellow and blue triangles in Fig. 4 show where trigger spots, trigger viewpoints, and behavioral areas are established. When the simulation in ActoViz is executed, VUsers move freely in the atypical space, and if they are located at this place, VUsers perform appropriate behaviors according to the characteristics of the VUser. Figure 4 shows the behavior of VUsers on ActoViz according to the specified trigger spots, trigger viewpoints, and behavioral areas.

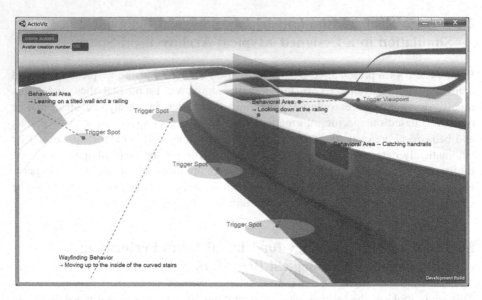

Fig. 2. Illustration of how to place trigger spots, trigger viewpoints, and behavioral areas in a designed, atypical building space [7].

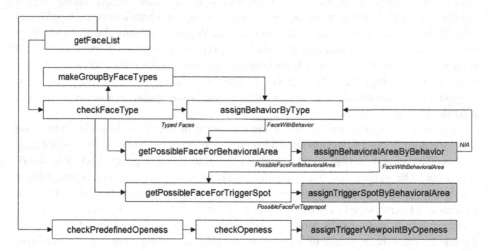

Fig. 3. The algorithm used to create trigger spots, trigger viewpoints, and behavioral areas in ActoViz.

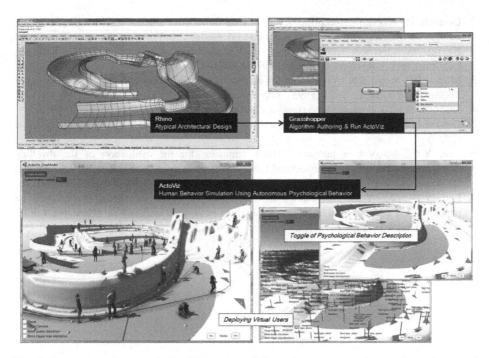

Fig. 4. Execution process of ActoViz and applying trigger spots, trigger viewpoints, and behavioral areas.

4   Conclusion and Discussion

This study proposed the developed expert system (ActoViz) based on the intelligent agents that engage in psychologically appropriate behaviors. This paper describes how to work with this idea in ActoViz systemically. The result of the study is to depict the technologies for deploying VUsers in a virtual place employing the ideas of trigger spot, trigger viewpoint, and behavioral area.

Through this study, we were able to realize VUsers' automated psychological behavior. However, in the future, it is necessary to review the system developed through the effectiveness examination for architects. In addition, it is necessary to develop technology and diversify behaviors to express advanced VUsers' actions.

Acknowledgement. This work was supported by the National Research Foundation of Korea (NRF) grant funded by the Korea government (MSIT) (NRF-2018R1A2B6005827).

References

1. Lee, Y.G., Park, C.H., Lim, D.H.: A study on the development of the user behavior simulation technology using a perceived action possibilities. J. Korea Multimed. Soc. **17**(11), 1335–1344 (2014)

2. Dourish, P.: Where the footprints lead: tracking down other roles for social navigation. In: Höök, K., Benyon, D., Munro, A.J. (eds.) Designing Information Spaces: The Social Navigation Approach. Computer Supported Cooperative Work, pp. 273–291. Springer, London (2003). https://doi.org/10.1007/978-1-4471-0035-5_12
3. Murase, H., Nayar, S.K.: Visual learning and recognition of 3-d objects from appearance. Int. J. Comput. Vis. 14(1), 5–24 (1995). https://doi.org/10.1007/BF01421486
4. Norman, D.A.: Affordances, conventions and design. Interactions 6(3), 38–43 (1999)
5. Gibson, J.J.: The Ecological Approach to Visual Perception. Houghton-Mifflin, Boston (1979)
6. Lee, Y.G.: ActoViz: a human behavior simulator for the evaluation of the dwelling performance of an atypical architectural space. In: Stephanidis, C. (ed.) HCII 2019. CCIS, vol. 1034, pp. 361–365. Springer, Cham (2019). https://doi.org/10.1007/978-3-030-23525-3_48
7. Lee, Y.L., Lee, Y.G.: Developing an autonomous behavior of virtual users based on psychological interpretation of human behavior to an atypical architectural shape. Int. J. ICT-Aided Archit. Civ. Eng. 6(1), 1–6 (2019)

Learning Technology

Visualization of Classification of Basic Level Schools in Mexico Based on Academic Performance and Infrastructure

Sergio V. Chapa-Vergara[1], Erika Hernández-Rubio[2],
Sergio D. Romero-García[1,2], and Amilcar Meneses-Viveros[1(✉)]

[1] Departamento de Computación, CINVESTAV-IPN, Mexico City, Mexico
{schapa,ameneses}@cs.cinvestav.mx
[2] Instituto Politécnico Nacional, SEPI-ESCOM, Mexico City, Mexico
ehernandezru@ipn.mx

Abstract. In Mexico, basic education schools can be classified as public and private. In Mexico the basic level of education consists of primary and secondary school. In Mexico there are government agencies such as INEGI and SEP (Ministry of Public Education), which are responsible for evaluating the academic performance of schools through knowledge exams or knowing the state of the infrastructure of school buildings. Measuring or determining the quality of a school is not a minor issue. Some authors suggest measuring the quality of a school based on models of program, comparison, dedication school, learner, absence, happiness and employment among others. Many of these models cannot be used in the context of Mexico or would be adapted. This paper presents a model based on quality indicators through its infrastructure and academic performance to obtain a classification of schools nationwide in Mexico.

Keywords: Basic level schools · Clustering · Data mining · Visualization

1 Introduction

In Mexico, basic education schools can be classified as public and private. According to INEGI (National Institute of Statistics and Geography), seven socioeconomic strata can be found in Mexico [8,9,14]. Public schools cover all regions, regardless of socioeconomic status. And private schools are only located in regions with medium, medium high and high socioeconomic strata. Knowing the quality level of a school is important for decision making [8,14].

In Mexico there are government agencies such as INEGI and SEP (Ministry of Public Education), which are responsible for evaluating the academic performance of schools through knowledge exams or knowing the state of the infrastructure of school buildings [9,10]. However, these data exist separately

© Springer Nature Switzerland AG 2020
C. Stephanidis and M. Antona (Eds.): HCII 2020, CCIS 1225, pp. 225–232, 2020.
https://doi.org/10.1007/978-3-030-50729-9_32

without making a correlation analysis of them. An analysis of this type would help to have indicators that allow measuring the quality of schools in a real way.

In Mexico the basic level of education consists of primary and secondary school. Public primaries can be 4 h a day or more than 4 h. In general, schools of 4 h per day are in areas with a high degree of marginalization. And schools of more than 4 h are given in so-called full-time schools (starting at 8AM and finish at 4PM). In public secondary school there are a group called Telesecundaria, a model for teaching with television support designed for rural areas with few infrastructure [5, 11].

Measuring or determining the quality of a school is not a minor issue [9]. The Organization for Economic Cooperation and Development (OECD) determines the level of education in a country through indicators such as the number of schools, results of tests to assess students' knowledge and conceptual elements (such as age, gender, place of birth, family income, and school grade) family, among others) [6]. Some authors suggest measuring the quality of a school based on models of school effectiveness [4], this models are ethic model, basic acquisition model, program model, comparison model, dedication school model, learner model, absence model, happiness model and employment model among others. Some works have build indicator Student Outcome based on school practices and contextual influences [10].

Many of these models cannot be used in the context of Mexico or would be adapted. For example, the conceptual elements of the OECD are taken from highly developed countries that contain migratory phenomena such as the reception of migrants and the difficulty of students to learn the official language of the country in which they are located, and in Mexico this conceptual element is not considered.

This paper presents a model based on quality indicators through its infrastructure and academic performance to obtain a classification of schools nationwide in Mexico. The students academic performance and school infrastructure was obtained from public information, this data bases are ENLACE and CEMABE. We extract, clean and transform this data into a datamart. Using datagrams it was possible to conclude that primary and secondary schools can be classified into three groups. Through clustering algorithms, we get the schools for each cluster. And then we get the association rule for each cluster. It is conclude that at the primary level the schools with the best performance were public and private ones in areas with few degree of marginalization, and the lowest were the public primary schools located in geographical areas with a high degree of marginalization. In secondary it was detected that the best schools are schools located in areas with few degree of marginalization and the lowest school were secondary schools in areas with high degree of marginalization and many of this are in the *telesecundaria* system. It's possible conclude the highest correlation between socioeconomic strata and academic performance of schools.

2   Related Work

Various works have been developed on the study of performance in education using data mining techniques. One of the indicators of educational quality efficiency is teacher performance. In [12] the authors design AI models for the evaluation of the performance of instructors at the university level. The system developed in [12] allows recommendations to improve teacher performance.

In this works [1, 7] the need arises to have models for educational evaluation of school performance. In [7] the author propose the use of data mining and genetic algorithms to do the evaluation in Mexico. In [1] a study of various classification techniques on different education indicators using data mining in Oman is made.

Other works have focused on the evaluation of LMS and e-learning systems on the web through data mining [3, 8, 13]. In [3] we seek to analyze the learning process of students and learn the methodology and usability of online courses. In [13] data mining is used to evaluate the contents of learning objects, the main idea is to use e-commerce approaches to improve interactivity with the contents of learning objects. In [8] the authors report a data mining model for analysis teaching and learning at the K-12 level.

In [2] it is sought to have an analysis of the various data of the educational system with the aim of finding patterns to predict student performance.

When reviewing the literature it is observed that there are different aspects that are evaluated: students, schools, teachers and IT systems. In addition the studies are carried out in very specific countries.

3   The Method

The public information was obtained from ENLACE test and CEMABE databases. The ENLACE test is an evaluation instrument that is applied in Mexico; It is standardized, objective, national in scope. The purpose of the ENLACE test is to provide, to researches, teachers and educational authorities, a valid, objective and reliable measure of current status of academic achievement of elementary school students.

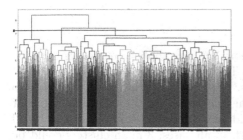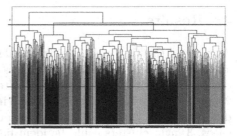

Fig. 1. Example of dendrogram for primary and secondary applied to a region of Mexico.

The CEMABE database is created by INEGI. The objective of CEMABE is to know statistically the educational system of Mexico through the geographical location of all educational establishments, to know the state of its infrastructure, equipment and school furniture, the registration of teaching, administrative and supervisory personnel.

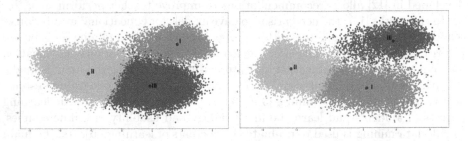

Fig. 2. K-means graphics for primary and secondary school.

The first step is to perform the process of extracting and cleaning the ENLACE and CEMABE databases. To work with this information, data cleaning algorithms must be considered, that is, processes that remove outliers so as not to alter the results. Then the datamart must be formed from the two databases. With the first version of the datamart we must reduce the dimensionality of the information, and this can be done by analyzing the main components. This step is important as it helps to have a smaller handling of the information without altering the final results.

Because of the type of information we are obtaining, in artificial intelligence, the classification of schools is an unsupervised learning problem. Therefore we must have procedures that help us to find the classification of schools. Then we must find the optimal number of clusters for this problem. Once we know this data, clustering algorithms can be used to obtain the groups we need. Finally we must to find the characteristics of the elements of each cluster to make the analysis to obtain relevant information.

4   Results

As part of the first step, the Tukey algorithm was applied to remove outliers. Then we proceed to union of data bases. The unions of ENLACE and CEMABE data base result in 400 attributes. After applying PCA we get a reduction to 25 principal variables. Then we applying the hierarchical cluster algorithm at different levels: national, by regions and by states, for example Fig. 1. In all cases, 3 main clusters could be identified. In all cases, 3 main clusters could be identified. Figure 1 shows the cut in two dendrograms and its possible to identify three hierarchical groups.

The next step the k-means algorithm was applied to obtain the three school groups for primary and secondary level. Figure 2 show the clusters for primary and secondary level. It's possible to observe the centroid.

Finally we employed the Apriori algorithm to get the association rules between components in every cluster. With this algorithm was possible to identify the type of clusters (I, II and III), Fig. 2. For primary, the clusters type I are schools with good academic performance and good infrastructure; schools in cluster II have a good performance but they still need to increase their infrastructure and schools of type III need attention to improve their performance and infrastructure. The characteristics of clusters for primary schools are presented in Table 1.

For secondary, the cluster type I are private schools, the clusters type II are public schools and schools in the cluster type III are public schools in the *Telesecundaria* system.

And the characteristics secondary schools clusters are presented in Table 2.

Table 1. Characteristics for primary school clusters

Cluster type I	Cluster type II	Cluster type III
Private schools are 99.2%	Public schools are 99.6%	Public schools are 85.7%
Mathematics performance is adequate in all grades	Mathematics performance is adequate in all grades	They have a high degree of marginalization
Mathematics performance for grades 2, 5 and 6 is above the national average	Performance in all subjects in all grades is above the national average	The average in mathematics in grades 5 and 6 is below the national average
The 97% in this group have internet access	The 84.6% in this group have internet access	The 85.6% in this group do not have internet access
The 71.3% in this group give internet access to their students	The 54% in this group don't have internet access to their students	The 92% in this group don't have internet access to their students
The 89.3% have computers for students	The 92.1% of schools do not have computers for students	The 58.6% of schools do not have computers for students
The 89.3% of schools do not belong to the national English program	The 70.2% of schools do not belong to the national English program	The 95.7% of schools do not belong to the national English program

Table 2. Characteristics for secondary school clusters

Cluster type 1	Cluster type 2	Cluster type 3
Private schools are 98.4%	Public schools are 61.3%	Public schools in *Telesecundaria* system are 93.2%
Spanish and civic and ethical training is above the national average	Mathematics is above the national average	The 71.4% of schools have a schedule less than the national average
The math average for grades 1 and 3 is above the national average	The math average for grades 1 and 2 is below the national average	The average in Spanish for grades 2 and 3, and the average in mathematics for first grade are below the national average
The 98.9% in this group have internet access	The 91.4% in this group have internet access	The 72.6% in this group do not have internet access
The 82.3% in this group give internet access to their students	The 64.8% in this group give internet access to their students	The 79% in this group don't have internet access to their students
The 82.3% have computers for students	The 67.6% of schools have computers for students	The 76.9% of schools have not computers for students
The 78.9% of schools do not belong to the national English program	The 77.6% of schools do not belong to the national English program	The 97.4% of schools do not belong to the national English program

5   Conclusions

The data for the analysis of this work were obtained from two different sources, ENLACE and CEMABE databases. The datamart is the union of this two sources. The algorithms PCA, hierarchical clustering, k-means and apriori were applied. The graphical representation of clusters helped in the process to determine the number of school groups. What is helpful in this unsupervised learning process.

By applying the PCA algorithm to reduce dimensionality and the use of the hierarchical algorithm, it can be determined that there are 3 main groups for primary and secondary nationally. This process was applied to different granularities in the data of primary and secondary schools that go to a) the entire Mexican Republic, b) regions of Mexico and c) states. In all cases it is observed that 3 can be considered as a good number of cut of the tree to obtain the groups of schools.

The k-means algorithm was used to obtain the three conjures. And finally, Apriori was used to know the common characteristics of each group of schools. Then we get that:

- For primary schools, type 1 schools are those public elementary schools that are located in areas with low economic development. Type 2 schools are public schools that are located in urban areas. Finally, type three schools are characterized in that 90% of the schools are private and that they are located in urban areas with a medium to high socioeconomic level.
- For secondary schools, type 1 schools are those secondary schools of telesecundaria type found in rural areas. Type 2 schools are public schools that are located in urban areas. Finally, type three schools are characterized in that 90% of the schools are private and that they are located in urban areas with a medium to high socioeconomic level.

We note that the most important infrastructure is the one that refers to internet access and having computers for students. Finally, it is observed that there is a very strong relationship between academic performance and the social stratum.

References

1. Almuniri, I., Said, A.M.: School's performance evaluation based on data mining. Int. J. Eng. Inf. Syst. **1**(9), 56–62 (2017)
2. Ayinde, A., Adetunji, A., Bello, M., Odeniyi, O.: Performance evaluation of Naive Bayes and decision stump algorithms in mining students' educational data. Int. J. Comput. Sci. Issues (IJCSI) **10**(4), 147 (2013)
3. Donnellan, D., Pahl, C.: Data mining technology for the evaluation of web-based teaching and learning systems. In: E-Learn: World Conference on E-Learning in Corporate, Government, Healthcare, and Higher Education, pp. 747–752. Association for the Advancement of Computing in Education (AACE) (2002)
4. Döş, İ.: Some model suggestions for measuring effective schools. Proc.-Soc. Behav. Sci. **116**, 1454–1458 (2014)
5. Durán, J.: The Mexican Telesecundaria: diversification, internationalization, change, and update. Open Learn.: J. Open Distance E-Learn. **16**(2), 169–177 (2001)
6. Organisation for Economic Co-operation and Development: La medición del aprendizaje de los alumnos: Mejores prácticas para evaluar el valor agregado de las escuelas. OECD Publishing (2011)
7. Galván, P.: Educational evaluation and prediction of school performance through data mining and genetic algorithms. In: 2016 Future Technologies Conference (FTC), pp.245–249. IEEE (2016)
8. Hung, J.-L., Hsu, Y.-C., Rice, K.: Integrating data mining in program evaluation of K-12 online education. J. Educ. Technol.Soc. **15**(3), 27–41 (2012)
9. Marchesi, Á.: Un sistema de indicadores de desigualdad educativa. Revista iberoamericana de educación **23**(1–21), 135–163 (2000)
10. Masters, G.N.: Measuring and rewarding school improvement (2012)

11. Mayo, J.K., McAnany, E.G., Klees, S.J.: The Mexican Telesecundaria: a cost-effectiveness analysis. Instr. Sci. **4**, 193–236 (1975). https://doi.org/10.1007/BF00053876
12. Ola, A., Pallaniappan, S.: A data mining model for evaluation of instructors' performance in higher institutions of learning using machine learning algorithms. Int. J. Concept. Comput. Inf. Technol. **1**(1), 17–22 (2013)
13. Pahl, C.: Data mining technology for the evaluation of learning content interaction. Int. J. E-Learn. **3**(4), 47–55 (2004)
14. Palomar Lever, J., Cienfuegos Martínez, Y.I., et al.: Pobreza y apoyo social: un estudio comparativo en tres niveles socioeconómicos (2007)

Case Study Course on the Development of Image and Text with Bronfenbrenner's Ecological Systems Theory

Miao-Hsien Chuang[1]([envelope]), Chin-Lung Chen[1], and Jui-Ping Ma[2]

[1] Department of Visual Communication Design, Ming Chi University of Technology, New Taipei City, Taiwan
joyceblog@gmail.com, lung@mail.mcut.edu.tw
[2] Center for Humanities and Arts Education, Kaohsiung Medical University, Kaohsiung, Taiwan
jpma@kmu.edu.tw

Abstract. In the internet age, people have become increasingly reliant on texting, videos, and emoticons to communicate, instead of talking, face-to-face interactions, and formal text writing. This has posed a problem because although many students, especially design students, upon graduation begin their professional career, a substantial number lack the ability to integrate at all in the workplace. Furthermore, students have become hesitant to and are even discouraged from obtaining advanced research degrees.In light of this, our research uses the "Case Study" course in the Department of Visual Communication Design that is held during the fourth year of undergraduate study as the experimental field. The research methods include conducting document analysis and innovative experimental teaching. This course is implemented in two stages: theoretical introduction and thematic text/graphics. The former provides students with an introductory concept of the theory, scope, methods, and applications of case studies while explaining the profound knowledge in simple terms. The latter uses Bronfenbrenner's ecosystem theory to plan three topics: microsystems (I wear therefore I am), the middle peripheral integration system (Embracing the stars), and the giant view system (Old objects with new stories). Using case studies and graphic displays, the aims are for students to show their concern for their families (e.g., their mother), for vulnerable groups, and for regional development or traditional culture. In addition, the revision of Bloom's taxonomy and implementation of PBL (preparation, implementation, publication, evaluation, and amendment) are adapted to explain the execution steps. Action Research will also be used in this study to collect researchers' reflection notes, students' self-assessments, learning outcomes, and feedback. Students are expected to execute professional and humanistic integration through the implementation of graphics and texts, cultivate communication, enhance systematic thinking and problem solving skills, and develop cross-domain learning skills, all of which can be practically applied once the students are in the workplace. The results of this research will then be shared with peers and thus contribute to education integration.

Keywords: Case study · Bronfenbrenner's ecological systems · Graphics and text · Design concern

© Springer Nature Switzerland AG 2020
C. Stephanidis and M. Antona (Eds.): HCII 2020, CCIS 1225, pp. 233–238, 2020.
https://doi.org/10.1007/978-3-030-50729-9_33

1 Research Background

With the emergence of the Internet and social media, which are generally replacing interpersonal communication, people have become accustomed to using simple text messages and stickers instead of face-to-face interaction and in-depth communication. The focus on images and neglect of formal text writing commonly occur in students and are particularly noticeable among design students. In addition to problems associated with professional knowledge and training, numerous students are faced with following four problems. (1) Design students are often immersed in drawing and computers, communications, and consumer electronics, in which images are prioritized and writing neglected, and these students engage in relatively few interpersonal interactions. (2) Although students have taken general education courses, the learning content and professional design topics have been rarely integrated. (3) Although most of the students at universities of science and technology have internship experience, they are often noted by supervisors to lack the independence, proactivity, expressiveness, and knowledge integration. (4) They are also unfamiliar with the research writing curriculum and research ability training. Overall, fourth-year students major in visual communication design were observed to require improvement and reinforcement in areas such as objective observation, record writing, appropriate communication, and analysis and knowledge integration, leading to their incompetence in final year projects, further studies, or entry into a business society in which project integration is emphasized.

2 Literature Review

2.1 Ecological Systems Theory, the Revision of Bloom's Taxonomy, and PBL

Ecological systems theory is a theory of human development research proposed by Bronfenbrenner in 1979. Development refers to a process in which an individual continuously perceives and responds to a changing environment. Bronfenbrenner asserted that understanding human development must go beyond merely directly observing the behavior of one or two people in the same place: It must examine multipersonal interaction systems in multiple environments and must consider other environments that can affect the research participants. Moreover, Bronfenbrenner claimed that the ecosystem is concentric with four-layered structure that extends outward. The innermost layer is called a microsystem, that most immediately and directly affect an individual's development, such as the influence of parents of one's family of origin. The second layer is called a mesosystem, which is further related to interconnections and relationships occurred in different environments, rather than just one environment, such as in home, school, or workplace socialization. The third layer is the exosystem, whereby uninvolved individuals are deeply affected by events that occur in other fields, such as campus learning environment and environments in which brothers and sisters in the family get along. Finally, the macrosystem encompasses the differences between cultures or subcultures, such as religious beliefs and social values (Bronfenbrenner 2010; translated by Tseng, Liu, & Chen).

Bloom (1956) proposed a cognitive domain educational goal taxonomy table, and the educational goal categories of cognitive domain were ranked at six levels from the simplest to the most complex and from concrete to abstract, namely, knowledge, comprehension, application, analysis, synthesis, and evaluation, with each level representing a mental function. In response to the evolution of educational theory, Anderson and Krathwohl (2001) published a revised version that included two dimensions: the knowledge dimension and the cognitive process dimension. The revised version separated knowledge levels into an independent dimension and subdivided this into factual knowledge, conceptual knowledge, procedural knowledge, and meta-cognitive Knowledge. Furthermore, the "comprehension" and "synthesis" in the old version were changed to "understand" and "create", respectively. In addition, Anderson and Krathwohl (2001) also compiled the knowledge dimension and cognitive process dimension into a two-way specification table (Anderson and Krathwohl 2001; Yeh and Lin 2003; Chen 2009) (shown in Table 1).

Table 1. Two-way specification table of the revision of Bloom's taxonomy

The knowledge dimension	The cognitive dimension			
	Remembering	Understanding	Applying	Analyzing
Factual knowledge	Listening	Summarizing	Classifying	Ordering
Conceptual knowledge	Describing	Interpreting	Experimenting	Explaining
Procedural knowledge	Tabulating	Predicting	Calculating	Differentiating
Meta-cognitive knowledge	Using appropriately	Executing	Constructing	Achieving

Source: Anderson and Krathwohl (2001)

Hsu (2001) defined project-based learning (PBL) as a construction-oriented learning method that provides students with highly complex and authentic thematic projects, allowing them to identify themes and design problems, develop action plans, collect information, perform problem solving, establish decision-making actions, complete inquiry processes, and present their final work. Piper is one of the PBL methods, describing five modes of project implementation, including preparation, implementation, presentation, evaluation, and revision. This study combined the revision of Bloom's taxonomy and PBL theory to develop a project implementation model suitable for this course.

2.2 Case Study

A case study is a scientific research method that uses techniques to develop a precise and in-depth understanding of a particular problem, to identify the problem and potential solutions. Case studies focus on the analysis of a particular matter instead of research on multiple individuals at one time (Chen 1995). Merriam (1988) stated that a case can be a person, an event, or an institution or unit used to examine a specific phenomenon. Stake (1995) considered a case to be a bounded system, which refers to a well-defined object rather than a general process. Scholars have listed the seven following characteristics of case studies, (Merriam 1988; Yin 2001, translated by Sheon; Lin 2000): particularistic, holistic, descriptive, interpretative, heuristic, inductive, and naturalistic generalization. Yin (2001, translated by Shang) noted that data collection contains three principles: the use of multiple sources of evidence, the establishment of a case study database, and the development of a chain of evidence; the six types of evidence included are documentation, archival records, interviews, direct observation, participant-observation, and physical artifacts.

2.3 Integration of Image and Text

Panofsky (1972) divided iconology into three levels to study fine art works and noted that the first level includes visually observable elements (object), the second level includes the imagery and message behind these visually observable elements (objects), and the third level includes the deep spiritual or cultural connotations behind the imagery and message conveyed by said elements. Rossiter and Percy (1980) proposed a dual loop theory, which they observed how the dual loop effect caused by graphical languages and verbal loops on advertising communication. According to this theory, consumers have both verbal and visual cognition responses when processing advertising information and memorize the information through decoding and encoding. Therefore, when consumers receive advertising information, the processing of verbal and visual information presents a complementary pattern, and the two types of information influence consumer decision-making. This study used interview and image combination methods to collect the opinions of targeted research participants for the extraction of concepts before creation.

3   Research Method

The research method of this study included literature analysis, innovative experimental teaching, and teaching effectiveness evaluation (i.e., teaching feedback, learning questionnaires, evaluation scale development, and expert evaluation). Literature analysis is in-depth reading and detailed analysis of related theories and consideration of how to utilize case study courses in taught for university design students, how to select and remove inappropriate contents, and how to translate these contents into related topics and applications. The teaching effectiveness evaluation was divided into three categories. (1) Teaching feedback: feedback on teaching materials for the theory of the three ecological-system layers, teaching reflection notes, and course satisfaction questionnaire. (2) Student learning outcomes: self-evaluation and peer evaluation. (3) Expert evaluation: Expert review, rating, and reliability testing.

4   Results and Discussion

This describes the ecological systems theory proposed by Urie Bronfenbrenner. Due to time limit for research, the theory's four layers were condensed to three layers by combining the second and third layers to form (1) the microsystem, (2) the mesosystem–exosystem, and (3) the macrosystem. The system extended outwards with the student as the central point and featured three themes, namely, "I Wear Therefore I am" (participant's mother or female family members), "Embracing the Stars" (the community, vulnerable groups, and patients with rare diseases), and "Old Objects with New Stories" (historical relics or culture), with the aim of invoking the concern of students toward families, communities, vulnerable groups, history, and cultures. Through the data collection, interviews, and work review, individuals reflect on their relationships with themselves and with others.

The simplified Bloom's two-way specification table combined with Piper of PBL (Hsu 2001) were developed into a syllabus, and a detailed implementation process was derived. (1) Conceptual knowledge: This describes the understanding and application of case study theory. (2) Procedural knowledge: This describes the implementation steps (e.g., listing, collection, analysis, and combination), that is, the implementation plan for a case study; case information collection, interviews with the case participants, and transcript compilation; analysis of the participant's characteristics; and the combination of keyword and symbol elements related to case characteristics. (3) Metacognitive knowledge: This describes the understanding, digestion, and graphic design output for tasks, which translated the symbolic concepts of graphics into visual images, constructed and arranged sketches as well as creating and publishing graphics, and evaluation.

5   Conclusions and Suggestions

This study used Bronfenbrenner's ecological systems theory and Bloom's two-way classification table to construct innovative teaching materials for a course on case studies designed for university design students, to establish implementation procedures for three-theme image–text implementation, and to collect learning outcomes and feedback questionnaires as references for the implementation and revision of the new semester's curriculum. Students are expected to have a basic understanding of course content through the introduction to case study theory. Moreover, the image–text project making can enable students to incorporate design-related knowledge with humanities and cultural knowledge they developed classes, thereby providing them with project management skills in workplace. The results of this study will also be shared with (vocational) high school teachers and designers in the design industry to obtain their opinions as a reference for future course planning, with the aim of sharing Taiwan's innovative teaching solutions and providing global scholars with cross-cultural analysis and references.

References

Anderson, L.W., Krathwohl, D.R.: A Taxonomy for Learning, Teaching, and Assessing. Longman, New York (2001)

Bloom, B.S.: Taxonomy of Educational Objectives: The Classification of Educational Goals. The Cognitive Domain. David McKay Co., Inc., New York (1956)

Bronfenbrenner, U.: The Ecology of Human Development: Experiments by Design and Nature. Harvard University Press, Cambridge (1979)

Bronfenbrenner, U.: The Ecology of Human Development: Experiments by Nature and Design. (Tseng, S.H., Liu, K., Chen, S.F. Trans.). Psychological Publishing, Taipei (2010)

Chen, F.H.: Newly revised theoretical connotation of Bloom's cognitive field goals and its application in history teaching. Hist. Educ. 15, 1–52 (2009)

Chen, Y.W.: Case study research. Dictionary of Library and Information Science (1995). http://terms.naer.edu.tw/detail/1681584/

Hsu, H.Y.: How to use internet to help children become research masters of? Web-based thematic learning and teaching innovation. Taiwan Educ. Rev. 607, 25–34 (2001)

Lin, P.H.: Case study and its application in educational research. In: Li-Wen (ed.) Qualitative Research Methods. National Chung Cheng University, Taipei (2000)

Merriam, S.B.: Case Study Research in Education. Jossey-Bass, Thousand Oaks (1988)

Panofsky, E.: Studies in Iconology: Humanistic Themes in the Art of the Renaissance. Harper & Row, New York (1972)

Rossiter, J.R., Percy, L.: Attitude change through visual imagery in advertising. J. Advert. 9(2), 10–16 (1980)

Stake, R.E.: The Art of Case Study Research. Sage, Thousand Oaks (1995)

Yeh, L.C., Lin, S.P.: Discussion on the revised edition of Bloom's cognitive educational goal classification. J. Educ. Res. 105, 94–106 (2003)

Yin, R.K.: Case study research: design and methods. (Shang, J.A. Trans.) (Original work published 1994). Hung-Chih, Taipei (2001)

Making Others' Efforts Tangible

– How Other Learners Affect Climate Fostering Long-Term Self-paced Learning in Virtual Environment

Shogo Imada[1], Naoko Hayashida[2](✉) ⓘ, Hideaki Kuzuoka[3] ⓘ,
Kenji Suzuki[1] ⓘ, and Mika Oki[1]

[1] University of Tsukuba, Tsukuba, Japan
[2] Fujitsu Laboratories Ltd., Kawasaki, Japan
hayashida.naoko@fujitsu.com
[3] The University of Tokyo, Tokyo, Japan

Abstract. For most learners, appropriate learning climates within spaces selected for self-study (e.g., libraries) are helpful in sustaining self-paced learning. To provide learners with appropriate self-study spaces, we have examined a virtual environment (VE) for self-paced English learning. To assess the influence of learning experience among other peer learners in a silent space, in this paper, we designed a VE in which others' efforts were made tangible by exaggerating their learning activities rather than the co-present peers themselves. The designed VE had no auditory communication capability. Over a seven-days-long experiment in a wild setting, we compared the designed VE and a VE with only a solo learner as a control condition. Participants in the co-present learning environment showed longer learning durations and higher learning gains than those in the solitary learning environment.

Keywords: Virtual reality · Intrinsic motivation · Self-paced learning

1 Introduction

For most learners, selecting appropriate learning environment is important for sustaining self-paced learning. Depending on learners' preferences, such environments vary from isolated spaces (e.g. a closed space in a library) to group study rooms (e.g. a room for a group fitness). Literatures show that social environment in a learning space, i.e., existence of other people, sometimes yield positive effects [14]. However, people in a same space sometimes negatively impact psychological safety. When the environment feels threatening, learners may pose challenging learning behaviors [3, 11]. To provide learners with appropriate self-study spaces, we have examined a virtual environment (VE) for self-paced English learning. To assess the influence of other learners being present in a VE, we have conducted exploratory studies. In this paper, to assess the positive influence of learning experiences among other peer learners in a silent space, we conducted a control study.

C. Stephanidis and M. Antona (Eds.): HCII 2020, CCIS 1225, pp. 239–247, 2020.
https://doi.org/10.1007/978-3-030-50729-9_34

2   Background

2.1   Issues with Online Learning and Effects of "Others"

The completion rate for most massive open online courses (MOOCs) was reported to be below 13% [10]. The increased use of computers as online learning tools has led to the creation of computer-based practice systems oriented towards self-study; however, persistent self-paced learning has not necessarily been achieved under the current online learning scenario.

The factors discriminating between online learners who complete their courses and dropouts were investigated in terms of both of learner factors and course/program factors [5, 7]. Regarding learner factors, Lee et al. showed that persistent students had higher levels of self-regulation skills [6]. To support learners' self-paced practices in line with the literature on self-regulated learning, user interfaces (UIs) for progress visualization have been studied [1].

Regarding course/program factors, interaction such as inter-student interaction has been discussed [7]. Self-determination theory (SDT) [4] explains that intrinsic motivation (the motivation to work hard on tasks for their own sake) can be promoted or thwarted according to the degree of fulfillment of the basic psychological needs of autonomy, competence, and relatedness. We think that how the climate of a learning environment fulfills the psychological need of relatedness including inter-student interaction is an important research factor that could lead to an online learning environment that fosters learners' challenging learning behaviors.

In a past quantitative study on articulating roles of psychological senses of community for online students, needs of stronger senses of community were indicated [12]. Moreover, the importance of a common identity in fostering a sense of community was shown rather than personal ties in online learning community [13]. In this study, we focus on the climate of a learning environment facilitated by common identity rather than personal inter-student communication.

2.2   Effects of "Peers in the Place"

Walton et al. showed that the activation or inhibition of goal pursuit can occur relatively strongly when people see their peers having minimal social links while tackling or completing a task [14]. In the setting of a real physical place in the context of phonetic language learning via videos, Lytle et al. highlighted the positive learning effect of having other children, mere peer learners present, as opposed to a tutor or a model learner [8]. These studies imply that the climate of a learning environment facilitated by co-present peer learners may increase humans' intrinsic motivation and in turn self-paced learning achievements.

2.3   State of the Art

Culbertson et al. showed that a 3D environment populated by both human- and computer-controlled characters has successfully created socially situated language learning experiences [2]. While social environment in a VE is expected to be an effective environment for distance learning, Meng-Yun et al. discussed that designers of VE classrooms should consider the tradeoff between learning experience and social interactivity [9]. For example, a VE full of friendly peers may be comfortable environment, but it may also hinder his/her challenging learning behaviors. In this study, we examined how a VE that creates a co-present learning experience among other peer learners without auditory communication capability positively affects the self-paced learning behaviors of a learner. We conducted a control study comparing two conditions—a solo learner condition as a control and an among-others condition for an investigation.

Our basic research question was:

RQ: How does a silent designed VE in which others' efforts were made tangible by exaggerating their learning activities positively affect learning climates and in turn learner's learning behaviors?

3   System

3.1   System Overview

This system was implemented in a web browser. Figure 1 (a) shows a bird-eye-perspective view of the entire hemispherical shaped world in the VE. When participants logged in to the VE, their avatar appeared at the center of the disk-shaped floor. White placard stands (standing objects) that had learning materials were set up, for a total of sixty. These were located along three lines having twenty of those for each. To start learning at each standing object, a learner moved around in the VE by controlling the avatar's location using a keyboard. Figure 1 (c) and (d) each display the versions of the VE that participants of a control group and an investigational group used.

After participants were close enough to a standing object, a question was asked. Each question asked for the meaning of an English word, and participants could answer from among four options. In the example shown in Fig. 1 (b), the four options were "habitat," "banquet," "evidence," and "education" written in Japanese characters located under a question for the word "evidence." In this figure, the location of each illustration is denoted with a gray square.

As shown in Fig. 1 (b), the viewpoint of the participants in the VE was always from a third-person perspective; thus, learners could always see the entirety of their own avatar's body from just behind the avatar.

The appearance of the avatar was common among all participants of both experimental groups, and the design was neutral with the aim of being non-reflective of any of the participant's demographic characteristics such as age and gender.

To avoid the participants in the investigational group accidentally logging in alone, the number of others was controlled by using non-player characters (NPSs); the numbers of NPCs were 5 at minimum and 10 at maximum.

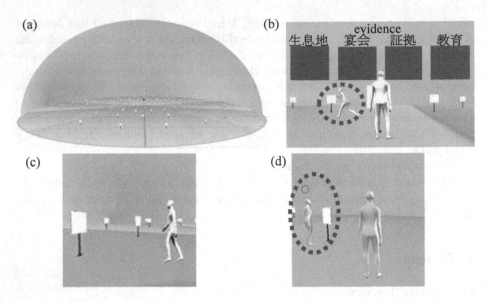

Fig. 1. VE overview.

3.2 Design for Making Other Learners' Efforts Tangible

To create an exaggerated learning experience in which the efforts of other learners are tangible, we designed a VE for an investigational group as follows. When a participant was tackling a question, other learners' learning activities, such as moving toward next question nearby, as shown in the red dotted line in Fig. 1 (b) were shared in the participant's spherical view. Moreover, an implicit notification was shared when a learner chose the right option in the form of a green circle displayed in the red dotted circle in Fig. 1 (d). We did not show any notification displaying learner's incompetence (i.e. when a learner chose an incorrect option). To avoid being too intrusive with other learners' learning activities, we also did not share any detailed learning progress of others.

4 Experiment

4.1 Participants

All participants confirmed prior to the experiment that they met participatory conditions such as whether they were a potential English learner motivated for some reason, had a pre-intermediate English skill level at least, and had a PC that could handle the VE during the experiment. Participants were assigned to one of the two conditions of subject design (i.e., the solo or among-others condition). Table 1 presents the characteristics of the two subsamples.

Table 1. Demographic characteristics of subsamples.

Characteristic	Solo (control)	Among-others (investigational)
N	12	12
Age		
Mean	23.08	21.00
Range	20–28	19–24
Gender	M 50%/F 50%	M 50%/F 50%

M = Male, F = Female

4.2   Materials

We designed a VE for each experimental condition, namely the solo condition as a control or the among-others condition for an investigation. In the solo condition, only the personal avatar was displayed in the VE, and the among-others condition had other learners' avatars in the VE.

The learning material set up for each condition was the same, 150 English words. These words were selected from a textbook for a pre-intermediate level learner in accordance with the participants' English skill level.

Each standing object in the VE was allocated with five English words at random from among the 150 English words.

4.3   Procedures

A pre-session and post-session were conducted at a laboratory. During the pre-session, procedures were explained, participants signed consent forms, they had a pre-test, and they learned how to use the VE. To avoid information of this experiment being openly available, particularly the difference between the two experimental conditions, to potential experiment participants, we asked all participants to not disclose experiment information during and after participating the experiment.

During the post-session, the participants had a post-test, filled out questionnaires, and were interviewed.

The pre-test and the post-test each consisted of the identical 150 English words that were included in the learning materials.

During the experiment session, the participants were allowed to access the VE anytime from anywhere using their own PC. The experiment participation was seven days during the indicated ten days.

On each day of participation in the experiment session, learners could move freely towards each standing object in the VE. The minimum required learning for each day of participation was five standing objects (twenty-five English words in total).

4.4   Measures

Psychological Responses to Learning Climates. To discuss RQ, particularly the psychological factors that are positively affected by learning climates, we asked how the learning experiences were in the VE as shown in Table 2.

Table 2. Questions on psychological responses in VE.

Question number	Question "Learning in the VE was:"
LE1_EJY	enjoyable
LE2_ATN	attention-getting
LE3_RLX	relaxing
LE4_ALN	aloneness-exerted

All items were measured on a six-point Likert-type scale ranging from one = "do not at all feel so" to six = "feel very much so."

Learning Behaviors. To estimate the differences between how people learned for each condition, we calculated the learning durations and the learning gain scores. The learning duration was calculated using only the time while a participant was learning at standing objects to avoid the influence of the time taken to move around the VE. The learning gain score was calculated as the percentage point that each participant gained from pre- to post-test.

4.5 Results

Statistical analyses were conducted using statistics software[1], considering a significance level of $p < 0.05$ (two-tailed). Each test effect size was estimated using r. We used nonparametric tests as statistical tests not only for questionnaire responses, but also for learning behaviors. This was because each data did not follow a normal distribution. To show data distributions, we used boxplots in Figs. 2 and 3. In these figures, an outlier was showed as a small circle.

Psychological Responses to Learning Climates. Figure 2 shows the psychological responses expressed by participants in the solo condition and the among-others condition. LE4_ALN had a significant difference between the two conditions in a Mann-Whitney test ($p = 0.01 < 0.05$, $Z = -2.51$, $r = 0.51$). The rest did not show significant differences.

Learning Behaviors. Figure 3 shows the learning durations and the learning gain scores by condition. Table 3 shows the statistical descriptions of those. Learning durations had significant differences between the two conditions in a Mann-Whitney test ($p = 0.02 < 0.05$, $Z = -2.37$, $r = 0.48$), and the learning gain scores also had significant differences between the two conditions in a Mann-Whitney test ($p = 0.01 < 0.05$, $Z = -2.49$, $r = 0.51$).

4.6 Discussion

In the case of both solo and among others in the VE, learners expressed almost the same positive psychological responses of enjoyment, attentiveness, and relaxation. The

---

[1] IBM SPSS Version 21.

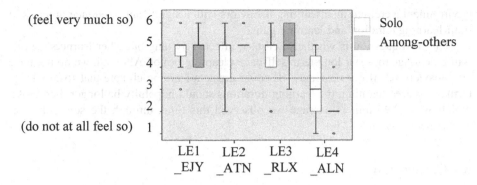

Fig. 2. Psychological responses by condition.

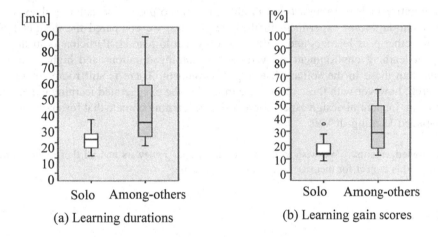

(a) Learning durations   (b) Learning gain scores

Fig. 3. Learning behaviors by condition.

Table 3. Statistical descriptions of learning behaviors.

Characteristic	Solo (control)	Among-others (investigational)
Learning durations [min]		
Mean	21.99	42.90
Median	22.04	33.11
Learning gain scores [%]		
Mean	17.33	32.22
Median	14.00	29.00

psychological responses while feeling alone were varied, particularly in the solo environment, and the existence of others in the VE mitigated this feeling of being alone with a significant difference. Moreover, participants in the co-present learning environment increased their learning behaviors with a significant difference in terms of both learning duration and learning gain.

The next question is whether a climate affected by tangible other learners' efforts will be enough to foster long-term self-paced learning or not. Although we do not have any answers yet, if our designed VE could create a learning climate that fosters long-term self-paced learning, the learning durations should hopefully be longer than those, which was 42.90 min in average we observed this time, through the seven days of experiment sessions.

5   Conclusion

To assess the positive influence of learning experiences among other peer learners in a silent space, we designed a silent VE in which others' efforts were made tangible by exaggerating their learning activities rather than the co-present peers themselves. Over the seven-days-long experiment in the wild setting, we compared the designed VE among other peer learners and a VE with only a solo learner. Participants in the co-present learning environment showed longer learning durations and higher learning gains than those in the solitary learning environment. There is still room for further research, however with these results, we think that the exaggerated learning experience can be an influential design aspect for a desirable learning climate that fosters long-term self-paced learning in VEs.

Acknowledgements.   We wish to thank the anonymous reviewers and all those who participated in this project for their useful comments and help.

References

1. Barria-Pineda, J., et al.: Concept-level knowledge visualization for supporting self-regulated learning. In: Proceedings of the 22nd International Conference on Intelligent User Interfaces, pp. 141–144. Limassol, Cyprus (2017). https://doi.org/10.1145/3030024.3038262
2. Culbertson, G., et al.: Social situational language learning through an online 3D game. In: Proceedings of the 2016 CHI Conference on Human Factors in Computing Systems, pp. 957–968. ACM, New York (2016). https://doi.org/10.1145/2858036.2858514
3. Dadds, M.: The feeling of thinking in professional self-study. Educ. Action Res. 1(2), 287–303 (1993)
4. Deci, E.L., Ryan, R.M.: The "What" and "Why" of goal pursuits: human needs and the self-determination of behavior. Psychol. Inq. 11(4), 227–268 (2000). https://doi.org/10.1207/S15327965PLI1104_01
5. Halawa, S., et al.: Dropout prediction in MOOCs using learner activity features. Proc. Second Eur. MOOC Stakehold. Summit. 37(1), 58–65 (2014)
6. Lee, Y., et al.: Discriminating factors between completers of and dropouts from online learning courses. Br. J. Educ. Technol. 44(2), 328–337 (2013)
7. Lee, Y., Choi, J.: A review of online course dropout research: implications for practice and future research. Educ. Tech. Res. Dev. 59(5), 593–618 (2011). https://doi.org/10.1007/s11423-010-9177-y

8. Lytle, S.R., et al.: Two are better than one: Infant language learning from video improves in the presence of peers. Proc. Natl. Acad. Sci. **115**(40), 9859–9866 (2018). https://doi.org/10.1073/pnas.1611621115

9. Meng-Yun, L., et al.: Virtual classmates: embodying historical learners messages as learning companions in a VR classroom through comment mapping. In: 2019 IEEE Conference on Virtual Reality and 3D User Interfaces (VR). IEEE, Osaka (2019)

10. Onah, D.F., et al.: Dropout rates of massive open online courses: behavioural patterns. In: Proceedings of EDULEARN 2014, pp. 5825–5834 (2014)

11. Porges, S.W.: The Polyvagal Theory: Neurophysiological Foundations of Emotions, Attachment, Communication, and Self-Regulation. W. W. Norton, New York (2011)

12. Rovai, A.P., et al.: School climate: sense of classroom and school communities in online and on-campus higher education courses. Q. Rev. Distance Educ. **6**, 4 (2005)

13. Sun, N., et al.: Where is community among online learners?: Identity, efficacy and personal ties. In: Proceedings of the Conference on Human Factors, CHI 2018, pp. 1–13. ACM Press, Montreal (2018). https://doi.org/10.1145/3173574.3173866

14. Walton, G.M., et al.: Mere belonging: the power of social connections. J. Pers. Social Psychol. **102**(3), 513 (2012)

Use of Force Simulator for Law Enforcement Handgun Qualification

Julie A. Kent[✉]

University of Central Florida, Orlando, FL 32816, USA
jakent@knights.ucf.edu

Abstract. Significant research has been done on the use of simulators for military weapons training from initial weapons handling to robust mission planning scenarios. In the United States, less has been done to validate the use of simulators in law enforcement training. A brief history of law enforcement training is provided followed by a discussion of some points on adult educational theory that may inform current law enforcement training practices. Following a review of other disciplines using simulators for training, current practices integrating simulators into law enforcement training is provided. A short selection of the different types of simulators available to law enforcement is presented as background to the presentation of a current study regarding the use of a weapons simulator for new law enforcement cadets.

The study evaluating the effectiveness of a use of force simulator in preparing new law enforcement cadets prior to their instruction on a live fire range, makes up the remainder of this paper. The study has a small sample size but supports the idea of training new recruits using a simulator prior to training at a live range. In the study one cohort of recruits had the opportunity to practice in a use of force simulator prior to range training. The results from this group were compared to results from previous cohorts who did not have the opportunity to train in the simulator. The results at the range support the benefits of training in the simulator for recruits.

Keywords: Law enforcement training · Use-of-force simulator · Handgun training

1 Simulation for Police Training

1.1 Training as a Reflection of Eras of Policing

Law enforcement officers are a part of everyday life in modern America. They have evolved with the changing of the country since colonial days. In the early years of the country laws were enforced and problems resolved by local groups of men, mostly interested in preserving the peace and the status quo. With the formation of professional police forces, these citizen groups evolved into an era called the political era. During this period very little training was supplied to police officers or recruits Todak [1]. In the early twentieth century, demands for police reform led to practices stemming from military procedures and more firmly rooted in the law as the source of police authority. Called the reform era, this period showed a marked increase in police

C. Stephanidis and M. Antona (Eds.): HCII 2020, CCIS 1225, pp. 248–255, 2020.
https://doi.org/10.1007/978-3-030-50729-9_35

training. Many of the tactics and procedures trained in this era were borrowed from the military [2]. These techniques promoted standardization and efficiency in police work based on the growing field of organizational theory [1]. These led to criticisms concerning the impersonal nature of police response. In the 1960s, racial tensions and the feelings of black citizens that they were unfairly treated by the police led to changes in police practices. Preoccupation with patrolling in high crime areas led to neglect of other services [3]. The advent of community policing reforms was to address some of these needs and bring the law enforcement officers back in contact with the law-abiding citizens needing protection.

The most recent era has been dubbed community policing emphasizing greater ties between the police force and the community. This era has been marked by increased attention to responding to problems that are not necessarily criminal acts. Paoline and Terrill [4] describe several approaches to community policing including focusing on quality of life issues that are a visible indicator of neighborhood decay, addressing underlying causes of specific problems and increasing interactions with citizens in the neighborhoods. This era also shows a marked increase in the use of technology for police activities. These initiatives included looking at crime statistics, locating crime hot spots, collating data to create intelligence related to crime and criminal activity and other forms of data driven activities [5]. Technology is of great benefit to policing, but training is required for responsible use of the technology.

With many different approaches used in different law enforcement agencies, there is no consensus on what constitutes good policing. Therefore, it is hard to agree on standards to determine if they are doing it well [1]. The responsibilities of the police force vary from municipality to municipality. Police draw their authority from the municipality and the legal system within which they operate. They have significant discretion in how they handle many public interactions. Often this discretion may be left to the individual officer [6].

As far back as 1986, Fyfe [7] writes police need to learn to manipulate events leading up to an encounter to reduce the likelihood that violence will occur. Officers are encouraged to learn more about the areas they patrol. Municipalities are encouraged to use data to determine locations that are most likely to require police support. Responding officers should take response time to analyze the information available to them and plan their approach to the encounter. Practice in a simulator with this type of planning and possible confrontation allows officers to try different options in a low risk environment.

1.2 Adult Learning Theories Supporting Training

The early part of the 20th century learning theory was dominated by behaviorists. One behaviorist theory from B. F. Skinner is known as operant conditioning. In this type of conditioning a stimulus results in a response, which is then reinforced in some manner [8]. An instructor asking a question is a stimulus to which a trainee responds, and the instructor praises the correct answer. For adults, the reinforcement may be the esteem of classmates or simply the opportunity to speak and hold attention. Behaviorist treat human learning as conditioning where people are programmed to respond to specific inputs.

Information processing theory treats human learning like a data repository where knowledge is linked to previous knowledge. In this theory additional processing that takes place with items in memory will serve to increase the ability to recall these items. Additional work with information will lead to better learning of that information [8].

In contrast to behaviorism, social cognitive theory emphasizes the importance of observation of others and of goal seeking behavior [9]. People act not simply in response to stimuli, but in response to their internal desires and goals. Learning is supported by the individual's desire to learn the material as opposed to the praise from others. People do not have to perform an action to learn from it but can learn from observing others. Bandura writes about reciprocal relations between personal thought, behavior, and the environment. The sense of accomplishment and self-efficacy can influence and individual to practice new behaviors [10].

1.3 Use of Simulation for Training

Simulation has long been used for various types of training. The game of chess is considered an early simulation of battlefield actions [11]. The modern military has proactively adopted simulation as a means of training and rehearsing battlefield actions [12]. Medicine has actively put simulation to use for physical patient care [13] and for coping with emotional impacts of medical interventions [14]. Additionally, professional and even amateur sports enthusiasts have taken up training with simulators as a way to improve athletic ability and provide more enjoyable practice. Police work may involve skills similar to the military in terms of tactics and weapons. It may include first aid and interventions with emotional content similar to the medical community and it may involve a certain amount of athleticism. The simulators in use in these professions may actively contribute to the development of simulation in the profession of policing.

Simulations allow the learner to become more actively involved in a situation. These may involve technology or may use role play and character actors to set up a scenario [15]. Clark [16] provides some guidelines for creating educational simulations. Better learning outcomes are achieved when initial goals are straight-forward, and complexity can be added with mastery. Explanatory feedback provided with the simulation also facilitates learning. This approach optimizes the pacing and the interfaces as appropriate for the learning task.

1.4 Training as a Reflection of Eras of Policing

Not all municipalities have access to simulators for use in training, but news articles and course descriptions indicate they are being adopted in many locations [17–19]. Driving simulators propagated, first among fire and rescue personnel, and then law enforcement. The initial adoption of these devices by fire and rescue was promoted by the high cost of accidents involving larger vehicles [20–22]. Departments may purchase or rent driving simulators to provide practice or training in conventional driving and emergency response. As simulators dropped in price, they were introduced into academy training. They are also being used to teach driving safety to other populations such as young adults or the elderly [23, 24]. The simulators can be used for basic driving practice, emergency driving, and pursuit driving. Different skills and attention to different details may be needed for different types of driving [25].

As departments adopt simulators, they may purchase both driving and use of force simulation [26]. Alternatively, law enforcement may repurpose military simulators especially when they are available at a reduced cost [27]. These may be useful for basic psychomotor training though they may not always be the best choice for decision making. Decisions to use force need to be made in the context of the situation. Therefore, training in use of force needs to be done in context. Thus, many Use of Force simulators focus on the scenario and availability of a wide variety of scenarios when marketing to law enforcement. However, these simulators may also be used for basic handgun qualification training and practice.

2   Use-of-Force Simulator for Initial Handgun Training

2.1   Simulator Practice Sessions

Valencia College of Criminal Justice Law Enforcement recruits go through two weeks of firearms range training towards the end of a 20-week law enforcement academy. Many of the recruits are accepted by local law enforcement services (Orange County Sheriff, Orlando Police Department, UCF Police Department and Seminole County Sheriff for the most part) prior to entering the academy or during their first weeks at the academy. These recruits obtain additional firearms instruction from their services prior to going to the range for training. Preservice recruits have been selected by a local law enforcement agency for eventual employment. This study focuses on recruits who are not preservice. These recruits are at a disadvantage when going to the range because they have not had the opportunity to obtain basic firearms instruction available to the others from their hiring agency.

The sessions were held on two consecutive Saturday mornings when the recruits were not otherwise engaged. The sessions were half hour blocks with three separate target arrangements in the simulator. In the first simulation recruits practice using a 6-pie plate target called "Plates of Steel" that is a generic scenario supplied by the equipment manufacturer. They shoot each plate going from left to right. The simulator reports the number of hits, misses, and the total time from the first shot to the last shot. A laser in the pistol tracks exactly where each shot hits. When all targets are down the operator replays the scene, so the shooter can check for shot placement. The instructor guides the recruit during the drill and shows how to improve accuracy based on information from the replay. Each recruit attempted the Plates of Steel two or three times at the start of each half hour session.

The second scenario is also supplied by the manufacturer and is called "Pepper Poppers". These targets feature a more human silhouette and the entire target collapses when hit. This scene uses all five screens starting from left to right. There are three targets on each screen and they get further away as the recruit progresses from left to right. Again, the operator replays the scene after each attempt allowing the recruit and instructor to view where shots hit and how to improve.

Finally, to culminate the practice sessions, the recruits ran through a Florida State qualification test in the simulator. This scene follows the steps of known Florida State test and was built by the Orange County Sheriff specifically for this simulator. In this scene, the recruits need to follow on screen instructions and each step is timed. The recruits noticed the time pressure and started to get a better sense of time intervals allowed for test. The scene has a single target which changes position during the test. At the end, the target is displayed on screen of the simulator and the location of each numbered shot is shown on the target. The overall qualification results with the number of hits and misses are also displayed. Again, the instructor helped interpret the results and provided feedback on how to improve.

No attempt was made to capture any scores during the simulator sessions. The primary hypothesis is that preservice cadets who use the simulator for training will do better at their qualification tests than previous cohorts who did not have the opportunity to use the simulator prior to range training. In this method, the simulator may serve as a type of scaffolding [15] allowing these recruits to attempt shooting with less risk than live fire. It also allows a low stakes opportunity to try different hand placement, eye movements, and body positioning. Finally, there may be emotional scaffolding of working one on one with an instructor without the added distractions of a group on a live range.

2.2   Results and Discussion

The state of Florida pistol qualification test for law enforcement [28] requires a passing score on two attempts in a row or on three out of six attempts. For the purpose of determining improvement based on the use of the simulator, the number of attempts required to successfully qualify was used as a metric. The number of attempts for the current group of preservice recruits is compared to the number of attempts required by preservice recruits from the previous two cohorts who did not have access to the simulator. Figure 1 shows the average number of attempts for the two groups. The number sitting above the median in each box plot is the total number of preservice recruits in each group.

The goal in using the simulator was to improve the ability of preservice recruits to qualify when they go to the range. As is evident recruits in the treatment group, passed in two attempts on average. By comparison the no treatment group required on average three attempts with several individuals requiring many more attempts. The differences in the means were compared using a t-test and found to be significant.

The results in this study are consistent with results found by Bennell, Jones and Corey [29] where simulator training was found to be of benefit for Canadian police recruits. A follow up longitudinal study showed that recruits first trained in the simulator did better on later requalification courses [30].

The current study is limited by the small sample size. This study focused on a simulator with a weapon having similar characteristics to the weapon the recruits will use on the qualification course. Results may be different if the simulator uses a weapon with a different shape or appearance from the weapon that will be used for qualification. While this study took place in Orlando Florida, there is no reason to believe the results would not generalize to other municipalities and training organizations.

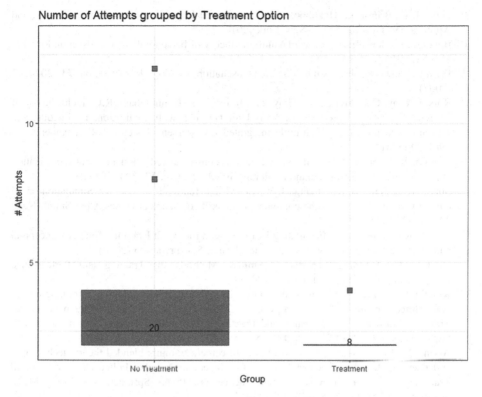

Number of Attempts grouped by Treatment Option

Fig. 1. The number of attempts required to qualify for preservice recruits in the treatment or no treatment groups. A minimum of two attempts is required to qualify.

References

1. Todak, N.: De-escalation in police-citizen encounters: a mixed methods study of a misunderstood policing strategy, vol. 79. ProQuest Information & Learning (2018)
2. Balko, R.: Rise of the Warrior Cop: The Militarization of America's Police Forces. PublicAffairs, New York (2013)
3. Hahn, H., Feagin, J.R.: Riot-precipitating police practices: attitudes in urban ghettos. Phylon **31**, 10 (1970)
4. Paoline, E.A., Terrill, W.: Police Culture: Adapting to the Strains of the Job. Carolina Academic Press, Durham (2014)
5. Gau, J.M.: Police Policy. Criminal Justice Policy (2019, manuscript submitted for publication)
6. Skolnick, J.H.: Justice Without Trial: Law Enforcement in Democratic Society. Quid Pro, LLC, Kindle (2013)
7. Fyfe, J.J.: The split-second syndrome and other determinants of police violence. In: Gibbs, J. J., Campbell, A. (eds.) Violent Transactions: The Limits of Personality, pp. 207–223. B. Blackwell, Oxford/New York (1986)
8. Schunk, D.H.: Learning Theories: An Educational Perspective. Pearson/Merrill/Prentice Hall, Upper Saddle River (2004)

9. Petty, R.E., Briñol, P.: Handbook of Implicit Social Cognition: Measurement, Theory, and Applications. Guilford Press, New York (2010)

10. Bandura, A.: Self-efficacy: toward a unifying theory of behavioral change. Psychol. Rev. **84**, 191–215 (1977)

11. Perkins, G.D.: Review: simulation in resuscitation training. Resuscitation **73**, 202–211 (2007)

12. Roberts-Gray, C., Clovis, E.R., Gray, T., Muller, T.H., Cunningham, R.F.: Field Survey of Current Practices and Problems in Army Unit Training, with Implications for Fielding and Training with the MILES (Multiple Integrated Engagement System), vol. 2, Appendixes, 1981-09 (1981)

13. Hebbar, K.B., et al.: A quality initiative: a system-wide reduction in serious medication events through targeted simulation training. Simul. Healthc. **13**, 324 (2018)

14. Shao, Y.N., Sun, H.M., Huang, J.W., Li, M.L., Huang, R.R., Li, N.: Simulation-based empathy training improves the communication skills of neonatal nurses. Clin. Simul. Nurs. **22**, 32–42 (2018)

15. Taylor, K., Marienau, C.: Facilitating Learning with the Adult Brain in Mind: A Conceptual and Practical Guide. Jossey-Bass, A Wiley Brand, San Francisco (2016)

16. Clark, R.C.: Building Expertise: Cognitive Methods for Training and Performance Improvement. Pfeiffer, San Francisco (2008)

17. Kratzig, G.P., Hudy, C.: From theory to practice: simulation technology as a training tool in law enforcement. In: Haberfeld, M., Clarke, C., Sheehan, D. (eds.) Police Organization and Training: Innovations in Research and Practice, pp. 65–79. Springer, New York (2012). https://doi.org/10.1007/978-1-4614-0745-4_5

18. Atkins, V., Norris, W.A.: Innovative law enforcement training: blended theory, technology, and research. In: Haberfeld, M., Clarke, C., Sheehan, D. (eds.) Police Organization and Training: Innovations in Research and Practice, pp. 45–63. Springer, New York (2012). https://doi.org/10.1007/978-1-4614-0745-4_4

19. Hickey, K.: Virtual training gets real: police, first responders use gaming technology and simulations for training and in the field, p. 16. 1105 Media, Inc. (2007)

20. Bui, D.P., et al.: Risk management of emergency service vehicle crashes in the United States fire service: process, outputs, and recommendations. BMC Public Health **17**, 885 (2017). https://doi.org/10.1186/s12889-017-4894-3

21. Donoughe, K., Whitestone, J., Gabler, H.C.: Analysis of firetruck crashes and associated firefighter injuries in the United States. Ann. Adv. Autom. Med. **56**, 69–76 (2012). Annual Scientific Conference

22. Burke, C.S., Salas, E., Kincaid, J.P.: Emergency vehicles that become accident statistics: understanding and limiting accidents involving emergency vehicles. Proc. Hum. Factors Ergon. Soc. Ann. Meet. **45**, 508–512 (2001)

23. Horrey, W.J., Lesch, M.F., Kramer, A.F., Melton, D.F.: Effects of a computer-based training module on drivers' willingness to engage in distracting activities (English). Hum. Factors **51**, 571–581 (2009)

24. Schreiner, M.B., Rothenberger, C.D., Sholtz, A.J.: Using brain research to drive college teaching: innovations in universal course design. J. Excell. Coll. Teach. **24**, 29 (2013)

25. Alpert, G.P., Lum, C.: Police Pursuit Driving. Policy and Research. Springer, New York (2014). https://doi.org/10.1007/978-1-4939-0712-0

26. O'Neill, L.: West Covina Simulators Train Police in Field Tactics: [Home Edition]. Los Angeles Times (pre-1997 Fulltext), Los Angeles, California, United States, p. 20 (1995)

27. Bumbak, A.R.: Dynamic Police Training. CRC Press, Boca Raton (2011)

28. Law Enforcement Officer Firearms Qualification Standard. Enforcement, F.D.o.L., USA (2013)

29. Bennell, C., Jones, N.J., Corey, S.: Does use-of-force simulation training in Canadian police agencies incorporate principles of effective training? Psychol. Public Policy Law **13**, 35–58 (2007)
30. Krätzig, G.P.: Pistol skill acquisition and retention: a 3-year longitudinal study. In: Interservice/Industry Training, Simulation, and Education Conference (I/ITSEC), Orlando, FL (2014)

Training Young Cybersecurity Talents – The Case of Estonia

Kaido Kikkas⬤ and Birgy Lorenz(✉)⬤

Tallinn University of Technology, Tallinn, Estonia
{Kaido.Kikkas,Birgy.lorenz}@taltech.ee

Abstract. The harsh reality of the online world today is that the survival of companies - and even countries - depends on the availability of adequate cybersecurity talent pool. Different countries run programs like CyberPatriot or the European Cyber Security Challenge to spark overall interest towards cybersecurity, but also to find those suitable for a cybersecurity career and start building it from an early age. Despite this, lack of qualified cybersecurity personnel is a growing problem as many educational facilities regard cybersecurity as a 'second-tier' field and keep targeting those who already come from IT background. As seen from Estonian experience, even if there is a growing trend of introducing robotics and programming at schools this is not sufficient. This paper describes the Estonian experience with the CyberOlympics/CyberSpike program from 2017–2019 and reflects on the lessons learned about talent building in cybersecurity. The data was collected using mixed methods, using both qualitative and quantitative analysis; it includes results from the competition, self-evaluation, external evaluation, discussion, and personal stories. The findings show the importance of building up security culture, the substantial impact from "bad/good neighborhoods" and role models as well as the importance of training (with a special notion on gamification), chances to test one's skills and also safely report bugs and security holes in online services. In addition, the results show that at the Capture the Flag (CTF) type of competitions, the younger age group outpaced their older peers, regardless of the latter having the advantages of the university and/or work experience.

Keywords: Cybersecurity · Competition · Gamification · Training · Hackers

1 Background

The cyber threat has started to develop at a rapid pace – the loss of data and money has reached the global impact level [3]. Comodo reports the rise of phishing, targeted attacks, and outbursts of malware in many spheres of society from business to the public sector to the military [4]. An organized crime assessment of De Bolle points out the rise of ransomware, crypto mining, exploits and more [6]. The cost of cybercrime rose by 72% in 2013–2018 [21].

Countries have tried to update their defenses by developing national strategies [10]; protecting the internet and different networking solutions to be also important as pointed out in International Frameworks on the Security of Network and Information

C. Stephanidis and M. Antona (Eds.): HCII 2020, CCIS 1225, pp. 256–263, 2020.
https://doi.org/10.1007/978-3-030-50729-9_36

Systems [14]. Concerns about the lack of cyber-aware common workers has made European Commission to take action by issuing "A new skills agenda for Europe" that focuses on IT and cybersecurity skills [12] as well as decreasing the gender gap [8], but the need to recruit more and more cybersecurity professionals can be seen all around the world [7, 19]. Therefore, those that focus less on technological measures and more on human resources will have the upper hand [11].

Skills that are needed for the future have likely been discussed from the beginning of humankind. Forbes lists skills that one needs to succeed in 2020 [13], OECD already discusses education and skills in 2030 [20], some others even try to figure out what will happen in 2050. However, instead of thinking about future skills and technology, we should be thinking about the culture and values that result in well-behaving, loyal and cyber-aware citizens [5, 15]. The old wisdom "Tell me who your friends are - I will tell you who you are" is still valid in both offline and online worlds, so staying clear from the online "bad neighborhoods" is increasingly important [17]. Also, the starting age matters - for IT/robotics/coding, the best time to begin could be at 8–11 and for cybersecurity, around 14 [2]. Using the common cybersecurity 'colored hats' - black (bad), white (good) and grey (in between), the future 'hat' of a curious newcomer largely depends on the culture and social learning [22].

There are many ways for finding these talents – besides the more established career models (universities, commercial training courses), there are extracurricular activities at various schools, and even correctional work with cyber offenders (offering them a legal alternative). As dedicated programs are still rare (due to the negative image of 'hackers' cultivated by media), the introduction is commonly made through programs like the Hour of Code – the more specific interest towards cybersecurity is usually sparked by personal experience in some 'grey' area. At the same time, there are several "Capture the Flag" - type talent competitions all over the world (CyberPatriot, European Cyber Security Challenge (ECSC)) to bring in skilled students in a variety of ways (as the organizers and levels vary a lot). For example, Estonia has held a cybersecurity competition for young talents called CyberSpike [1]. The CyberSpike consists of two rounds (4 h preliminary and final using defense (blue) and attack (red) skills through various challenges), a CyberCamp and other that is listed under the CyberOlympic program.

Cybersecurity education usually focuses on the development of IT professionals (having some administration, crypto, forensics, management, InfoSec, legal, etc. competencies). In the competitions, people are divided into blue (defenders) and the red (attackers) teams. For example, the CyberPatriot exercises measure the "blue team" technical IT administrator skills. CTFs are usually hacker community events that measure red, but sometimes also blue skills. Mäses (2018) has suggested a division of cyber skills into 4 categories: technical cybersecurity skills, technical skills (e.g. programming), non-technical cybersecurity skills (human-related skills, digital safety/awareness, social manipulation), and generic (presentation, reporting, leadership) skills [16, 18].

In cybersecurity, building a community with shared "white hat" values is crucial. From the 3-year working experience with cybersecurity talents aged 14–25, we have drawn some guidelines how to work with these people, how to help them navigate through several competitions and cyber camps to raise their ethical and technical competencies becoming a white hat hacker (a security specialist that everyone wants to hire). Therefore, our research questions are a. What are the mechanisms determining if one becomes a cyber-talent or not; b. What are the supporting structures needed to push the talents towards getting better?

2 Methods

The comparative data for this study has been collected over 3 years (2017–2019) from the participants (aged 14–24 divided into 14–20 (younger) and 21–24 (older) group) of the CyberSpike competition and CyberOlympic program (see Table 1). We used mixed methods and coding to detect patterns and attempted to outline possible solutions to help in bringing up cyber talents in Estonia. The data about competitions are mostly quantitative, while qualitative data was collected about self-assessment, discussion groups, and personal stories. We also used an external assessment to analyze participant progress, this data is also qualitative.

Table 1. Numbers of participants in CyberSpike, CyberCamp, and International competitions

Year	CyberSpike Preliminary (4 h online)	CyberSpikeMain (4 h, invited)	CyberCamp	International competitions
2017	104	28	16	10
2018	171	40	26	18
2019	145	39	24	24

The choice of skills focused upon are following the topics of the ECSC curriculum guidelines - Web hack, Malware analysis, Reverse engineering, Mobile security, Steganography, Database security, Secure code analysis and programming, Pentesting, Network security, Forensic analysis, Crypto, Smart Card and Hardware [9]. Cyber-Camp with its 2–3 sessions of training (one training session lasts usually for 2–3 days) also includes social manipulation techniques as well as general social topics such as ethics, cooperation, presentation, teamwork, mentoring, and leadership. The program also strives to connect the participants in the larger cybersecurity community that meets in different competitions, training events and meetups, and shares information in different online channels (e.g. Facebook, Slack). The goal is to bring together the older and younger generations of cybersecurity enthusiasts and experts to provide a safe discussion and learning ground. The program is supported by the Ministry of Defense and industry but is led by academics from Tallinn University of Technology.

The collected data includes the participants' results from CyberSpike 2017–2019 (competition data from both the preliminary round and main competition); the participants' reflection on their skills (self-assessment); evaluation matrix of ECSC topics and external analysis of the participants' performance and overall skills; other data: a. personal stories b. personal feedback on their career and development choices c. discussions involving participants and event organizers.

3 Results and Discussion

In the preliminary round, the exercises were easier than at the main competition, but they involved more participants (the main computer involved only the best). In 2017 and 2019, both defense and offense skills were included, in 2018 the focus was on the defense. The results show older participants having better "blue" (IT administrator; reflecting that they usually have some academic or practical background in the field) skills, while the younger participants were more keen on using "red" (offensive) skills – to the point that in 2018, this resulted in getting a lot of "minuses" lowering the total score for the younger group (usually, due to inadequate understanding of the provided tools, leading to disrupted services and servers) (see Fig. 1).

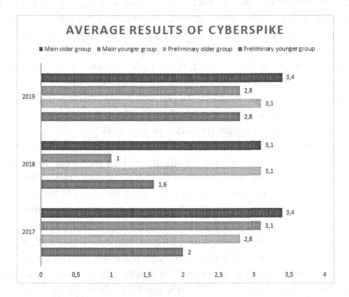

Fig. 1. Results of CyberSpike competition 2017–2019 for different age groups

The assessment results (combining self- and external assessment) suggest that the participants have a stronger background in web hacking, social manipulation, secure programming, operating system security, and presentation skills. The weaker side includes cryptography, penetration testing, malware analysis, network, and database security, mobile devices security, and steganography. The most common programming languages mentioned are Python, C#, Java, JavaScript, and PHP. The evaluators also report high levels of creativity in other fields like music, art, and entrepreneurship.

We note that the participants of the CyberCamps strived to understand and learn from their mistakes, also showing democratic principles in leadership and team building (e.g. offering a leading role to a rather young participant who was deemed capable). There were also cases where team building details (rules, punishments, etc.) took over and wasted the precious time meant to solve the actual problem – but the more specific and technical the task, the less likely this proved to be.

Also, while 25% of the participants were successful university students (reported their university average score to be over 4.5 out of 5), for another 25% university was not a priority in life at all. The remaining 50% were undecided whether they wanted to pursue an academic career or go straight working in the industry.

Some excerpts from the discussion and personal stories:

- **How one starts to become a hacker or grow interested in cybersecurity?** I had a slow computer and I wanted it to become more efficient. I wanted to win the game, so I changed the code. I found some scripts online and tested them, it was so easy so I started to learn about what else I can do. A friend showed me and then I was better than him. A teacher recommended to take part in the competition and then I was good at it. I did not have an internet connection so I hacked a neighbor's to use it;
- **How do you improve your skills?** I go online and search for CTFs or hacking exercises, I look for online communities. Sometimes I need to go to the Dark Web to get some data that I am interested in. I learn different programming languages and participate in online hacking courses. I develop something like a game or website or install services and then I try to hack it, so I play around inside my computer a lot. I help less knowledgeable people to solve their mistakes. I meet up with my friends, usually online and discuss things or try out new tools, discuss what they have heard or done (there are not so many friends though). I work in the IT – administrator or developer and I need it to become better at my work;
- **What is missing to support your goals to become better in cybersecurity?** More hacking events, gatherings, meeting with others like me. This hobby is not always understood by my parents and peers, so I have no one to discuss these things with. I have no role models. I don't know how I can use these skills for real work. I would like to do something good, but when I approach those whose webs I have hacked, then they get mad and will call the police on me - so I can't tell them, and it bothers me because other people get hurt because of the holes and data breaches in the system. There are not enough native language materials for beginners - schools also don't teach us anything that is needed for future life as teachers are incompetent. There are no girls in this field, but it's hard for them as they are not probably interested in going so deep – and they have already been left behind so much. Hacking is not considered to be a good thing, and girls want to be good. I need to update my skills in other fields as well - the example I don't like to interact with people and it can become a weakness. I need to understand more "blue" team skills as well, as I don't have anywhere to test and learn it; I need to go to study at university, as I need the diploma if I want to have a career in it.

The discussions suggest that to start as a cyber-talent, one simply needs a basic understanding of IT plus information retrieval, languages (Estonian and/or Russian, English), and overall out of box thinking. Teaching oneself different computer languages is highly beneficial, so are participating in different online pieces of training as well as solving exercises and puzzles.

For intermediate and advanced levels, the recommendations focused on four skillsets for both red and blue teams - application, operating system, network, and hardware, with cryptography included in all four. The role of leadership skills was also stressed.

Additionally, six typical roles for an efficient competition team were outlined:

- **Leader** – develops strategy, deals with planning and risk assessment. Other areas could include ethics, legislation, presentations, communication and social manipulation.
- **Defender** – IT administrator to set up and repair services and systems. A cross between system administrator (Linux/Windows/mobile) and network administrator (firewalls, architect). On novice level can only solve basic problems, the intermediate ones can create rules, and advanced ones develop structures. They should be able to detect and analyze problems, collect evidence and make decisions.
- **Scripter** – analyzes code and writes scripts for automation. Good secure programming skills are needed.
- **Pentester** – deals with vulnerabilities and attacks. Knows a lot about different operating systems (Windows, Linux, Mac, and Mobile) as well as web/database development as well as finding and exploiting vulnerabilities. Understands rootkits, reverse engineering, OSINT, and other related concepts.
- **Hardware specialist** – finds hardware vulnerabilities and has good skills in forensics – mobile, smart cards, Arduino, lock picking. Good skills in engineering, new devices development and "how stuff works"/"what is inside the device".
- **Crypto specialist** – creates ciphers and breaks them (algorithms, secure programming, open and secret key). Knowledge of logic, blockchain, steganography is beneficial.

Another thing that surfaced was the social aspect. Hacking has a tainted image in society (largely due to the image cultivated by media). There are limited ways to use 'white hat' skills, especially if one already has done something 'black' - even notifying about real security problems anonymously is difficult. Due to all this, many 'naturals' are left on their own. Learning by doing is also difficult, as suitable training facilities are scarce and experimenting with 'real things' may result in major (even if unintended) damage. To develop cyber skills safely and responsibly, a safe training environment and ethical guidance are needed. Young talents would also need role models explaining different paths in cybersecurity as well as possible career choices (one way to do it would be to include them to competitions). Right now in Estonia (and likely elsewhere), the older InfoSec community keeps on their own and the young ones run wild in different online channels. This means also that the ethics are not discussed, a harmful mindset can be developed, and when it comes to a future career, it would often be planned outside Europe (perpetuating the talent drain from the EU).

Hacker community and CTFs are good for developing red team skills. There are red team courses targeting pentesters which are usually not accessible for the youth. Younger participants ask for these types of lessons to feel more empowered as the results are immediately visible - service is down, access is granted, etc. Conversely, participating in official competitions and academic or vocational courses improves "blue" team skills that are valued in the labor market - security IT administrator skills, InfoSec, etc. At the same time, as the results do not give immediate feedback, they tend to be not the traits that 14-year-old beginner talent would want to acquire. Not that many "blue" team materials available for self-study that suit younger people due to the language and terminology used, but also a high level of previous knowledge assumed (e.g. about large networks). And while the social skills as a whole can be deemed as adequate for the competition context, they do not always translate well into the workplace (reporting to superiors, training employees), as the mindsets are often too different (i.e. the skills work only if everyone is technically on the same level).

Suggestions:

- support talent competitions, training camps, and interaction with experts and companies:
  - find ways to test skills against academic standards and explain what is expected from the competitions and how it translates to real life;
  - help develop both technical and nontechnical skills that contribute to success in later life;
  - build a community for young talents, but include experts as well
- bring talents to use their skills for good: test skills in competitions, develop educational content, organize events for others, give speeches, provide supervised pentesting services (e.g. Hacker One: Bounty Bug service in US or Trace Lab, that provides a service to look up missing persons). Teaching "white" hacker ways and ethics are important to properly direct the young talents and help them to make ethical choices.
- develop an anonymous system where one can report unsecured systems without revealing his/her identity.

4 Conclusion

The career model of old – go to school, get a diploma, get training and be an expert – is largely not valid in today's cybersecurity. One can become an expert at the age of seven, by hacking an Xbox. Young talents have a lot of time in their hands and the world is full of insecure systems. Therefore, it is crucial to building up security culture for youth, complete with competitions, training, ethics, and community support. At the same time, while both hacker community skills and academic knowledge are useful, they are different – and these differences must be identified and explained. And finally, to properly guide the new generation, a code of ethics should be formulated (in fact, several historical models can be built upon).

References

1. About the project: Cyber olympic program in Estonia using Whirlpool method (2018). Cyber Olympia website. https://sites.google.com/view/kyberolympia/eng/about-the-project
2. Antropoloogia: Tuleviku tegija teekond startup ökosüsteemi (2018). http://www.antropoloogia.ee/uuringud
3. Cambridge Centre for Risk Studies: Global risk outlook for 2018; Cambridge Centre for Risk Studies, University of Cambridge (2018). https://www.jbs.cam.ac.uk/fileadmin/user_upload/research/centres/risk/downloads/crs-lloyds-world-cities_2018-index.pdf

4. Comodo Security: Cybersecurity 2018/Global threat report Q3 2018 Edition (2018). https://www.comodo.com/public/report/communications.php
5. Da Veiga, A., Eloff, J.H.: A framework and assessment instrument for information security culture. Comput. Secur. **29**(2), 196–207 (2010)
6. De Bolle, C.: Internet organised crime threat assessment 2018, Europol (2018). https://www.europol.europa.eu/internet-organised-crime-threat-assessment-2018
7. De Zan, T.: Mind the gap: the cyber security skills shortage and public policy interventions. University of Oxford/GCSEC (2019). https://gcsec.org/wp-content/uploads/2019/02/cyber-ebook-definitivo.pdf
8. Digital Single Market: Increase in the gender gap in the digital sector - Study on Women in the Digital Age (2018). https://ec.europa.eu/digital-single-market/en/news/increase-gender-gap-digital-sector-study-women-digital-age
9. ECSC: Cyber security curriculum for European cyber security challenge, ENISA project restricted website/database (2017)
10. ENISA: An evaluation framework for cyber security strategies (2014). https://www.enisa.europa.eu/publications/an-evaluation-framework-for-cyber-security-strategies
11. Estonian Ministry of Economic Affairs and Communications: Estonian cybersecurity strategy (2019). https://www.mkm.ee/sites/default/files/kuberturvalisuse_strateegia_2019_vv-s_kinnitatud.docx
12. European Commission: A new skills agenda for Europe (2016). https://eur-lex.europa.eu/legal-content/EN/TXT/?uri=CELEX:52016DC0381
13. Forbes: The skills you need to succeed in 2020 (2018). https://www.forbes.com/sites/ellevate/2018/08/06/the-skills-you-need-to-succeed-in-2020/
14. International Frameworks on the Security of Network and Information Systems Article 7: Measures for a high common level of security of network and information systems across the Union (2016). https://eur-lex.europa.eu/legal-content/EN/TXT/?uri=uriserv:OJ.L_.2016.194.01.0001.01.ENG&toc=OJ:L:2016:194:TOC
15. Karie, N.M., Karume, S.M.: Digital forensic readiness in organizations: issues and challenges. J. Digit. Forensics Secur. Law **12**(4), 5 (2017)
16. Landwher, C.: A pedagogic cybersecurity framework (2018). http://peterswire.net/wp-content/uploads/Pedagogic-cybersecurity-framework.pdf
17. Moura, G.C.: Internet bad neighborhoods (No. 12). Giovane Cesar Moreira Moura (2013)
18. Mäses, S., Randmann, L., Maennel, O., Lorenz, B.: Stenmap: framework for evaluating cybersecurity-related skills based on computer simulations. In: Zaphiris, P., Ioannou, A. (eds.) LCT 2018. LNCS, vol. 10925, pp. 492–504. Springer, Cham (2018). https://doi.org/10.1007/978-3-319-91152-6_38
19. OECD: Computers and the future of skill demand (2017). http://www.oecd.org/publications/computers-and-the-future-of-skill-demand-9789264284395-en.htm
20. OECD: The future of education and skills, education 2030 (2018). http://www.oecd.org/education/2030/E2030%20Position%20Paper%20(05.04.2018).pdf
21. Accenture/Ponemon Institute: Cost of cybercrime study (2019). https://www.accenture.com/_acnmedia/pdf-96/accenture-2019-cost-of-cybercrime-study-final.pdf
22. Xu, Z., Hu, Q., Zhang, C.: Why computer talents become computer hackers. Commun. ACM, **56**(4), 64–74 (2013). http://www.yildiz.edu.tr/~aktas/courses/CE-0112822/08-04-3-1.pdf. Author F.: Article title. Journal 2(5), 99–110 (2016)

A Framework to Analyze Comments for Educational Apps on Google Play Store

Atharva Kimbahune[1]([✉]), Niharika Srivastav[1],
and Snehal Kimbahune[2]

[1] Ramrao Adik Institute of Technology, Nerul,
Navi Mumbai 400706, MH, India
atharva.ssk@gmail.com, niharika.belle@gmail.com
[2] Nagpur University, Nagpur 440033, MH, India
snehal.kimbahune@gmail.com

Abstract. School going students are often juggling between their studies and their parents' expectations to perform well, often leading to educational stress. After a quick survey of 10th Grade students in India, it was found that difficulty in understanding mathematics is one of the leading causes of stress. To moderate such stress and help towards making mathematics a joyful experience, ReviseOnTheGo, a suite of mobile apps were developed. These applications were published to the Google Play Store and there are about 30000+ downloads in total to date. A lot of feedback through 484 ratings, about 100+ ratings with comments were received. Young students express their feedbacks differently, for instance, their ratings and comments may not be aligned. These comments and ratings are the only interface between the developer and the students, hence they are crucial for the fine-tuning of User Interface, Information Architecture, and its contents. There is a lack of analytics frameworks which differentiate between the choice of words and their intended meaning of these young students. The developed framework attempts to bridge this gap by performing sentiment analysis based on parameters such as discrepancy between the rating and tone of the comment, the student's gender, feedback persona, use of slang, number of words used and grammatical errors. The framework provides a better view by objectively looking at these parameters and unequivocally classifying the emotional response.

Keywords: Educational stress · Analytics frameworks · Feedback

1 Introduction

Educational stress is one of the leading issues that students face. Students are burdened by studies and expectations to perform well in their examinations. After a quick short survey, it was found that the common source of the stress is mathematics and its formulas [1]. At the time of examination, students see the question, interpret the steps required to solve it and then start solving the question. The problem arises when the student has to recollect the formulas to use and all the intricacies of the formula. So, developed few mobile applications under the name ReviseOnTheGo to reduce the stress for these students [11, 12]. These applications are basically audio-visual formula

© Springer Nature Switzerland AG 2020
C. Stephanidis and M. Antona (Eds.): HCII 2020, CCIS 1225, pp. 264–268, 2020.
https://doi.org/10.1007/978-3-030-50729-9_37

based revision applications. The formulas are displayed and a recorded voice can be played which reads the formulas with a very short description of the terms of the formula. There were about 30000+ total downloads on the Google Play Store, many more via popular offline sharing applications and about 100+ comments. However, the feedback provided by the students who have actually used these applications, have very positive, positive, and negative and a neutral nature [2]. Figure 1 is a representation for comments like: "Loved it very helpful This app is needed for my neighbour because of weakness in algebra so thanks atharva kimbhaune", "Very very useful for us to get good mks by revising all the steps", help us realize that these applications have been actually used by students and the students have indeed benefited from these applications.

1	Name	App	Comment	Rating	Sex	Dicripency comment .T vs rating (y/n)	No of words	spelling mistakes	Punctuation mistakes	Feedback normaliz ed with rating	Feedback aspect 1 persona	Slang
2	Rohan Arron		Its good Thanks for the efforts put in by you people for this concept but there are spelling mistakes.I hope you see to it .(In geometry as well as algebra	4	M	N	31	0	1	positive	corrective	n
3	Dattu Khakale		Useful app Very useful app for me	4	M	N	7	0	1	very positive	appreciative	n
4	Rohit Singh		It is nce Awesome	1	M	Y	4	1	1	very positive	appreciative	n
5	Ajay Dadilwar		Interesting	2	M	N	1	0	0	positive	appreciative	n

Fig. 1. Sample of feedback received on ReviseOnTheGo applications

It helped us understand and to conclude decisively that the students feel less stressed and the applications have helped them to score better marks in their examinations. There is a plethora of education related applications on the Google Play Store which generate a huge data amount of data through feedback. The developers are always working towards improving their applications. So the question arises, can process of understanding this large feedback be automated through sentiment analysis? [4]. The Google Play Console offers some preliminary insights but fails to provide a better understanding of the emotional response of the user [6]. There is a lack of analytics frameworks which differentiate between the choice of words and their intended meaning of these young students. Generic sentiment analysis frameworks such as TextBlob, LingPipe and GATE to name a few, exist which might help us get some basic idea of the emotional response of the user. However, none of these frameworks are specialized towards the students' feedback. The proposed sentiment analysis framework aims to better understand the feedback received on the Educational Applications on the Google Play Store [12].

2 Methods

This framework uses the dataset generated by extracting the feedback from all the ReviseonTheGo Applications published on the Google Play Store [1, 12]. The dataset contains the feedback as ratings and comments. We find that out of the total feedback, only about 26% users wrote comments, among them about 10% users were female and the reset were male, about 6% users had discrepancies between the rating and the comment and about 12% used slang words in the comments. Considering these statistics, the data is first classified into six main categories on the basis of the gender of the user, rating [3], comment, number of words in the comments, number of spelling mistakes, use of slang words, feedback normalized with the comment and discrepancy between rating and the comment [3, 4] as described in Fig. 2. Records 3 and 4 in Fig. 1 show the presence of discrepancy [3, 7] between the meaning of the comment and the rating provided. Hence, the intended meaning has to be understood as it cannot be determined due this issue.

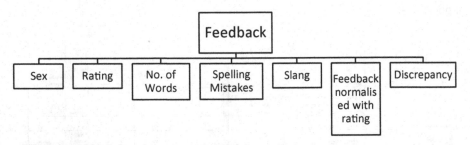

Fig. 2. Categorization of data

This categorization was done manually as the users include words from regional languages, presence of slang and discrepancy, which cannot be understood by the machine learning algorithms. As shown in Fig. 3, the feedback normalized with rating is subcategorized as Very Positive, Positive, Neutral and Negative individually [2]. This data is stored as the dataset in the csv format.

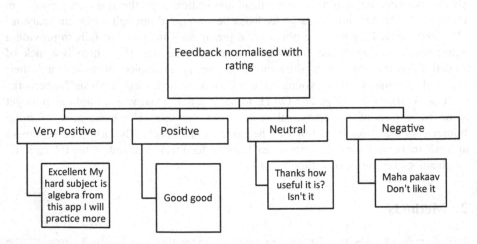

Fig. 3. Categorization of feedback normalized with the corresponding rating

Preprocessing of the data is done in the initial step. Blank data, incomplete data is removed and the data is split into training set and test set (80:20) as shown in Fig. 4. After preprocessing the data, 98 records are present in the dataset. In the next step, this dataset is fed into a Neural Network Classifier. The neural network is designed using the scikit-learn machine learning library. Since the dataset is labelled, supervised learning is used. The system was trained with respect to gender of the user, rating [3], comment, number of words in the comments, number of spelling mistakes, use of slang words, feedback normalized with the comment and discrepancy, as shown in Fig. 5. A total of 98 records were analyzed.

Fig. 4. Sample of processed dataset

```
#Classifier Training
#'lbfgs', 'sgd', 'adam'
clf = MLPClassifier(solver='adam', alpha = 1e-5, hidden_layer_sizes=(50,50,50,50),
random_state=1, max_iter=5000 )
clf.fit(train_input,train_output)
print("no of outputs ", clf.n_outputs_)
print("test acc", clf.score(test_input,test_output))
print("train acc", clf.score(train_input,train_output))
```

Fig. 5. Training the neural network classifier

3   Results and Discussion

In this project, a sentiment analysis was done manually and processing of feedback is carried out with the aim of creating a novel prototype sentiment analysis framework. The Neural Network generates a model after the classification is performed. The model is then tested using the test data. As compared to other frameworks such as Textblob, LingPipe and GATE, our framework is not only specialized for the feedback of educational applications but also provides high accuracy of 93.5%.

The framework can be used to gain better insights into the feedback of other educational applications [4]. Developers can gain a better understanding of the user's actual experience of using the applications rather than simply interpreting the comments and ratings to improve the User Interface, Information Architecture and the application's contents and so on, to provide a better experience [5].

4   Conclusion

The aim of this project was to create a prototype framework pertaining to the feedback received on relevant educational applications on the Google Play Store with high accuracy [4]. The feedback dataset was input into a classification neural network which generated a model. This model can be used to perform the sentiment analysis for gaining better insights on the feedback [4]. We used 98 records present in the dataset to train the model. In the future, feedback from multiple educational applications can be used to increase the scope of the results.

References

1. Kimbahune, A., Kimbahune, S., Kimbahune, S.: ReviseOnTheGo – immersive mobile applications for accelerated mathematics learning. In: Thampi, S.M., Krishnan, S., Corchado Rodriguez, J., Das, S., Wozniak, M., Al-Jumeily, D. (eds.) SIRS 2017. AISC, vol. 678, pp. 383–389. Springer, Cham (2018). https://doi.org/10.1007/978-3-319-67934-1_34
2. Handani, S., Saputra, D., Hasirun, Arino, R., Ramadhan, G.: Sentiment analysis for Go-Jek on Google Play Store. In: IOP Conference Series: Journal of Physics: Conference Series, vol. 1196, p. 012032 (2019)
3. Islam, M.R.: Numeric rating of apps on Google Play Store by sentiment analysis on user reviews. In: International Conference on Electrical Engineering and Information & Communication Technology (ICEEICT) (2014)
4. Bin, F., Jialiu, L., Christos, F., Jason, H., Sadeh, N.: Why people hate your app—making sense of user feedback in a mobile app store. In: KDD 2013, Chicago, Illinois, USA, 11–14 August 2013, 978-1-4503-2174-7/13/08. ACM (2013)
5. McIlroy, S., Shang, W., Ali, N., Hussan, A.: Is it worth responding to reviews? A case study of the top free apps in the Google Play Store. IEEE Softw. 34(3) (2017)
6. Hassan, S., Tantithamthavorn, C., Bezemer, C., et al.: Studying the dialogue between users and developers of free apps in the Google Play Store. Empir. Softw. Eng. 23, 1275–1312 (2018). https://doi.org/10.1007/s10664-017-9538-9
7. Aralikatte, R., Sridhara, G., Gantayat, N., Mani, S.: Fault in yours tars: an analysis of android app reviews (2018). arXiv:1708.04968v2 [cs.LG]. Accessed 11 Aug 2018
8. https://timesofindia.indiatimes.com/city/thane/18-yr-old-comes-up-with-app-for-last-minute-SSC-revision/articleshow/51664433.cms
9. Rizk, N.M., Ebada, A., Nasr, E.S.: Investigating mobile applications' requirements evolution through sentiment analysis of users' reviews. In: 2015 11th International Computer Engineering Conference (ICENCO), Cairo, pp. 123–130 (2015)
10. https://www.youtube.com/watch?v=NojYPeMifWk
11. https://www.youtube.com/watch?v=iUV2UitQ3WQ
12. https://play.google.com/store/apps/developer?id=Atharva+Kimbahune

Implementation of Computational Thinking in School Curriculums Across Asia

Kasper Kristensen[✉]

University of Southern Denmark (SDU), Odense, Denmark
kakr@mmmi.sdu.dk

Abstract. Computational Thinking (CT) has seen a tremendous rise within the educational sector. Being adopted into the curriculums for secondary and primary schools across the globe. This paper covers early finds from an initial literature review, aimed at a larger comparative study between Europe and Asia concerning the pedagogy of CT. A survey mapping the current approach to Information and Communication Technology (ICT) in the East Asian region. The primary focus is on the countries' current and future implementation of CT in primary and secondary education. Interestingly, a similar rate of adoption can be found also in Europa [1]. Moreover, this paper analyzes the complexities inherent in attempting a characterization and comparison of the CT approach of different countries, starting from the lack of a universally accepted definition for CT, including an uneven distribution of articles on the topic. Our main contribution is to propose an extended set of categories to support a critical comparison.

Keywords: Computational thinking · Pedagogy

1 Introduction

Since the conception of the personal computer, its potential to transform education has been widely recognized. Not merely as a method to acquire and assimilate new knowledge, but as a tool to apply, use and transform what we learn. Indeed, the near-universal application, and therefore, the appeal of the personal computer was envisioned to serve as a motivator for learning [2]. Since those early years, the influence and importance of computers and ICT have increased dramatically. In recent years, it has become apparent computers will continue to transform and alter society, as such technology cannot be limited as an aid or facilitator for learning but needs to be an integral part of what we learn, a domain of its own [3].

CT has seen a rapid and widespread adoption internationally, as an element of compulsory school subjects central around ICT and computer science. While most countries agree on the urgency of teaching CT as a 21st-century skill [3], the implementation strategy and specific subject matter vary. Some choose to omit the term to improve the longevity of official legislation. Making a comparison between countries is difficult, but no less relevant since many countries share the same goals and face similar problems in this transition. This paper is part of a larger study, aiming at identifying and compare relevant countries in the East Asian region, to offer better support to the

© Springer Nature Switzerland AG 2020
C. Stephanidis and M. Antona (Eds.): HCII 2020, CCIS 1225, pp. 269–276, 2020.
https://doi.org/10.1007/978-3-030-50729-9_38

current ongoing work towards implementing CT into the curriculums in Danish elementary education. The first part of this larger study requires a survey on the current state of implementation across the region, and to identify countries with similar characteristics as Denmark.

In this context, this paper aims at defining the CT approach of entire countries and analyzing the development and integration of CT, ICT and digital literacy, focusing on new legislation and changes to school curriculums, and core development in the field in East Asia.

This paper is based on data from a literature review, focusing on papers related to CT for primary and secondary education. Here we will follow the framework used by Bocconi et al. [1] for European countries. However, we will also identify limitations of the Bocconi framework, and define an extended set of categories, our proposed framework for comparing CT implementations in various countries.

2 Computational Thinking

The following section will focus on CT within primary and secondary schools. CT has recently seen a near-universal recognition by countries across the world, as this paper will show in the next section. School systems across the world are in various stages of implementation of new curriculums which include digital literacy, ICT and CT as central points.

In order to compare CT adoption and implementation in different countries, we need to first look at the current definitions of CT, and possibly identify the most accepted. Unfortunately, a widely agreed-upon definition of Computational Thinking has not been reached, but the current development within the field and interest from school legislation can be traced back to Wing [3], which identified CT as an essential skill for the 21st Century [4]. Therefore, in this paper, we will focus on CT as stated by Wing (2006), which defines CT as a systematic method for problem-solving. Interestingly the term was originally coined in Mindstorm by Papert [2] 30 years ago. Unsurprisingly the definition and focus have changed slightly over the decades. Papert [2] originally envisioned the personal computer as a great facilitator for assimilation of knowledge, as the personal computer's adaptive nature would allow it to be tailored to an individual's interests, functioning as a catalyst for intrinsic motivation. Papert laments the fact that computers were yet not powerful enough to create fully engaging activities, but stating than when the technology is sufficiently mature, it will allow CT to be integrated into everyday life [2]. Current ICT is clearly not yet mature, and each country must now somehow figure out how a person becomes a computational thinker. In short, Papert's definition of CT was to be able to use computers for everyday tasks, which could sound already surpassed given the average computer skills of today's pupils and students.

To utilize computers not just as a user and for the breadth of possible applications today, no matter how accommodating the program, means being proficient at problem-solving. So, another definition could be that CT is the method by which one efficiently solves a problem computationally. It is this computational methodology that Wing [3] identifies as a fundamental skill for the 21st century.

In this paper, we need to categorize the constituting elements of CT, which is a problem on its own, given that there is no universally agreed-upon definition of CT. Our solution is to look at a simple categorization, designed and widely used for teaching notably in the USA, England and Taiwan [5], as it gives a general overview of the different components to CT. The elements are; decomposition, pattern recognition, abstraction, and algorithms.

Decomposition is the first step in the process of dividing a problem into discrete parts. Each part can then be tackled individually, flattening the complexity of the overall problem.

Pattern Recognition in the second step, where commonalities are identified, which could be repeating sequences, generalized categories or other similarities observed in the problem.

Abstraction: in the third step the solutions are modeled and abstracted. A good solution should be general, solving multiple problems of a similar nature and not merely the initial specific problem.

The last step is represented by algorithms, where the problem is expressed as a series of steps necessary for finding the solution to the problem.

The question of what a universally accepted definition of CT could be is still unanswered, and that implies that each country is adopting a customized blending of elements from different international and national sources [6].

Moreover, practical implementation of CT, especially when it concerns primary school requires to look at many more aspects than simply the core elements of CT itself; for instance, classroom orchestration, support for ICT competences of teachers, and development of suitable textbook and online materials, in the appropriate language.

3 Data Gathering

In our literature review, we aim at painting a picture, showing the direction in which the field is progressing in each country. Our strategy is to collect papers from prominent conferences in Asia: we are focusing in particular on Asian conferences as we presume they contain a more representative sample of the field as they contain a larger sample of material with a broad range, from large CT-related projects to small-scale studies. However, further studies might be needed to verify this assumption. Our methodology for the collection and categorization of the studies is rather standard: we started collecting papers from two of the most prominent conferences in Asia (identified thanks to our network of researchers in CT and education in Asia). Papers were selected corresponding to the following criteria: they must be centered around CT by the authors' own statement, authors must be primarily located in the East Asian Region. The paper should not be a meta-study as they often focus on studies internationally. Finally, the paper must be written in English. Papers might belong to multiple categories, in cases where multiple approaches are used, or subjects covered; in those cases, they will be categorized according to what the authors emphasize as a primary focus.

We started basing our classification on Bocconi et al. [1], but to properly cover the material we worked in an inductive way, loosely inspired by grounded theory [7]. Hence, we conducted a thematic analysis of the papers identifying emerging categories, as a result, in our method the papers will be assessed according to the following parameters:

Level of education under study, mapped to k-12 education:

- First elementary school, Second elementary, High school, University

Area of study

- Curriculum, Teachers, Students

Scientific approach:

- Quantitative, Qualitative; and also, completion stage: planned, work in progress, completed.

Attitudes and disposition:

- Career Learning, Transferable Skills, General Education

Nationality

We need to extend and complement [1] in various ways, during our analysis of the literature. For example, we added the category "area of study" to be able to differentiate papers with respect to how the curriculum is covered, and whether the paper looks mainly at students or teachers.

Curriculum refers to discussion or proposition for school curriculums. In cases where propositions are based on surveys or tests from teachers or students. The text would belong to the respective category instead. Career learning is taught to emphasize a profession or career path, in our case often computer science or engineering. Transferable is taught to improve the students across a wide area of competencies. The aim of General education is to prepare the student to be a competent member of society.

Finally, we have looked at the availability of pedagogical material: some countries are overrepresented, while others are rarely covered. This presents us with an issue of representativeness and significance of our papers sample; to cope with this we are currently adopting a qualitative approach, following discourse analysis techniques for our categorization and data analysis [7] However, in the scope of our larger Asian comparison project, we will consider enlarging the sample and involve our network of experts to address the significance of our data.

3.1   Our Approach in Action

From our initial survey, the countries that seem to be of most interest for future study in Hong Kong, South Korea, and Taiwan. These countries share a similar agile nature to Denmark and size. As an example of the results our method can provide, we can outline the CT approach in each of these three countries, based on the papers analyzed so far in our review.

Hong Kong ICT and CT are central to Hong Kong's education system. Interestingly the change has been spearheaded by the Hong Kong Jockey Club, a nonprofit organization. The organization holds a legal monopoly on gambling and betting.

Information literacy is one of the seven core competencies for secondary education, and "Information Technology for Interactive Learning" is one of four key tasks as stated by the Educational Bureau. CT has integrated into the curriculum since 2017 [8]. Additionally, the Educational Bureau has currently finalized a supplementary curriculum specifically for CT [8].

South Korea fully implemented a new curriculum integrating computational thinking [9]. The process started with a nationwide pilot in 2015 and was implemented as a compulsory part of the curriculum for primary and secondary schools in 2018 [10].

Taiwan began in August of 2019 to require every student in secondary school to be fostered with computational thinking competences. This has so far been achieved by integrating computational thinking into the curriculums of other courses [5].

For Hong Kong, Taiwan and South Korea we also created a detailed comparison, summarized in Tables 1, 2 and 3; the tables show some of the papers for each country, using the categories in our method. In the tables (*) indicates early studies describing something they want to test, but have not yet tested, what we call planned in our Scientific Approach category.

Table 1. Hong Kong.

Authors	Level of education	Area of study	Scientific approach	Attitude
Wong and Cheung 2015	Primary, Secondary	Teachers	Quantitative	Career learning
Kong and Li 2016	Primary	Curriculum	Qualitative	General education
Kong and Lao 2017	Primary	Students	Qualitative	Career learning
Wong, Tang, Zhang and Cheung 2015	Primary	Students	Quantitative	Transferable skills
Liu, Li, Kong and Lo 2016	University	Students	Qualitative	General education

Our overall goal here is to describe and compare the CT approach of countries, eventually to take advantage of the findings to support educational institutions in Denmark in their efforts to implement CT.

4 Summary of Our Early Results

We present here a summary of early findings from our literary review. We used our method and looked at the state of implementation of curriculums for primary and secondary school integrating CT, ICT and digital literacy. Our study follows the overview of European countries by Bocconi et al. [1]. The different degree of details is due not only to the early stage of our survey but also on the uneven distribution of studies for the different countries.

Table 2. Taiwan.

Authors	Level of education	Area of study	Scientific approach	Attitude
Tseng et al. 2018	High School	Curriculum	Qualitative*	Career learning
Kong and Li 2016	University	Students	Quantitative	General education
Kong and Lao 2017	Primary	Curriculum	Qualitative*	General education
Wong, Tang, Zhang and Cheung 2015	Primary	Curriculum	Qualitative*	General education
Liu, Li, Kong and Lo 2016	University	Students	Quantitative	General education

Table 3. South Korea.

Authors	Level of education	Area of study	Scientific approach	Attitude
Song and Han 2018	Primary	Students	Quantitative	General education
Lee 2017	All	Teachers	Qualitative	General education
Jeon, Jeong and Song 2018	Primary	Students	Quantitative	General education
Byun, Ryu and Han 2018	Primary	Curriculum	Quantitative*	General education
Choi and Lee 2018	Primary	Students	Quantitative	General education

China started in 2007 to restructure and centralize its computer education at the university level [9]. Furthermore, China implemented a new national curriculum in 2017, which included computational thinking [11].

Japan is currently in the process of implementing a new curriculum, which was finalized in 2018 and includes programming as a compulsory subject for students in primary and secondary schools [12] and should be fully implemented by 2022 [11]

Macau has not officially moved towards implementing CT in a centralized fashion. Macau is instead focused on computer literacy and the usage of digital tools such as word processing, spreadsheets, and database applications [13]. Which is taught at the primary and secondary level, in a non-centralized fashion with no unifying curriculum at the governmental level [13].

Mongolia aims to increase the incorporation of ICT in the classroom and has the general goal to increase the digital literacy of the entire population [14]. Does not currently plan to integrate computational thinking into the curriculum.

Information about North Korea's educational system is scarce, as only a few papers are published. According to Lee [15], North Korea moved away from teaching primarily usage of software tools and towards learning programming skills in 2014.

5 Discussion

In general, we can state that ICT and CT are being implemented in an array of different local conditions. In our literary review, we have noticed a tendency for countries to first integrate ICT into the classroom, which is a necessity for teaching usage of word processing and database software. General ICT skills and computing equipment seem to be considered prerequisites to introducing CT. In fact, while CT could be taught using unplugged activities, this approach is usually not supported at a governmental level, even in countries where overall ICT adoption is low; it is possible that individual teachers could still use unplugged activities.

However, the teachers' discretion is also another factor that changes dramatically from country to country. In Scandinavia, the tendency is to leave many practical details of the implementation of courses to the teachers, so we expect CT in Denmark to possibly follow that approach too [6].

The framework from Bocconi et al., categorized studies according to subtheme of CT [1], it was not possible to replicate this method for this study as must papers were found to cover CT in a broad or holistic way, either focusing on general issues such as how to empower and facilitate teachers or by presenting tools and materials which facilitated learning many subdomains of CT at once. This might be a result of the early stage of implementations in the various countries, as the field matures it could be interesting to see if more focused research will emerge.

Furthermore, we see the adoption of CT into school curriculums for the East Asian region is developing at a similar timescale as seen in Europe [1]. No government in the East Asian region is completely disregarding ICT, and we see a clear tendency for continuous improvement. If not teaching CT, then working towards integrating ICT into the school day. It is very likely countries will move towards a curriculum integrating CT as the proliferation of everyday ICT matures.

6 Conclusion and Future Work

This paper discusses the problems in attempting a characterization and comparison of the Computational Thinking approaches of different Asian countries and proposes an extended set of categories to support the comparison, based on the work of [1] with respect to CT in Europe. Early results from a few specific countries are also presented. Future work includes completing a more extensive version of the early literature review presented in this paper, assessing the significance of the sample in the review, and compiling a more complete matrix of the approaches to CT in Asian countries most relevant for our goal.

References

1. Bocconi, S., Chioccariello, A., Dettori, G., Ferrari, A., Engelhardt, K.: Developing computational thinking in compulsory education-Implications for policy and practice. Joint Research Centre (Seville site) (2016)
2. Seymour, P.: Mindstorms; Children, Computers and Powerful Ideas, 1st edn. Basic Book, New York (1980)
3. Wing, J.M.: Computational thinking. Commun. ACM **49**(3), 33–35 (2006)
4. Mohaghegh, D.M., McCauley, M.: Computational thinking: the skill set of the 21st century. Int. J. Comput. Sci. Inf. Technol. **7**(3), 1524–1530 (2016)
5. Hsu, T.-C.: A study of the readiness of implementing computational thinking in compulsory education in Taiwan. In: Kong, S.-C., Abelson, H. (eds.) Computational Thinking Education, pp. 295–314. Springer, Singapore (2019). https://doi.org/10.1007/978-981-13-6528-7_17
6. Kristensen, K.: Towards computational thinking in Scandinavia. In: 27th International Conference on Computers in Education, ICCE 2019, pp. 47–49. Asia-Pacific Society for Computers in Education (2019)
7. Drotner, K., Iversen, S.M.: Digitale metoder: At skabe, analysere og dele data. Samfundslitteratur (2017)
8. Education Bureau. https://www.edb.gov.hk/en/index.html. Accessed 20 Mar 2020
9. Hsu, Y.-C., Irie, N.R., Ching, Y.-H.: Computational thinking educational policy initiatives (CTEPI) across the globe. TechTrends **63**(3), 260–270 (2019). https://doi.org/10.1007/s11528-019-00384-4
10. Lee, M.: Computational thinking: efforts in Korea. In: Rich, P.J., Hodges, C.B. (eds.) Emerging Research, Practice, and Policy on Computational Thinking. ECTII, pp. 363–366. Springer, Cham (2017). https://doi.org/10.1007/978-3-319-52691-1_22
11. Wu, L., et al.: Teacher's perceptions and readiness to teach coding skills: a comparative study between Finland, Mainland China, Singapore, Taiwan, and South Korea. Asia-Pac. Educ. Res. **29**(1), 21–34 (2019). https://doi.org/10.1007/s40299-019-00485-x
12. Kanemune, S., Shirai, S., Tani, S.: Informatics and programming education at primary and secondary schools in Japan. Olymp. Inform. **11**(2017), 143–150 (2017)
13. Wong, K., Negreiros, J., Neves, A.: Computer literacy teaching using peer-tutoring: the Macao, China, experience. Proc. MAC-ETL **2016**, 10–17 (2016)
14. Gaspard-Richards, D.: Flipped classroom, mlearning and the integration of ICT in teaching and learning. Int. J. Educ. Dev. Using Inf. Commun. Technol. **15**(2), 2–4 (2019)
15. Lee, Y.B.: Analysis on computer education in elementary schools in North Korea and South Korea with further prospect. J. Korea Converg. Soc. **5**(4), 49–60 (2014)

Proposal of a Career Selection Support System for High School Students by Visualizing Occupations

Ryuhei Kubota and Tomofumi Uetake(✉)

School of Business Administration, Senshu University, Kawasaki, Kanagawa,
Japan
uetake@isc.senshu-u.ac.jp

Abstract. Recently, high schools have been required to promote career education. Many high schools have been conducting workplace experiences and vocational lectures to raise high school students' career awareness. However, it is difficult for high school students to find the path they really want by receiving these career education attempts. In this study, we propose a support system for high school students who refrain from choosing a career path, by suggesting occupations related to the interests of high school students. Our proposed system visualizes the relationships between occupations from the viewpoint of high school students by using the connections between occupations and shows their information in an easy-to-understand manner.

Keywords: Information visualization system · Career education in high school · Network diagram

1 Introduction

In recent years, MEXT (the Ministry of Education, Culture, Sports, Science and Technology) is promoting "career education" at each school, considering the characteristics of the school and the actual conditions of the community [1]. In response, many high schools have been conducting workplace experiences and vocational lectures to raise high school students' career awareness [6, 7]. Moreover, there are many online and offline services for career education (e.g. "Job Guidance for the 13-year-olds and all triers" [4], "Carrimaga" [5]).

However, it is difficult for high school students to find the path they really want by receiving these career education attempts, because not only are the interests of high school students diverse, but they do not have enough understanding and awareness of occupations themselves. Therefore, the current career education has a problem that the needs of high school students are not sufficiently satisfied.

© Springer Nature Switzerland AG 2020
C. Stephanidis and M. Antona (Eds.): HCII 2020, CCIS 1225, pp. 277–283, 2020.
https://doi.org/10.1007/978-3-030-50729-9_39

2 Objective of This Study

In this study, we propose a system for high school students who refrain from choosing a career path, by suggesting information on related occupations considering the interests of high school students and supporting their career choice.

3 Analysis of the Career Education in High School

3.1 Analysis of the Interests of High School Students and Existing Services for Career Education

We analyzed the questionnaire results [2] about the items that a high school student values when choosing occupations and clarified the following points.

- Items such as "work" and "job content" are most valued
- Items such as "stability" and "seniority" are not valued
- Items such as "worthwhile" and "work atmosphere" are valued

Next, as a result of analyzing existing services [3–5] for knowing occupations, the following points became clear.

- Because occupations are displayed for each category, prior knowledge is required to make full use of them
- It is difficult to get to the information of the occupations that they are interested in unless they search by occupation name or related words.

3.2 Analysis of the Activities of High Schools' Career Education

Next, as a result of analyzing the activities of high schools' career education [6, 7], the following points became clear.

- The opportunities for real life and occupation are incorporated in their activities.
- However, students' interests are not fully reflected in their activities.

3.3 Summary of the Analysis

Analysis of the interests of high school students showed that their interests were diverse, but also showed that they did not have enough knowledge. And analysis of previous cases showed that although the curriculum incorporated opportunities to touch the real world and occupations, students' interests were not fully reflected. These results indicated that there was a mismatch between the interests of high school students and the information of occupations provided by the existed system (see Fig. 1).

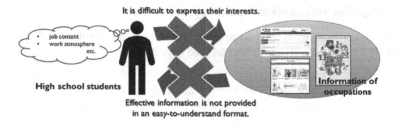

Fig. 1. Mismatch between the interests of high school students and provided information of occupations

4 Proposal of a Career Selection Support System for High School Students

We propose a system that can widely visualize occupations considering their interests of high school students, and present information about the occupations in an easy-to-understand manner. Specifically, we proposed following 3 functions.

(1) Occupation information filter function
(2) Occupation information visualization function
(3) Occupation information comparison function

The overview of our proposed system is showed in Fig. 2.

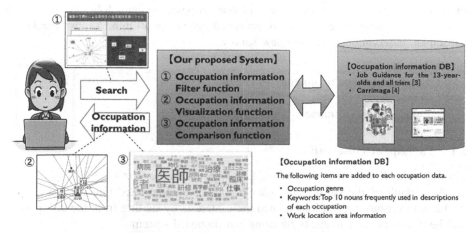

Fig. 2. Overview of our proposed system

4.1 Occupation Information Filter Function

Function to extract related occupations considering various high school students' interests based on the "keyword", "occupation", and "work area" entered by the user.

4.2   Occupation Information Visualization Function

Function to visualize extracted occupation information in a network diagram using NodeXL [8] based on a dynamic model (see Fig. 3).

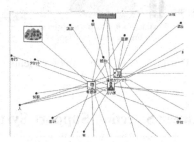

Fig. 3. Network diagram visualizing the relationship between occupations

4.3   Occupation Information Comparison Function

Function that presents a "word cloud" created with descriptions of each occupation [9] to facilitate visual grasp and comparison of occupations and their job contents.

5   Evaluation

In order to evaluate the effectiveness of our proposed system, following two high school students were asked to use our proposed system for 30 min. And we conducted participant observations and interview survey.

– Participant A:
  11th grade, Interests: treatment
– Participant B:
  11th grade, Interests: nurse.

5.1   Participant Observations

The following Fig. 4 shows the usage history of the participant A.

As a result of the participant observation, it was confirmed that the participants could learn various occupations related their interests by starting from the occupations and keywords of their interests by using our proposed system.

5.2   Interview Survey

The following comments were obtained during the interview survey.

- Expressing occupations in the word cloud makes it easier to understand unknown occupations.
- I don't care much about the "work area" when searching for occupations.

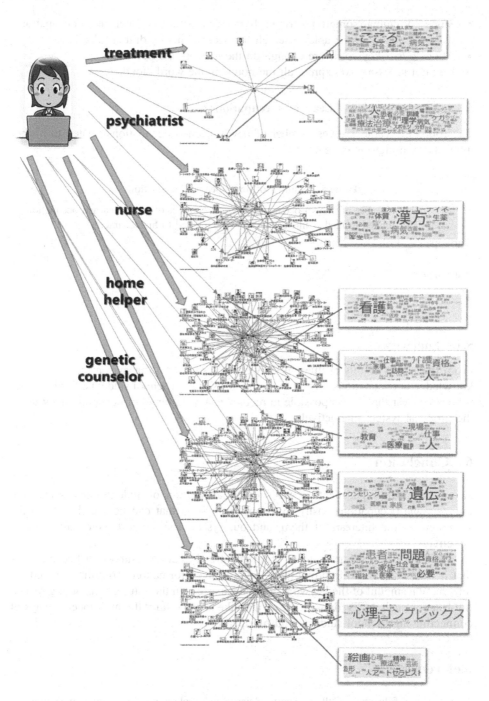

Fig. 4. Usage history of the participant A

- Since TV dramas sometimes trigger high school students' interests in occupations, it would be nice to be able to search for occupations by drama title.
- About 6 to 7 keywords are enough on the network diagram.
- It is not necessary to express all the nouns in the word cloud.

5.3   Number of Newly Learned Occupations

The following Table 1 gives number of newly learned occupations related to his/her interests by using our system.

Table 1. Number of newly learned occupations

	Number of known occupations related to his/her interests	Number of newly learned occupations related to his/her interests
Participant A	10	31
Participant B	13	29

5.4   Summary

From the results of this evaluation showed that the use of our system could increase knowledge of occupations related to the interests of high school students. Furthermore, it became clear that it was possible to recognize a wide range of occupations by using the proposal system interactively.

6   Conclusion

As a result of the experiments, it was shown that high school students can associate the interests and occupations easily by using our system that can be searched from the viewpoint of the interests of them, and our system can support their career choice effectively.

However, from the participant observation and interview survey, it became clear that it was necessary to improve the validity of the information about the area and the information amount of the keywords to be visualized. In the future, considering related information such as TV dramas, we would like to reconsider the multifaceted ways of connecting high school students and occupations.

References

1. Ministry of Education, Culture, Sports, Science and Technology. http://www.mext.go.jp/
2. Big Life21. http://www.biglife21.com/. Accessed 5 Mar 2020
3. Ministry of Internal Affairs and Communications. http://www.soumu.go.jp/

4. Ryu, M.: Job guidance for the 13-year-olds and all triers. https://www.13hw.com/home/index. html
5. Carrimaga. https://www.nikki.ne.jp/magazine/. Accessed 5 Mar 2020
6. Will Project: Noshiro Senior High School. http://www.noshiro-h.akita-pref.ed.jp/NWPpf.pdf. Accessed 5 Mar 2020
7. Empowerment school: Fusekita High School. https://www.osaka-c.ed.jp/fusekita/others/ enpowerment.html. Accessed 5 Mar 2020
8. NodeXL. https://www.smrfoundation.org/. Accessed 5 Mar 2020
9. lab.fanbright. http://lab.fanbright.jp/lod/text. Accessed 5 Mar 2020

Different Ways of Interacting with Videos During Learning in Secondary Physics Lessons

David Leisner[1]([⊠]) [iD], Carmen Zahn[1] [iD], Alessia Ruf[1] [iD],
and Alberto Cattaneo[2] [iD]

[1] Institute of Research and Development of Collaborative Processes (ifk),
FHNW University of Applied Sciences and Arts of Northwestern Switzerland,
Olten, Switzerland
{david.leisner,carmen.zahn,alessia.ruf}@fhnw.ch
[2] Swiss Federal Institute for Vocational Education and Training (SFIVET),
Lugano, Switzerland
alberto.cattaneo@iuffp.swiss

Abstract. In times of rapid technological change towards digital technologies, educational institutions increasingly use interactive videos to support effective learning both in online and face-to-face lessons and across many subjects. However, the mechanisms underlying video-based learning – especially *active* learning - have not yet been conclusively clarified. Research into active video-based learning, which has been significant to date, has been conducted mostly in higher education and with university students. Consequently, systematic studies on how interactive videos can be used for meaningful learning in school-based education is crucial. The present contribution describes a field experiment with 16-year-old school students ($N = 78$) and realistic video-based physics lessons at secondary school level II. Students' learning was supported by the video tool "*ivideo.education*". The study investigated three learning conditions in order to explore the influences of in-video quizzes and writing annotations on learning success and interest. Data was collected by means of pre-, post- and delayed post-tests. Results show a consistent tendency on a descriptive level that the combination of in-video quizzes and continuous writing of annotations leads to higher learning success and interest than post-video quizzes or post-video annotation writings.

Keywords: Interactive videos · Annotations · In-video quizzes · Post-video quizzes · Active and constructivist learning · Multimedia

1 Introduction

Video-based learning materials provide unique possibilities to illustrate, demonstrate and present complex topics and processes, that cannot – or not easily - be shown in real-life scenarios [14]. Consequently, in times of rapid technological development, educational institutions have made particular use of video-based materials to support learning and conceptual understanding in various areas [16]. In addition, videos are inevitable for distance learning and open education.

© Springer Nature Switzerland AG 2020
C. Stephanidis and M. Antona (Eds.): HCII 2020, CCIS 1225, pp. 284–291, 2020.
https://doi.org/10.1007/978-3-030-50729-9_40

However, research on the effects of video-based learning is conflicting: while various studies have shown that learning with videos leads to significantly higher learning success compared to text-based learning [6, 13] other studies could not show any significant difference [5, 7]. Possible explanations for the controversial findings are different types of video presentation (interactive vs. non-interactive). Dale's cone of experience suggests that learners remember 90% of what they have learned when they experience it directly, for example through interactive videos [18]. Interactive videos encourage active and constructivist engagement with the learning content which results in a better recall of it.

Thereby, not only basic interaction (such as play, pause buttons) but also extended interaction features (such as self-written summaries i.e. annotations and in-video quiz) have been shown to have a positive effect on learning success [19, 20] and interest [10, 11].

In sum, while research on video-based learning is still conflicting, the positive aspects of enabling interactions in such learning environments are evident. Therefore, the empirical findings regarding interaction features are subsequently reported in more detail, before the aim and added value of the present study are clarified.

1.1 Interactive Video Features

The role of interactivity in video-based learning becomes evident in the fact that even basic *control features* in form of sliders, or toolbars with play, pause and rewind/forward buttons enable learners to adapt the information flow from videos to their individual needs and capacities and thus minimize the risk of cognitive overload [2]. This is in line with research showing positive correlations of learning success with the intensity of use of video interaction features and individual mental effort [20]. More complex interaction features such as in-video quizzes (e.g. multiple choice, true/false) and annotations (e.g. annotated self-written summaries) offer additional possibilities to support learning. *In-video quizzes*, on the one hand, can be embedded directly at any point in the video and allow immediate feedback [1, 2], which has especially in multimedia learning a positive impact on learners' engagement [1, 3] and motivation [9]. However, in-video quizzes can also have a distracting effect, if not meaningfully implemented. This, in turn can lead to a decrease in interest in learners or even to them missing the main message in the video [12]. Research suggests that such a distraction effect can best be minimized when quizzes are implemented as a continuation and not an extension of the video content [12]. In other words, quizzes should appear in the same place as the learning content in order to simulate the interactive discussion between teachers – or a learning environment – and learners [3]. *Annotations*, on the other hand, allow learners to actively contribute their own content and thus transform the video into an enriched information structure respectively self-created learning product [19]. Previous research suggests that the continuous writing of annotations in videos promotes the connection between previous knowledge and new information [21, 22] and that conceptual understanding can be enhanced by this active contribution of learners through adding self-written summaries into the learning material [17]. In sum, from previous research it becomes clear, that enabling video interactions is supportive for learning success [19, 20] and increase of interest in the learning topic [10, 11].

However, what is missing so far is a systematic comparison of different extended interaction features on learning success and interest.

1.2 Present Study

In the present study we focused on in-video quizzes and annotations as they have been proven to be supportive for learning success and interest. Moreover, both interaction features are closely related as shown in a study by Szpunar, Jing and Schacter [15] suggesting that learners write more notes when in-video quizzes were available.

Furthermore, although in-video quizzes have been researched in several cases, a systematic experimental comparison between post and in-video quizzes is still missing [3]. To the authors' knowledge a similar comparison for annotations has also not yet be done. Finally, the authors are not aware of investigations of long-term memory effects of extended interactive features.

Hence, the present study pursued two main objectives: (1) the simultaneous and systematical considering of two closely related extended interaction features (i.e. in-video quizzes and annotations) and investigation of their effects on learning success and interest (with additional consideration of long-term effects); and (2) the consideration of the position or rather the time (in-video vs. post-video) of offering these interaction features in the learning material. This leads us to the following research question and hypothesis:

RQ1: To which extend do *different positions* of quizzes and *different positions of prompts* for writing annotations in interactive learning videos have an impact on learning success and interest?

In order to answer this question, we investigated variants of positioning quizzes and prompts for writing annotations (in-video vs. post-video and combinations). Precisely, we tested the following hypotheses:

H1: Interactive videos with in-video quizzes plus continuous in-video annotations lead to better learning success than videos with in-video quizzes plus post-video annotations.

H2: Interactive videos with in-video quizzes plus continuous in-video annotations lead to higher learning success than videos with in-video annotations plus post-video quizzes.

In order to answer this research question and hypotheses we set up a field study in the classroom (high school) that is described in the next section in more detail.

2 Methodology

2.1 Participants and Experimental Design

Seventy-eight learners from four different classes – taught by the same physics teacher – of a Swiss high school (secondary level II) participated voluntarily in our study (32 female; average age of 16.4 (*SD* = .65, range: 15–18 years). The classes participated in the experiment one after the other while the learners in each class were randomly allocated to the conditions.

The experimental design was a 3 × 2 mixed design. The first factor (between-subject) represented the type of treatment the learners received while working with the video. Learners in *condition 1* ($n = 28$) worked with in-video quizzes and were only asked to write notes at the end of the learning video (post-video annotation). Learners in *condition 2* ($n = 25$) worked with in-video quizzes and were asked to continuously write annotations in the video (in-video annotations). Taking into account findings regarding interaction features (c.f. 1.1) *condition 2* corresponded to an optimal learning environment. Learners in *condition 3* ($n = 25$) were as well asked to continuously write annotations in the video (in-video annotations) while the quizzes appeared one after the other at the end of the video (post-video quizzes). Regardless of the condition, the video could be watched over again. The second factor (within-subject) was the measuring-time (immediate post-test, delayed post-test five weeks later). Dependent variables were short and long-term learning success and interest.

2.2 Materials, Measurements and Procedure

The learning content used in this study was about *hydraulic energy transport*. The video was created by the teacher, mainly by using PowerPoint and slightly optimized by an expert at our university in consideration of multimedia theories [8]. The video was accompanied by a pre- and post-instruction video. The entire interactive video had a duration of about ten minutes. The video was then uploaded into the interactive video tool *ivideo.education* developed by the Swiss Federal Institute for Vocational Education and Training (SFIVET). The ivideo.education player interface allows both embedding quizzes and taking annotations. For learning, the students received an iPad (9.7 in.) each with a keyboard, touchpen and headphones.

Learning success was measured by objective measures and self-assessment. The *self-assessed knowledge* (one item: *"I know what hydraulic energy transport is"*) was based on three points in time (prior, immediate & delayed post) and on a five-point Likert scale. The *objective measures* of learning success were immediate post-test and delayed post-test of knowledge. The test consisted of ten multiple choice questions developed by an expert and teacher, each with four options and only one correct answer. *Interest* in the topic was measured twice (prior interest and immediate post-measurement) based on the *Intrinsic Motivation Inventory* [4] and a five-point Likert scale.

The field experiment took place in class during a 45-min physics lesson. After five weeks, the learners answered the delayed post-test again during normal physics lesson.

3 Results

Prior knowledge, *pre-experimental interest* and *demographic variables* (gender, class) did not differ significantly between conditions. The groups were therefore considered comparable.

3.1   Learning Success

Self-assessments. Table 1 shows that learners from *condition 3* rated their short-term learning success (immediate post-test) as the highest. In contrast, learners from *condition 2* assess their long-term learning success (delayed post-test) as the highest. In addition, learners from *condition 2* showed the highest increase in self-assessed knowledge between pre- and immediate post-test as well as between pre- and delayed post-test.

Table 1. Descriptive data on self-assessed learning success

Condition	n	Measuring time point		
		Pretest	Immediate post-test	Delayed post-test
		M(SD)	M(SD)	M(SD)
1	28	2.04(.84)	4.14(.45)	2.32(.98)
2	25	1.76(.72)	4.20(.87)	2.84(.85)
3	25	2.08(.81)	4.28(.68)	2.76(1.09)

Note. The self-assessment of knowledge was measured via a five-point Likert scale.

However, Kruskal-Wallis tests showed that neither short ($\chi^2(2) = 1.44$, $p = .49$, $N = 78$) nor long-term subjective learning success ($\chi^2(2) = 4.89$, $p = .09$, $N = 78$) differed significantly between conditions. Furthermore, it has been shown that self-assessed knowledge increased significantly after learning with the interactive video in all treatment groups, while a Kruskal-Wallis test showed that this increase between pre- and immediate post-test did not differ significantly between conditions ($\chi^2(2) = 2.18$, $p = .34$, $N = 78$). In contrast, a Kruskal-Wallis test showed that the increase in knowledge between pre- and delayed post-test differs significantly between conditions ($\chi^2(2) = 7.95$, $p = .02$, $N = 78$). Subsequent post-hoc tests (Dunn-Bonferroni) indicated that this increase was only significantly higher in *condition 2* compared to *condition 1* ($z = -2.82$, $p = .01$) with medium effect ($r = .39$).

Objective Measures. Table 2 shows that learners from *condition 2* achieved the highest average score in the knowledge test at both measurement points. However, a one-way ANOVA showed no significant differences between the conditions regarding short-term learning success ($F(2,75) = 2.15$, $p = .12$, partial $\eta^2 = .05$, $N = 78$). A Kruskal-Wallis test also showed no significant differences between the conditions regarding long-term learning success ($\chi^2(2) = .14$, $p = .93$, $N = 78$).

Table 2. Descriptive data on learning success (objective measurement)

Condition	n	Measuring time point	
		Immediate post-test	Delayed post-test
		M(SD)	M(SD)
1	28	13.36(4.46)	9.86(4.45)
2	25	15.60(3.71)	10.96(4.99)
3	25	14.32(3.50)	10.24(4.04)

Note. In each knowledge test 24 points (10 items) could be achieved.

3.2 Interest

On average, learners from *condition 2* showed the highest increase in interest between the two measuring points, as shown in Table 3.

Table 3. Descriptive data on interest in the topic

Condition	n	Measuring time point	
		Pretest	Immediate post-test
		M(SD)	M(SD)
1	28	2.99(.59)	3.32(.68)
2	25	2.88(.57)	3.59(.75)
3	25	3.10(.67)	3.63(.73)

Note. Interest was measured using 7 items and a five-point Likert scale.

Although interest increased significantly in all conditions between the two measurement points, a two-way ANOVA with repeated measures showed that there are no significant differences between the conditions regarding the increase in interest (F $(2,75) = .90$, $p = .41$, partial $\eta^2 = .02$, $N = 78$).

4 Discussion

The current study examined the effects of two different extended interaction features (in-video quiz and annotation) in a classroom context and the impact of their position within the learning material, on learning success and interest.

Our results show, that learning about *hydraulic energy transport* with interactive videos lead to significant self-assessed learning success and interest, independent of condition. Interactive videos therefore seem to be well suited to foster learning success and interest in physical learning topics. Besides, descriptive results for the self-assessed learning success show that *condition 3* (post-video quiz, in-video annotation) rated their short-term learning success highest. This might be due to the fact that these learners answered all quizzes and received *immediate* feedback before the subjective knowledge assessment and therefore they may have felt most confident. Another explanation for the lower average short-term learning success in *condition 2* (in-video quiz & annotation) and *1* (in-video quiz, post-video annotation) might be that learners were distracted by in-video quizzes or even felt that they had missed the main message of the learning video [12].

In contrast, *objectively measured* learning success have shown that the continuous writing of annotations in videos (condition 2 & 3) fosters the generation of associations between previous knowledge and new information respectively the conceptual understanding, which is consistent with previous findings [22]. Moreover, taking into account that learners from *condition 2* achieved on average a higher short and long-term learning success compared to learners from *condition 3*, it can only be concluded that the combination of in-video quizzes and continuous writing of annotations leads to higher learning success or in other words: An evidence-based design of interactive videos leads to higher learning success.

However, the study had several limitations that should be taken into account in further research: For ethical reasons the learning content had no influence on the learners' physics grade. Hence, there was no prospect of being rewarded for good efforts, so the learners' performance was merely the result of their intrinsic motivation. This may have minimized possible effects of different design parameters in interactive videos. Moreover, the intensity of use of control features as well as the potential confidence induced by the immediate feedback through the quizzes could not be tracked. This data would have contributed to further findings. Finally, it should be noted that the results of the present study are based on one high school and thus are not to be applied without consideration to the entire secondary school level II.

In conclusion, our study provides deeper insights into video-based and interactive learning of physics learning content in high school. Despite the fact that there were no significant effects of different design parameters in interactive videos, the descriptive data showed a clear tendency. On average, an evidence-based design respectively the combination of in-video quizzes and continuous annotation writing leads to higher learning success and interest.

References

1. Baker, A.: Active learning with interactive videos: creating student-guided learning materials. J. Libr. Inf. Serv. Distance Learn. 10(3–4), 79–87 (2016)
2. Cattaneo, A.A.P., van der Meij, H., Aprea, C., Sauli, F., Zahn, C.: A model for designing hypervideo-based instructional scenarios. Interact. Learn. Environ. 27(4), 508–529 (2019)
3. Cummins, S., Beresford, A.R., Rice, A.: Investigating engagement with in-video quiz questions in a programming course. IEEE Trans. Learn. Technol. 9(1), 57–66 (2016)
4. Deci, E.L., Ryan, R.M.: Intrinsic Motivation Inventory (2003)
5. Donkor, F.: The comparative instructional effectiveness of print-based and video-based instructional materials for teaching practical skills at a distance. Int. Rev. Res. Open Distrib. Learn. 11(1), 96–116 (2010)

6. Kay, R., Edwards, J.: Examining the use of worked example video podcasts in middle school mathematics classrooms: a formative analysis. Can. J. Learn. Technol. **38**(3), 1 (2012)
7. Lindgren, R., Pea, R., Lewis, S., Rosen, J.: Learning from digital video: an exploration of how interactions affect outcomes. In: Proceedings of the 8th International Conference on Computer Supported Collaborative Learning, pp. 447–449. International Society of the Learning Sciences (2007)
8. Mayer, R.E.: Multimedia Learning, 2nd edn. Cambridge University Press, Cambridge (2009)
9. Merkt, M., Weigand, S., Heier, A., Schwan, S.: Learning with videos vs. learning with print: the role of interactive features. Learn. Instr. **21**(6), 687–704 (2011)
10. Montazemi, A.R.: The effect of video presentation in a CBT environment. Educ. Technol. Soc. **9**(4), 123–138 (2006)
11. Nikopoulou-Smyrni, P., Nikopoulos, C.: Evaluating the impact of video-based versus traditional lectures on student learning. Educ. Res. **1**(8), 304–311 (2010)
12. Rice, P., Beeson, P., Blackmore-Wright, J.: Evaluating the Impact of a quiz question within an educational video. TechTrends **63**(5), 522–532 (2019)
13. Santagata, R.: Designing video-based professional development for mathematics teachers in low-performing schools. J. Teach. Educ. **60**(1), 38–51 (2009)
14. Schön, S.: Klappe zu! Film ab! – Gute Lernvideos kinderleicht erstellen. In: Pauschenwein, J. (ed.) Tagungsband zum 12. E-Learning Tag der FH JOANNEUM, pp. 3–10 (2013)
15. Szpunar, K., Jing, H., Schacter, L.: Overcoming overconfidence in learning from video-recorded lectures: implications of interpolated testing for online educators. J. Appl. Res. Mem. Cogn. **3**(3), 161–164 (2014)
16. Tiernan, P.: An inquiry into the current and future uses of digital video in University teaching. Educ. Inf. Technol. **20**(1), 75–90 (2015)
17. Wittrock, M.C.: Generative learning processes of the brain. Educ. Psychol. **27**(4), 531–541 (1992)
18. Yousef, A.M.F., Chatti, M.A., Schroeder, U.: The state of video-based learning: a review and future perspectives. Int. J. Adv. Life Sci. **6**(3/4), 122–135 (2014)
19. Yousef, A.M.F., Chatti, M.A., Danoyan, N., Thüs, H., Schroeder, U.: Video-mapper: a video annotation tool to support collaborative learning in MOOCs. In: Proceedings of the Third European MOOCs Stakeholders Summit EMOOCs, pp. 131–140 (2015)
20. Zahn, C., Barquero, B., Schwan, S.: Learning with hyperlinked videos – design criteria and efficient strategies of using audiovisual hypermedia. Learn. Instr. **14**(3), 275–291 (2004)
21. Zahn, C., Pea, R., Hesse, F.W., Rosen, J.: Comparing simple and advanced video tools as supports for complex collaborative design processes. J. Learn. Sci. **19**(3), 403–440 (2010)
22. Zahn, C., Krauskopf, K., Hesse, F.W., Pea, R.: How to improve collaborative learning with video tools in the classroom? Social vs. cognitive guidance for student teams. Int. J. Comput.-Supp. Collab. Learn. **7**(2), 259–285 (2012)

Combining Gamification and Active Learning in Higher Education

Giada Marinensi[1(✉)], Marc Romero Carbonell[2],
and Carlo Maria Medaglia[1]

[1] Link Campus University, Via del Casale di San Pio V, 44, 00165 Rome, Italy
g.marinensi@unilink.it
[2] Universitat Oberta de Catalunya, Rambla Poblenou, 156, 08018 Barcelona,
Spain

Abstract. European Higher Education Institutions (HEIs) have undertaken a path of structural reforms, outlined by the Bologna Process, to progress towards quality education and the creation of more learner-centred and engaging learning environments.

As a result, HEIs have tried to foster the adoption of active learning methodologies. Among them, flipped classroom has recently attracted much attention. Flipped classroom can be defined as an instructional approach where students gain first exposure to a subject through out-of-class self-paced learning activities (readings, video lectures, etc.). Thus, class time can be devoted to deepening their learning through activities facilitated by the teacher. However, for flipped classroom to be effective, students should not skip out-of-class learning activities. Gamification, that is the use of game elements in non-game contexts, can be helpful to foster students' engagement and motivation. This doctoral research aims to design, implement and refine an instructional approach which combines flipped classroom and gamification.

Keywords: Gamification · Flipped classroom · Active learning · Motivation · Engagement · HEIs

1 Introduction

In recent decades, European Higher Education Institutions (HEIs) have undertaken a difficult path of structural reforms, outlined by the Bologna Process launched in 1998–1999, aiming at achieving progress towards quality education. The Bologna Process established a set of goals to be reached and fostered the adoption of shared tools, such as the European Standards and Guidelines for Quality Assurance in the European Higher Education Area (2015). According to these Guidelines: "Institutions should ensure that the programmes are delivered in a way that encourages students to take an active role in creating the learning process" (p. 12).

However, shifting from the traditional lecture-focused classroom setting to more learner-centred environments is still an ongoing, complex transition for all the involved subjects: academic bodies, teachers and students. To be successful, this process needs that all these subjects are equally engaged and motivated. Therefore, finding effective

C. Stephanidis and M. Antona (Eds.): HCII 2020, CCIS 1225, pp. 292–296, 2020.
https://doi.org/10.1007/978-3-030-50729-9_41

ways to counteract students' lack of engagement and motivation has never been more crucial.

Extensive literature about active learning strategies as a way to implement more learner-centred and engaging learning environments is already available (Misseyanni et al. 2018; Hammond et al. 2010; Zepke and Leach 2010; Felder and Brent 2009). Among active learning strategies, flipped classroom has recently attracted much attention and has been widely applied in HEIs.

In essence, flipped classroom can be defined as an instructional approach where students gain first exposure to a subject through self-paced learning activities taking place outside of the classroom (readings, video lectures, etc.). Thus, class time can be devoted to deepening their learning through problem-solving activities facilitated by the teacher, discussion with peers, debates, etc. (Brame 2013).

One of the most relevant benefits of this approach is the promotion of students' active involvement. Moreover, it offers a chance to focus class time on the higher forms of cognitive work (application, analysis, synthesis, and/or evaluation), as described by Bloom's revised taxonomy (Anderson and Krathwohl 2001), by engaging students in complex tasks with the support of the teacher and the involvement of the group of peers.

Therefore, flipped classroom seems to be a powerful instructional strategy, but one of its main critical aspects is the fact that, for it to be effective, students should not skip out-of-class learning activities.

Here is where gamification, that is the "use of game design elements to motivate user behavior in non-game contexts" (Deterding 2011), can be helpful. The use of gamification in HEIs, which has increased considerably over the past years, seems to have led to the achievement of very positive results improve students' engagement and motivation (Ferreria et al. 2019; Rahman et al. 2018; Costello and Lambert 2018; Leaning 2015; Villagrasa et al. 2014). Moreover, some recent experimental studies have even already reached encouraging results analysing the effect of implementing gamification strategies to promote student engagement in the out-of-class learning activities of flipped university courses (Huang et al. 2018).

Hence, this doctoral research aims to design, implement and refine an instructional approach which combines flipped classroom and gamification to try solving the problem of students' lack of engagement and motivation.

2   Research Questions and Objectives

The research will specifically address the following research questions:

1. Can a gamification-enhanced flipped classroom approach foster students level of engagement and participation in both out-of-class and in-class learning activities?
   1.1. How does the students' perception of this approach change over time?
   1.2. Can this approach have a positive impact on tasks' completion rate?
2. Which impact may have a gamification-enhanced flipped classroom approach on students learning outcomes?

2.1. How students involved in gamification-enhanced flipped classroom score in the post-course test?
2.2. Do students involved in gamification-enhanced flipped classroom produce high quality artefacts?

According with the above research questions, the main research objective will be to understand if the combination of flipped classroom and gamification can enhance students' engagement and motivation, facilitating their learning process and the achievement of good learning results.

3   Research Methodology

In this doctoral study, the Design-Based Research (DBR) methodology will be adopted. Design-Based Research is underpinned by the pragmatic paradigm (Alghamdi and Li 2013). As stated by Corbin and Strauss, DBR is a research approach that has the main advantage of addressing the issue of linking theory and practice in educational research (Corbin and Strauss 2014). At its core, in fact, DBR is a process aiming at developing solutions to practical problems in learning environments. In the frame of DBR, the researcher can examine processes while also analyzing the effectiveness of the research design with participants, in order to re-shape, with participants' active involvement, the processes which are the object of the study (Gravemeijer and Cobb 2006).

Herrington et al. (2007) provided a set of guidelines for preparing a dissertation proposal adopting DBR approach. Taking into account the general research process structure they suggested, this doctoral study will be articulated in four main phases, briefly described as follows:

- Phase 1: Analysis of the problem
- Phase 2: Design of the proposed intervention
- Phase 3: Iterative cycles of testing and refinement of solutions in practice
- Phase 4: Reflection to produce "Guidelines for the implementation of the gamification-enhanced flipped classroom approach".

4   Data Collection

The research will use a mixed-method strategy, it will combine quantitative data from questionnaire surveys, with qualitative data gathered from interviews and focus groups. In particular:

- During "Phase 1: Analysis of the problem" a qualitative approach will be used to better understand teachers perspectives (expectations about gamification, issues related to engagement, etc.). Focus groups with University teachers will be carried out to get a better understanding of how they usually foster students' engagement and motivation and of their expectations about gamification. Qualitative interviews will be organized as well, to understand the expectations and the level of commitment of academic bodies. A questionnaire will be distributed to a group of students, to keep into account their expectations and their needs.

- During "Phase 2": The data collected during Phase 1 will be analysed and, together with the literature review, will be used to develop draft principles to guide the design of the intervention and then define the proposed intervention.
- During "Phase 3: Iterative cycles of testing and refinement of solutions in practice" Data about students' experience will be collected through observation and through a questionnaire, then in-depth interviews with teachers will be conducted in order to gain a deeper understanding of their perspective.

References

Alghamdi, A.H., Li, L.: Adapting design-based research as a research methodology in educational settings. Int. J. Educ. Res. **1**(10), 1–12 (2013)

Anderson, L.W., Krathwohl, D.R.: A taxonomy for learning, teaching, and assessing: a revision of Bloom's taxonomy of educational objectives (2001). https://doi.org/10.1207/s15430421tip4104_2

Brame, C.: Flipping the Classroom. Vanderbilt University Center for Teaching (2013). http://cft.vanderbilt.edu/guides-sub-pages/flipping-the-classroom/

Corbin, J., Strauss, A.: Basics of Qualitative Research: Techniques and Procedures for Developing Grounded Theory. Sage Publications, London (2014)

Costello, R., Lambert, M.: Motivational Influences for higher education (HE) students. Int. J. Online Pedag. Course Des. **9**(1), 38–50 (2018)

Deterding, S., Khaled, R., Nacke, L., Dixon, D.: Gamification: toward a definition. In: Forthcoming in Gamification Workshop, CHI 2011 (2011)

Felder, R.M., Brent, R.: Active learning: an introduction. Am. Soc. Qual. High. Educ. Brief **2**(4), 1–5 (2009)

Ferreira, M.J., Algoritmi, C., Moreira, F., Escudero, D.F., Gretel, L.S.: Gamification in higher education: the learning perspective. In: Experiences and perceptions of pedagogical practices with Game-Based Learning & Gamification, p. 195 (2019)

Gravemeijer, K., Cobb, P.: Design research from a learning design perspective. In: Van den Akker, J., Gravemeijer, K., McKenney, S., Nieveen, N. (eds.) Educational Design Research, pp. 17–51. Routledge, London (2006)

Hammond, J.A., Bithell, C.P., Jones, L., Bidgood, P.: Act. Learn. High. Educ. **11**(3), 201–212 (2010). https://doi.org/10.1177/1469787410379683

Herrington, J., McKenney, S., Reeves, T., Oliver, R.: Design-based research and doctoral students: guidelines for preparing a dissertation proposal. In: Montgomerie, C., Seale, J. (eds.) Proceedings of World Conference on Educational Multimedia, Hypermedia and Telecommunications 2007, pp. 4089–4097. AACE, Chesapeake (2007)

Huang, B., Hew, K.F., Lo, C.K.: Investigating the effects of gamification-enhanced flipped learning on undergraduate students' behavioral and cognitive engagement. Interact. Learn. Environ. 1–21 (2018). https://doi.org/10.1080/10494820.2018.1495653

Leaning, M.: A study of the use of games and gamification to enhance student engagement, experience and achievement on a theory-based course of an undergraduate media degree. J. Media Pract. **16**(2), 155–170 (2015)

Misseyanni, A., Papadopoulou, P., Marouli, C., Lytras, M.D. (eds.): Active Learning Strategies in Higher Education: Teaching for Leadership, Innovation, and Creativity (2018). https://0-ebookcentral-proquest-com.cataleg.uoc.edu

Rahman, R.A., Ahmad, S., Hashim, U.R.: The effectiveness of gamification technique for higher education students engagement in polytechnic Muadzam Shah Pahang, Malaysia. Int. J. Educ. Technol. High. Educ. **15**(1), 41 (2018). https://doi.org/10.1186/s41239-018-0123-0

Standards and Guidelines for Quality Assurance in the European Higher Education Area (ESG): Brussels, Belgium (2015)

Villagrasa, S., Fonseca, D., Redondo, E., Duran, J.: Teaching case of gamification and visual technologies for education. J. Cases Inf. Technol. **16**(4), 38–57 (2014)

Zepke, N., Leach, L.: Improving student engagement: ten proposals for action. Act. Learn. High Educ. **11**(3), 167–177 (2010). https://doi.org/10.1177/1469787410379680

Development of a Real Time Page Transition Feedback System and Its Impact on Learning Behavior

Daiki Mori[1(✉)], Yasuhiro Mori[2], Komei Sakamoto[2], and Takahiko Mendori[1]

[1] School of Information, Kochi University of Technology, Kami, Japan
210383t@ugs.kochi-tech.ac.jp, mendori.takahiko@kochi-tech.ac.jp
[2] Graduate School of Engineering, Kochi University of Technology, Kami, Japan

Abstract. In recent years, LMS such as Moodle or Canvas have enabled collect large scale learning logs easily. xAPI is a technical specification of the learning logs that specifies a structure to describe learning experiences and defines how these descriptions can be store LRS. LRS is database system for standardized learning logs by xAPI. According, we can analyze the learning logs to figure out the learner's achievement level and problems. LA catch a great deal of attention in learning research domain. The latest study focuses on analyzing learning logs and method for giving analysis results feedback to teachers and learners. The analysis results provide evidence of individual learning and class improvement. This paper described our real time viewing status feedback system and its experimental result. Our study focused to give real time feedback to learners by during class based on Social Constructivism. We developed a real time viewing status feedback system. The system gave the status feedback to teachers and learners. We conducted experiments of to give real time viewing status feedback. Through the experiments, the teacher could confirm the learner's situation whether they could follow her/his lecture by checking the real time viewing status feedback. In addition, the learners could confirm how many learners are viewing the previous or subsequent pages or same page as the teacher. As the result, the visualization of page transition had suggested that giving feedback affected learner's learning activities.

Keywords: LMS · xAPI · Learning analytics

1 Introduction

In recent years, learning environment in which many learners participate is widespread and many educational institutions introduce LMS (Learning Management System) and carry out long term operation. LMS such as Moodle or Canvas have enabled collect large scale learning logs easily. ADL (Advanced Distributed Learning) defined xAPI (Experience API) [1]. xAPI is a technical specification of the learning logs that specifies a structure to describe learning experiences and defines how these descriptions can be store LRS (Learning

© Springer Nature Switzerland AG 2020
C. Stephanidis and M. Antona (Eds.): HCII 2020, CCIS 1225, pp. 297–303, 2020.
https://doi.org/10.1007/978-3-030-50729-9_42

Record Store). LRS is database system for standardized learning logs by xAPI. According, we can analyze the learning logs to figure out the learner's achievement level and problems. LA (Learning Analytics) catch a great deal of attention in learning research domain. SoLAR (Society for Learning Analytics and Research) defined LA as the measurement, collection, analysis and reporting of data about learners and their contexts, for purposes of understanding and optimizing learning and the environments in which it occurs [2]. The latest study focuses on analyzing learning logs and method for giving analysis results feedback to teachers and learners. The analysis results provide evidence of individual learning and class improvement.

The study of Shimada (2018) gave feedback to teachers and provided the following potential benefits [3]. Teachers can adjust the lecture speed based on the real-time visualization of learner's activities and slow down to allow learners to catch up. This study did not give feedback to learners.

Our study focuses to give real time feedback to learners by during class based on Social Constructivism. Social Constructivism is a sociological theory of knowledge according to which human development is socially situated and knowledge is constructed through interaction with others [4]. In this study, we develop a real time viewing status feedback system. The system gives the status feedback to learners. We report impact for learner's learning activities.

2   Our LA Environment

We developed a LA environment. Figure 1 shows our LA environment. Moodle (Modular Object-Oriented Dynamic Learning Environment) is a free and open-source LMS [5,6]. Moodle manages online learning such as e-learning. Moodle stores learning logs such as login and logout. We installed a plugin on the Moodle that standardizes the pseudonymous learning logs by xAPI and store the learning logs in LRS. Learning Locker is a free and open-source LRS [7]. Our previous study, we developed STELLA (Storing and Treating the Experience of Learning for Learning Analytics) [8]. STELLA is Moodle module. Teachers can upload teaching materials of PDF format in STELLA linked to the Moodle. Teachers and learners uses STELLA for viewing the teaching materials. STELLA outputs their viewing behavior as learning logs and records pseudonymously the learning logs. The learning logs are including such as pseudonymously userID, the teaching materials name, page number and viewing time. STELLA standardizes the learning logs by xAPI and store the learning logs in LRS. The visualization tool visualizes their page transition of the teaching materials from the stored learning logs.

The environment is introduced few classes of Kochi University of Technology. A few teachers introduced the environment to 9 classes and used the environment from 15 January 2018 until 7 March 2020. Number of the stored learning logs were 591688.

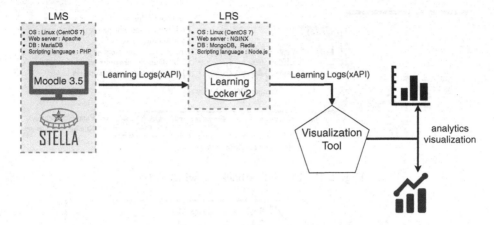

Fig. 1. Our LA environment

3   Real Time Page Transition Feedback System

Learners can receive teacher's explanation and teaching materials as compositions of learning. In this study, based on social constructivism, we give feedback that the learners can mutual inference with the others as a composition of learning. The feedback is the viewing status of the others who are viewing teaching materials at the same time. The learners can change in learning behavior by the feedback. We developed a real time viewing status feedback system on STELLA.

Figure 2 and Fig. 3 shows our real time viewing status feedback system on STELLA. The belt graph shows page number of learners in color. The table shows the number of learners viewing each page. Teachers and learners can confirm how many learners are viewing the previous or subsequent pages or same page as the teacher. The teachers can determine whether the learners are following lecture pace or are not following lecture pace in real time by the visualization. The object list is a list of teaching materials that the others are viewing in real time. The teachers and the learners can confirm kind of the teaching materials by the list. The learners can be aware of the others by the visualization.

4   Experimental of the Feedback

We evaluated operation of real time feedback system by asking students to use STELLA in classes held at Kochi University of Technology in 2018 and 2019 as a verification of the operation of the real time feedback system. Then, we gave learners with real time feedback on the viewing status of teacher materials. In addition, we accumulated learning histories in order to verify the effect of on learning behavior and achievement of tasks by awareness the others.

In the experiment, the learner was able to select whether to have real time feedback during class. This makes it possible to analyze differences in learning

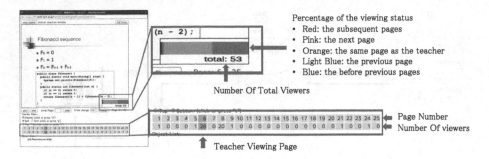

Fig. 2. Real time feedback: viewing status

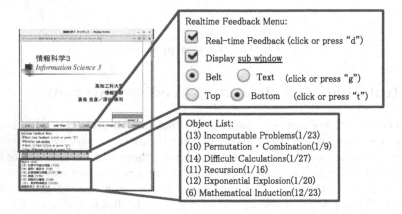

Fig. 3. Real time feedback: real time feedback menu and object list

behavior that do not depend on the content of the lesson from the learning history. The target lecture is the first half class of Information Science 3 which was started in 2019. We accumulated each learning history from 25 to 50 students out of 123 students. We divided the experiment into the following three cases.

– When we give real-time feedback
– When we did not give real time feedback
– When the learners can choose real time feedback

Figure 4 and Fig. 5 shows the learner in the same lecture separated by presence or absence of feedback, and visualized the learning history of entire lecture with heat map. Figure 6 and Fig. 7 are graphs of the page transitions of the learners in same lecture with or without feedback. Figure 4 and Fig. 6 shows page transitions for learner who have selected real time feedback, and Fig. 5 and Fig. 7 shows page transitions for learner who have not selected real time feedback. From the figures, it can be seen that tendency of learner page transitions differs slightly depending on presence or absence of real time feedback. We suggest from graph visualized from the learning history that presence or absence of feedback has some effect on learning behavior. However, when learning

(4) Logic 2 / Surplus (12/16) Heatmap Feedback Yes

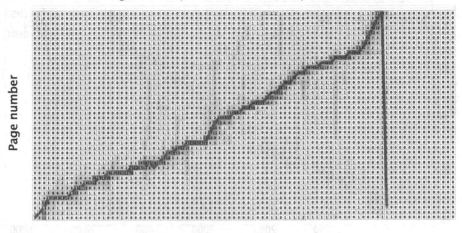

Elapsed time (minute)

Fig. 4. Heatmap: feedback yes

(4) Logic 2 / Surplus (12/16) Heatmap Feedback No

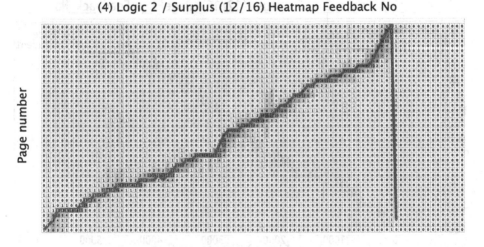

Elapsed time (minute)

Fig. 5. Heatmap: feedback no

behavior such as "next forward" or "jump to teacher's page" was counted from the learning history, no significant difference was found in the number of learning behavior depending on presence or absence of feedback.

As the result, the visualization of page transition had suggested that giving feedback affected learner's learning activities. However, no significant difference was found the number of learning behavior compare presence to absence of feedback.

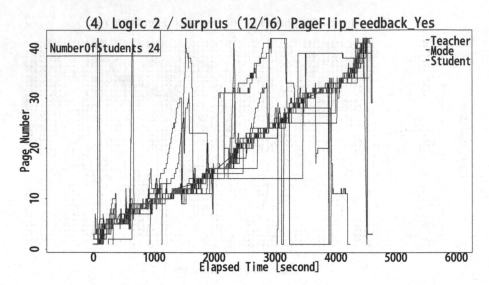

Fig. 6. PageFlip: feedback yes

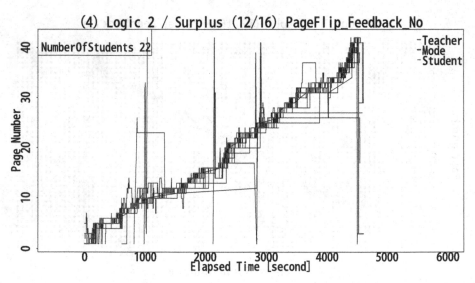

Fig. 7. PageFlip: feedback no

5   Conclusion

This paper described our real time viewing status feedback system and its experimental result. Our study focused to give real time feedback to learners by during class based on Social Constructivism. We developed a real time viewing status feedback system. The system gave the status feedback to teachers and learners. We conducted experiments of to give real time viewing status feedback. Through the experiments, the teacher could confirm the learner's situation whether they could follow her/his lecture by checking the real time viewing status feedback. In addition, the learners could confirm how many learners are viewing the previous or subsequent pages or same page as the teacher. As the result, the visualization of page transition had suggested that giving feedback affected learner's learning activities.

In our future work, we continue to use the real time viewing status feedback system for the other classes. We hypothesize that learners expand an understanding of the class by to give real time feedback. Besides, we will analyze the relationship between the learning behavior and performance of learners. We will predict learners who are at risk of failing a course or dropping out by the analysis results.

References

1. ADLNet. https://github.com/adlnet/xAPI-Spec/. Accessed 5 Mar 2020
2. Society for Learning Analytics Research (SoLAR). https://www.solaresearch.org/about/what-is-learning-analytics/. Accessed 5 Mar 2020
3. Shimada, A., Konomi, S., Ogata, H.: Real-time learning analytics system for improvement of on-site lectures. Interact. Technol. Smart Educ. **15**(4), 314–331 (2018). https://doi.org/10.1108/ITSE-05-2018-0026
4. McKinley, J.: Critical argument and writer identity: social constructivism as a theoretical framework for EFL academic writing. Crit. Inq. Lang. Stud. **12**(3), 184–207 (2015). https://doi.org/10.1080/15427587.2015.1060558
5. Moodle. https://moodle.org/. Accessed 5 Mar 2020
6. Wild, L.: Moodle 3.x Developer's Guide. Packt Publishing, Birmingham (2017)
7. HT2Labs. https://www.ht2labs.com/learning-locker-community/overview/. Accessed 5 Mar 2020
8. Mori, Y., Sakamoto, K., Mendori, T.: Development of a real time viewing status feedback system and its impact. In: Companion Proceedings of the 9th International Conference on Learning Analytics & Knowledge, LAK 2019, pp. 174–175 (2019)

Development and Initial Feasibility Testing of the Virtual Research Navigator (VRN): A Public-Facing Agent-Based Educational System for Clinical Research Participation

Sharon Mozgai[1,2]([✉]), Arno Hartholt[1,2], Dayo Akinyemi[1,2], Katarina Kubicek[1,2], Albert (Skip) Rizzo[1,2], and Michele Kipke[1,2]

[1] Institute for Creative Technologies, University of Southern California, 12015 Waterfront Dr., Playa Vista, CA 90094, USA
mozgai@ict.usc.edu
[2] Children's Hospital Los Angeles, 4650 Sunset Blvd., Los Angeles, CA 90027, USA
http://ict.usc.edu
http://chla.usc.edu

Abstract. The overall goal of VRN is to develop a novel technology solution at Children's Hospital Los Angeles (CHLA) to overcome barriers that prevent the recruitment of diverse patient populations to clinical trials by providing both caregivers and children with an interactive educational experience. This system consists of 1) an intelligent agent called Zippy that users interact with by keyboard or voice input, 2) a series of videos covering topics including Privacy, Consent and Benefits, and 3) a UI that guides users through all available content. Pre- and post-questionnaires assessed willingness to participate in clinical research and found participants either increased or maintained their level of willingness to participate in research studies. Additionally, qualitative analysis of interview data revealed participants rated the overall interaction favorably and believed Zippy to be more fun, less judgmental and less threatening than interacting with a human. Future iterations are in-progress based on the user-feedback.

Keywords: Human-computer interaction · Digital agent · Clinical trial

1 Introduction

Pediatric patients and their families may not have access to the most up-to-date information about research, treatment protocols, examples of important research findings, and opportunities to participate in clinical research studies. This leads to barriers to participation, that include a lack of knowledge about research, misconceptions or fears about participating in research studies, and not

© Springer Nature Switzerland AG 2020
C. Stephanidis and M. Antona (Eds.): HCII 2020, CCIS 1225, pp. 304–307, 2020.
https://doi.org/10.1007/978-3-030-50729-9_43

Fig. 1. Ava (left) and Zippy (right) who guide the users through the interactive experience.

knowing how to talk to their pediatrician about research opportunities [1–3]. The overall goal of the Virtual Research Navigator (VRN) system is to develop a new technology solution at Children's Hospital Los Angeles (CHLA) to overcome these major barriers to clinical and translational science engagement and the recruitment of diverse patients in clinical trials.

VRN aims to achieve this goal by providing both parents/caregivers and children with an interactive educational experience. The experience is led by a virtual characters designed to be both kid- and parent-friendly. Zippy and friend Ava (see Fig. 1) can discuss and provide information on diverse topics related to clinical research and address user questions to answer what it means to participate in research and why research participation is important to advancing health and healthcare. This system consists of 1) an intelligent agent that users can interact with by either keyboard or voice input, 2) a series of animated shorts that cover specific topics including Privacy, Consent and Benefits, and 3) a User Interface (UI) that guides the user through all available content. In effect, VRN is designed to take people on a journey through the research process, and ideally, all the way to enrolling them in an actual study. The clinical trial educational content was provided by CHLA in a text-based format and was adapted for this interactive system.

2   Methods

Twenty-two subjects (n = 16 parents/caregivers ages 37–53, n = 6 children ages 12–18) were recruited to be part of an initial feasibility study at CHLA. Participants reported their racial/ethnic background as Latino (n = 9), White (n = 5), Black/African American (n = 3), White/Latino/Native American (n = 2), White/ Latino (n = 1), White/Asian/Pacific Islander (n = 1), and Other(n = 1). Participants interacted with Zippy and his friend Ava via a web interface to learn about clinical research and better understand what it means to be involved in a research study. Pre- and post-questionnaires were given to assess knowledge level and willingness to participate in clinical research. Participants were also asked to give qualitative feedback on the system in five core areas (1) Appearance (2) Usability (3) Acceptability (4) Technology Experience and (5) Content.

3   Results

Participants in the study either maintained or increased their level of willingness to participate in research studies; the sample size was too small to conduct a Wilcoxon signed-rank test [4]. Qualitative analysis of interview data revealed that overall participants rated the interaction favorably and believed Zippy to be more fun, less judgmental and less threatening than interacting with a human.

Participants provided actionable feedback in the five core areas. Regarding **appearance**, general consensus was a desire for larger UI elements, including larger buttons, text and video screen for the deployment of educational video content. The participants expressed general satisfaction with the **usability** of the interface, but multiple participant's submitted a request that subtitles be provided as the content is currently deployed in English, however English may not be the first language of the end-users. In the category of **acceptability**, the feedback was positive, however specific requests for adding a theme song to Zippy's animation suite were recorded. Regarding **technological experience**, actionable feedback was given for the video player; participants expressed a desire to have the videos play automatically. Additionally, there were several requests for longer record-time for participants' responses. For **content**, participant's feedback addressed tailoring the video content to be more brief and to focus more on questions regarding the safety of the research protocol. Future iterations are in-progress based on this user-feedback (see Fig. 2).

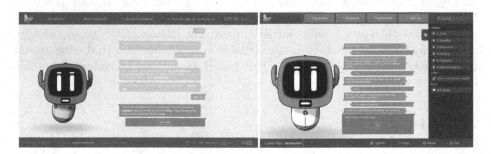

Fig. 2. Figure 2 Original UI (left) and current work-in-progress UI addressing user feedback (right), including larger UI elements, more prominent Zippy character, and streamlined navigation (e.g., additional short cuts, clearer labels, etc.).

4   Discussion

This project seeks to engage children (and their parents/caregivers) in the Los Angeles area who are receiving care at CHLA with Zippy, a Virtual Research Navigator, designed to educate users on the research process and ultimately enroll them in an actual study. Zippy's intent is to address the mistrust and the misconceptions many have about research and get more people involved by helping them understand more fully what's involved in clinical studies—including the regulations and ethical guidelines that govern clinical research. Zippy has been designed to appeal to a wide audience at CHLA and to involve both parents/caregivers and children. Younger children understandably find it difficult to digest details about medicine and research delivered by their doctors that is typically written in legalize designed for an adult audience, but an animated robot can be fun to talk to—and might break the ice better than a human doctor.

Users in this study are provided the opportunity to ask questions about different aspects of the clinical research process, and Zippy can answer verbally, using everyday terminology that kids and laypeople can understand. Initial tests of Zippy conducted with patients at CHLA are promising in this area. In fact, participants rated the interaction favorably and believed Zippy to be more fun, less judgmental and less threatening than interacting with a human. A second iteration is currently being finalized. Next steps include a pilot study that will insert Zippy into the clinical workflow when patients see their doctor at CHLA. The long term goal of this project is to introduce the Zippy platform into different sorts of hospitals, working with different populations and different health research aims.

Acknowledgements. The authors would like to thank all of our collaborators at CHLA and the USC Institute for Creative Technologies who worked on making VRN a success. In particular, Matt Liewer and Wendy Whitcup.

References

1. Elliott, D., Husbands, S., Hamdy, F.C., Holmberg, L., Donovan, J.L.: Understanding and improving recruitment to randomised controlled trials: qualitative research approaches. Eur. Urol. **72**(5), 789–798 (2017)
2. Featherstone, K., Donovan, J.L.: "Why don't they just tell me straight, why allocate it?" The struggle to make sense of participating in a randomised controlled trial. Soc. Sci. Med. **55**(5), 709–719 (2002)
3. Unger, J.M., Cook, E., Tai, E., Bleyer, A.: The role of clinical trial participation in cancer research: barriers, evidence, and strategies. Am. Soc. Clin. Oncol. Educ. Book **36**, 185–198 (2016)
4. Zimmerman, D.W., Zumbo, B.D.: Relative power of the Wilcoxon test, the Friedman test, and repeated-measures ANOVA on ranks. J. Exp. Educ. **62**(1), 75–86 (1993)

Development of a Learning Analytics Environment Introducing Mentoring History

Tatsuya Shishibori[1]($\boxtimes$), Komei Sakamoto[2], Yasuhiro Mori[2],
and Takahiko Mendori[1]

[1] School of Information, Kochi University of Technology, Kami, Japan
210323t@ugs.kochi-tech.ac.jp, mendori.takahiko@kochi-tech.ac.jp
[2] Graduate School of Engineering, Kochi University of Technology, Kami, Japan

Abstract. In recent years, learning environment in which many learners participate is widespread. Many educational institutions introduce LMS (Learning Management System) and carry out long term operation. LMS such as Moodle or Canvas have enabled collect large scale learning logs easily. Accordingly, LA(Learning Analytics) catch a great deal of attention. We can find problem and check learner's achievement level by LA. The study of Majumdar (2019) record teacher's behavior after class hours. However, mentoring (teaching behavior) affects learners not only after class hours but also during class hours. Usual LA researches dose not focus on the face-to-face mentoring. In this study, we propose that store mentoring history in our LA environment. Besides, we develop LA environment that store and analyze mentoring history. We visualized the stored mentoring history. The visualization had suggested that Mentoring impact on learning behavior. In addition, we analyzed the stored mentoring history. Result of analysis, number of Mentoring had an impact on achievement level of exercise.

Keywords: LMS · Mentoring · Mentoring history

1 Introduction

In recent years, learning environment in which many learners participate is widespread. Many educational institutions introduce LMS (Learning Management System) and carry out long term operation. LMS manages online learning such as e-learning. In addition, LMS stores learning logs such as login and logout. Therefore, LMS such as Moodle or Canvas have enabled collect large scale learning logs easily. The ADL (Advanced Distributed Learning) defined xAPI (Experience API) that is a technical specification of the learning logs [1]. xAPI specifies a structure to describe learning experiences and defines how these descriptions can be store LRS (Learning Record Store). LRS is database system for standardized learning logs by xAPI. According, it is easy to analyze the learning logs to figure out the learner's achievement level and some

C. Stephanidis and M. Antona (Eds.): HCII 2020, CCIS 1225, pp. 308–315, 2020.
https://doi.org/10.1007/978-3-030-50729-9_44

problems. LA (Learning Analytics) catch a great deal of attention in learning research domain. SoLAR (Society for Learning Analytics and Research) defined LA as the measurement, collection, analysis and reporting of data about learners and their contexts, for purposes of understanding and optimizing learning and the environments in which it occurs [2]. The latest study focuses record not only learner's learning logs but also teacher's teaching behavior after class hours. Analysis of teaching logs provide important teaching behavior and corroborating of learner's behavior.

The study of Majumdar (2019) record teacher's behavior after class hours [3]. However, learners usually learn individually during class hours especially exercise. In addition, learners question and receive advice during class hours from mentor(teacher and teaching assistant). Accordingly, mentoring (teaching behavior) affects learners not only after class hours but also during class hours. Usual LA researches dose not focus on the face-to-face mentoring.

The previous our study, we developed STELLA (Storing and Treating the Experience of Learning for Learning Analytics) [4]. STELLA standardizes learner's detailed learning history by xAPI, store the learning history in LRS. However, we also didn't consider face-to-face mentoring to learners. Therefore, we need to develop system which store mentoring history during class hours.

In this study, we propose that store mentoring history in our LA environment. Besides, we develop LA environment that store and analyze mentoring history. To realize the environment, we developed MLR (Mentoring Log Recorder) and MRS (Mentoring Record Store). MLR stores mentoring log during class hours as a mentoring history in MRS. In addition, MLR can share storing mentoring history between mentor. Furthermore, we report impact of mentoring for learner's learning behavior and achievement level of exercise.

2   Our LA Environment

We developed former LA environment. Figure 1 shows our former LA environment. The previous study, we developed STELLA. STELLA is module of LMS. Teachers can upload teaching materials of PDF format in STELLA linked to the LMS. Teachers and learners use STELLA for viewing the teaching materials. STELLA outputs their viewing behavior as learning logs and records pseudonymously the learning logs. The learning logs are including such as pseudonymously userID, the teaching materials name, page number and viewing time. STELLA standardizes the learning logs by xAPI and store the learning logs in LRS. The visualization tool visualizes their page transition of the teaching materials from the stored learning logs.

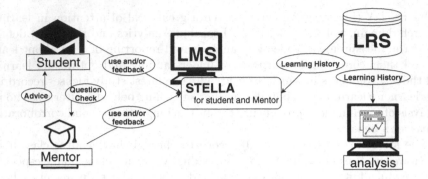

Fig. 1. Our LA environment

3   LA Environment Introducing Mentoring History

Figure 2 shows our LA environment introducing mentoring history. MLR has two functions. One is to store mentoring performed by mentors as a mentoring history in MRS (Meontoring Record Store). The other is to share how each learner received instruction during class hours among mentors.

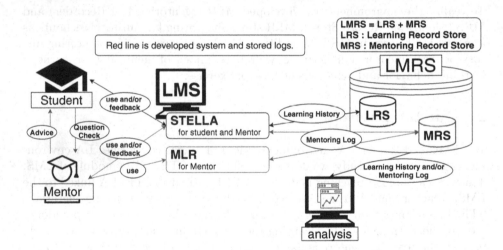

Fig. 2. LA environment introducing mentoring history

3.1   Mentoring History Storing Function

MLR stores the mentoring history in MRS. Details of the mentoring history are as follows; timestamp: mentoring history occurrence time, actor: mentored learners, checker: mentor who performed mentoring, course: class name, exercise name: exercise name, number of exercise: number of exercises, exercise num: exercise number, evaluation: exercise score, comment: advices and questions. By collecting mentoring histories with MLR and storing the histories, it is possible to share mentoring during class hours and analyze the relationship between the degree of achievement and the mentoring history.

3.2   Mentoring Sharing Function

MLR is improved real-time sharing and management system for exercise progress in practical and exercises. MLR has two pages. One is to confirm exercise achievement of the entire each learner. The other is to confirm the exercise achievement of individual. Mentors can check and evaluate for exercise using MLR. MLR has exercise pages for evaluating the entire each learner. Also, MLR has personal exercise pages for evaluating each learner. In addition, in order to use student information registered in LMS, the Moodle module is used to store detailed mentoring history in MRS.

Exercise Page

Exercise page have a function to check whether each student has achieved exercises. MLR is LMS module. Therefore, we can create by referring to the student number and the name of the learner who belongs to the course in exercise page. Mentors can refer to it when checking the percentage of attendees and the percentage of exercise achievements. Also, announcements can advise the entire learner when the learner is performing exercises. The history of advices displays when the entire learner receive advice. Regarding the contents of MLR table, the number of cells changes according to the number of exercises. The five choices of a four-step evaluation and question as to whether the learner has achieved exercises, can evaluate the learner's exercise. When we perform the evaluation, the time at which we performed the evaluation is displayed at the final check time, and "done" indicating that transmission has finished is displayed in the evaluated cell. Also, when the learner has achieved exercises, the number of persons achieving exercises is counted. The background color of the learner's cell changes yellow-green (Fig. 3).

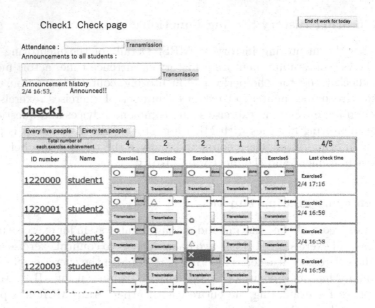

Fig. 3. Exercise page (Color figure online)

Personal Exercise Page

Personal exercise page has functions to perform students' advice, responses to questions, and evaluations. The page can not only evaluate each exercise but also leave comments for the learner. Mentor can check the comments for each learner to understand which exercise the student has stumbled on and where they could not understand. The learner's situation can understand by leaving a comment in the student information. For example, exercises could not be completed due to poor physical condition.

4   Experimental Result

The purpose of this experiment is to verify whether mentor behavior influence learner based on timing of mentoring, changing of learner behavior or achievement of exercises. We also visualize learning history and mentoring history. Therefore, we collected the learning history and mentoring history that occurred in the class held at Kochi University of Technology.

4.1   Experiment Outline

We collected the learning history and mentoring history for programming experiment 1. The period is six times between July 2 and July 19, 2019. The class hours are the third and fourth classes on Tuesday and Friday, and the location is PC room. In the first half of each class, lesson explanations are given, and in the second half, three to five exercises are asked. The collection of learning histories targets at students who have used STELLA among 109 registered students. So that students who do not use STELLA can view class materials, KUTLMS of Kochi University of Technology display the same class materials. Students must complete exercises during class hours and have the mentor evaluate exercises. The maximum number of mentors who evaluate exercises is about 10 mentors(2 teachers and 8 Teaching Assistants).

4.2 Stored Mentoring History

Table 1 shows the number of mentoring logs the mentor gave to each student in the six classes. We also used mentoring history and exercise achievement to analyze.

Table 1. The number of mentoring logs

The day of class	7/2	7/5	7/9	7/12	7/16	7/19
The number of questions	0	17	2	9	8	6
The number of advices	5	7	8	25	10	50
The number of exercise	359	206	375	390	412	282
The number of exercises	4	3	4	4	4	4

4.3 Result

Analysis Method

We use all student exercise achievements in each class to analyze. In addition, mentoring histories use advice to students, responses to questions from students, and evaluation of student exercises. The analysis method uses Welch's t-test. We find the significant difference between the average of the exercise achievements of two independent groups in each exercise. This time, we conducted an analysis to find the significant difference between the average of exercise achievements of students who received advice from the mentor and students who never received advice from the mentor (Table 2).

Table 2. The number of mentorings

The day of class	Received advice once ()	Never received any advice ()	p-value
2 July	0.95	0.7311	5.716154e−1
5 July	0.8571	0.4825	1.653e−4
9 July	0.875	0.7623	1.0634e−2
12 July	0.88	0.75	2.1263e−3
16 July	0.85	0.7649	8.92674e−2
19 july	0.57	0.4618	2.6608e−2

Visualization of Learning Behavior and Mentoring

Figure 4 shows the timing of learning behavior and mentoring. it is possible to confirm the change in learning behavior and the timing of mentoring.

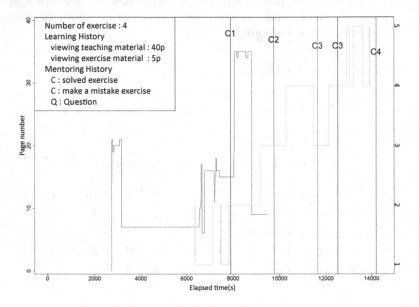

Fig. 4. Visualization of learning behavior and mentoring

5   Conclusion

This paper described our LA environment introducing mentoring history and analysis of mentoring history. Our study, we developed MLR and MRS. MLR store mentoring during class hours as a mentoring history in MRS. MLR can share storing mentoring history between mentor. We conducted experiments of to store and share mentoring history. In addition, we visualized and analyzed impact of mentoring for learner's learning behavior and achievement level of exercise. As the result, the visualization had suggested that mentoring impact on learning behavior. Besides, we confirmed that mentoring impact on achievement level of exercise.

In our future work, we continue to use MLR for other classes. We hypothesize that mentoring affects learning behavior. We will analyze some relationship of learning behavior and timing of mentoring. In addition, we will analyze learning behavior and content of mentoring. We will research mentoring that expand an understanding of class of learner.

References

1. adlnet. https://github.com/adlnet/xAPI-Spec/. Accessed 5 Mar 2020
2. Society for Learning Analytics Research (SoLAR). https://www.solaresearch.org/about/what-is-learning-analytics/. Accessed 5 Mar 2020
3. Majumdar, R., Akcapinar, A., Akcapinar, G., Flanagan, B., Ogata, H.: LAViEW: learning analytics dashboard towards evidence-based education, companion. In: Proceedings 9th International Conference on Learning Analytics & Knowledge (LAK 2019), pp. 68–73 (2019)
4. Mori, Y., Sakamoto, K., Mendori, T.: Development of a real time viewing status feedback system and its impact, companion. In: Proceedings of the 9th International Conference on Learning Analytics & Knowledge (LAK 2019), pp. 174–175 (2019)

Developing an Interactive Tabletop Mediated Activity to Induce Collaboration by Implementing Design Considerations Based on Cooperative Learning Principles

Patrick Sunnen[1]([⊠]), Béatrice Arend[1], Svenja Heuser[1],
Hoorieh Afkari[2], and Valérie Maquil[2]

[1] University of Luxembourg,
Porte des Sciences 11, 4366 Esch-sur-Alzette, Luxembourg
{patrick.sunnen,beatrice.arend,svenja.heuser}@uni.lu
[2] Luxembourg Institute of Science and Technology,
Avenue des Hauts-Fourneaux, 4362 Esch-sur-Alzette, Luxembourg
{hoorieh.afkari,valerie.maquil}@list.lu

Abstract. Constructive collaboration can be a difficult matter. For this reason, we are implementing and studying an interactive-tabletop-mediated activity that aims at inducing collaboration among participants. The resulting activity 'Orbitia' is designed as a serious game. Participants are asked to act as a space-mining crew, which has to collect minerals with a rover and rely on a camera-drone for reconnaissance, while keeping the rover out of harm and managing limited resources. In this paper we provide an account of how we designed Orbitia's pedagogical structuring by relying on the Johnsons' cooperative learning approach whose fundamental concept is "positive interdependence". More particularly, we show how we worked on resource, role and task inter-dependence to design three collaboration-inducing 'flagship' devices: the rover-steering-device (RSD), the item-locating-device (ILD) and the responsibility-activating-device (RAD).

Keywords: Interactive tabletop · Collaboration · Cooperative learning

1 Introduction

There is an increasing recognition that societal and intellectual challenges will be (resp. are already) so complicated or complex that they can only be tackled collabo-ratively. However, constructive collaboration on new challenges is a difficult matter and the mere joining of people's forces does not help unless people know *how* to collaborate [1]. Hence, learning to learn and to work together must become an important goal in education and professional training. So, the design research project ORBIT (Overcoming Breakdowns in Teams with Interactive Tabletops) aims at implementing and studying a joint problem-solving activity at an interactive tabletop (ITT) [2].

C. Stephanidis and M. Antona (Eds.): HCII 2020, CCIS 1225, pp. 316–324, 2020.
https://doi.org/10.1007/978-3-030-50729-9_45

In reference to the project name we called this activity 'Orbitia' (see Fig. 1). Orbitia is designed as a serious game where adult participants are asked to act as a space-mining crew. The latter has to collect minerals with a rover and rely on a camera-drone for reconnaissance, while keeping the rover out of harm and managing limited resources. The activity consists of two phases. The first one is designed to induce 'smooth' collaboration among the participants. In the second one, the underlying foundational rules are unexpectedly modified in order to put to the test participants' previously established collaboration procedures. Thus, in order to cope successfully with this advanced dynamic situation, participants will have to re-establish and expand their collaboration procedures.

Stahl [3] rightfully points out that every technology in order to achieve a desirable educational outcome requires "considerable interface design, user evaluation, peda-gogical structuring, and collaborative culture" (p. 486). While the implementation of ORBIT's multidisciplinary design-based research process as well as results of the video-taped trials are resp. will be presented elsewhere [4], the purpose of this paper is to provide an account of how a cooperative learning approach [5, 6] provided for the pedagogical structuring and informed the design of the now accomplished first phase of Orbitia.

2 Theoretical Design Considerations

2.1 Collaboration

In everyday life and even in many scientific accounts, the term 'collaboration' is often used very broadly to describe two or more persons working together on the same task. Hence, before we can begin to conceive Orbitia as an interactive tabletop activity inducing collaboration in a face-to-face setting, we have to become more specific about the conduct we seek to solicit here.

In line with a process-oriented meaning-making approach on collaboration [7], we rely on Roschelle and Teasley [8], who define "collaboration" as a "coordinated, synchronous activity that is the result of a continued attempt to construct and maintain a shared conception of a problem" (p. 70). So, the design of Orbitia aims at imple-menting a co-located activity, that provides a mediational framework supporting par-ticipants' mutual engagement, pointing their orientation to a shared goal, facilitating the description of the current problem state, and raising their awareness of problem-solving actions [4].

2.2 Collaboration and Interactive Tabletops

Interactive tabletops can integrate physical and digital artefacts, spoken and written texts to provide groups with a focal point and dynamic resource to support collabo-ration [3]. In other words, they are inherently designed as shareable interfaces (see Fig. 2): their input modalities support more than one participant [9] and their horizontal orientation enables face-to-face communication around a large surface that provides participants with a shared overview and focus point [10].

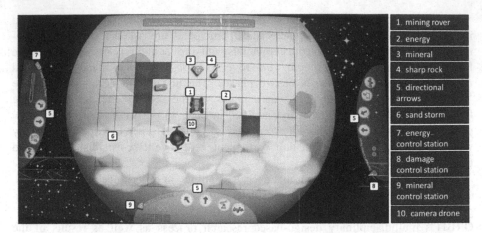

| 1. mining rover |
| 2. energy |
| 3. mineral |
| 4. sharp rock |
| 5. directional arrows |
| 6. sand storm |
| 7. energy control station |
| 8. damage control station |
| 9. mineral control station |
| 10. camera drone |

Fig. 1. Annotated screenshot of 'Orbitia'.

Fig. 2. A group of participants engaging with 'Orbitia'

Pointing to relevant studies Ioannou and Antoniou [11] (p. 165) summarize that tabletops enhance the sense of teamwork, induce interaction and willingness to participate in group tasks, foster equity in physical interaction, promote joint attention on the task, and improve the (learning) experience and engagement with the task. Indeed, when participants' attention is drawn to the tabletop, they can see each other's actions as well as the system's feedback, potentially changing the nature of the collaboration: for example, the explicit awareness of other's hand actions facilitates exploration and increases collaborative forms of construction and meaning making [12] (p. 319).

However, none of these promising study outcomes can be taken for granted and, as we pointed out above, the pedagogical framework that is designed into the ITT-mediated activity is a crucial issue here. For this reason, we shall now outline the essential features of Orbitia's pedagogical structuring and how we implemented them.

2.3 Cooperative Learning

In instructional contexts "cooperative learning" and "collaborative learning" are either used interchangeably or presented as having considerable overlap. At times, cooperative learning is considered as the more structured approach where "the structure is imposed by the teacher" and "is designed to achieve a specific goal or end-product" [13] (p. 71). During our literature research we found that a number of researchers [14, 15] take inspiration in Johnson & Johnson's work on *cooperative learning* [5, 6] to develop educational *collaborative* game scenarios. The latter are defined as games where "all the participants work together as a team, sharing the pay-offs and outcomes; if the team wins or loses, everyone wins or loses" [16] (p. 25).

The Johnsons rely on a social interdependence perspective and "cooperation" is described as "positive interdependence", which exists "when students perceive that they are linked with groupmates in a way that makes it impossible for anyone to succeed unless the entire group succeeds (and vice versa) and that they must coordinate their efforts with their groupmates to complete a task" [5] (p. 27). Research indicates that participants engaged in cooperative settings spend considerable time on task, show positive attitudes toward the experience of working on the task, take accurate perspectives, generate new ideas and readily transfer their cooperative efforts to new tasks [17].

Such a defined approach of cooperative learning is suitable for creating a group-worthy task which calls for participants to rely on multiple resources that cannot be mobilised by one person alone, and aims at creating a situation in which participants "work interdependently and reciprocally, and where the exchange of ideas and information" and "the joint construction of understanding" are key to success [18] (p. 115).

In order to construct the pedagogical structuring of 'Orbitia' we relied on the following interdependence principles of "cooperative learning": *fantasy* (the task is embedded in a compelling narrative, here: space-mining), *environmental* (group members are bound by the physical environment; here: the tabletop and the graphical representation of a planetary surface), *identity* (establishment of a group identity, here: participants are positioned as a space mining crew by the narrative), *goal* (only the group can accomplish the set goal, here: collecting the minerals), *task* (each participant has to complete a sub-task for the group goal to be achieved, here: steering and retrieving manoeuvres), *role* (complementary task-relevant responsibilities are distributed among the participants, here: being in charge of mining, repairing or energy matters), *resource* (every participant holds only a portion of the needed resources, here: for example, individually allocated steering options) and *reward* (every participant receives the same reward when the group goal is reached, here: moving to the next level and eventually winning the game). To avoid putting pressure on an emerging group, we have not yet implemented an *outside enemy* interdependence (the group is put in competition with other groups, standards or time). Nevertheless, this feature may be applied in the second phase of the activity where the collaboration procedures established by the participants are to be challenged.

3   Implementing Cooperative Learning Design Considerations

More particularly, we worked on resource, role and task interdependence to guide the design of three collaboration-inducing 'flagship' devices: the rover-steering-device (RSD), the item-locating-device (ILD) and the responsibility-activating-device (RAD).

(1) The *rover-steering-device* consists of a virtual manoeuvrable rover with distributed control buttons. Every control station is equipped with two touch-controlled arrows (Fig. 1, no 5; Fig. 3a) enabling each participant to steer the rover into two different directions. This particular distribution of the control options aims at ensuring that every participant has to bring in a specific *resource* (two unique directions) assigned to him/her in order to move the group's rover to a targeted spot. The steering movements have to be performed in an appropriate order and thus every movement correspond to sub-*tasks* to be done by the responsible participants. This is reinforced by the fact that two directions (see Fig. 3b) can only be taken through the composition of two other directions, thus requiring the intervention of two participants in close coordination. The distribution of the steering options contributes to the establishment of *roles*, further strengthened through the organisation of the ILD and the RAD.

(2) The *item-locating-device* consists of one tangible shared object (drone) with an integrated display, a surrounding 3 × 3 digital grid and four mini-maps in each control station (see Fig. 4). The drone can be operated by every participant to disclose the hidden items in the sandstorm area. While being moved over the surface the display shows the number of (hidden) items in the surrounding grid. After pushing a button, the nature of the surrounding items (mineral, energy stack, sharp rock) and their location is briefly revealed in the grid. This information is then distributed to the corresponding mini-maps[1] in the three control stations. Thus, every participant has a particular complementary *resource* at his/her disposal, i.e. the information on the location and the amount of the type of items that are associated with his/her control station. This feature aims at supporting the establishment of a specific *role* for every participant, which is materialised in the RAD.

(3) The *responsibility-activating-device* offers three different positions materialized as energy, damage, and mineral control stations located in three separate places (Fig. 1, no. 7–9; Fig. 5). Every participant is expected to take the responsibility of one area: energy, mining, or damage management). According to the assumed responsibility, s/he has to monitor the number of attributed items (energy units, number of spare wheels or number of minerals collected) and the corresponding locations of the collectable (energy, minerals) and dangerous items (rocks). The

---

[1] This feature is inspired by the quadrants in the game "Chase the Cheese" [15].

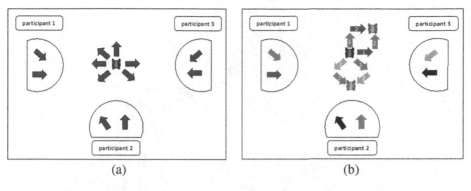

Fig. 3. (a) Distribution of directions (b) Composing missing directions

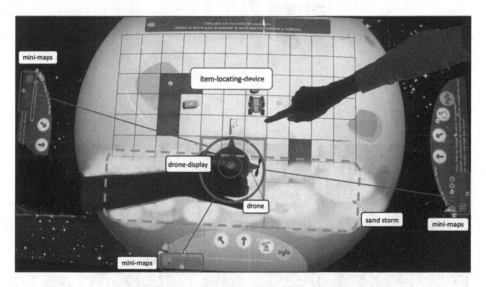

Fig. 4. Participants applying the item-locating-device

different items are marked on the respective mini-maps as dots meaning that the dots appearing in the mini-maps of the mining control station point to the location of the minerals and so on. Thus, according to his/her *role*, every participant has a particular complementary *resource* at his/her disposal, which is the information on the location and the amount of the type of items that are associated with his/her control station. This *role-* or responsibility-related distribution also applies to the information shown in the display area of every control station (Fig. 5, blue rounded rectangle). On pushing the info button first (Fig. 5, red circle) and then the appearing crosses (not visible in the figures), the participant receives responsibility-

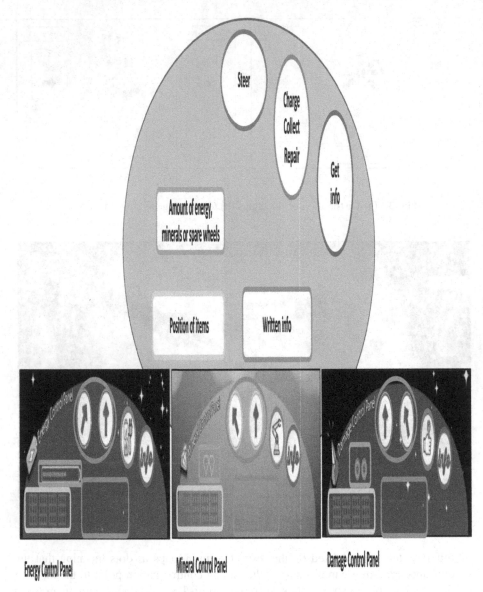

Fig. 5. Responsibility-activating-device (Color figure online)

specific written information[2] with regard to the features of his/her station. Furthermore, every participant has to perform the related pick-up respectively the

---

[2] Other less specific information – for example, the mission objective, some features of the map (base, sandstorm, etc.) – is available right away for every participant in a display field above the grid or around the drone. For reasons of space and to ensure better readability, we chose not to elaborate here on how we provided the participants with written operating instructions.

wheel-changing action by pushing the button on his/her control station provided for this purpose (*task* interdependence).

4 Conclusion

Taking Stahl's [3] caution seriously, we conceptualised the pedagogical design of our collaboration-inducing ITT-mediated activity Orbitia by relying on a sound and validated cooperative learning approach developed by the Johnsons [5, 6]. We are aware that all the other considerations listed by Stahl [3] – interface design, user evaluation and collaboration culture – are equally important and closely intertwined. That's why we plan to address these issues in subsequent publications. In this paper, we elaborated on how we implemented the concept of "positive interdependence" [5, 6] in the design of Orbitia. So far, our ongoing user evaluation and video analyses indicate that participants experience the engagement with Orbitia as collaborative, display collaborative conduct in the sense of [8], and actively engage with and appropriate the three developed flagship devices the rover-steering-device, the item-locating-device and the responsibility-activating-device.

Acknowledgements. We thank the Luxembourg National Research Fund (FNR) for funding this research under the CORE scheme.

References

1. Schwarz, B.B., de Grootet, R., Mavrikis, M., Dragon, T.: Learning to learn together with CSCL tools. Int. J. Comput.-Supported Collab. Learn. **10**(3), 239–271 (2015)
2. Sunnen, P., Arend, B., Maquil, V.: ORBIT - overcoming breakdowns in teams with interactive tabletops. In: Rethinking Learning in the Digital Age: Making the Learning Sciences Count, 13th International Conference of the Learning Sciences (ICLS) 2018, London (2018)
3. Stahl, G.: Collaborating around the tabletop. Int. J. Comput. Support. Collab. Learn. **6**(4), 485–490 (2011)
4. Sunnen, P., Arend, B., Heuser, S., Afkari, H., Maquil, V.: Designing collaborative scenarios on tangible tabletop interfaces - insights from the implementation of paper prototypes in the context of a multidisciplinary design workshop. In: 17th European Conference on Computer-Supported Cooperative Work, Salzburg (2019)
5. Johnson, D.W., Johnson, R.T., Johnson Holubec, E.: The New Circles of Learning. Cooperation in the Classroom. ASCD, Alexandria (1994)
6. Johnson, D., Johnson, R.: Positive Interdependence. The Heart of Cooperative Learning. Interaction Book Company, Edina (1992)
7. Stahl, G., Koschmann, T., Suthers, D.: Computer-supported collaborative learning. In: Sawyer, R.K. (ed.) The Cambridge Handbook of the Learning Sciences, 2nd edn, pp. 479–499. Cambridge University Press, New York (2014)
8. Roschelle, J., Teasley, S.: The construction of shared knowledge in collaborative problem solving. In: O'Malley, C. (ed.) Computer Supported Collaborative Learning, pp. 69–97. Springer, Berlin (1995). https://doi.org/10.1007/978-3-642-85098-1_5

9. Evans, M.A., Rick, J.: Supporting learning with interactive surfaces and spaces. In: Spector, J.M., Merill, M.D., Elen, J., Bishop, M. (eds.) Handbook of Research on Educational Communications and Technology, pp. 689–701. Springer, New York (2014). https://doi.org/10.1007/978-1-4614-3185-5_55

10. Brudy, F., Marquard, N.: The tabletop is dead? – long live the table's top! submitted to the workshop: "the disappearing tabletop - social and technical challenges for cross-surface collaboration". In: conjunction with the ACM Conference on Interactive Surfaces and Spaces 2017. ISS, Brighton (2017)

11. Ioannou, A., Antoniou, C.: Tabletops for peace: technology enhanced peacemaking in school contexts. Educ. Technol. Soc. **19**(2), 164–176 (2016)

12. Price, S.: Tangibles: technologies and interaction for learning. In: Price, S., Jewitt, C., Brown, B. (eds.) The Sage Handbook of Digital Technology Research, pp. 307–325. Sage, London (2013)

13. McWhaw, K., Schnackenberg, H., Sclater, J., Arambi, P.-C.: From co-operation to collaboration. In: Gillies, R., Brown, B. (eds.) Co-operative Learning, pp. 307–325. Sage, London, New York (2003)

14. Oskanen, K., Hämäläinen, R.: Game mechanics in the design of a collaborative 3D serious game. Simul. Gaming **45**(2), 255–278 (2014)

15. Collazos, C.A., Guerrero, L.A., Pino, J.A., Ochoa, S.F.: Collaborative scenarios to promote positive interdependence among group members. In: Favela, J., Decouchant, D. (eds.) CRIWG 2003. LNCS, vol. 2806, pp. 356–370. Springer, Heidelberg (2003). https://doi.org/10.1007/978-3-540-39850-9_30

16. Zagal, J.P., Rick, J., Hsi, I.: Collaborative games: lessons learned from board games. Simul. Gaming **37**(1), 24–40 (2006)

17. Johnson, D.W., Johnson, R.T.: Cooperative, competitive, and individualistic learning environments. In: Hattie, J., Anderman, E.M. (eds.) International Guide to Student Achievement, pp. 372–374. Routledge, New York (2013)

18. Vass, E., Littleton, K.: Peer collaboration and learning in the classroom. In: Littleton, K., Wood, C., Staarman, K.J. (eds.) International Handbook of Psychology in Education, pp. 105–135. Emerald Group Publishing Limited, Bingley (2010)

Using Emoji as Image Resources
in Educational Programming Tools

Ryo Suzuki[(✉)] and Ikuro Choh

Waseda University, Lambdax Bldg 3F, 2-4-12 Okubo,
Shinjuku, Tokyo 169-0072, Japan
reputeless@gmail.com

Abstract. In this paper, we describe techniques and considerations for using emoji effectively in educational programming tools. Introducing emoji gives users access to more than 3,000 different image assets for game and other application development. Since the font files installed in the user's computer vary by its operating software and device vendor, it is preferable that programming tools bundle common emoji font files for users. Emojis have a variety of gender and skin color patterns, which reduces the artist's effort to bring diversity to the illustrations of the people. Some emojis contain violent or vulgar expressions. Tool providers can filter some emojis to prevent children from accessing inappropriate emojis in schools, or they can adjust visuals to mitigate aggressiveness. Advanced visuals and applications can be obtained by extracting contour and geometry information or adding shadows. In order to help users quickly find the emoji they are looking for from many emojis, a utility system should be implemented that classifies emojis by category, searches for emojis by word, and suggests random emojis.

Keywords: Programming tool · Emoji · Visual programming · Visual design

1 Introduction

1.1 Visual Elements in Programming Tools

A typical educational programming tool uses user code to animate visual elements, such as pictures of animals or people. Scratch [1] allows users to use many image assets provided by the tool, as well as image files uploaded by the users and illustrations drawn by the users on the tool. Image assets make it easy to get started coding quickly, and learners who aren't good at drawing or don't paint well with the mouse can easily get involved in the development of an application.

In developing our new programming tool, we chose a policy of providing users with a sufficient amount of image assets, as existing tools do, and used emojis as a resource for image data (Fig. 1).

1.2 Emoji

Emoji are pictograms used inline in text. In recent years, they are frequently seen in e-mails, messengers, and texts posted on social networks. Emoji are standardized by the

© Springer Nature Switzerland AG 2020
C. Stephanidis and M. Antona (Eds.): HCII 2020, CCIS 1225, pp. 325–331, 2020.
https://doi.org/10.1007/978-3-030-50729-9_46

Fig. 1. Our programming tools provide users with emojis as image assets that can be used for game development.

Unicode Consortium and its Unicode Emoji [2] defines pairs of one or a few code points and a corresponding example pictogram. Currently, 3,053 emoji types are listed in the latest standard, Unicode Emoji 12.0 published in 2019.

Emoji symbols cover a variety of things such as animals, food, vehicles, buildings, and occupations, allowing users to express a diverse and complex world and story without having to draw pictures by themselves. Emoji encourages users to challenge themselves to code movement, for example, making a bouncing ball, a running tiger, a flapping butterfly, or a flame spreading.

One of the features of emojis is that they are designed to be acceptable to a diverse group of people. For example, the technologist, as defined by the Unicode emoji, has three genders and six skin colors, for a total of 18 patterns (Fig. 2). The same is true for other professional emoji, such as firefighters and pilots.

Fig. 2. Three gender patterns and six skin-tone options are available for each profession (Twemoji [3]). (Color figure online)

2 Implementation

2.1 Bundling Emoji

The type of emoji font file preinstalled on a user's computer depends on the type and version of the operating system and the vendor of the device. Even if the font name is the same, the type and design of the emoji included depends on the version of the font. When a user's font file does not contain the desired emoji data, a renderer such as a Web browser displays a fallback box glyph called "tofu" or a list of individual emoji decomposed based on ZWJ (zero width joiner) as shown in Fig. 3. Usually, in such cases, it is difficult for the user to read the original meaning. Therefore, when using emojis in programming tools, it is desirable to bundle and distribute a common set of fonts for all users to use on the tool.

Fig. 3. A font fallback box glyph (left) and decomposed emojis (right). Emojis that cannot be represented by the user's font file are rendered in these styles.

2.2 Licensing

Only a small number of vendors produce emoji typefaces compared to the alphabetic typefaces. Table 1 shows a list of the major emoji fonts. Most of the emoji font vendors are platformers with huge users, like operating software and SNS. In terms of font licensing, there are only four fonts that can be distributed as part of a programming tool.

Table 1. Major emoji fonts and their licenses.

Emoji	Example	License and URL
Twitter Twemoji		CC-BY 4.0 https://github.com/twitter/twemoji
Google Noto Emoji		Apache License 2.0 https://github.com/googlefonts/noto-emoji
Apple		proprietary
Microsoft		See https://docs.microsoft.com/en-us/typography/fonts/font-faq
Samsung		proprietary
Facebook		proprietary
OpenMoji		CC BY-SA 4.0 https://github.com/hfg-gmuend/openmoji
WhatsApp		proprietary

2.3   Rendering

Some emoji fonts are not vector data but a set of PNG compressed bitmap data (100–200 pixels wide per character) stored in the font file. Rendering such image beyond their original size will result in artifacts (Fig. 4). On the other hand, rendering many vector data requires either pre-rendering the emoji offline, or an efficient way to draw the vector data in real time.

Fig. 4. Sharpness is lost due to enlargement of low-resolution emoji.

For monochromatic emojis, signed distance field (SDF) [4] or multi-channel signed distance field (MSDF) [5] can be used to produce huge rendering results from images with a few tens of pixels per side (Fig. 5), while keeping sharpness (Fig. 6). More research is needed on how to efficiently render vector data for emojis containing multiple colors [6].

Fig. 5. MSDF-encoded image (44 × 48 pixels) of an emoji depicting a rocket (see Fig. 6). (Color figure online)

2.4   Orientation

When using emojis in programming tools, the orientation of the emoji symbols should be handled with care. If not handled properly, for example, a marathon runner in the game will run backwards. Unicode Emoji does not specify the orientation of symbols in most cases, except for some symbols such as arrows. Programming tool developers should manually tag the orientation of the emoji or allow users to flip the orientation of the symbol left or right in the tools.

A proposal to use ZWJ to add orientation information to emojis is being discussed in the Unicode Consortium [7]. Therefore, future implementations could use this to determine orientation.

Fig. 6. MSDF can generate sharp, high-resolution images from low-resolution data (see Fig. 5).

2.5 Reducing Aggressiveness

Some emojis contain violent expressions and vulgar gestures. Especially in educational use, programming tool developers need to consider removing these emojis, or they can just provide a configuration to filter these emojis. We found a technique to mitigate the aggressiveness of some emojis by fattening the outline of the emoji, as shown in Fig. 7, to give the illusion that it is a sticker depicting a knife rather than a real knife.

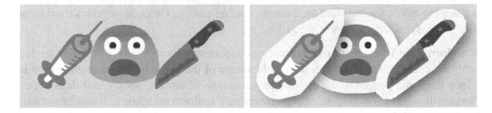

Fig. 7. The wide white outline reduces the aggressiveness of some symbols.

A pistol was once depicted in emojis as a classic handgun, but after Apple changed its design to a toy gun in 2016, all the major emoji vendors have shifted these to depicting water guns [8].

2.6 Taking More Out of the Emoji

If many emojis appear in the game, it can be difficult to tell which objects are important (e.g., controllable player characters). The presence of emojis of important characters and objects can be emphasized by adding round shadows to the background (Fig. 8).

The geometry data retrieved from the emoji is useful for games using physics simulations (see Fig. 1, center).

2.7 Searching for an Emoji

Since there are more than 3000 emojis, programming tools need to assist users to quickly find the emoji they want to use.

Fig. 8. Round shadow under the character enhances the presence of the emoji in the screen.

Classification by Category. Emojis can be categorized according to their meaning. It is useful to be presented with all the animal emojis when the user wants to create a zoo. Unicode provides official emoji categories and subcategories in its list [9].

Searching for Emojis Associated with a Word. A system can be provided to display multiple emojis associated with a search term. It is useful when users are looking for a specific national flag from more than 200 flags, or for emojis that are difficult to categorize, such as a spoon (food or tools). The programming tool needs to implement a mapping table of words and their corresponding emojis. Unicode provides short name and some keywords for each emoji [9].

Random Emoji Suggestions. Presenting random emojis to users is one way to deal with the complexity. Users can decide the theme of the game based on random emojis. Since flags and people make up a large percentage of emojis, people and flags appear frequently when randomly selecting emojis with uniform weighting. It can be avoided by biased weights.

3   Future Work

The productivity of emoji searches needs to be improved, as the number of emojis is expected to continue to grow [10]. To cope with the increasing resolution of users' devices, a method of rendering emojis with better runtime performance is required. It would be useful to be able to create a new custom emoji (such as a facial expression) in the same style as the tool's emoji when the user cannot find the desired emoji.

Acknowledgement.   This work was supported by I-O DATA Foundation.

References

1. Scratch Homepage. https://scratch.mit.edu/. Accessed 20 Jan 2020
2. The Unicode Consortium, Unicode Emoji. http://www.unicode.org/Public/emoji/12.0/. Accessed 20 Jan 2020
3. Twitter/Twemoji GitHub. https://github.com/twitter/twemoji. Accessed 20 Jan 2020

4. Green, C.: Improved alpha-tested magnification for vector textures and special effects. In: ACM SIGGRAPH 2007 Courses, pp. 9–18 (2007)
5. Chlumský, V., Sloup, J., Šimeček, I.: Improved corners with multi-channel signed distance fields. Comput. Graph. Forum **37**, 273–287 (2018)
6. Eri, L.: GPU-centered font rendering directly from glyph outlines. J. Comput. Graph. Tech. (JCGT) **6**(2), 31–47 (2017)
7. The Unicode Consortium: Working Draft for Proposed Update Unicode Technical Standard #51 (2019). https://www.unicode.org/L2/L2019/19203r2-wd-uts51-17-draft.pdf
8. Apple and The Gun Emoji. https://blog.emojipedia.org/apple-and-the-gun-emoji/. Accessed 20 Jan 2020
9. Unicode Emoji List. https://www.unicode.org/emoji/charts/emoji-list.html/. Accessed 20 Jan 2020
10. The Unicode Consortium, Draft Emoji Candidates. https://unicode.org/emoji/future/emoji-candidates.html. Accessed 20 Jan 2020

Developing Evaluation System that Scientifically Presents the Rotation Ability of the Top as a Score: "Koma Scouter"

Hiroshi Suzuki[✉] and Hisahi Sato

Kanagawa Institute of Technology, Shimoogino 1030, Atsugi, Kanagawa, Japan
hsuzuki@ic.kanagawa-it.ac.jp

Abstract. Using by the compact disc are able to easily make an original top. This CD top will support in the learning of the gyroscopic and moment of inertia. Therefore, sometimes it become to a theme of experience course of Science Museum. We using on this CD tops, has developed a "Koma Scouter" as a system to connect the original tops making and edutainment. This system first shooting top of arranging the color nut on the CD in USB camera. Next, the system presents to user the score of rotation ability of the tops taken by image analysis. By presenting the rotation score top the user own, the user can recognize performance of the top that own it. In this paper, we describe a method for recognizing the color nuts, which are arranged in the CD, and a method of evaluating the rotation score of the CD top. As a result of using this system in scientific events, Kids of about 40% has reworked the top.

Keywords: Top · Science education · Edutainment · Interaction · OpenCV

1 Background

In recent years at science museums and large shopping centers, there have been a lot of interactive edutainment projects [1, 2] that make use of things children make themselves [3, 4]. However, with these sorts of projects, none of the things the children make are evaluated scientifically. That is why we offer a "Koma Scouter" as a system that can scientifically evaluate the original spinning tops (works) made by the children. Colored nuts are arranged on a CD that will be a spinning top, and by that image being analyzed by this system, the center of gravity and moment of inertia are measured from the size and placement of the nuts, and a score is presented for that spinning top's rotational ability. This will give the children an understanding of rotation, and it can be expected to act as a motivation for them to remake it.

2 Related Work

Interactive system using the tops has been developed a few so far. "Moving, Hitting, Expending" [5] are media-art systems that extend Tops with audio and visual effects by tracking the Top moving in real time. Matoba et al. has developed a playground

© Springer Nature Switzerland AG 2020

C. Stephanidis and M. Antona (Eds.): HCII 2020, CCIS 1225, pp. 332–337, 2020.
https://doi.org/10.1007/978-3-030-50729-9_47

equipment system that expands the top play experience [6]. In this system, an original top-and-bottom controller equipped with an electric motor is used to rotate without touching the top, and visual effects and dynamic feedback are added to the top play. MRSPINTOP [7], which we previously developed, is a camera-based augmented reality entertainment system that observes the top with an overhead camera and overlays three-dimensional characters on the camera image. Such an interactive system that extends the rotational movement of a top is based on the premise that the top is prepared as a special system, and it is not assumed that a kid creates and uses an original works. For this reason, the cost per tops kids tends to be high, and it is not to say that this system is for everyone to play.

3 Overview of the Koma Scouter

Anyone can easily make a spinning top, and so as to display the score for that top, our research representatives developed a top construction kit, a top photography case, and a program to measure the top. Figure 1 displays a diagram with an overview of this system, and the specifics for the top construction kit and the top photography case.

3.1 Original Spinning Top Construction Kit

As the main part of the spinning top the children make, it uses a normal 12 cm size CD with a white background. On top of the children using markers to draw anything they like on the white background, they glue on JIS standard M4, M5, and M6 nuts colored either red, green, or blue.

3.2 Spinning Top Photography Case

This is a case that photographs the top of the spinning top with a USB camera and measures the score for that top from the acquired image. In addition to the camera, the case also includes LED lights, and a QR code reader. The guide portion on this case has a QR code reader that automatically reads the QR code underneath the original top the children make, and it recognizes each top individually.

3.3 Spinning Top Measurement Program

The spinning top measurement program is an image recognition program that recognizes the placement of the nuts and measures the center of gravity and moment of inertia. So as to obtain the position of each nut, it uses the photographed image to detect the nuts from matching it to a template. It calculates a KomaScore for each spinning top from the obtained size and position of each nut. The algorithm to calculate the KomaScore is as follows. With the number of nuts as i, the placement vector of the nuts as p, and each nut's mass as m, it is possible to calculate the spinning top's center of gravity vector G with (1)'s equation. So as to take vector G and turn it into a score, the radius of the CD is converted into centimeters, and with it set as 6, the GScore is calculated with (2)'s equation. For the moment of inertia score, the moment of inertia I

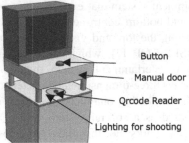

Button

Manual door

Qrcode Reader

Lighting for shooting

A. Original spinning top construction kit

B. Detail of Spinning top photography case

Fig. 1 Overview of Koma Scouter, original spinning top construction kit and spinning top photography case

is calculated from (3)'s equation from the number of nuts as i, each nut's mass as m, and the distance from the center of the spinning top as r. The calculated value for I is very small, so to be able to use it as a score, it is multiplied by 100 to produce the IScore for this value.

$$G = \frac{\sum_i m^i p^i}{\sum_i m^i} \tag{1}$$

$$GScore = -\left(\frac{|G|}{6} - 1\right) * 100 \tag{2}$$

$$I = \frac{\sum_i m^i r^{2i}}{\sum_i m^i} \tag{3}$$

$$IScore = I * 100 \tag{4}$$

4 Field Research from Events

In order to use the Koma Scouter was developed in the present study in the actual children's events, creative event was carried out "made by Let's play! Spinning disk". This event, to 8 days until August 10 to 18 days 2019, was carried out as a summer event of Toshiba Future Science Museum. Flow of this event are, at first, kids making the original top by reference a sample of the top. Then they were checked the Koma score of the made top by using the Koma Scouter. Finally, Kids freely played with their original tops using a special table. Figure 2 shows children trying it out. According to the historical data, the total number of people who tried it out was 2,854, and there were a total of 6,538 measurements done. According to Table 1, there were 1,152 participants who did two or more measurements (repeat measurers), and about 40% of participants remade their spinning top. The Improvement Rate heading in Table 1 displays the percentage of scores done for repeat measurers whose later scores had improved compared to their initial score, and a trend can be seen that as the number of measurements increased, the improvement rate also increased. Figure 3 displays the percentages of the number of times participants did repeat measurements. According to the historical data, as the measurements were repeated three or more times, the improvement rate increased, suggesting that the participants who did it three or more times were intentionally trying to raise their scores.

Fig. 2 Kids making a top and measuring Koma score

5 Discussion

Analysis of historical data and Discussion Total experience person number of people during the event from the history data of the Koma Scouter was 2852 people. The number of total measurement was found to be was 6538 times. The average top score of the number of measurements and the number of user is shown in Table 1. According to Table 1, experience who made the measurement of two or more times (repeat measurement person) is 1152 people, it can be seen that about 40% of the user had been re-create the top. Table and improvement rate in the third column shows the percentage of people of the score than subsequent that score of the initial measurement of the repeat measurement person is high, that there is a tendency to go up is about improvement overlaying the number of measurements It is seen. The percentage of repeat measurement number of user is shown in Fig. 3.

Table 1 Event logging data and users average score

Times	User	Improved persons	Improvement rate	Score average	Score median
1	1700			73.65	74.06
2	492	279	57%	73.65	73.99
3	249	192	77%	73.74	74.60
4	119	98	82%	74.44	75.19
5	86	77	90%	76.18	76.76
6	54	47	87%	75.77	75.24
More	152	143	94%	76.34	76.13

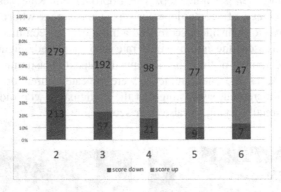

Fig. 3 Rate of score up users

From historical data, it can be seen that the improvement rate is increased from three or more repeat measurements. In other words, experience who are measuring more than three times, is considered as an attempt to raise the intentionally score. In the event, easily from infant to adult, it had been making each of the original top. In around the Koma Scouter.

6 Conclusion

We proposed a "Koma Scouter" as a system that can measure the rotational force of the original top that children were produced. In this system, it obtains the surface image of the original top using a USB camera. Then, recognizing the position and size of the arranged colored nut from the acquired image. And,

To measure the center of gravity and moment of inertia of the top, it is presented to the user as Koma score. Koma Score was made using the present system have been found to function as an index to know the rotation ability is spinning tops.

However, there recognize undetected or erroneous in the detection of color nut, an error of about 10% measured KomaScore occurs. At present, there is a problem that the top score will change slightly in the case of the same top again measured.

Such as to apply a deep learning technology, we believe that it is necessary to increase the detection accuracy by using a new method.

References

1. Team Labo: SketchAquarium. https://futurepark.teamlab.art/playinstallations/sketch_aquarium
2. Hiroshi, S., Sato, H., Hayami, H.: Fight our shadow robot! In: ACM SIGGRAPH 2013 Studio Talks, SIGGRAPH 2013 (2013). Article no. 15
3. Cowan, K.: Multimodal technologies in LEGO house: a social semiotic perspective. Multimodal Technol. Interact. **2**, 70 (2018). https://doi.org/10.3390/mti2040070
4. 1-10 Works: OmochanoKunitofushiginakamihikouki. https://works.1-10.com/product/fushiginakamihikouki/
5. Switch: Mawaru, Utu, Hirogaru. http://switch-project.jp
6. Yagimoto, K., Sato, H., Cho, S., Shimojima, A., Suzuki, H.: MRSPINTOP. Laval Virtual ReVolution (2011). In press
7. Matoba, Y., Sato, T., Koike, H.: Enhanced interaction with physical toys. In: Proceedings of the ACM International Conference on Interactive Tabletops and Surfaces, ITS 2011, Kobe, Japan, pp. 57–60 (2011)
8. He, K., Zhang, X., Ren, S., Sun, J.: Deep residual learning for image recognition. In: 2016 IEEE Conference on Computer Vision and Pattern Recognition (CVPR), pp. 770–778 (2016)

Deep Learning-Based Automatic Pronunciation Assessment for Second Language Learners

Kohichi Takai[1,2], Panikos Heracleous[2(✉)], Keiji Yasuda[1,2], and Akio Yoneyama[2]

[1] Nara Institute of Science and Technology, Nara, Japan
takai.koichi.tc1@is.naist.jp, ke-yasuda@dsc.naist.jp
[2] KDDI Research, Inc., Fujimino, Japan
{pa-heracleous,yoneyama}@kddi-research.jp

Abstract. For second language learners, computer-aided language learning (CALL) is of high importance. In recent years, the use of smart phones, tablets, and laptops has become increasingly popular; with this change, more people can use CALL to learn a second language. In CALL, automatic pronunciation assessment can be applied to provide feedback to teachers regarding the efficiency of teaching approaches. Furthermore, with automatic pronunciation assessment, students can monitor their language skills and improvements over time while using the system. In the current study, a text-independent method for pronunciation assessment based on deep neural networks (DNNs) is proposed and evaluated. In the proposed method, only acoustic features are applied, and native acoustic models and teachers' reference speech are not required. The method was evaluated using speech from a large number of Japanese students who studied English as a second language.

Keywords: Automatic pronunciation assessment · Acoustic features · Deep neural networks

1 Introduction

English is one of the most widely spoken languages in the world and many people learn English as a second language (ESL). In addition to conventional in-class English learning, the importance of computer-aided language learning (CALL) increases. ESL includes four components namely, listening, reading, speaking, and writing. The current research focuses on English pronunciation assessment, which plays an important role in the speaking component of second language learning.

Previously, several studies addressed the problem of automatic pronunciation assessment using different features and grading approaches [4,7,11]. However, the majority of the studies reported require accurate native acoustic models

© Springer Nature Switzerland AG 2020
C. Stephanidis and M. Antona (Eds.): HCII 2020, CCIS 1225, pp. 338–342, 2020.
https://doi.org/10.1007/978-3-030-50729-9_48

with a large amount of training data, reference teachers' speech, and are usually text-dependent (i.e., known text of the uttered speech). These automatic assessments are only useful for shadowing-based pronunciation learning. In contrast, text-independent automatic pronunciation assessment without teacher's reference speech can expand possibility of CALL applications.

2   Methods

2.1   Overview of Data Collection

In the proposed method, automatic pronunciation assessment without reference native speech and known text of the uttered speech is being considered. Because of the simplicity in collecting the speech data, in the current study a speech shadowing framework and materials were used.

To evaluate the effectiveness of the proposed method for automatic pronunciation assessment, speech data on various materials and a large number of speakers were collected. Following the data collection, human raters were employed to annotate the collected speech samples. In this section, the data collection procedure and the data annotation are described.

Speaking Materials and Collected Speech Data. For speaking material, 3,388 sentences of shadowing samples extracted from daily conversations were used. The materials were classified into five subsets reflecting the English proficiency level. In the current study, the TOEIC listening and reading test score was used to define difficulties of materials.

The materials also included the native reference speech samples, and, therefore, the speakers could use the native speech as a reference before producing the desired speech sample. This made it easy for speakers to produce difficult sentences and reduced the need for dictionaries. The speakers who participated in the data collection included Japanese students (45.53%), native Japanese English teachers (11.24%), and native English teachers (43.23%).

In total, 924 speakers produced speech samples from a part of the shadowing materials. Details of the collected speech data are shown in Table 1.

Table 1. Details of collected speech samples.

TOEIC score	# of sentences in shadowing materials	# of collected speech samples
~400	729	57,601
400~500	777	67,090
500~600	938	65,060
700~800	521	34,391
800~	423	23,214
Total	3,388	247,356

Annotation by Manual Pronunciation Evaluation. A part of the collected speech data which consists of 96,993 speech samples were evaluated by human raters using four criteria as shown in Table 2.

Table 2. Criteria of subjective evaluation.

Criteria	Check point	Rank 5	Rank 4	Rank 3	Rank 2	Rank 1
Overall	Intelligibility	Near native	3∼5	Intermediate	1∼3	Beginner
Pronunciation	Stress	>90%	>70%	>50%	>50%<40%	<40%
Intonation	Intonation/stress	Appropriate tone place and pitch	3∼5	Often appropriate	1∼3	Not appropriate
Fluency	Rhythm/linking/speed	Natural	3∼5	Fairly natural	1∼3	Not natural

Each speech sample was evaluated by two different English native raters using a 5-rank scale for each criteria. The two scores were averaged to provide the final score. Tables 3 shows the annotation results of overall annotation criterion.

Table 3. Subjective evaluation results in overall criterion.

Rank in overall criterion	Rank 1	Rank 2	Rank 3	Rank 4	Rank 5	Total
# of speech samples	3,433	6,698	11,165	11,737	63,960	96,993

2.2   Results

The data set for preliminary DNN experiments were created by using a subset of data shown in Table 3. For pronunciation assessment, a 3-level scale was used, namely, below average (rank1 and rank2), average (rank3), and above average (rank4 and rank5) by merging the corresponding ranks. In the experiments reported in the current study, 935 speech samples for each class were used for training the DNN [6]. Other 924 speech samples for each class were used for the DNN evaluation.

For the evaluation, the recalls of each class, the unweighted average recall (UAR) (i.e., mean of the class recalls), and the Pearson correlation coefficient metrics were used. Mel-frequency cepstral coefficients (MFCCs) [8] concatenated with shifted delta cepstral (SDC) coefficients [1,9] were extracted from the speech signal every 10 ms with a time window of 20 ms. The MFCC and SDC features were used to construct the i-vectors [3] used for training and evaluation.

Gaussian mixture models (GMMs) supervectors are widely used in speaker recognition. The GMM supervectors are obtained by concatenating the means of an adapted GMM. The main disadvantage of supervectors is the high dimensionality, which imposes high computational and memory costs. To overcome these problems, the i-vectors were introduced, which represent the whole utterance by a small number of factors, explaining also the variability of speaker, language, emotion, and channel. In the current method, the i-vectors are used as features for pronunciation scoring. Following i-vector extraction, linear discriminant analysis (LDA) [5] was also applied to further improve the class discrimination ability.

The classification experiments were based on DNNs. A DNN is a feed-forward neural network with many (i.e., more than one) hidden layers. The main advantage of DNNs compared to shallow networks is the better feature expression and the ability to perform complex mapping. In the current study, four hidden layers with 64 units and ReLu activation function were used. On top, a fully-connected Softmax layer was added. The number of batches was set to 512, and 500 epochs were used.

Table 4 shows the results achieved. As shown, when using LDA, significant improvements were obtained. When using MFCC and SDC features with LDA, a 64.4% UAR and a 0.48 correlation were achieved. These results are comparable or even superior to other similar state-of-the-art approaches [2, 10].

Table 4. Individual recalls for the three classes.

Features (ivector extraction)	Below average	Average	Above average	UAR	Pearson CC
MFCC	56.24	23.98	25.18	35.13	0.0236
MFCC + SDC	42.45	31.53	35.01	36.33	0.0568
MFCC + LDA	50.96	62.95	60.67	58.19	0.3928
MFCC + SDC + LDA	63.14	57.30	72.75	64.40	0.4803

3   Conclusions

In the current paper, a method for automatic pronunciation assessment for second language learners was presented. The method is based on DNNs, and the results obtained were very promising. Data collection of a large number of speakers was also introduced. Evaluating the method using a larger amount of non-native speech data is currently in progress.

References

1. Bielefeld, B.: Language identification using shifted delta cepstrum. In: Fourteenth Annual Speech Research Symposium (1994)
2. Chen, L.Y., Jang, J.S.R.: Automatic pronunciation scoring using learning to rank and DP-based score segmentation. In: Proceedings of Interspeech, pp. 761–764 (2010)
3. Dehak, N., Kenny, P.J., Dehak, R., Dumouchel, P., Ouellet, P.: Front-end factor analysis for speaker verification. IEEE Trans. Audio Speech Lang. Process. **19**(4), 788–798 (2011)

4. Franco, H., Neumeyer, L., Ramos, M., Bratt, H.: Exploring deep learning architecures for automatically grading non-native spontaneous speech. In: Proceedings of ICASSP, pp. 6140–6144 (2016)
5. Fukunaga, K.: Introduction to Statistical Pattern Recognition, 2nd edn. Academic Press, New York (1990). Ch. 10
6. Hinton, G., et al.: Deep neural networks for acoustic modeling in speech recognition: the shared views of four research groups. IEEE Sig. Process. Mag. 29(6), 82–97 (2012)
7. Nicolao, M., Beeston, A.V., Hain, T.: Automatic assesement of English learner pronunciation using discriminative classifiers. In: Proceedings of ICASSP, pp. 5351–5355 (2015)
8. Sahidullah, M., Saha, G.: Design, analysis and experimental evaluation of block based transformation in MFCC computation for speaker recognition. Speech Commun. 54(4), 543–565 (2012). https://doi.org/10.1016/j.specom.2011.11.004
9. Torres-Carrasquillo, P., Singer, E., Kohler, M.A., Greene, R.J., Reynolds, D.A., Deller Jr, J.R.: Approaches to language identification using gaussian mixture models and shifted delta cepstral features. In: Proceedings of ICSLP 2002-INTERSPEECH 2002, pp. 16–20 (2002)
10. Witt, S., Young, S.: Phone-level pronunciation scoring and assessment for interactive language learning. Speech Commun. 30, 95–108 (2000)
11. Yue, J., et al.: Automatic scoring of shadowing speech based on DNN posteriors and their DTW. In: proceedings of Interspeech, pp. 1422–1426 (2017)

"Ad Meliora": Towards an Improved Approach to Global Software Engineering Curriculum

Simona Vasilache[(✉)]

Graduate School of Systems and Information Engineering,
University of Tsukuba, Tsukuba, Japan
simona@cs.tsukuba.ac.jp

Abstract. Software engineering education in Japan is an established field, with more students being increasingly attracted to this area. However, many Japanese academic institutions lack a vision of the global aspects of software engineering teaching. This work will present some of the lessons learned during an introductory software engineering course held at a Japanese university, in a multicultural classroom.

Besides the contents of the taught material, the various in-class activities and assignments are meant to make the students aware of the importance of cultural differences, not only when teaching software engineering, but also in future software development centered workplaces. Class participation levels during these activities of Japanese students vs. international students will be highlighted. This work will emphasize the need for culturally responsive teaching to be applied in a software engineering classroom and will offer a glimpse into a multicultural environment at an academic institution in Japan.

Keywords: Multicultural environments · Global software engineering · Class participation

1 Introduction

When it comes to learning in general, culturally responsive teaching, a term introduced by Ladson-Billings in 1995, is a pedagogy that recognizes the importance of including students' cultural references in all aspects of learning [1]. This applies to all learned disciplined, including software engineering (SE). Moreover, the field of global software engineering has gained particular interest in recent years, as a reality for even the smallest companies [2]. Numerous educational aspects, as well as work style and habits are culturally specific, and this is visible in the SE field as well. Software engineering educators need to prepare the students for their future workplaces, which are often these days international and distributed.

Software engineering education in Japan is an established field, with more students being increasingly attracted to this area. However, many Japanese academic institutions lack a vision of the global aspects of SE teaching. Our previous work highlighted some of the students' perceptions of global aspects of software engineering, as shown in [3] and [4]. This work will present some of the lessons learned during an introductory SE

C. Stephanidis and M. Antona (Eds.): HCII 2020, CCIS 1225, pp. 343–348, 2020.
https://doi.org/10.1007/978-3-030-50729-9_49

course held at a Japanese university, in a multicultural classroom. The results presented in this paper are based on the instructor's empirical observations, on questionnaires and after-class informal discussions, gathered since 2016, when this course was held in English for the first time at the institution where the author teaches. The contents of the taught material, together with the in-class activities and assignments, are meant to make the students aware of the importance of cultural differences, not only when teaching SE, but also in future SE-related workplaces.

2   Course Description and Evolution

2.1   Basic Course Description

The focus of this work is a course named "Principles of Software Engineering", taught in the past 4 years at the University of Tsukuba in Japan. This is an introductory course which aims to introduce basic software engineering principles, covering topics like: software development models, life cycle, requirements gathering and specification, system design, user interface design, testing (verification and validation), project planning and management, business aspects of software development etc.

This course is mainly intended for computer science graduate students, but it is also available to students belonging to other majors, as well as undergraduate students. In its first year, i.e. 2016, 15 students enrolled, followed by 26 students in 2017 and 35 students in 2018. In 2019, the course attracted 66 students. The language of instruction is English, unlike the majority of the other courses, which are offered in the local Japanese language. The classes were made up of a mixture of local Japanese students and international students, as shown in Table 1. Most participants were computer science students enrolled in the master's course. There was one undergraduate student in each 2016 and 2018; two undergraduate students enrolled in 2019. In each 2018 and 2019, one student belonging to a different major enrolled; moreover, two exchange students participated in the course held in 2018.

Table 1. International students' participation in the SE course

Year	Total number of students	Number of international students	Percentage of international students
2016	15	9	60
2017	26	18	69.2
2018	35	24	68.5
2019	66	33	50

2.2   Course Evolution

Whereas the main topics of the course remained the same throughout the 4 years since its inception, the structure of the classes evolved, as this section will describe.

The first and the second year resembled mostly a classical lecture style course, where most of the time was spent by the instructor lecturing in front of the students and the participants listening for the most part. However, the instructor insisted on involving the students, thus asking questions and eliciting answers from the students. In the first year of holding the course, it already became clear to the instructor that cultural differences are present in the classroom. In line with many cultural-differences theories (e.g. [5, 6]), it was obvious that the Japanese students, as members of a collectivistic type of society, are more used to listening to the lecturer, without questioning him/her, whereas many of the students belonging to more individualistic societies are eager to express their opinions, to question what they are being taught. The efforts to involve the Japanese students did not yield immediate results. Unless individually asked to give an opinion, these students generally preferred a passive attitude during the discussions. It was at this point that the instructor realized that she must find alternative ways to involve the students more actively.

Starting with 2018, the number of class activities increased. Mini teams were created in class and the students had clear tasks which involved communicating with their teammates. After fulfilling their tasks, the teams were asked to report in front of the classroom and/or compare results with other teams and discuss outcomes. The teams were created in such a way that the members belonged to at least two different cultures and, as much as possible, they had to speak English amongst. It is worth mentioning here that often Chinese students are fluent in Japanese and, when working with Japanese classmates, they can easily speak their language, thus, not all team interactions took place in English. However, reporting results or discussing outcomes with the whole class was always performed in English. At first, the Japanese team members were tempted to ask their non-Japanese teammates to speak in front of the whole class; however, the instructor made sure to elicit some form of active participation, either in the form of confirming what their teammates reported or by asking them to make extra comments.

The latest teaching year, i.e. 2019, was particularly fruitful. Each lecture included at least one class activity. The groups were created such that they each contained members from different cultural background. With such a large number of students, i.e. 66, out of which 33 were Japanese and 33 were international students (from 6 different countries), there was no difficulty to create different groups every time, with different combinations of students' nationalities. The number of class activities was higher than in the previous year and the types of activities were more diverse.

In one example, using *manaba* [7], i.e. the learning management system available for the class, a micro-project was carried out; its purpose was supporting the teaching of issues entailed by the requirements elicitation phase in the development of a software product. Seven teams were created beforehand by the instructor; the class activity is described below.

Part I:
- *5 min: within the team created beforehand by the instructor, on manaba, choose two members acting as "customers" and 4–6 members acting as "developers"*
- *10 min: "developers" create a questionnaire for the "customers"*

- *10 min: "customers" answer questionnaire in writing ("customers" and "developers" do not communicate directly)*
- *15 min: "developers" create a requirement document, using "shall", "should" and "unclear" items (the "shall" items include requirements that the product must have, whereas the "should" items refer to those that would be helpful, but not absolutely necessary)*

Part II: swap "customers" with another team developing the same product
- *5 min: "customers" write what they disagree with, what pleasantly surprises them, what is missing in the requirements document*

Part III: share the documents with the whole class and discuss

After completing the activity, the instructor asked questions like: *was there a leader among developers? did everyone participate? did the customers collaborate? which is better, small development teams or larger ones? would interviews be more helpful than questionnaires?*

This activity was just one of several activities highlighting the importance of cultural differences within teams who participate in various software development phases.

With regard to the method of assessing students' work and grading, one of our previous small-scale studies highlighted the students' preferred grading style [3]. As was shown in this work, most participants preferred either individual assignments or team projects, with no student choosing a final exam as their preference. This result is in line with the instructor's decision to abolish the final exam after the first year and use assignments as the main grading method in subsequent years.

3 Discussion and Lessons Learned

Due to the fact that it is taught in English, the instructor believes that, at first, there was reluctance at registering for this course, anticipating difficulties in understanding the course materials and performing assignments or taking exams. However, the instructor made sure to accommodate the lack of confidence in writing in English and thus allowed the students to write their assignments in Japanese, provided that the assignments are submitted in electronic form (i.e. not hand-written, in order to facilitate translation in English for the instructor, if needed). All class materials were available in electronic form, as well. As students learned about these provisions, more of them had the confidence to register for a class taught in English. At the same time, in the beginning, the students enrolled were not aware of the number of interactions that they would have with the other non-Japanese class participants and which would have to take place in English. As previously described, year by year, this course entailed an increasing number of class activities. On the one hand, the potential class participants learned that they can use Japanese for their assignments, even though the class is taught in English; on the other hand, they learned that they would need to interact with their classmates in English, through class activities. The benefits of interacting with other students appear to have weighed more than the lack of self-confidence when it comes to communicating in English, as the continuously increasing number of students shows (from 15 in 2019 to 66 in 2019 – see Table 1). The instructor believes that the success of the class activities provides a valuable lesson for students as future employees in multicultural environments.

Experience with these 4 years of teaching this course taught the instructor that whereas the content of the teaching material can be more or less fixed, the approach to teaching this content is very much culturally dependent. Whether more discussions are involved or more lecture-style teaching is present depends on the students preference and on how they respond to various teaching styles. The in-class activities showed that it is important to adjust the team componence, the work style and even the content itself, based on who takes part in them.

The success of the class was reflected in the comments received from the students at the end of the course. According to the university's rules, each course ends with an evaluation questionnaire given to students in which they rate how well the class was prepared and conducted, how much time they needed to prepare for each class etc. The questionnaire also contains open questions in which students point out good aspects of the course, aspects that need to be improved, expectations, as well as other opinions and recommendations.

Many students praised the "lively atmosphere", the "dynamic class", the interaction between teacher and students and the chance to communicate with others. The fact that students were always involved in eliciting answers to various questions was highly valued. Most students enjoyed the many questions, comments from class and "side topics" discussions. Interestingly, some students felt they would have talked more, but that there was always "someone else in the class who would talk before". Thus, the suggestion for more pair work came up, i.e. the opportunity to express personal thoughts, at least in front of one other person, if not in front of the whole class.

One of the most rewarding comments came from one the students stating the following good aspect of the course: "the lecturer changed the students' silence into discussion and projects". The instructor sees this comment as a success in overcoming cultural differences and language barriers, i.e. making the students who are traditionally more inclined to silence participate more in class. One other student stated that "the principles that I learned in the class changed the way I approach problem solving in general", illustrating that the gained benefits go beyond the software engineering area.

Nevertheless, not all students shared the same opinion. At the end of the course in 2019, one interesting comment came to light, stating that "group work is a big waste of time", as many students are "not interested in participating or too shy to speak up". This comment came from one of the more active students, who observed the big difference between himself and those less interested in participating. This shows that there is still much work to be done by the instructor, to persuade those less active to participate more during class. More than this, the students need to be exposed to more interactive classes, so that active learning becomes the norm and they participate in class activities and group work with more ease, regardless of the class componence or of the language involved.

4 Conclusions and Future Work

This work highlighted the need for culturally responsive teaching to be applied in a software engineering classroom and offered a glimpse into a multicultural environment at an academic institution in Japan. The experience gained in the classroom mimics some aspects of actual working places in international environments; different cultural norms and behavior are visible in the classroom, just like they are in a working environment.

One important direction for future work would be implementing a real-life project in a truly distributed environment: collaborating with a university abroad, with students organizing the distributed teams, taking into consideration the spatial, temporal and cultural differences and carrying out the project.

References

1. Ladson-Billings, G.: Toward a theory of culturally relevant pedagogy. Am. Educ. Res. J. **32** (3), 465–491 (1995)
2. Beecham, S., Clear, T., Damian, D., Barr, J., Noll, J., Scacchi, W.: How best to teach global software engineering? Educators are divided. IEEE Softw. **1**, 16–19 (2017)
3. Vasilache, S.: From an international classroom to a distributed work environment: student perspectives on global software engineering. In: 2018 IEEE International Conference on Teaching, Assessment, and Learning for Engineering, pp. 825–828. IEEE (2018)
4. Vasilache, S.: Teaching software engineering in a multicultural environment. In: Auer, M.E., Guralnick, D., Simonics, I. (eds.) ICL 2017. AISC, vol. 716, pp. 360–365. Springer, Cham (2018). https://doi.org/10.1007/978-3-319-73204-6_40
5. Hofstede, G., Hofstede, G.J., Minkow, M.: Cultures and Organizations: Software of the Mind: Intercultural Cooperation and its Importance for Survival. McGraw-Hill, New York (2010)
6. Mercier, H., Deguchi, M., Van der Henst, J.B., Yama, H.: The benefits of argumentation are cross-culturally robust: the case of Japan. Think. Reason. **22**(1), 1–15 (2016)
7. Manaba. https://manaba.jp/products/. Accessed 20 Mar 2020

The Learning Behaviors Analysis in a Language Learning Support System – A Pilot Study

Jingyun Wang[1(✉)], Ching-ju Chao[2], and Likun Liu[1]

[1] Kyushu University, Fukuoka, Japan
warmplam@gmail.com, likunliu@hdi.ait.kyushu-u.ac.jp
[2] Tung Fang Design University, Kaohsiung, Taiwan
chingju@mail.tf.edu.tw

Abstract. In this paper, we present an ontology-based visualization language learning support system (VLLSS) which provide learning materials based on topic maps. A pilot experiment was conducted to study the learning behaviors features of learners who studied with VLLSS. One class of 11 intermediates and one class of 19 beginners from a university in Taiwan studied with the system for learning Japanese grammar. Not only the reported learning perception but also the learning logs recorded by VLLSS are analyzed. In terms of learning perception, no significant difference was found in other scales except in a tendency of significant difference in mental load. It is found that compared to intermediates who studied more difficult grammar points, the beginners reported significant higher pressure when studied with the system. In terms of learning logs, we analyzed the ratio of studied related grammar points to the target grammar points, the ratio of studied relations to the target ones, and the number of the target grammar points. We also studied the relation between those three parameters and the learning habit.

Keywords: Learning behaviors · Language learning support · Topic maps

1 Introduction

Recently years, numerous of language learning support system [1, 2] were developed to support the traditional language learning. The learning achievement and learning perception of the learners were normally analyzed for proving the learning effectiveness [3–5]. However, few discussed the learning behaviors based on the log data recorded by systems.

In our previous work [3, 4], an ontology-based Japanese language learning support system (called CLLSS) were designed and developed to help instructors organize learning materials based on topic maps and also provide learners learning materials based on topic maps. The examination of learning achievement and learning perception of the learners were discussed from various perspective. In this paper, the learning behaviors based on the log data recorded by the new version of CLLSS (ontology-based visualization Japanese language learning support system, called VLLSS) is analyzed in addition to the learning perception.

C. Stephanidis and M. Antona (Eds.): HCII 2020, CCIS 1225, pp. 349–355, 2020.
https://doi.org/10.1007/978-3-030-50729-9_50

2   An Ontology-Based Visualization Language Learning Support System

Figure 1 shows the main interface of VLLSS. As an example shown in Fig. 1, when the learner studies with a target Japanese grammar point "～ta i" (displayed in the red), all its related grammar points (nodes displayed in yellow), and the relations (displayed in different colors in response to the relation name) between them will be shown in a map. (Since the target grammar point is located in the center of the topic map, in this work it is also called center node in the topic map). When the mouse hovers over any node, the attributes of the node (such as pattern, example and so on) will be displayed; when the mouse hover over any line, the name of the relation will be displayed [4]. Furthermore, from the map the learner can access the learning materials (including explanations and practices) not only addressing each grammar point by right-clicking the node but also addressing each relation by right-clicking the line.

KnowledgePointName知識ポイント ～たい
                                      ～ta i

----Related Knowledge Point 関連知識ポイント：----

動詞の連用形 ～たがる

Conjunctions of verbs   ～ta ga ru

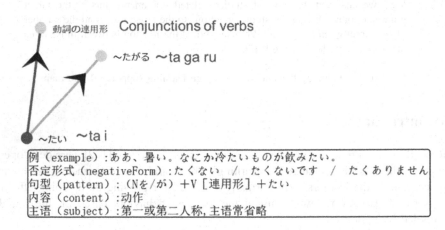

動詞の連用形 Conjunctions of verbs

～たがる ～ta ga ru

～たい ～ta i

例（example）：ああ、暑い。なにか冷たいものが飲みたい。
否定形式（negativeForm）：たくない ／ たくないです ／ たくありません
句型（pattern）：（Nを／が）＋V［連用形］＋たい
内容（content）：动作
主语（subject）：第一或第二人称, 主语常省略

Fig. 1. An example of displayed topic map (Color figure online)

3   Experimental Procedures

We conducted a pilot experiment to study the learning behaviors features of learners who studied with VLLSS. One class of 11 intermediates and one class of 20 beginners from a university in Taiwan studied with the system for learning Japanese grammar.

Before the learning activity, both classes took the learning habit questionnaire and then a 20 min training about how to use the system. After that, the participants were required to study with the system to study for one hour. Finally, all the participants took a learning perception questionnaire [4], which involved the satisfaction for learning mode,technology acceptance measures and cognitive load.

4 Results

4.1 Learning Perception Analysis

The feedback about the learning activity and the system evaluation from both classes, are shown in Table 1. According to this table, for the answers to "What is the maximum number of the relations shown in the relation panel of the system at one time that do not make you feel pressure and disturbed?", the average number given by the intermediates and beginner are 5.09 and 4.68, respectively; this means that when a GP involves more than 4 relations in the course the optimum number of its related GPs to be shown in the relation panel at one time is 4 for beginner and 5 for intermediates. This result suggests that the system should encourage the instructors describe the priority of the relations and just show not more than 4 of them in the relation panel while making the rest selectable.

The average ratings of "Effort for understanding the purpose and the explanation of learning activity" (the maximum is 7) of the intermediates and beginner are 4.55 and 4.95, respectively; this means most participant could understand the learning purpose of this activity. The average ratings of "Effort for understanding the target GPs" (the maximum is 7) of the intermediates and beginner are 4.55 and 4.89, respectively; this suggest the learning activity was moderate (neither too easy nor too difficult) for the participants.

In terms of mental load, the average rating of the degree of distraction of both classes are lower than 4 (neutral), implying that using VLLSS the learners could concentrate on learning with low pressure; however, the average rating of the degree of pressure of intermediates is lower than 3 while the degree of pressure of intermediates are slightly higher than 4.

In terms of technology acceptance measures of the experimental group, the average rating of the item "It is easy to use this Comparison function of the system". (1–3: strongly to slightly disagree, 4–6: slightly to strongly agree) are 4.82 for intermediates and 4.95 for beginners; this means that most participants felt that it was easy to operate and get familiar with the system. The item "This Comparison function of the system is useful for study." (1–3: strongly to slightly disagree, 4–6: slightly to strongly agree) received the average rating 5.27 from intermediates and 4.89 from beginners, implying that most of participants identified the usefulness of VLLSS in improving their learning performances.

We further compare the learning perception difference between these two classes. No significant difference was found in other scales except a significant tendency in the mental load ($F_{(2,27)} = 3.08$, $p < 0.1$). It is found that compared to intermediates who

Table 1. The analysis results of learning perception.

Group	Item	Optimum number of relations	Mental effort		Mental load		Technology acceptance	
			Understand the purpose (1–7)	Learn the GPs (1–7)	Distraction (1–7)	Pressure (1–7)	Easiness (1–3: no 4–6: yes)	Usefulness (1–3: no 4–6: yes)
Intermediates	Mean	5.09	4.55	4.55	3.00	2.91	4.82	5.27
	S.D.	1.38	1.21	1.29	1.61	1.30	1.17	1.49
Beginners	Mean	4.68	4.95	4.89	3.84	4.08	4.95	4.89
	S.D.	1.97	1.13	0.94	1.31	1.32	1.43	1.45
MANCOVA (Wilks' Lambda)	F (2,27)		0.621		3.08*		0.877	
Levene's test	F (1,28)	1.421	0.007	0.728	1.116	0.004	0.953	0.380
One-way ANOVA	F (1,28)	0.362	1.278	0.898	2.721	6.061**	0.064	0.465

*<0.1 **<0.025

studied more difficult grammar points, the beginners reported significant higher pressure ($F_{(1,28)} = 6.061$*, $p < 0.025$) when studied with the system.

4.2 The Analysis of Learning Logs

Besides the reported learning perception, the learning logs recorded by VLLSS are also analyzed. Whenever a user accessed a node or a relation to visit the addressing learning materials, one data entry containing user id, corresponding node/relation name and time will be recorded as a log. In this paper, we analyzed the ratio of studied related grammar points (related nodes in topic maps) to the target grammar points (center nodes in topic maps), the ratio of studied relations to the target ones, and the number of the accessed target grammar points (center nodes in topic maps).

As shown in Table 2, although studied with different contents, the average number of visited target grammar points are around 22 for both intermediates and beginners. It is found that compared to the beginners, the intermediates checked learning materials of significantly more related grammar points ($t = 5.39$) and more relations ($t = 4.33$) when they studied target grammar points.

Table 2. The log data result of intermediates and beginners

Group	Items	Accessed related nodes VS center nodes	Accessed relations VS center nodes	The number of the accessed center nodes
Intermediates	Mean	0.79	0.17	21.73
	S.D.	0.23	0.13	13.99
Beginners	Mean	0.25	0.01	22.05
	S.D.	0.33	0.02	18.61
T-test	t	5.39**	4.33*	−.054

**<0.001 *<0.01

The Pearson correlation between those three parameters and the learning habit are analyzed. Based on the answers to the question about learning habit in questionnaire before the learning activity, there were 14 participants (4 intermediates and 10 beginners) who completely did not have the comparison habit, 11 participants (5 intermediates and 6 beginners) who sometime would compare the related KPs while reminded by the instructor or other learners, and 5 participants (4 intermediates and 1 beginners) who most of the time would realize the relations between acquired GPs and new GP and would like to compare them to increase the understanding of the knowledge. Significance (Pearson correlation = 0.41, p < 0.05) is found between the learning habit level and the ratio of studied relations to the target grammar points; this suggests that the higher level of the comparison habit a learner has, more frequently she/he tends to access more relations between target grammar points and their related ones.

To further exam the learning behaviors, K-means clustering is considered. In virtue of the K-means clustering, we were able to assign learners into different clusters in conformity with similar features [6]. In this work, we have performed basic K-Means clustering under the condition where K = 2, K = 3 and K = 4 respectively. Here the result of 4-mean clustering is discussed.

To profile learners' behaviour, we have utilized 4 sets of features: Average accessed related node count verses accessed center nodes, average accessed relations verses accessed center nodes, average accessed center node number and the habit level. The 4-means clustering result is shown in Table 3. Cluster 0 (Accessed related nodes vs center nodes: Mean = 0.36, SD = 0.23; accessed relations vs center nodes: Mean = 0.15, SD = 0.19; accessed center node number: Mean = 2.14, SD = 0.90) owns the highest average habit level (Mean = 2.14, S.D. = 0.90) while students in other clusters possess a relatively lower habit level (Cluster 1: Mean = 1.33, S.D. = 0.57; Cluster 2: Mean = 1.55, S.D. = 0.69; Cluster 3: Mean = 1.67, S.D. = 0.71). Cluster 1 (Accessed related nodes vs center nodes: Mean = 0.57, SD = 0.41; Accessed relations vs center nodes: Mean = 0.04, SD = 0.05; Average habit level: Mean = 1.33, SD = 0.58) and Cluster 2 (Accessed related nodes vs center nodes: Mean = 0.58, SD = 0.48; Accessed relations vs center nodes: Mean = 0.05, SD = 0.07; habit level: Mean = 1.55, SD = 0.69) were having a relatively close parameter on all other features except the Average center node number (Mean = 56.33, SD = 8.08 verses: Mean = 5.27, SD = 3.35). Among which cluster 1 possess the highest accessed center node number while cluster 2 was the lowest among all clusters. This could indicate that learners who target too many or too few grammar points could potentially have the same learning behaviour in visiting related grammar points and relations between grammar points. By comparison, all parameters of Cluster 3 stayed in the middle range among all 4 clusters (accessed related nodes vs center nodes: Mean = 0.31, SD = 0.37; accessed relations vs center nodes: Mean = 0.04, SD = 0.05; average accessed center node number: Mean = 32.78, SD = 4.02; habit level: Mean = 1.67, SD = 0.71).

To better illustrate the general behavior in all the four clusters, one student is selected from each cluster and each scatter plot shown in Fig. 1 represents their study path (Fig. 2).

Table 3. The 4-means clustering result by considering 4 parameters as features

Cluster	Class name	Average accessed related nodes vs center nodes	Average relations vs center nodes	Average accessed center nodes	Average habit level	N	Percentage in label	Percentage in cluster (%)
0	Intermediates	0.58	0.35	20.33	2.67	3	27.27	42.86
	Beginners	0.20	0	18.75	1.75	4	21.05	57.14
1	Intermediates	0.92	0.10	49.0	1.0	1	9.09	33.33
	Beginners	0.40	0.01	60.0	1.5	2	10.53	66.67
2	Intermediates	0.96	0.13	8.0	1.5	4	36.36	36.36
	Beginners	0.36	0	3.71	1.57	7	36.84	63.64
3	Intermediates	0.75	0.08	32.33	1.67	3	27.27	33.33
	Beginners	0.10	0.02	33.0	1.67	6	31.58	66.67

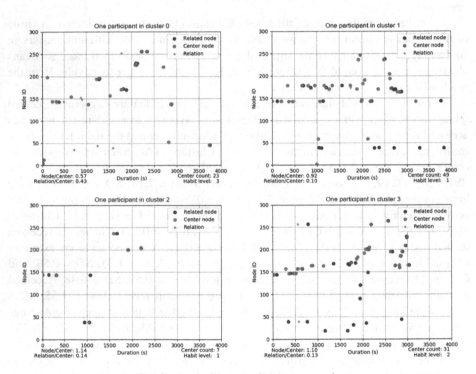

Fig. 2. Students' access log in scatter plot

5 Conclusion and Future Work

In this paper, we present a visualization language learning support system which provide topic map as virtual catalogue for learning materials addressing the interested knowledge and its relations with other knowledge. This paper described the results of a pilot study. Besides the learning perception of the participants, the learning behaviors based on log data recorded in the system are also discussed.

In terms of learning perception, no significant difference was found except a significant tendency in the mental load. It is suggested that compared to intermediates who studied more difficult grammar points, the beginners reported significant higher pressure when studied with the system. The learning logs suggests that the higher level of the comparison habit a learner has, more frequently she/he tends to access the learning material of more relations from topic map. K-mean crusting was also used to further group the learning behaviors.

However, due to the small number of the participants and short duration of study of this polite study, the conclusion needs to be further confirmed. In future, we enhance the system function and conduct a serious of long-term experiment with more participants and tract their learning paths for a semester period.

Acknowledgements. The research is supported by JSPS KAKENHI Grant-in-Aid for Young Scientists Grant Number 20K19938, and 2019 Kyushu University Research Activity Support for Women Returning from Maternity and Parental Leave.

References

1. Goto, T., Kojiri, T., Watanabe, T., Yamada, T., Iwata, T.: English grammar learning system based on knowledge network of fill-in-the-blank exercises. In: Lovrek, I., Howlett, R.J., Jain, L.C. (eds.) KES 2008. LNCS (LNAI), vol. 5179, pp. 588–595. Springer, Heidelberg (2008). https://doi.org/10.1007/978-3-540-85567-5_73
2. Sunar, A.S., Hayashi, Y., Watanabe, T.: Multiple-choice cloze exercise generation through English grammar learning support. Int. J. Know. Web Intell. **4**(1), 79–92 (2013)
3. Wang, J., Mendori, T., Xiong, J.: A language learning support system using course-centered ontology and its evaluation. Comput. Educ. **78**, 278–293 (2014)
4. Wang, J., Mendori, T., Xiong, J.: A customizable language learning support system using ontology-driven engine. Int. J. Distance Educ. Technol. **11**(4), 81–97 (2013)
5. Wang, J., Mendori, T.: An evaluation of the learning attitude and motivation in a language learning support system. In: Proceedings of 15th IEEE International Conference on Advanced Learning Technologies, (ICALT 2015), pp. 358–361(2015)
6. Wang, J., Shimada, A., Okubo, F.: E-book learner behaviors difference under two meaningful learning support environments. In: The Proceedings of the 27th International Conference on Computers in Education, (ICCE 2019), vol. 1, pp. 342–347 (2019)

Practice of Sandbox Game in Higher Education Based on Graphic and Game Programming Environment

Tengfei Xian[✉]

University of Finance and Economics of Guangdong, China, 21, Luntou Road,
Guangzhou 510320, Guangdong, People's Republic of China
xiantengfei@gdufe.edu.cn

Abstract. The graphical and game programming environment provides a practical way to improve the learning process, especially the motivation of game creators. However, the research on students seldom uses graphic and game programming in higher education. Therefore, this study takes Ylands, a sandbox game of Tencent, as an example to investigate the creative thinking of higher education curriculum games and explore the factors that affect higher education's acceptance of graphic programming. Based on FSLSM results, the students' initial learning based on the sandbox game has different preferences for creative content. In addition, the early experience of students with a lot of game experience has become an important factor affecting students' acceptance of sandbox and game creation. Other factors, such as self exploration ability, sense of achievement, expectation of effort, degree of realization of ideas, social influence, convenience, participation, skills and control, are also important factors. According to the results of this study, the instructional designer can control the content of sand box game creation course, improve the efficiency and effectiveness of the course.

Keywords: Flow theory · Learning style · FSLSM · UTAUT

1 Introduction

The Use of visual programming to learn and design games. visualization and Gamification will become another important trend in the field of training and development. Now, More and more people and many researches have revealed some meanings of Gamification. However, up to now, there are few researches on visualization and game design. Therefore, the purpose of this study is to explore the visual programming of sandbox game platform in higher education, and to explore the main factors that affect the use of visualization and Gamification in higher education. In addition, it constructs a game learning behavior style model suitable for college students. Using the method of game making platform and questionnaire to study the learning style. This is of great significance for learners, teachers and game developers in sandbox. The results of this study can be used as a reference for instructional design or educators to design better game training programs for higher education.

© Springer Nature Switzerland AG 2020
C. Stephanidis and M. Antona (Eds.): HCII 2020, CCIS 1225, pp. 356–364, 2020.
https://doi.org/10.1007/978-3-030-50729-9_51

In this study, Tencent's online game "Ylands" is a sandbox online game produced by Tencent's game. There are visual programming tools in the editor. Players can freely edit terrain, game logic, etc. players can make various types of games through the editor, including role-playing games, shooting games, survival exploration games, etc. The built-in game scene and editor of Ylands not only provide the known game mode, but also have the greatest feature that players can design their own map scene according to the materials provided in the editor or in combination with programming, so as to give full play to their creativity. Here, the production of the game is mainly through visual programming. The process of programming is to select the corresponding roles, and drag the existing modules such as "motion", "appearance", "control" required by the characters in the code, and set the modules accordingly.

In universities, Ylands cooperates with the school of art and design of Guangdong University of Finance and economics. After six weeks of study, 56 students of the school have produced a total of 20 games. At the beginning of this study, we use the Felder Silverman learning style questionnaire to classify the learning styles. After the game is made, we use flow theory to test the game. At last, we use the UTAUT model to put forward conjecture and test the acceptance of college students to the sandbox game platform in this course.

1.1 Study 1 Felder Silverman Learning Style Model

Learning style can be defined as individual psychological, emotional and emotional characteristics, which can be regarded as perception, interpretation, interaction and response to learning content (Felder and Spurling 2005; Keefe 1987) the theory of learning style was put forward by Herbert theren, an American scholar, in 1954. Among them, the Felder Silverman learning style model draws on many learning style models, with better integrity and practicability. In addition, Felder Silverman model can get the information of four dimensions of learners through questionnaire measurement, so as to better guide learners' learning behavior. Therefore, it is widely used in the study of learning behavior and has been recognized by more and more researchers. The study also uses the Felder Silverman model to research learning style. In the system of sandbox game teaching course, their action behavior, data and path of learning activities will be recorded through the sandbox game platform. By collecting, sorting, analyzing and summarizing the data, students' relatively objective learning behavior characteristics can be obtained.

The classification of Felder Silverman learning style model plays an important role in learners' learning. Learners with different styles can learn according to different teaching designs, such as sequential learners can learn step by step, active learners can arrange active communication and discussion links, visual learners can use videos and pictures Mainly for explanation.

The design of personalized demand customization system based on sandbox game creation platform. The game creation provides the Creator with a developer introduction, developer foundation from semester, new version function learning, component learning, advanced module. Each platform can record the length of learning time.

After the classification and definition of the Felder Silverman learning style model, we have made the learning style index questionnaire based on the theory and practice of graphical programming and game teaching. After several improvements, the latest version of the questionnaire has been formed. There are 44 questions in the learning style test scale. Each question has a, B the two options correspond to different types of learners in corresponding dimensions. The purpose of this scale is to study the stability and personality of learning style of students who choose to make different types of sand box games.

From the analysis of the relevant elements of various learning styles, we can find that there are differences in learning behaviors among learners with different learning styles. Many researchers found that the Felder Silverman learning style model can also be applied to the learning of visual programming platform. There is also a correlation between learners' learning style, behavior characteristics and content. For example, for active learners, they like to communicate with others in the production process. There is a special forum for developers to communicate in Ylands. Learners like this may post and reply more in the forum. Therefore, in the follow-up study, we will explore the relationship between learners' learning styles and the characteristics of various game learning behavior patterns.

2 Study 2 Flow Theory

GEQ questionnaire is a common method to measure immersion experience. Many researchers use questionnaire survey to measure the dimensions of immersion experience, the difference between immersion experience in situations and individual immersion experience (Nakamura and Csikszentmihalyi 2002). At present, the most widely used immersion experience scales are: flow state scale and disposition flow scale compiled by Jackson, etc., which are built on the basis of nine dimensional models of immersion experience (Kawabata et al. 2008).

56 students participated in the evaluation (N = 56, 38 male), the age range is 19–22, The students are from different grades and majors. After six weeks of course, a total of 20 different types of games have been made by using the Yland, including 5 shooting games, 2 role-playing games, 4 tower defense games, 6 leisure games and 3 racing games. After the completion of production, the course requires 20 games to experience the game and use GEQ to measure. Participants need to play an average of 16 h of games per week.

The game experience questionnaire (GEQ) game experience scale consists of three modules: core scale, post game experience scale and social presence scale. It provides the player with a series of statements describing the state, and then evaluates the degree of agreement between the player's feelings in the process of the game (/after playing) and these statements, i.e. the player's five options from 0 (totally disagree) to 4 (fully agree) for each topic content. The dimensions corresponding to the items in the scale are different. By calculating the average score of each dimension, the experience differences of different games/versions in different dimensions can be achieved.

The game experience made by students was measured from 7 dimensions: immersion, fluency, ability, positive emotion, challenge, negative emotion and restlessness/fidgety. Descriptive statistics for the originally proposed seven-factor GEQ are presented in Table 1 below.

Table 1. Descriptive statistics for the GEQ sub-scales (as originally proposed)

Subscale	Min.	Max.	Mean	SD	Skew.	Kurt
Competence	1.78	5.0	3.932	0.619	−0.478	0.075
Sensory & imag.imm	1.15	5.0	3.669	0.772	−0.538	−0.193
Flow	1.00	5.0	3.	0.894	−0.380	−0.302
Tension	1.00	5.0	1.992	0.892	1.117	0.968
Challenge	1.00	5.0	3.002	0.776	0.051	−0.308
Neg. affect	1.00	4.0	1.762	0.574	0.949	0.931
Pos. affect	2.40	5.0	4.255	0.564	−0.826	0.394

After verification, the results from Table 2 shows that the different kinds of games generated by sandbox platform, on the whole, bring the players a sense of satisfaction, achievement and pleasure, participation, satisfaction, as well as rich fun and the playability of the game itself. Their overall experience can be positive. However, it is relatively low in the continuous immersion test, which reflects the lower intensity of the subsequent playability. The common problem is that the story length of each game is not long, and the difficulty continues to decrease during the process, which leads to the reduction of player's sense of achievement.

Table 2. Item content and factor loadings for the GEQ exploratory factor analysis in Study 2.

Item code	Label	Factors				
		1	2	3	4	5
P	I feel satisfied	0.595	−0.008	0.060	0.032	0.141
P	I have the skill of making	0.672	0.036	0.149	0.117	0.010
P	I'm interested in making stories	0.596	−0.037	0.047	0.108	−0.014
P	I think the story is interesting	0.831	−0.200	−0.048	−0.101	−0.005
I	I'm totally in the game	0.645	−0.166	0.012	−0.004	0.107
P	I feel happy	0.576	−0.036	0.097	−0.033	−0.006
N	Playing this game makes me feel bad	−0.088	0.408	0.006	−0.059	0.009
T	I'm thinking about something else when I play this game	−0.068	0.360	−0.035	0.179	0.150
T	I feel tired	−0.054	0.703	−0.032	−0.049	0.024
c	I can play this game well	0.235	0.091	0.485	0.064	−0.066
T	I find this game hard	0.174	−0.021	0.671	0.071	0.024
F	Playing this game is a visual pleasure	0.235	0.104	0.883	0.275	−0.042
I	I forgot everything else when I played the game	0.275	0.097	0.482	0.064	−0.007

(*continued*)

Table 2. (*continued*)

Item code	Label	Factors				
		1	2	3	4	5
P	I feel good	0.028	−0.047	−0.005	0.647	−0.042
c	I have a good time in this game	−0.085	−0.029	−0.091	0.782	0.077
T	I'm bored	0.158	0.048	−0.029	0.543	0.015
H	I have a great sense of achievement	−0.021	0.046	−0.017	0.858	−0.056
I	I am immersed in imagination	0.164	0.079	0.134	0.543	−0.029
F	I think I can explore more	−0.048	0.081	0.057	0.030	0.571
F	I enjoy the game	0.201	−0.015	−0.003	0.263	0.426
F	I soon finished the goal of the game	−0.021	-0.091	0.482	0.163	−0.067
T	I'm upset	0.086	0.703	−0.032	−0.049	0.024
T	I feel pressure	0.063	0.408	−0.077	0.085	−0.059
T	I feel anxious	−0.047	0.790	−.035	0.275	−0.126
F	I don't have a sense of time	−0.085	−0.029	−0.017	0.782	0.015
H	I think the game is challenging	0.158	−0.017	0.571	0.117	0.047
F	I'm very impressed with the game	−0.006	−0.060	−0.029	−0.030	0.810
F	I'm very focused on games	0.188	0.016	−0.003	0.162	0.419
N	I feel depressed	−0.045	0.408	−0.035	0.163	−0.029
I	Playing this game is a rich experience	−0.048	−0.029	−0.030	−0.015	0.810
I	I feel disconnected from the outside world	−0.269	−0.089	−0.060	-0.060	0.581
H	I feel pressed for time	0.174	0.016	−0.003	0.162	0.430
T	I've put in a lot of effort	−0.057	0.061	0.061	0.030	0.571

Note: The code number corresponds to the items number from the original GEQ scale. The code letters represent the originally hypothesized factor labels: P = positive affect; N = negative affect; T = Tension; H = Challenge, C = competence; F = flow; I = immersion.

3   Study 3 UTAUT Model

Based on the Unified Theory of Acceptance and Use of Technology (UTAUT). Structural equation model was used in the study, online questionnaire was used to obtain the research data, and Likert 5-point scale was used to measure the variables. Each item in the questionnaire is given a grade, which is represented by difference data.

In this paper, 5 subscales are used, i.e. 5 alternative comment answers are given for each question in the scale, with the score from 1 to 5, 1 indicating extremely disagree, 2 indicating disagree, 3 indicating general, 4 indicating agree, and 5 tables I agree. The research is based on the integrated technology acceptance model, combined with data survey, to retain the core variables (performance expectation, effort expectation, social impact and promotion factors). In order to make the research more consistent with the theme and characteristics of the sandbox game creation platform, this paper introduces the "content quality" factor, and puts forward the basic research hypothesis based on the adjustment variables.

3.1   Research Method

Because this study explored the acceptance of sandbox game creation platform by college students, the participants were limited to art college students of Guangdong University of Finance and economics.

Descriptive statistics:

The questionnaire was distributed in the Art College of Guangdong University of Finance and economics by convenient sampling. In this survey, 56 questionnaires were sent out, and 56 effective questionnaires were collected through online survey. The effective rate of the questionnaires was 100%. Using spss22.0 software, when the Cronbach reliability coefficient value is above 0.7, the reliability of the study is better, the coefficient value of each variable of the study is between 0.8–1, and the questionnaire has a high reliability (Table 3).

It can be seen from the above that performance expectation, promotion factors, teaching willingness, social influence and content quality all have a significant positive impact on the acceptance of game making education. The satisfaction of college students to the sandbox game platform is significantly affected by the promotion factors (path coefficient is 0.71, P < 0.001). That is to say, the convenience and novelty of the sandbox game platform can improve the learning efficiency and enthusiasm of students' learning game making education. Performance expectation has a significant positive impact on the degree of acceptance (path coefficient is 0.20, P < 0.001), which shows that sandbox game platform has the nature of exceeding the limit of time and space use, and can meet the needs of students' game making and learning. Content quality and recognition show a significantly lower positive impact (path coefficient is 0.14, P < 0.05), indicating that education should not ignore the role of network media while focusing on content richness and timeliness. Social influence also affects the acceptance (path coefficient is 0.13, P < 0.05). Students will spontaneously tend to learn the content of sandbox game education online.

Table 3. UHAUT analysis in study 3.

Category	Latent variable	Measure term	CRC	KMO	SFC
Subject of acceptance	Performance expectation (PE)	Sandbox platform learning can meet my game making learning needs Sandbox platform learning for all kinds of time Sandbox platform learning can improve my knowledge, I think it's easy Sandbox platform is easy to use	0.868	0.772	0.810 0.878 0.881 0.817
Subject of acceptance	Effort Expectancy (EE)	Sandbox platform is easy to operate For sandbox platform, I can adapt quickly For sandbox platform to find knowledge points, I think it is easy If everyone around me uses sandbox platform to learn how to make games, I will try	0.897	0.832	0.905 0.876 0.841 0.902
Accepting environment	Social Influence (SI)	Teachers or friends recommend me to use sandbox platform to study ideological and political education. I will try I have the necessary resources for sandbox platform Education Using sandbox platform is in line with my learning style	0.838	0.735	0.907 0.796 0.886 0.876
Receiving media	Facilitating Conditions (FC)	I think sandbox platform can improve my enthusiasm for learning politics I think sandbox platform is convenient and novel for education and learning Compared with the traditional, Sandbox platform can improve my game learning efficiency I think sandbox platform provides rich learning content	0.906	0.840	0.902 0.868 0.876 0.903

(continued)

Table 3. (*continued*)

Category	Latent variable	Measure term	CRC	KMO	SFC
Object of acceptance	Content Qualities (CQ)	I think the educational content of sandbox platform is more timely I think the content of sandbox platform is clear and concise, which can highlight the key points	0.879	0.743	0.901 0.889
Subject of acceptance	Acceptability	I think it's better to use sandbox platform to learn ideological and political content than traditional teaching methods I think sandbox platform is very helpful to my game making and learning Generally speaking, I recognize and accept the sandbox platform of colleges and Universities	0.929	0.860	0.896 0.922 0.911

4 Conclusion

According to the test results of making games on the sand box platform of Ylands, students with positive and balanced styles have higher learning efficiency and stability in making games. From the GEQ analysis, it is found that the students' acceptance of the game produced by sandbox platform is relatively high. In the game test, the immersion index is relatively high, which proves that sandbox game has certain advantages over traditional games. Finally, after the analysis of Utaut model, the students are more satisfied with the use of sandbox game platform in Colleges and universities.

References

1. Ryan, R.M., Rigby, C.S., Przybylski, A.: The motivational pull of video games: a self-determination theory approach. Motiv. Emot. **30**(4), 344–360 (2006). https://doi.org/10.1007/s11031-006-9051-8
2. Pieter, W., Esmee, S.M.: The role of learning styles in game-based learning [IJGBL]. Int. J. Game-Based Learn. **10**(1), 54–69 (2020)
3. Fullerton, T.: Games Design Workshop: A Playcentric Approach to Creating Innovative Games. Morgan Kaufmann, Burlington (2008)
4. Roodt, S., Ryklief, Y.: Using digital game-based learning to improve the academic efficiency of vocational education students [IJGBL]. Int. J. Game-Based Learn. **9**(4), 45–69 (2019)

5. Bozkurt, A., Durak, G.: A systematic review of gamification research: in pursuit of homo ludens [IJGBL]. Int. J. Game-Based Learn. **8**(3), 15–33 (2018)
6. Wong, L.H., Hsu, C.K.: Effects of learning styles on learners' collaborative patterns in a mobileassisted, Chinese character-forming game based on a flexible grouping approach. Technol. Pedag. Educ. **25**(1), 61–77 (2016)
7. Kapp, K.: The Gamification of Learning and Instruction. Pfeiffer, San Francisco (2012)
8. Landers, R.N., Bauer, K.N., Callan, R.C.: Gamification of task performance with leaderboards: a goal setting experiment. Comput. Human Behav. **71**, 508–515 (2017)
9. Rumeser, D., Emsley, M.: Learning style and learning method preference in project management education: what happens when things get more complex? In: Proceedings of the European Conference on Games Based Learning, pp. 860–865. Academic Conferences International Limited (2017)
10. Chung, C.H., Shen, C., Qiu, Y.Z.: Students' acceptance of gamification in higher education [IJGBL]. Int. J. Game-Based Learn. **9**(2), 1–19 (2019)

Emotional Pathways of Successful College Essays

Eric Xu[1] and Qiping Zhang[2(✉)]

[1] Stuyvesant High School, 345 Chambers Street, New York, NY 10282, USA
ericxu113@gmail.com
[2] Long Island University, 720, Brookville, NY 11548, USA
qiping.zhang@liu.edu

Abstract. The quality of college personal essays impacts the future of millions of high school seniors every year. While the content of such an essay may be easily rated, the emotional impact of the style and wording is more difficult to quantify. Previous work has been done on emotional evaluations of specific genres such as movie reviews and blogs. This paper intends to reveal how common or different emotional expressions evolve, from opening, to body, to closing among the "successful" college essays. Adhering to the widely-accepted dimensions of emotion, valence ("positive or negative connotation of an emotion") and arousal ("intensity") were coded on a 9-Likert scale for each coding unit- a paragraph. Additionally, emotional assessments were aggregated over the structure of each essay (opening, body, closing). MANOVA analysis was conducted on the effect of structure and content type (Achievements and Passion, Characteristics and Identity, and Overcoming Obstacles and Learning From Experience) on the valence and arousal scores. On average, successful college essays have a slightly positive valence and above-average arousal. Results further revealed that nearly all successful college essays had a positive valence closing. There also seems to be significant correlations between the specific content of college essays and specific structural elements, suggesting that these combinations are effective and overrepresented in the pool of successful college essays. The implications of the research can not only be used to help future college applicants optimize their emotional pathways but may also be extended into other genres like novels and fiction.

Keywords: Emotional expression · College essay · Valence · Arousal

1 Introduction

Text communicates informative contents and attitudinal information such as emotional states. Previous work has been done on emotional evaluations of specific genres such as movie reviews [1] and blogs [2]. In contrast, this paper reports an empirical study of emotion evaluation on college essays, a genre of text that impacts the future of millions of high school students every year.

College essays are inherently emotion-rich, because they are meant to communicate an applicant's character and personality within a limited space. Due to intrinsic differences in each applicant's background and writing style, a diverse range of emotional

© Springer Nature Switzerland AG 2020
C. Stephanidis and M. Antona (Eds.): HCII 2020, CCIS 1225, pp. 365–371, 2020.
https://doi.org/10.1007/978-3-030-50729-9_52

expression patterns is expected. It is commonly agreed that the structure of personal essays consists of 3 parts: opening, body, and closing [3, 4]. This paper intends to reveal how common or different emotional expressions evolve, from opening, to body, to closing among the "successful" college essays. The findings of this study will reveal what lead those essays to be successful in terms of their emotional expression development.

2 Literature Review

2.1 College Essay in Common App

Since the development of common application for college application, college essays are required. It usually has 6–7 prompts for any high school student applicant to choose from [5].

Prompt #1: Share your story.

- Some students have a background, identity, interest, or talent so meaningful they believe their application would be incomplete without it. If this sounds like you, please share your story.

Prompt #2: Learning from obstacles.

- The lessons we take from obstacles we encounter can be fundamental to later success. Recount a time when you faced a challenge, setback, or failure. How did it affect you, and what did you learn from the experience?

Prompt #3: Challenging a belief.

- Reflect on a time when you questioned or challenged a belief or idea. What prompted your thinking? What was the outcome?

Prompt #4: Solving a problem

- Describe a problem you've solved or a problem you'd like to solve. It can be an intellectual challenge, a research query, an ethical dilemma—anything of personal importance, no matter the scale. Explain its significance to you and what steps you took or could be taken to identify a solution.

Prompt #5: Personal growth.

- Discuss an accomplishment, event, or realization that sparked a period of personal growth and a new understanding of yourself or others.

Prompt #6: What captivates you?

- Describe a topic, idea, or concept you find so engaging it makes you lose all track of time. Why does it captivate you? What or who do you turn to when you want to learn more?

Prompt #7: Topic of your choice.

- Share an essay on any topic of your choice. It can be one you've already written, one that responds to a different prompt, or one of your own design.

2.2   Analysis of Emotional Expression

Work on sentiment analysis has typically focused on recognizing valence – positive or negative orientation. In addition to this measuring tool of valence, we also used intensity or arousal. In this work, we address the task of identifying expressions of emotion in text.

In a work focused on learning specific emotions from text, Alm et al. [6] have explored automatic classification of sentences in children's fairy tales according to the basic emotions identified by Ekman [7]. The data used in their experiments was manually annotated with emotion information, and is targeted for use in a text-to-speech synthesis system for expressive rendering of stories.

Many other research papers on emotion detection used machine learning to provide more specific categories of emotion and quicker coding. Ultimately, rule-based emotional coding used in [8] may be a little too robotic and not enough human. There are all sorts of sarcastic and subtle tones conveyed through text that is sometimes impossible for strict rules to measure emotion-wise.

3   Method

3.1   Dataset

The study utilized a total of 45 college essays from featured in high-profile public sources (such as New York Times [9] and the Harvard Crimson [10]) within the past 5 years. All of them are within 650 words as commonly required. Essays that did not follow the traditional Opening-Body-Closing structure were excluded.

3.2   Emotional Expression

Valence and Arousal are two popular dimensions in emotion research [11, 12]. Valence refers to the degree of positive or negative connotation of an emotion, while Arousal refers to how calming or exciting an emotion is. They were coded on a Likert-scale of 1 to 9.

3.3   Content Type

Three categories describing the primary essay topic were identified based on related literature [13, 14]: Achievements and Passion (**AP**), Characteristics and Identity (**CI**), and Overcoming Obstacles and Learning From Experience (**OE**).

3.4   Content Analysis

Structure, valence, and arousal were coded for each coding unit- a paragraph. Additionally, each essay was assigned a content type (**AP, CI, OE**). Two coders coded a sample of 10 essays based on the coding manual that was developed for this study until the inter-coder reliability reached an acceptable level (Cohen's Kappa = .74 for valence, .87 for arousal). Two coders reached a complete agreement on coding of structure and content type. After that, one coder coded the rest of the essays.

4   Results

In order to explore what emotional characteristics successful college essays have, we analyzed the emotional qualities of each paragraph and sorted them by essay structure (opening-body-closing).

First, we analyzed the emotional expression over development of the story (structure) in terms of essay content (**AP, CI, OE**) (Fig. 1, Table 1 and 2). The main effects of structure was significant (valence: $F(2,84) = 20.88$, $p < .01$; arousal: $F(2,84) = 5.65$, $p < .01$). The post-hoc Tukey analysis showed that closing was significantly higher than opening and body on both valence and arousal ($p < .01$). The main effect of content on Valence was significant ($F(2,42) = 3.50$, $p < .05$), but on Arousal was not significant ($F(2,42) = .05$, $p > .05$). The post-hoc Tukey analysis showed that emotional valence of AP essays is significantly higher than that of OE essays ($p < .05$).

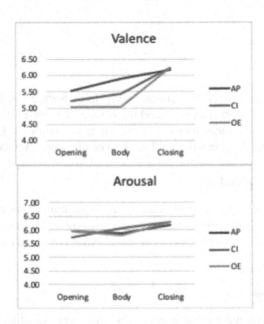

Fig. 1. Effect of structure and content on emotional valence and arousal

Then, we analyzed emotional expression in terms of valence types and arousal types (Fig. 2 and 3). Five emotional archetypes (bump, valley, upward, downhill, and flatline) were identified based on the change in valence/arousal over the structure. For

Table 1. Emotional valence by content type and essay structure: Mean (Std. Dev.) (1 = most negative, 9 = most positive)

	Opening	Body	Closing	Overall
AP	5.53 (.77)	5.90 (.44)	6.18 (.53)	5.84 (.30)
CI	5.22 (.88)	5.45 (.93)	6.23 (.54)	5.51 (.51)
OE	5.04 (.94)	5.04 (.80)	6.23 (.56)	5.32 (.62)
Total	5.27 (.87)	5.47 (.80)	6.21 (.53)	5.56 (.53)

Table 2. Emotional arousal by content type and essay structure: Mean (Std. Dev.) (1 = most calm, 9 = most alert)

	Opening	Body	Closing	Overall
AP	5.98 (.65)	5.87 (.70)	6.20 (.56)	5.97 (.32)
CI	5.72 (.47)	6.08 (.55)	6.28 (.50)	6.00 (.33)
OE	5.96 (.76)	5.81 (.56)	6.30 (.53)	5.98 (.44)
Total	5.88 (.63)	5.92 (.53	6.26 (.60)	5.98 (.35)

example, a bump essay refers to one with valence/arousal of the body higher than opening and closing, while a valley refers to one with valence/arousal of the body lower than opening and closing. The interaction effect of valence type and structure was significant ($F(6,82) = 17.99$, $p < .01$), so did the interaction effect of arousal type and structure ($F(8, 80) = 23.29$, $p < .01$).

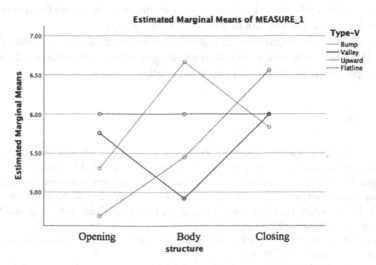

Fig. 2. Effect of structure and valence type on emotional valence

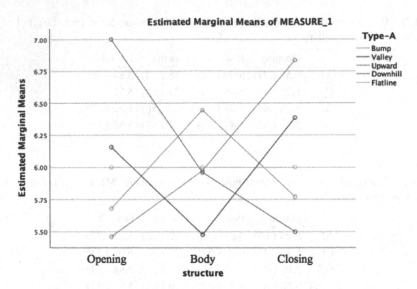

Fig. 3. Effect of structure and arousal type on emotional arousal

5 Discussion and Conclusion

Ultimately, many successful college essays have on average a slightly positive valence. This only makes sense, as most authors would want to paint a positive image of themselves to make themselves seem a better candidate for admission. Similarly, the arousal was also slightly higher than the middle point of 5 on a 9-likert scale, most likely because students wanted to emphasize specific qualities about them and because a lot of subject material was condensed into a limited space.

There seems to be significant correlations between the specific content of college essays and specific structural elements, suggesting that these combinations are effective and overrepresented in the pool of successful college essays.

References

1. Pang, B., Lee, L., Vaithyanathan, S.: Thumbs up? Sentiment classification using machine learning techniques. In: Proceedings of the Conference on EMNLP (2002)
2. Mishne, G., Glance, N.: Predicting movie sales from blogger sentiment. In: AAAI 2006 Spring Symposium on Computational Approaches to Analysing Weblogs (2006)
3. Frank, J.F.: Crushing the Common App Essay: A Foolproof Guide to Getting into Your Top College. Follettbound (2018)
4. Wissner-Gross, E.: Write Your College Essay in Less Than a Day. Ballantine Books Trade Paperbacks, New York (2009)
5. Commonapp 2019–2020 College Essay Prompts. https://www.commonapp.org/apply/2019-essay-prompts. Accessed 9 Oct 2019
6. Alm, C.O., Roth, D., Sproat, R.: Emotions from text: machine learning for text-based emotion prediction. In: Proceedings of the Conference on Human Language Technology and

Empirical Methods in Natural Language Processing, pp. 579–586. Association for Computational Linguistics (2005)

7. Ekman, P.: An argument for basic emotions. Cogn. Emot. **6**(3–4), 169–200 (1992)
8. Lee, S.Y.M., Chen, Y., Huang, C.R., Li, S.: Detecting emotion causes with a linguistic rule-based approach. Comput. Intell. **29**(3), 390–416 (2013)
9. Lieber, R.: Trash, the Library and a Worn, Brown Table: The 2019 College Essays on Money (2019). https://www.nytimes.com/2019/05/09/your-money/college-application-essays-money.html
10. Successful Harvard Application Essays. https://www.thecrimson.com/topic/sponsored-successful-harvard-essays-2018/. Accessed 27 Sept 2019
11. Russell, J.A., Barrett, L.F.: Core affect, prototypical emotional episodes, and other things called emotion: dissecting the elephant. J. Pers. Soc. Psychol. **76**(5), 805–819 (1999)
12. Hepach, R., Kliemann, D., Grüneisen, S., Heekeren, H.R., Dziobek, I.: Conceptualizing emotions along the dimensions of valence, arousal, and communicative frequency–implications for social-cognitive tests and training tools. Front. Psychol. **2**, 266 (2011)
13. Fiske, E.B., Hammond, B.: Real College Essays that Work. Sourcebooks Inc., Naperville (2009)
14. St. Martins Griffin: 50 Successful Harvard Application Essays: What Worked for Them Can Help You Get Into the College of Your Choice, New York (2017)

Development of Nudge System: To Nudge Other Students Through Their Tablet

Kyoichi Yokoyama[1]([✉]), Tadashi Misono[2], Rieko Inaba[3],
and Yuki Watanabe[1]

[1] Tokyo University of Science, Tokyo, Japan
1719528@ed.tus.ac.jp, wat@rs.tus.ac.jp
[2] Shimane University, Matsue, Shimane, Japan
misono@edu.shimane-u.ac.jp
[3] Tsuda University, Tokyo, Japan
inaba@tsuda.ac.jp

Abstract. We develop a system that students can use to nudge other students thought their tablet, thus developing self-regulation learning skills during class. This paper presents the nudge system functions and interface design. A key feature of the nudge system is its division into four components: note taking, learning log collection, visualization of learning, and learning log confirmation. The note-taking function enable learners to write, delete, and underline notes directly on distributed materials. The visualization function of learning from distributed materials is related to the lesson (.pdf) that has been sent to the tablet device; when multiple learners take notes or underlines the same materials, the approximate section of the materials on other learners' tablet devices can be highlighted in color. As more learners take notes in the same section, the section color becomes darker. We think that this function will enable learners to use reflection, forethought, and performance assessment to evaluate their own learning strategies during class. The learning log collection function collects contents written on the class materials by hand. Additionally, the learning log collection function records to the note completion of the learners. The learning log confirmation function enables the teacher to see the note-taking process of all of the learners after class.

Keywords: Self-regulated learning · Note-taking · CSCL · Nudge

1 Introduction

Self-Regulated Learning (SRL) is cyclical and comprises situations in which learners receive feedback on their own learning. Through this feedback, learners then use meta-cognitive, motivation, and learning strategies to improve their own learning processes (Zimmerman 2001). SRL involves the following triadic processes (see Fig. 1): forethought, performance, and reflection (Zimmerman 2000). During the forethought phase, the learner spends considerable time thinking and planning, and individuals both analyze the task ahead and motivate themselves to act by what they believe about themselves and their situation. During the performance phase, self-regulation involves monitoring one's own thoughts and behaviors within given performance contexts and

© Springer Nature Switzerland AG 2020
C. Stephanidis and M. Antona (Eds.): HCII 2020, CCIS 1225, pp. 372–380, 2020.
https://doi.org/10.1007/978-3-030-50729-9_53

selecting or modifying one's strategies. During the self-reflection phase, the learner reviews the outcomes of their efforts and the behaviors that led to them, and searches to make attributions for what has happened (Usher and Schunk 2018). Schunk and Zimmerman (2008) have suggested that the advantages of being a good self-regulator include being able to: (a) set better learning goals, (b) implement more effective learning strategies, (c) monitor and assess one's own goal progress successfully, (d) seek assistance occasionally, and (e) adjust strategies more efficiently. Consequently, teacher should provide learning environments and supportive intervention in order to facilitate the cyclical process of SRL.

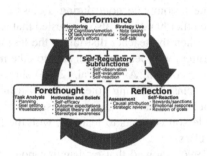

Fig. 1. Cyclical process of SRL

In relation to mathematics and SRL, Corte et al. (2000) states that the ultimate goal for people learning mathematics is to become adaptive competence learners. Adaptive competence learners gain the ability to apply meaningful mathematical knowledge and skills both flexibly and creatively in a variety of contexts. For example, in the problem-solving process in mathematics, learners not only use conventional methods but also seek new ones. Corte and Verschaffel (2006) perceives SRL skills as an important factor in acquiring adaptive competence. As a result of such findings, students clearly need SRL skills to learn mathematics and become adaptive learners. However, Schunk (2001) notes that students do not become self-regulated learners voluntarily or automatically. In other words, they become self-regulated learners as a result of help from others. Based on these findings, it is necessary to implement instructional designs in which the teachers stimulate SRL in school environments and train students to become self-regulated learners.

Zimmerman et al. (1996) introduced five viewpoints through which learners could be conscious of their own learning improvement: (a) planning and using study time more effectively, (b) understanding and summarizing, (c) improving methods of note taking, (d) anticipating and preparing better for examinations, and (e) writing more effectively. These can facilitate learners to become proficient in SRL skills via support from their teachers. Through these, learners can observe their current study practices more accurately, ascertain for themselves which study methods are ineffective and replace them with better ones, and be more personally aware of their improved effectiveness. Therefore, when the teacher develops the SRL skills of students, it is necessary to promote their ability to self-regulate their learning via these five viewpoints and to establish a complementary teaching environment and teaching methods.

Note-taking is defined as taking notes and underlining notes, distributed material, and texts by learners in instructor-learning situations, such as during classes and while reading texts (Kobayashi 2000). Di Vesta and Gray (1972) divided note-taking into encoding and storage functions. Kiewra (1989) says that note-taking and reviewing actions facilitate understanding and memory of knowledge. The encoding function facilitates recognition processing by combining the teaching contents with the prior knowledge of the learner through writing notes. The storage function enables effective review by writing notes. With respect to note-taking, Kiewra (1989) has suggested that it is not possible to write a complete note during a class because of the speed and density of classes. On the other hand, it is also suggested that learners can easily narrow down the gist of a class when the teacher distributes the lesson materials in which the outline of the class is written, with learners thus able to take notes on the materials. In terms of understanding the content, Avval et al. (2013) showed that learners promote their understanding of the class by taking notes on the distributed lesson materials. On the basis of these facts, it is necessary to design a class in which the teacher distributes materials describing the lesson contents to learners, with the learner then taking notes on the materials during class.

Zimmerman et al. (1996) showed that exchanging notes with others during class help to develop a learner's SRL skills. Learners can review their learning strategies, set goals, and implement them with help from others. In this way, the development of SRL skills requires new learning experiences, as new skills are required after clarifying the limitations of existing strategies. Therefore, receiving assistance, such as feedback from another person, is one of the strategies of SRL (Zimmerman 2001). In addition, there is a gradual level for the development regarding learners' ability to self-regulate their learning, and external approaches and supports are necessary in the early stages of development (Zimmerman 2000). Teachers play an essential role in the instructional design, enabling learners to receive feedback from during class in order to help them develop SRL skills.

Molnar and Lukac (2015) suggested that the Internet provides a variety of educational portals and interactive applications designed to support active learning. In recent years, the schools that provide Information and Communication Technology (ICT) facilities, such as computers, large presentation devices, ultra-high-speed Internet, and wireless LAN, has increased in terms of Japanese secondary schools. In particular, high schools that have already adopted ICT-based forms of education have implemented classes using applications offering electronic blackboards and tablet terminals. As an example, LoiLoNote—an application software application available on a tablet terminal—offers a flipped classroom, making it possible to collect homework from learners before a class, return it, and provide feedback to the student by adding comments. In this way, feedback has been effectively provided to learners by utilizing ICT equipment. However, providing immediate feedback in class settings using ICT has hardly been carried out. This is because the system load is significant, and moreover, it is impractical for the teacher to offer feedback to all students during a class.

Recently, the number of classes using ICT equipment has increased due to the advances made in ICT equipment. The same is true for receiving feedback from others. There are many studies on feedback in terms of different learning strategies. In particular, in recent years, there many studies have been conducted on providing feedback using ICT equipment (e.g., Oura et al. 2008). Due to the recent advancements in ICT equipment, educational facilities have begun to prepare environments that utilize these equipment during classes. As the result, it seems that environments in which ideas are transmitted between learners in real time are becoming more common, while learners are also able to receive feedback during class as a result of these changes.

People often need nudges to help them make decisions that are difficult and rare, for which they do not get feedback, and which contain aspects they have trouble translating into terms that they can easily understand (Thaler and Sustein 2008, p. 74). Thaler and Sustein (2008) define a nudge as any aspect of the choice architecture that alters people's behavior in a predictable way without forbidding any options or significantly changing their economic incentive. That is to say, by incorporating the nudge in a class, it is possible to promote the learning of a learner who does not know what to do.

Nudge studies have been conducted in a variety of educational fields, and Damagaard and Nielsen (2018) have identified twelve categories of research and practice that use nudges: default, framing, peer-group manipulations, deadlines, goal setting, reminders, informational, assistance, boosting skills to alleviate self-control problems, social comparison, extrinsic motivation, and social belonging identity activation and mindset. Among them, deadlines, goal setting, and reminders are necessary for development of SRL, as external factors intervene and induce behavior. In addition, it is possible for the learner to make active selection action by receiving information and assistance from another person. Based on these facts, in order to promote active action selection and SRL, this study incorporates a nudge system.

2 Purpose

By focusing on note-taking in the context of a secondary education mathematics course, this study aims to develop a system that can create a cyclical SRL process during class. This system visualizes how and when other learners are learning based on information regarding other learners' note-taking using tablet devices, which offers immediate feedback. By monitoring the learning strategies of others, one's own learning is also reviewed and reflected in terms of one's own learning strategies. By visualizing the learning strategy of others, we can thus promote learning between learners on the tablet, with the aim of developing a collaborative learning strategy.

This paper introduces the interface of the system and presents the policy of future evaluation. First, we introduce both the functions implemented in the Nudge System and the tools displayed on the screen. We then explain how to visualize learning on the tablet devices and for nudge learners, while also introducing how a learner's learning processes are recorded in the system. As a guideline for the analysis, we will conduct the analysis from three viewpoints designed to measure the usefulness of the system.

Furthermore, the interface evaluation of the system is evaluated based on how useful it is.

The study was conducted on a class in which each student had a tablet device in a wireless LAN environment. In the class, the material (PDF) was distributed to the tablet device of each user, with the material working as a notebook. The material included PowerPoints and blackboard contents prepared by the teacher in advance. Using this approach, it is possible to shorten the length of the class. The learner writes, underlines, or notes the points explained by the teacher in the material.

3   System Overview

The system (Below: Nudge System) is a web application that can be accessed by up to 45 people at a time, excluding teachers. Nudge System is a system utilized during class.

On Nudge System, the learner directly writes on the material that has been distributed via the table device. Then, the system collects the information written by all the learners, enabling the learners to review their own learning strategies, and the visualization is carried out based on the information, thereby facilitating learning (see Fig. 2). The system encourages learners to learn from other learners during class and asks them to display their learning strategies in a notebook on their tablet device, thereby enabling metacognition, review of their learning strategies, and reflection on how to proceed with their learning in terms of putting strategies into action. During class, learners learn how and when to improve their learning through the use of their peers' nudging. It is also possible for teachers to ask questions where there are many gaps to fill in, which might expedite deeper learning.

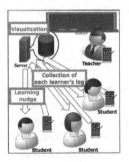

Fig. 2. How Nudge work

The key information here is not the content that the student wrote on the tablet, but the information showing the place and timing of their writing. This timing records the points at which other learners are writing in color, at these are then successively updated.

A key feature of the system is its division into four components: note-taking, collection of learning log, visualization of learning, and confirmation of learning log.

The details of each function and the reasons why we implement these functions are described below.

3.1 Note-Taking Function

The note-taking function enables learners to write, delete, and underline notes directly on materials distributed by hand on the tablet. This function can remove incorrectly written notes and underlining.

This function uses pens and markers as tools, and we will examine which has a stronger impact on learners when we analyze whether learners can make active decisions via Nudge System.

3.2 Collection of Learning Log Function

The collection of learning log function collects the contents that learners write and underline as notes in the learning log. The teacher can confirm the recorded learning log after the class. The collection learning log function records each time a learner writes on the lesson materials. Then, the system updates the records and reflects them as colors in the visualization of learning.

3.3 Visualization of Learning Function

The learning visualization function distributes materials related to the lesson (PDF) to the tablet device. When the learner takes notes or underlines on the same materials, the approximate parts of the materials written on other students' tablet devices can be visualized by color. The higher the number of entries in the same section, the darker the color. However, this function does not indicate specific contents for notes.

This function not only presents the learning strategy information of others to the learner, but also confirms what kind of learning behavior the learner's actions are an example of, based on the visualized information. This confirms whether or not there was decision making and behavioral change as a result of the nudge, as well as whether the learner engages in SRL during class.

3.4 Confirmation of Learning Function

The confirmation of learning function can check the learning log of each learner by specifying the date and time, teaching materials, and the users. This function is not available to learners, and only the teacher can check the process from the first notes to latest notes of all students after class. This function enables us to examine the long-term changes in the note taking of each learner, as well as to check whether the system affected the note-taking process.

4   System Interface

The interface of the system can be seen in Fig. 3. The upper toolbar consists of the Delete button, Select button, Marker button, Pen button, Swipe button, Shrink button, Zoom button, Page Select button (Show All Pages Drop-down), Next Page button, and Previous Page button.

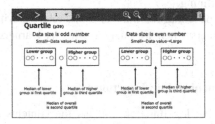

Fig. 3.   System interface

The following is an explanation of how the visualization is carried out when Learner 1 and Learner 2 listen to the class and respectively write on the distributed lesson material. We also present a learner's screen, which changes over time (see Fig. 4):

1. Each learner takes notes and underlines during class to promote their own understanding and memory.
2. The system adds the thickness of the line written by the learner, the thickness of the marker, and the thickness of the set value set beforehand by the instructor. Then, a PNG image in which a line thicker than the line actually written by the learner is created. This PNG image is called a visualization layer. The visualization of the learning is feasible by superimposing the visualization layer on the lesson material.
3. When combined with the visualization layers created at the same time by others, the areas with more writing are highlighted. The visualization layer updates at regular intervals, providing information on how and at what time other learners are writing.

The thickness of the note, the thickness and color of the marker, and the transparency and color of the visualization layer can be changed by setting them before the class. The set value added to the memo is set so that other learners cannot judge the contents of the memo.

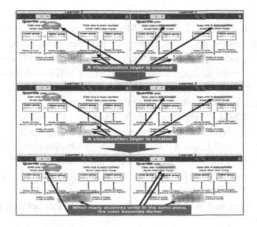

Fig. 4. Learner's screen, which changes over time

5   Evaluation Guideline

The practice using Nudge System is scheduled for June to July, 2020. Therefore, this paper introduces the viewpoints through which we will evaluate the interface of the system, and we will announce the results in an announcement on the day.

We will evaluate the system from three viewpoints. First, we will evaluate whether the cyclical process of SRL changes as a result of utilizing this system during class. This is possible because we will be able to see how many times learners try to improve their learning during class. The second viewpoint is the transformation of note-taking. In terms of whether the cyclical process of SRL shifts during class, we will observe potential modifications in the note-taking process during class. We will also observe and evaluate the quantitative and qualitative modification of note taking in long term. The third viewpoint is to conduct a questionnaire survey on whether there was a change in learners' own behavior and decision making by receiving a nudge from others during class. This will be done by assessing if learners used the Nudge System to assess whether nudges from others influenced their own thoughts and decisions.

References

Zimmerman, B.J.: Theories of self-regulated learning and academic achievement: an overview and analysis. In: Zimmerman, B.J., Schunk, D.H. (eds.) Self-Regulated Learning and Academic Achievement: Theoretical Perspectives, 2nd edn., pp. 1–38. Lawrence Erlbaum Associates, Mahwah (2001)

Zimmerman, B.J.: Attaining self-regulation a social cognitive perspective. In: Boekaerts, M., Pintrich, P.R., Zeidner, M. (eds.) Handbooks of Self-Regulation, pp. 19–35. Elsevier, America (2000)

Usher, E.L., Schunk, D.H.: Social cognitive theoretical perspective of self-regulation. In: Schunk, D.H., Greene, J.A. (eds.) Handbook of Self-Regulation of Learning and Performance, pp. 19–35. Routledge, New York (2018)

Schunk, D.H., Zimmerman, B.J.: Motivation an essential dimension of self-regulated learning. In: Schunk, D.H., Zimmerman, B.J. (eds.) Motivation and Self-Regulated Learning. Theory, Research and Applications, pp. 1–30. Lawrence Erlbaum Associates, New York (2008)

Corte, E.D., Mason, L., Depaepe, F., Verscha, L.: Self-regulation of mathematical knowledge and skills. In: Zimmerman, B.J., Schunk, D.H. (eds.) Handbooks of Self-Regulation of Learning and Performance, pp. 155–172. Taylor & Francis Group, London (2000)

Corte, E.D., Verschaffel, L.: Mathematical thinking and learning. In: Renninger, K.A., Sigel, I.E. (eds.) Handbook of Child Psychology, vol. 4, pp. 103–152. Wiley, Canada (2006)

Schunk, D.H.: Social cognitive theory and self-regulated learning. In: Zimmerman, B.J., Schunk, D.H. (eds.) Self-Regulated Learning and Academic Achievement: Theoretical Perspectives, 2nd edn, pp. 119–144. Lawrence Erlbaum Associates, Mahwah (2001)

Zimmerman, B.J., Bonner, S., Kovach, R.: Developing Self-Regulated Learners Beyond Achievement to Self-Efficacy. American Psychological Association, Washington, DC (1996)

Kobayashi, K.: Note-taking and note-reviewing in a seminar class setting. Jpn. J. Educ. Psychol. **48**, 154–164 (2000)

Di Vesta, F.J., Gray, G.S.: Listening and note-taking. J. Educ. Psychol. **63**(1), 8–14 (1972)

Kiewra, K.A.: A review of note-taking: the encoding-storage paradigm and beyond. Educ. Psychol. Rev. **1**(2), 147–172 (1989). https://doi.org/10.1007/BF01326640

Avval, F.Z., Jarahi, L., Ghazvini, K., Youssefi, M.: Distribution of handouts in undergraduate class to create more effective educational environment. Int. J. Educ. Res. **1**(12), 1–6 (2013)

Molnar, P., Lukac, S.: Dynamic geometry systems in mathematics education: attitudes of teachers. Int. J. Inf. Commun. Technol. Educ. **4**(4), 19–33 (2015)

Oura, H., Kato, H., Akahori, K.: Anchored feedback: deictic indicator providing cognitive guidance in a classroom feedback system. Jpn. Soc. Educ. Technol. **31**, 25–32 (2008)

Thaler, R.H., Sunstein, C.R.: Nudge: Improving Decisions About Health, Wealth, and Happiness. The Penguin Group, New York (2008)

Damgaard, M.T., Nielsen, H.S.: Nudge in education. Econ. Educ. Rev. **64**, 313–342 (2018)

Author Index

Printed in the United States
By Bookmasters